KORN FERRY

FYI®

for your improvement

Competencies
development
guide

New 38 global competency framework
Korn Ferry Leadership Architect™

Table of contents

Competencies

Note: Italicized words are not alphabetized.

Career stallers and stoppers

Introduction

Who is this guide for?

We know that for development to make a lasting difference, people must be clear on what skill or behavior they need to improve, be motivated to make the change, and know what steps to take. This guide provides you with ideas and strategies on how to improve where you need to be stronger or work around a need so that you can be as effective as possible. You just need to bring the insight and the motivation. Obviously, anyone who doesn't recognize their development needs will not be helped by this guide. If this is you, seek additional feedback and counsel before going any further.

Similarly, if you aren't motivated to take the steps needed to improve, or you don't think your need matters, talk to your mentor or someone who understands your role and aspirations. Ask them why this need is important for your development. See how the need plays out for you. Consider the consequences of not addressing the need. Think about the benefits of developing to meet the need.

The tips in this guide provide practical guidance to help you develop. If you recognize your needs and are motivated to do something about them, read on.

What is in this guide? Where did it come from?

This guide focuses on the Korn Ferry Leadership Architect™, a global competency framework. The Korn Ferry Leadership Architect™ was designed based on thorough, comprehensive, and rigorous analysis. This global competency framework was derived based on a combination of quantitative, qualitative, and market-based data, sourcing from Korn Ferry's own extensive data stores and external research literature sources.

Leveraging decades of expertise and knowledge from the hundreds of thousands of leadership assessments Korn Ferry has amassed, the development of the Korn Ferry Leadership Architect™ was based on the following criteria and principles:

- Skills that matter most for performance.
- Skills that are most relevant in the 21st century context.

- Validity across global regions.
- A user-friendly framework.
- Content that can be used for multiple purposes including selection, development, performance, and competency modeling.

The Korn Ferry Leadership Architect™ global competency framework comprises:

4 Factors	Factors are groups of competencies that form a cohesive theme. These competencies share some thematic similarities. Factors can be derived from statistics or content analysis.
12 Clusters	Clusters are statistically supported groupings of related competencies that represent a broader scope of skills and behaviors that contribute to success in the skill.
38 Competencies	Competencies are skills and behaviors required for success that can be observed.
10 Career stallers and stoppers	The Korn Ferry Leadership Architect™ contains 10 Career stallers and stoppers that are further grouped into 3 Clusters. Stallers and stoppers are behaviors generally considered problematic or harmful to career success.

Korn Ferry Leadership Architect™ Global competency framework

FACTOR I: THOUGHT

A. Understanding the business
5. Business insight
11. Customer focus
17. Financial acumen
35. Tech savvy

B. Making complex decisions
8. *Manages* complexity
12. Decision quality
32. *Balances* stakeholders

C. Creating the new and different
18. Global perspective
19. *Cultivates* innovation
33. Strategic mindset

FACTOR II: RESULTS

D. Taking initiative
2. Action oriented
27. Resourcefulness

E. Managing execution
15. Directs work
25. Plans and aligns
38. *Optimizes* work processes

F. Focusing on performance
1. *Ensures* accountability
28. *Drives* results

FACTOR III: PEOPLE

G. Building collaborative relationships
6. Collaborates
9. *Manages* conflict
20. Interpersonal savvy
21. *Builds* networks

H. Optimizing diverse talent
4. Attracts top talent
13. Develops talent
14. *Values* differences
34. *Builds effective* teams

I. Influencing people
7. Communicates effectively
16. *Drives* engagement
23. Organizational savvy
24. Persuades
37. *Drives* vision and purpose

FACTOR IV: SELF

J. Being authentic
10. Courage
36. *Instills* trust

K. Being open
29. *Demonstrates* self-awareness
30. Self-development

L. Being flexible and adaptable
3. *Manages* ambiguity
22. Nimble learning
26. *Being* resilient
31. Situational adaptability

CAREER STALLERS AND STOPPERS

M. Trouble with people
102. Blocked personal learner
103. *Lack of* ethics and values
110. Political missteps

N. Doesn't inspire or build talent
101. *Poor* administrator
104. Failure to build a team
105. Failure to staff effectively

O. Too narrow
106. Key skill deficiencies
107. Non-strategic
108. Overdependence on an advocate
109. Overdependence on a single skill

|

How do I use this guide?

Strategies for improvement

First, determine the need.

The key to using this guide is to identify the right development need. Five of the most typical development needs fall into two major categories—the need to build skill or the need to reduce noise.

Developmental strategies to build skill in competencies are straightforward. In all cases, you can attack the need directly or at least deal with it by working around the need. Consider these three cases that indicate a need to build skill:

1. You are average in a skill that is critically important and needs to be stronger.

2. You are weak (unskilled) in an important area and you'd like to get better (skilled) or move from negative to neutral.

3. You are untested (maybe unskilled) in an important area.

When your focus is to reduce noise in order to avoid derailment, it's a bit different. If you receive feedback that you have a *Lack of* ethics and values (103), this is a serious problem, and your goal should be to neutralize this potentially career-stopping issue. Working on a staller is not the same as building a competency. A staller is much more serious and likely results from many sources—what you underdo, such as Interpersonal savvy (20) and what you overdo, such as *Drives* results (28) or Persuades (24). For this reason, we have written separate remedies for the stallers and stoppers that cover tips you won't find if you simply go to Interpersonal savvy (20), for example. Consider these two needs that require you to reduce noise:

1. You overuse a strength to the point that it is causing problems for you.

2. You have a staller/stopper that is causing serious problems for you that you need to neutralize.

Then, take action.

When you have identified a need, start to put your development plan together. List the competency and the "before" description that applies to you (from either the Less skilled or Overused skill definitions). Or, list the staller/stopper and the "before" description that applies to you from the Problem definition. Review and record Causes as well as your learnings from the Context for each chapter. Then you are ready to create an action plan. There are four possible strategies for taking action, depending on your need.

1. *Develop.* You don't have to be good at everything. Most successful leaders have four to six major strengths, but tend to lack glaring weaknesses. Developing in all 38 Competencies is unlikely, so select wisely. If you are committed to developing a competency, create a plan using these suggestions:

    -   Choose from the development tips. Look at the specific tips and pick the ones that apply. Each tip addresses a specific manifestation of being unskilled at the competency. It is unlikely that all of the topics or tips will apply to any one person. Think back to the Causes you checked and what you learned from the Context.

    -   Seek further feedback. Little happens without feedback. Get a developmental partner, get formal 360 feedback, and poll people you work with about what you should start doing, keep doing, keep doing with slight modifications, and stop doing.

    -   Use jobs or assignments for development. The number one developer of competence by far is stretching, challenging jobs—not feedback, not courses, not role models, but jobs where you develop and exercise significant and varied competencies. If you really want to grow, these are the best places to do it. You'll have to stretch in uncomfortable areas. A challenging job or assignment requires you to work on your downsides more vigorously because you either perform or fail. Real development happens when it's not practice but it's the real thing and the stakes are high. Use your new job or assignment to learn from experience—this ability has been shown to be linked to potential.

    -   Lay out a plan and a schedule. Your plan should include at least three items you will work on immediately.

2. *Work around the need to neutralize the weakness.* Self-knowledge is essential to this approach. You have to know you have the need and acknowledge its importance. You can use any of these four workaround strategies to cover for your lack of skill. The goal of a workaround is to reduce the noise caused by the need. While there may or may not be any learning attached to the workaround, this

accomplishes what must be done without directly addressing the personal need.

– People workarounds...
Find an internal or external person to stand in for you when the weakness is in play. This could be a peer, a friend, someone from your staff, or a consultant. For example, if you are a marginal presenter, get someone who is a good presenter to present your material. Hire people for your team who are good in the areas you are not. Delegate the tasks that bring the weakness into play.

– Task workarounds...
Trade tasks or share tasks with a peer. For example, you help a peer with their strategic planning, and they help you with your presentations to senior management. Structure the weakness out. Redesign your job (with your boss) so that you are not responsible for the task(s) that brings your weakness into play. Change your job so that you no longer have to give lots of speeches to strangers. Assign that task to another unit.

– Change workarounds...
If you decide that you don't want to work on your needs, do an honest assessment of your strengths and find an organization, a job, another unit, or another career that fits those strengths. If you are in sales promotion and are not a comfortable presenter or cold caller, then find a sales job where leads are provided or customers come to you, or consider marketing analysis where those two requirements are greatly decreased.

– Self workarounds...
Acknowledge your weaknesses and be honest with yourself and others. Research shows that admitting weaknesses (within limits) actually increases people's evaluations of you. So if you start by saying, "As most of you know, speaking is not one of my strengths," people will not be as critical. Make a conscious decision to live with a weakness. If you decide not to address the need, concentrate harder on the things you do well.

3. *Compensate for an overused strength.* Using the strengths that got you where you are today is fine, of course, until something changes—a new strategy, a change in job responsibilities, a new leadership direction in the organization. Then new skills are called for, and the current skill portfolio needs an overhaul. You come to a fork in the road, and the path you choose makes a big difference. One path is taken by the open, learning agile, curious, continuous

improvers. They detect that the assignment is going to require a break from the past, a new direction. They figure out what the new ways of thinking or new skills need to be and develop them or use workarounds or compensators. The other path is taken by the larger group. When things are not going the way they are used to, when they are stretched to their limit, they turn up the volume on the handful of strengths that they already have. Their operating theory is that if a lot is good, more must be even better. If you have been given feedback that you do too much of a good thing—here are some general strategies to address this problem:

- Isn't it obvious? Stop overdoing it. Do it less. But when your mentor says be less smart, be less results oriented, do less yourself, you have trouble with that advice. Why? Because those are the things that account for your success to date. Those are the things you have been rewarded for. It's pretty scary thinking about *doing less* of what you are good at. It's really hard in real life to crank back on your strengths, but it can work.

- Add some other skills you have to lessen the noise and the damage you are causing by the overuse. Keep driving results, but do so in a softer way by adding more effective communication or Interpersonal savvy (20).

- You may not have the skills that could compensate for your weaknesses. In that case, you can use a workaround strategy or develop the compensating skills that are needed. For that, think about which of the competencies would help and use the developmental tips listed in those chapters.

4. *Live with it.* You can just live with a weakness. At least you know what it is and are willing to admit that you have a lack of skills in this area. Recognize and deploy your strengths. In this case, find your highest competencies or performance dimensions and leverage them. If you excel at balancing stakeholders or collaborating, get into more situations that allow you to use and hone your strengths. Get into roles, jobs, organizations, and career paths that use your specific current and existing strengths.

vii

Organization of FYI® for your improvement

Where do I find what I need?

Competency name and number.

Definition of the competency.

Context – Gives you the lay of the land. The Context reviews the general case for the competency, how it operates, and why it's important.

Quotes – Each chapter has two quotes to inspire you and to give you food for thought.

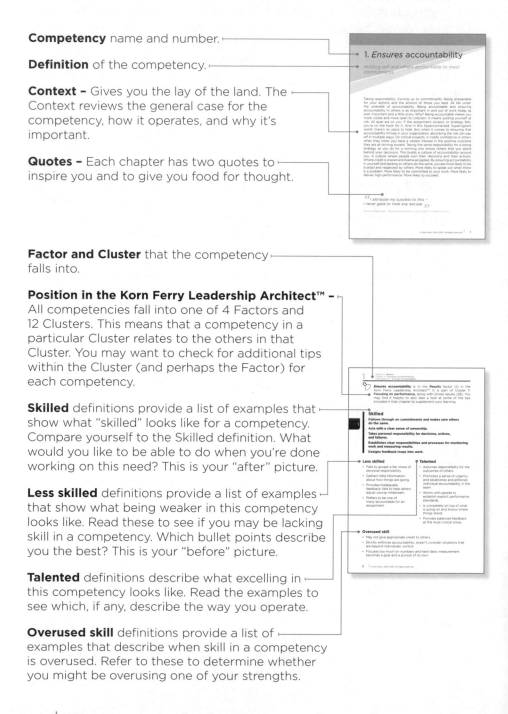

Factor and Cluster that the competency falls into.

Position in the Korn Ferry Leadership Architect™ – All competencies fall into one of 4 Factors and 12 Clusters. This means that a competency in a particular Cluster relates to the others in that Cluster. You may want to check for additional tips within the Cluster (and perhaps the Factor) for each competency.

Skilled definitions provide a list of examples that show what "skilled" looks like for a competency. Compare yourself to the Skilled definition. What would you like to be able to do when you're done working on this need? This is your "after" picture.

Less skilled definitions provide a list of examples that show what being weaker in this competency looks like. Read these to see if you may be lacking skill in a competency. Which bullet points describe you the best? This is your "before" picture.

Talented definitions describe what excelling in this competency looks like. Read the examples to see which, if any, describe the way you operate.

Overused skill definitions provide a list of examples that describe when skill in a competency is overused. Refer to these to determine whether you might be overusing one of your strengths.

Some possible causes of lower skill – We list numerous reasons why you might have this need. Check the causes that could apply to you. Many developmental efforts have floundered because the plan attacked the wrong problem. Write down your particular need—what it looks like, what causes it, whom it plays out with and in what situations. If your causes aren't listed, add them to the list.

Callout – We've included a short case study in each chapter to bring the competency to life. "Did you know?" provides interesting facts from our research. "Does it best" describes a person or organization that is well recognized for their strength in the competency, and "Culture card" identifies how cultural factors impact the competency. We've also included "Brain boosters," which are full of facts and information from a neuroscience perspective.

Development tips were developed from research on competencies—what experiences teach them, what they look like, what their elements are. They are also tested ideas from working with executives on what's getting in their way and how to fix it. We kept these tips brief, doable, and action oriented. Ten or more tips are included to work directly on a need. Although a few may be longer-term, many are things you can start working on today. We wanted to give motivated people a way to get started right away and see results quickly. Based on our research and experience, these are the tips that are most likely to work. Choose one or two of these to include in your development plan.

Want to learn more? Take a deep dive...

Interspersed with the development tips are some resources to help you explore developing the competency further. They range from video clips to journal articles to websites that will allow you to dive more deeply into some of the areas covered by the tips.

Job assignments denote situations that require application of certain competencies. Research shows that 70% of development happens on the job, and jobs differ in development power and in the competencies they address. You can't always change jobs for development reasons alone, but there is almost always a job assignment that you can select in your current role to address your development need.

Take time to reflect... leaves you with some thought-provoking statements regarding things you might want to consider as you develop the competency. Read these to see which areas of concern relate to you and take some inspiration from the guidance offered.

Learn more about... provides a small number of texts selected from expert reviews, best-seller lists, and reputable publishers that will support your development in the competency. We chose them because they're current and full of practical suggestions. We've also provided the links to the deep dive resources referenced earlier in the chapter. So, there's a wide variety of resources to help you develop each competency.

Recommended search terms – In case you'd
like to search the web for additional guidance
on developing the competency, we have
provided some search terms to get you started.

**More help... ** All of the links provided in the
deep dives interspersed throughout the
development tips are available at this location.
Additional resources and insights are also
provided to further your development. Keep
the site open while reading for easy access to
the resources associated with development tips
that resonate with you.

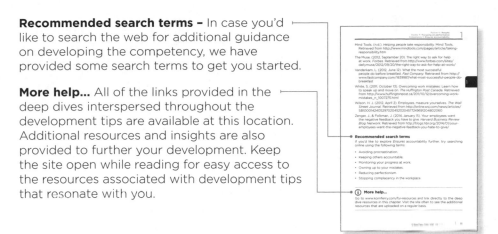

Specific to Career stallers and stoppers chapters...

A problem – Statements that describe examples
of what a staller/stopper looks like when it is "a
problem." Read these to see if a staller/stopper
might be an issue for you.

Not a problem – Statements that describe
examples of what a staller/stopper looks like
when it is "not a problem." Read these to see if a
staller/stopper is not a concern for you.

Other causes – Being less skilled at or overusing
some competencies may also be the cause of an
issue with a staller/stopper. We have selected the
most significant causes, based on our research.

A staller results from many sources—what you
underdo (Less skilled), such as Interpersonal savvy
(20) and what you overdo (Overused skill), such
as *Drives* results (28). Review the list to see if any
of the unskilled or overused competencies match
your profile. Use this information to help you
decide what to focus on in your development plan.

About the editor

Heather Barnfield is Director, Intellectual Property Development for Korn Ferry. In addition to serving as editor and co-author for this guide, Heather was part of the team who developed the Korn Ferry Leadership Architect™ global competency framework and was a contributing writer for the Korn Ferry Institute competencies best practices paper titled *Define, Distill, Deploy*. She edited and co-wrote the Korn Ferry *Talent Review* product suite, as well as the Korn Ferry *Interview Architect™* and is the series editor for Korn Ferry's *Career Architect® Express*. Heather has over twenty years of experience in leadership development, talent management, and engagement. Her career has spanned a variety of leadership positions, as well as consultancy, across a wide range of industries both in the UK and the US, where she has been based since 2009.

| xiii

Acknowledgments

The creation of this guide would not have been possible without the tireless efforts and commitment of the talented team who made it happen.

Thanks to the team of writers who worked with Heather to create the practical tips for developing skill in the competencies. Jill Wachholz, Evelyn Orr, Stephanie Busby, Kevin Hedman, Tanya Just, Katie Cooney, and Louise Grinsdale, we couldn't have done it without you.

Appreciation must also be shown for the extensive research carried out by Guangrong Dai, Jon Feil, and King Yii (Lulu) Tang. Your work helped us provide rich examples to support our suggestions, as well as a wide variety of additional learning resources. And the research and support of Gustavo Gisbert and Dave McMonagle helped us over the finish line.

Vicki Swisher, we thank you for your insightful review of everything we wrote. Your keen eye and vast experience were invaluable.

The translation of the guide into several languages would not have been possible without Valérie Petit. Thank you for enabling us to reach people across the globe.

We must also thank those who kept us in line – Karen Opp for your essential legal guidance and Diana Vaicius for managing the whole project from start to finish.

The creation of this guide would not have been complete without the skill and dedication of our design and production team of Lesley Kurke, Doug Lodermeier, and Paul Montei. And lastly, a huge thank you to Bonnie Parks for doing such a wonderful job of editing and proofing, not to mention providing us with moral support and the benefit of your extensive experience.

The rich legacy of research and intellectual property created by Bob Eichinger and Mike Lombardo formed the foundation upon which this guide is built. Their work provided inspiration for many of the ideas expressed within.

It took a village, and in the words of Helen Keller, "Alone we can do so little; together we can do so much."

1. *Ensures* accountability

Holding self and others accountable to meet commitments.

Taking responsibility. Owning up to commitments. Being answerable for your actions and the actions of those you lead. All fall under the umbrella of accountability. Being accountable and ensuring accountability in others is as important in and out of work today as ever. Important and a little scary. Why? Being accountable makes you more visible and more open to criticism. It means putting yourself at risk. All eyes are on you. If the assignment, project, or strategy fails, you're on the hook for it. And in this hyperconnected, hypervigilant world, there's no place to hide. But when it comes to ensuring that accountability thrives in your organization, absorbing the risk can pay off in multiple ways. On critical projects, it instills confidence in others when they know you have a vested interest in the positive outcome they are all striving toward. Taking the same responsibility for a losing strategy as you do for a winning one shows others that you stand behind your decisions. This builds a culture of accountability around you. A culture where people own their decisions and their actions. Where credit is shared and blame accepted. By ensuring accountability in yourself and leading so others do the same, you are more likely to be trusted and respected by others. More likely to speak out when there is a problem. More likely to be committed to your work. More likely to deliver high performance. More likely to succeed.

" *I attribute my success to this –*
I never gave or took any excuse. **"**

Florence Nightingale – English social reformer and founder of modern nursing

| 1

***Ensures* accountability** is in the **Results** factor (II) in the Korn Ferry Leadership Architect™. It is part of Cluster F, **Focusing on performance,** along with *Drives* results (28). You may find it helpful to also take a look at some of the tips included in that chapter to supplement your learning.

Skilled

Follows through on commitments and makes sure others do the same.

Acts with a clear sense of ownership.

Takes personal responsibility for decisions, actions, and failures.

Establishes clear responsibilities and processes for monitoring work and measuring results.

Designs feedback loops into work.

Less skilled

- Fails to accept a fair share of personal responsibility.
- Gathers little information about how things are going.
- Provides inadequate feedback; fails to help others adjust course midstream.
- Prefers to be one of many accountable for an assignment.

Talented

- Assumes responsibility for the outcomes of others.
- Promotes a sense of urgency and establishes and enforces individual accountability in the team.
- Works with people to establish explicit performance standards.
- Is completely on top of what is going on and knows where things stand.
- Provides balanced feedback at the most critical times.

Overused skill

- May not give appropriate credit to others.
- Strictly enforces accountability; doesn't consider situations that are beyond individuals' control.
- Focuses too much on numbers and hard data; measurement becomes a goal and a pursuit of its own.

Some possible causes of lower skill

Causes help explain *why* a person may have trouble with *Ensures* accountability. When seeking to increase skill, it's helpful to consider how these might play out in certain situations. And remember that all of these can be addressed if you are motivated to do so.

- Not goal oriented.
- Afraid of making a mistake.
- Low self-confidence.
- Narrow comfort zone.
- Lacks commitment.
- Unsure how to measure performance.
- Disregards the bigger picture.
- Shies away from tough problems.
- Has unrealistic expectations.

 Culture card

Accountability plays out differently in different cultures. Collaborating across international boundaries means recognizing and respecting this. A Brazilian team working with an American team might feel the tension of different priorities. Both may take responsibility for performance excellence. Both may have a sense of urgency. But both see different things as critical. To a Brazilian, relationships are seen as paramount to delivering the result. Too much planning gets in the way of that. The American is likely to see the project plan as essential. Socializing is not essential to the task and may even get in the way. Accountability to the process versus accountability to the people. One culture doesn't want to fail people. The other doesn't want to fail the plan. So how do cross-cultural teams reconcile their different views of accountability? Through recognition of differences. Appreciation of what's valued by others. Willingness to compromise and adapt. The Brazilian team could position a project plan as integral to forging a relationship with their colleagues. The American team could invest more time socializing and connecting. Establishing common accountability across cultures means accommodating what is most important to others.[1]

Tips to develop *Ensures* accountability

1. **Unsure of the target? Establish clear goals.** How can you take charge of where you're headed unless you know your destination? Before you can take accountability for anything, you need to know what's expected. Have a set of clearly articulated goals that specifically states the outcome required and defines your target result—a clear picture of what success looks like. Goals help focus time and effort. They make things fairer. They provide an objective way to measure someone against what's required of them. They can be used to stretch people. Learn how to create SMART (Specific, Measurable, Achievable, Relevant, Time-bound) goals. Set SMART goals for projects and other work tasks when you assign them to yourself or others.

2. **Tend to put things off? Identify procrastination triggers.** Procrastination is a common way of avoiding responsibility or putting off dealing with a situation. Often, it means that someone else has to take responsibility. Others may start to see you as unreliable. Not accountable. Identify why you procrastinate. Slow to act because you don't think you're up to the task? Talk it through with someone who will bolster your confidence. Waiting until you have 100% of the information and resources you need to get started? Start doing the things you can do with the resources you have. Find it too overwhelming? Break it down into smaller, more manageable pieces. Commit to doing a piece a day. Don't even think of the larger goal. Just do something on it each day. Do you find the task boring? Focus on the sense of achievement you will have from getting it done and off your desk. Or is it something else? Once you understand why you put things off, you can take steps to fix the problem. Support others in identifying their reasons too.

3. **Afraid to fail? Redefine success.** Need things to go right the first time? Have to finish what you've started? Must complete tasks and wrap them up into nice clean packages? View it as a failure if you are unable to achieve this 100% of the time? Things won't always go right the first time. As John F. Kennedy once said, "Nothing worthwhile has ever been accomplished with a guarantee of success." Often, things worth doing take repeated effort. A midcourse correction might be needed. Sometimes it's right that a task be abandoned, never finished. Develop a philosophical view of failure. Change your internal reward system from one that only celebrates completion to one that recognizes effort. Give yourself credit for successfully moving things forward incrementally. Praise yourself for seeking feedback and fixing mistakes. Have the courage to rethink

the plan. Salute your bold decisions to change direction or halt, if that is the right thing to do.

4. **Unsure why your contribution matters? Find the connection.** It can be hard to engage your head and heart if you can't see how your efforts fit into the big picture. Everyone needs a clear line of sight from their personal goals to the goals of the organization. Make it your business to learn all you can about the vision, the overall objectives, the future direction. Read the mission statement and annual reports. Talk to people who know. Then find a way to articulate how your responsibilities fit in. How you contribute to success through the tasks you do each day. Why your efforts matter. Take pride in the fact that you're responsible for the achievement of something bigger than yourself and your immediate team.

Want to learn more? Take a deep dive...

Ashkenas, R. (2012, July 9). Seven mistakes leaders make in setting goals. *Forbes.*

Chua, C. (2010, June 3). *11 Practical ways to stop procrastinating.* Lifehack.

Doherty, K. (2008). *Strategies to reduce perfectionism.* Psych Central.

Mind Tools. (n.d.). *Helping people take responsibility.* Mind Tools.

5. **Stuck in first gear on a new assignment? Focus to move forward.** Write down where you are now and where you want to be. Ask yourself: What are the benefits of achieving this goal? What do I need in order to succeed? How will I get there? What paths could I take? Who else needs to be involved? What could help/hinder my progress? How else could I achieve the required outcome? Write down your answers. Use them to create actions. Start with what *you* will do *now*. Break big action steps into a few smaller, more manageable ones. Arrange them in chronological order. Give yourself a date by which each will be accomplished. Hold yourself accountable for each one. Review your progress regularly and tick them off as you go. Use your plan to stay on top of what is going on.

6. **Need to stay focused? Monitor progress regularly.** How will you know you've delivered a successful outcome? What will you see? Hear? Feel? How will you know you're on track? What formal and informal metrics will you use to measure progress? Take a look at

| 5

1

what you're responsible for. Can you confidently answer each of those questions? If not, spend time clarifying. Discuss with others where you need to. Set up a process to monitor progress toward goal achievement. Be creative. Explore using visual aids. Maybe a thermometer or a running track with a finish line. Show progress as you go. Create a sense of urgency by showing "hot spots" or where standards are slipping. Indicate key milestones. Celebrate as each one is reached. Display team or departmental goals and visual aids on the wall—somewhere prominent, where everyone will see them. If you are setting goals for others, involve them in defining success measures. They'll often come up with measures that are important to them and that are different from formal measures. Monitoring progress must motivate, so let them decide what will spur them on.

7. **Not sure how you're doing? Find ways to gauge your impact.** It's up to you to ensure you're doing the right things, at the right time, in the right way. That you're delivering to the required standard. Causing the right outcomes. Having the right impact on others. As well as using formal measures to monitor how you're doing, introduce feedback loops into your work. Invite others to comment on the impact of your actions and behaviors as they experience them. The faster and the more frequent the cycles, the more opportunities you have to learn. Reflect on what you learn. Evaluate the feedback in line with what you need to achieve. Make necessary adjustments.

8. **Don't like asking for help? Cast pride aside.** If you find it difficult to ask for help, try to establish why. Perhaps you see it as a sign of weakness? Feel you should be able to deal with situations alone? The fact is that sometimes two (or more) minds are better than one. It's likely you often won't have all the answers. Especially when it comes to dealing with tough problems. Ask for help when you need it; don't wait for a crisis to occur. When it is offered, accept it in good faith. You'll gather more information. Gain a broader perspective of the issue. Be better equipped to make the right decisions. Able to act more quickly. Learn new ways of operating. Start seeing the value of interdependence with others. Remember that asking for and accepting help from others does not make you less accountable. It also doesn't mean you are shirking responsibility. It means you're committed to doing the best job you can.

Want to learn more? Take a deep dive...

Fox, J. (2013, December 13). You can get some big things done when it's not all about you. *Harvard Business Review Blog Network.*

The Muse. (2012, September 20). The right way to ask for help at work. *Forbes.*

Vanderkam, L. (2012, June 12). What the most successful people do before breakfast. *Fast Company.*

Wilson, H. J. (2012, April 2). Employees, measure yourselves. *The Wall Street Journal.*

9. **Run away from mistakes? Own up to them.** Everyone makes mistakes. Mistakes go with being human. When a mistake happens, it's tempting to cover it up, get defensive, or even go on the attack. Avoid the blame game, whether it's blaming circumstances or, worse, placing the blame on someone else. Admit your mistake early. Make it public. Especially if the error could impact other people or other projects. Let people know quickly to limit the damage. You may have created the problem; now become part of the solution. You can't change what happened, but you can help make it right. Talk about the mistake matter-of-factly. One way to get some good from a misstep is to always ask, "What can I learn from this?" Turn a bad situation into a valuable lesson—don't waste it. Apply what you have learned so the mistake does not happen again. Make learning from mistakes a good habit. Move on, don't dwell on it. Learn to be more comfortable admitting your mistakes. Don't run for cover, face the music. In doing so, you'll encourage others to do the same.

10. **Assured you're doing a good job? Do it better.** When you're consistently meeting the required standards of performance, it's easy to get comfortable. Complacent. To get stuck in a routine of doing what you've always done. And why not? After all, you're doing a good job, right? While the answer to that may be yes today, over time it is likely to become no. Don't get left behind. Raise your personal standards. Set stretching goals. Push yourself to the next level of success. Proactively find ways that you can do an even better job. Challenge limiting beliefs about what you can achieve. Have the courage to step outside your comfort zone. It's where you'll reap the biggest rewards.

11. **Shy away from giving feedback? Learn the principles of constructive feedback.** Honest feedback lets people know how they are performing. It can confirm they are meeting the expected standards. Or it can let them know they are falling short. Keep it factual. Talk about behaviors—the things you have seen and heard the person do. Don't make statements about their identity—who they are or their values. Be specific about what has gone well and what needs adjusting. Guide them to make midcourse corrections. Give the feedback "in the moment"—while the event is still fresh enough for your comments to resonate. Don't put it off for days or weeks. Point out an error before it becomes a problem. Remember, feedback should be balanced when it makes sense. Catch people doing something right. Make giving regular feedback a priority. Being accountable for giving feedback helps others become accountable for their own actions.

Want to learn more? Take a deep dive...

Klobucher, T. (2011, October 24). The danger of complacency in the workplace. The Great Workplace Revolution [YouTube].

Llopis, G. (2013, July 8). 10 Signs your employees are growing complacent in their careers. *Forbes*.

White, S. (2011, October 13). Overcoming work mistakes: Learn how to speak up and move on. *The Huffington Post Canada*.

Zenger, J., & Folkman, J. (2014, January 15). Your employees want the negative feedback you have to give. *Harvard Business Review Blog Network*.

Job assignments

- Put yourself forward to lead the resolution of a tough problem that requires help from others. Recognize what others have to offer and how they can support you.

- Volunteer to present a proposal to a senior team that you know will provoke contention, raise challenging questions, and encourage debate. Be prepared to fight your corner.

- Volunteer to lead the definition of SMART goals for a new or evolving project.

- Work on a project that analyzes performance and results and take responsibility for feeding back the outcome to those involved.

- Design a set of formal and informal measures of progress for your current responsibilities. Share them with your boss. Review your progress on an ongoing basis.

Take time to reflect...

If you're worried about being blamed when things go wrong...

> ...then consider that taking accountability also means you're likely to get the credit when things go right. Accountability involves taking the rough with the smooth.

If you let things slide rather than challenging others to deliver...

> ...then remember that success often depends on each person in the team contributing. If someone isn't getting the job done, they will need to improve or accept the consequences. Otherwise, the whole team may suffer.

If you take accountability yourself, but don't instill it in others...

> ...then find out how to make the work matter for your team. What will success bring? What are the consequences of missing targets? Show them why excellence is essential.

"Few things can help an individual more
than to place responsibility upon him,
and to let him know that you trust him. **"**

Booker T. Washington – American educator, author, and orator

Learn more about *Ensures* accountability

Burka, J. B., & Yuen, L. M. (2008). Procrastination: *Why you do it and what to do about it now* [25th Anniversary ed.]. Cambridge, MA: Da Capo Press.

Evans, H. J. (2008). *Winning with accountability: The secret language of high-performing organizations.* Dallas, TX: CornerStone Leadership Institute.

Grimshaw, J., & Baron, G. (2010). *Leadership without excuses: How to create accountability and high performance (instead of just talking about it).* New York, NY: McGraw-Hill.

Pychyl, T. A. (2013). *Solving the procrastination puzzle: A concise guide to strategies for change.* New York, NY: Penguin Group.

Samov, P. (2010). *Present perfect: A mindfulness approach to letting go of perfectionism and the need for control.* Oakland, CA: New Harbinger Publications, Inc.

Deep dive learning resource links

Ashkenas, R. (2012, July 9). Seven mistakes leaders make in setting goals. *Forbes.* Retrieved from http://www.forbes.com/sites/ronashkenas/2012/07/09/seven-mistakes-leaders-make-in-setting-goals/

Chua, C. (2010, June 3). *11 Practical ways to stop procrastinating.* Lifehack. Retrieved from http://www.lifehack.org/articles/lifehack/11-practical-ways-to-stop-procrastination.html

Doheny, K. (2008). *Strategies to reduce perfectionism.* Psych Central. Retrieved from http://psychcentral.com/lib/strategies-to-reduce-perfectionism/0001526

Fox, J. (2013, December 13). You can get some big things done when it's not all about you. *Harvard Business Review Blog Network.* Retrieved from http://blogs.hbr.org/2013/12/you-can-get-some-big-things-done-when-its-not-all-about-you/

Klobucher, T. (2011, October 24). The danger of complacency in the workplace. The Great Workplace Revolution [YouTube]. Retrieved from http://www.youtube.com/watch?v=kez4J7l-Swg

Llopis, G. (2013, July 8). 10 Signs your employees are growing complacent in their careers. *Forbes.* Retrieved from http://www.forbes.com/sites/glennllopis/2013/07/08/10-signs-your-employees-are-growing-complacent-in-their-careers/

Mind Tools. (n.d.). *Helping people take responsibility.* Mind Tools. Retrieved from http://www.mindtools.com/pages/article/taking-responsibility.htm

The Muse. (2012, September 20). The right way to ask for help at work. *Forbes.* Retrieved from http://www.forbes.com/sites/dailymuse/2012/09/20/the-right-way-to-ask-for-help-at-work/

Vanderkam, L. (2012, June 12). What the most successful people do before breakfast. *Fast Company.* Retrieved from http://www.fastcompany.com/1839987/what-most-successful-people-do-breakfast

White, S. (2011, October 13). Overcoming work mistakes: Learn how to speak up and move on. *The Huffington Post Canada.* Retrieved from http://www.huffingtonpost.ca/2011/10/12/overcoming-work-mistakes_n_1007275.html

Wilson, H. J. (2012, April 2). Employees, measure yourselves. *The Wall Street Journal.* Retrieved from http://online.wsj.com/news/articles/SB10001424052970204520204577249691204802060

Zenger, J., & Folkman, J. (2014, January 15). Your employees want the negative feedback you have to give. *Harvard Business Review Blog Network.* Retrieved from http://blogs.hbr.org/2014/01/your-employees-want-the-negative-feedback-you-hate-to-give/

Recommended search terms

If you'd like to explore *Ensures* accountability further, try searching online using the following terms:

- Avoiding procrastination.
- Keeping others accountable.
- Monitoring your progress at work.
- Owning up to your mistakes.
- Reducing perfectionism.
- Stopping complacency in the workplace.

 More help...

Go to www.kornferry.com/fyi-resources and link directly to the deep dive resources in this chapter. Visit the site often to see the additional resources that are uploaded on a regular basis.

2. Action oriented

Taking on new opportunities and tough challenges with a sense of urgency, high energy, and enthusiasm.

In our fast-moving world, opportunities can pass by in a flash. Blink and a chance is missed. Organizations depend on great ideas to keep them ahead of the pack, but without implementation, they're just good ideas. Thoughts, initiatives, plans, designs, strategies—all critically important, but none of them will make a difference without execution. And that's where action oriented people come in. They make things happen. Ideas become plans. Plans become reality. They get things moving. When things get tough, they rise to the occasion and switch to solution focus. They quickly move from "Why did this happen?" to "How can this work?" And they inspire others to do the same. So don't just think it, do it. Take some risks. Seize opportunities. Drive things forward.

"Vision is not enough.
It must be combined with venture.
It is not enough to stare up the steps;
we must also step up the stairs."

Vaclav Havel – Czech politician and writer

Action oriented is in the **Results** factor (II) in the Korn Ferry Leadership Architect™. It is part of Cluster D, **Taking initiative,** along with **Resourcefulness** (27). You may find it helpful to also take a look at some of the tips included in that chapter to supplement your learning.

Skilled

Readily takes action on challenges, without unnecessary planning.

Identifies and seizes new opportunities.

Displays a can-do attitude in good and bad times.

Steps up to handle tough issues.

Less skilled

- Is slow to act on an opportunity.

- Spends too much time planning and looking for information.

- May be overly methodical, taking too long to act on a problem.

- Is reluctant to step up to challenges; waits for someone else to take action.

Talented

- Quickly and decisively takes action in fast-changing, unpredictable situations.

- Shows a tremendous amount of initiative in tough situations; is exceptional at spotting and seizing opportunities.

Overused skill

- Pushes solutions before adequate analysis.

- May waste energy by immediately tackling an issue, forcing rework along the way.

- Is so ready to act alone, misses counsel from others.

Some possible causes of lower skill

Causes help explain *why* a person may have trouble with Action oriented. When seeking to increase skill, it's helpful to consider how these might play out in certain situations. And remember that all of these can be addressed if you are motivated to do so.

- Burned out.
- Hesitates too much.
- Reluctant to make a decision.
- Not motivated, bored.
- Not passionate enough about work.
- Perfectionist.
- Procrastinates.
- Lacks self-confidence.
- Slow to grab opportunities.
- Won't take a risk.

Brain booster

Are you a multi-tasker? Action-oriented people often try to do more than one thing at once. Check e-mail while cooking dinner, carry on two conversations at once, wrap up writing two or more reports at the same time. What we think of as multi-tasking is really just juggling. Switching your attention between tasks quickly may feel like a necessary survival skill, but toggling between tasks has a cost. Studies that look at divided attention show that when we are distracted, we remember less, we perform worse, and it decreases our brain power. But in today's frenetic world, focusing purely on one thing at a time is not always realistic. Think carefully about how you manage your tasks. What can you do simultaneously without affecting your productivity? Don't try to juggle several cognitively demanding tasks. Working on a task that requires a lot of thinking alongside one that requires less brain energy is more feasible. If a task needs your intense concentration, treat yourself to a break by working on something more mindless.[2]

Tips to develop Action oriented

1. **Tend to procrastinate? Get an early start.** Do you put things off until the last minute? Is there always another day to get something started? Do you think you perform at your best when time is tight and you have an "impossible" deadline? Some people genuinely do work more effectively under pressure. Maybe it's because they need a fire under them to get them moving. Having too much time makes distractions tempting. Whatever the reason, pushing things to the last minute is risky. Things can go wrong. Unexpected events present themselves with no warning. Plans get thrown off track. Procrastinate and you reduce your ability to flex when unforeseen events come your way. Start early. Always complete 10% of each task as soon as it's assigned. Take some preemptive action to get you moving. Make some notes. Call a stakeholder. Source some materials. Anything to get the ball rolling. If you need to feel the heat, create some by breaking the task down into smaller stages, each with their own tight deadline. If the overall task seems overwhelming, focus instead on each step that will get you there.

2. **Moving, but in the wrong direction? Get your priorities right.** Some people take action but on the wrong things. Effective leaders typically spend about half their time on two or three key priorities. What should you spend half your time on? Can you name five things that you have to do that are less critical? If you can't, you're not differentiating well. People without priorities see their jobs as 97 things that need to be done right now—that will actually slow you down. Pick a few mission-critical things and get them done. Don't get diverted by trivia. Clear the clutter.

3. **Perfectionist? Curb your appetite for 100%.** Need everything to be just so before you can progress? Do you worry when every "t" isn't crossed? Perfectionism is tough to let go of, especially if you pride yourself on it. Recognize what might be at the root of your perfectionism. Collecting information to build your confidence? Recognize that you don't have to be right all the time. Afraid of criticism? Remember that others are unlikely to scrutinize as much as you do. Worried about being mediocre? Celebrate your strengths. Each week let go of some of your need to be perfect—even just a little. Practice tolerating less-than-perfect away from work. Resist ironing every wrinkle out of your shirt. Accept that the paint on the back door is not quite streak free. Live with the picture that's slightly lopsided. Make similar allowances in the work environment. Let things go. Sometimes good enough is good enough. You just need

to be able to figure out when. The time you save striving for perfection can be put toward actually getting things done.

4. **Stuck in analysis paralysis? Balance thought with action.** Break out of your "examine it to death" mode and just do it. Sometimes you hold back on acting because you don't have all the information. You like to be sure before you act. The real test is who can act the soonest with a reasonable amount of data, but not necessarily all of it. If you learn to make smaller decisions more quickly, you can change course along the way. Build your confidence with less analysis and more experimenting. Choose some tasks that affect only a small number of people. Set yourself an absolute deadline to move forward and go for it. Act, get feedback on the results, refine, and act again. Be brave with some bigger tasks. Pessimist? You may examine things to death because you're a chronic worrier who focuses on the downsides of action. Write down your worries, and for each one, assign an upside—a pro for each con. Once you consider both sides of the issue, you will be more willing to take action.

Want to learn more? Take a deep dive...

AsapScience. (2012, December 12). The science of productivity [YouTube]. AsapScience.

Branson, R. (2011, September 27). Richard Branson on time management. *Entrepreneur*

Shellenbarger, S. (2009, November 18). No time to read this? Read this. *The Wall Street Journal.*

5. **Don't like risk? Start small.** Sometimes taking action involves pushing yourself, taking chances, and trying bold new initiatives. Doing those things leads to more misfires and mistakes. Research says that successful executives have made more mistakes in their careers than less successful ones. Treat any mistakes or failures as chances to learn. Nothing ventured, nothing gained. Increase your comfort with risk. Start small so you can recover more quickly. Go for small wins. Don't blast into a major task to prove your boldness. Break it down into smaller tasks. Start with the one you find easiest. Then build up to the tougher ones. Try out new approaches. Review each task to see what you did well. What did you not do well? Set goals so you'll do something differently and better each time. Challenge yourself. See how creative you can be in taking action a number of different ways.

6. **Not sure if you can do it? Build your confidence.** Maybe you're slow to act because you don't think you're up to the task. If you boldly act, others will shoot you down. If you don't get it right the first time, you'll never be able to do it. Think about when you first rode your bike without training wheels. Did you read a manual? Study other kids riding before you climbed onto the seat? Probably not. You just did it, likely falling off more times than you could count. Then climbed back on and kept at it until you got it. That "just do it" spirit can get stifled by the desire to be cautious. Being successful right away becomes more important than taking a chance by acting. Take a course or work with a mentor to bolster your confidence in one skill area at a time. Focus on the strengths you do have; think of ways you can use these strengths when taking nerve-wracking actions. If you are interpersonally skilled, for example, see yourself smoothly dealing with questions and objections to your actions. The only way you will ever know what you can do is to act and find out.

7. **Bruised by failure? Focus on opportunities.** Did something go wrong and you swore never to try it again? Are you still smarting from the sting of a failed attempt? Mistakes happen. To everyone. When Dr. Spencer Silver produced a low-tack glue instead of the super strength adhesive he was aiming for, he could have discarded it as a failure. But, instead, he talked up its potential uses for six years. Finally a colleague, Art Fry, recognized its practical application. And the ubiquitous sticky note was born. Not every mistake leads to a game-changing product, but learning and opportunity are there for the taking when things don't work out. Reflect on three things that didn't work out as you'd planned. How did you deal with them? What could you have done differently in handling those situations? What did you learn from the experience? What opportunities could have emerged from not achieving what you set out to do?

8. **Afraid to get others involved? Polish your sales pitch.** Taking action requires that you get others on board. You need their input, their support, their ideas. Work on your influencing and selling skills. Lay out the business reason for the action. Think about how you can help everybody win by taking action. Get others to buy in before you have to take action. Involved people are easier to influence. Learn better negotiation skills. Learn to bargain and trade.

Want to learn more? Take a deep dive...

Ancowitz, N. (2009, September 18). Introverts: Manage your perfectionism and reduce your agita! *Psychology Today.*

Editor in Chief, Pick the Brain. (2007, October 3). *7 Ways to overcome the fear of failure.* Pick the Brain.

Litt, M. (2012). Why you have to fail to have a great career: Michael Litt at TEDxUW [YouTube]. TED.

9. **Don't see the importance? Get the bigger picture.** Sometimes a task or a project seems pointless. You just don't see why you have to expend time and energy on it. You'd much rather focus on something else. Well, you were given this assignment for a reason. The goal you set to get the job done defines *what* you need to do and *how* you'll get there. What's sometimes missing is the *why*. What does your task contribute to? What difference does it make to the organization? Where does your piece of the puzzle fit in? If you don't know, chances are you'll be lacking the motivation to get it done. Find out what's going on in the organization. Understand where your function fits in. Read the latest financial report. Familiarize yourself with the organizational goals. Learn how important the work of your team is to achieving these. Read marketing literature. Talk to colleagues in different functions. Track the path from your goal to the overall objectives of the organization. See it as part of the full picture. Describe the consequences if you don't move forward with a sense of urgency.

10. **Lost your passion? Focus on your interests.** Have you run out of gas? Is your heart not in it anymore? Not 100% committed? Been doing the same sort of work a long time and bored with it? Made the same decisions time and time again? Worked with the same people? You may not be able to change all of this, but you can make the best of it. List what you like and don't like to do. Concentrate on doing at least a couple of your preferred activities each day. Work to delegate or task trade the things that are no longer motivating to you. Do your least favorite activities first; focus not on the activity, but your sense of accomplishment. Change your work activity to mirror your interests as much as you can. Volunteer for new projects that will stretch your skills and make you flex different muscles.

11. **Can't get motivated? Find a compelling purpose to pull you along.** Some assignments have you leaping out of bed in the morning to

get going. Others make you want to reset the alarm. Throwing yourself into something you're not inspired to do is hard going. A status update report you loathe writing. Sales activity number-crunching that is so tedious to pull together. The Pacific Institute's Lou Tice emphasized the importance of turning "have tos" into "want tos." An update report is just a report until it enables the CEO to recognize employees for the fantastic community support project it describes. Sales stats are just numbers until they're turned into the success reported to shareholders. Focus on the end result of your tedious task. What does it enable? Who's going to benefit? What difference will it make to them? Turn your have to into a want to. Now you have a great reason to get the job done.

Want to learn more? Take a deep dive...

Klein, P. (2012, June 6). How to find work with purpose. *Forbes.*

Pink, D. (2009, August 25). Dan Pink: The puzzle of motivation [YouTube]. TED.

Taylor, J. (2012, January 2). Personal growth: Motivation: The drive to change. *Psychology Today.*

Job assignments

- Volunteer to lead a project that will require driving many actions within very aggressive time frames.

- Take on a daunting task such as stepping in to fix a critical initiative that has stalled, lost focus, or encountered major obstacles.

- Identify and pursue a bold new opportunity for the organization. Make a case for the new idea, draft a plan of action, and carry forward the steps needed to ensure successful returns.

- Turn around the performance of a project team or group that has become bogged down by many competing priorities. Provide a clear path forward and execute the vital actions necessary for success.

- Take responsibility for a task or a target that people have grown weary of and instill a feeling of renewed purpose, energy, and drive in the team.

Take time to reflect...

If you shy away from getting started and find yourself hesitating instead of acting...

> ...then recognize that thinking about it, analyzing it, and planning it are all important, but they don't get the job done. You have to take the plunge and get going.

If you worry your course of action is not correct and may fail...

> ...then be aware that putting things off is not going to help. Even if the way isn't certain, take a few preliminary steps. As you push ahead, the right path will likely grow clearer.

If you often lose sight of the purpose and goal...

> ...then reflect on the "Why?" behind what you are doing. Busy does not mean effective. Keeping focused on the overall goal is critical to staying productive and aligned.

❝‍*You are what you do, not what you say you'll do.* **❞**

Carl Jung – Swiss psychiatrist

Learn more about Action oriented

Baldoni, J. (2005). *Great motivation secrets of great leaders.* New York, NY: McGraw-Hill.

Covey, S. M. R. (1989). *The 7 habits of highly effective people: Powerful lessons in personal change.* New York, NY: Simon & Schuster.

Hiam, A. (2003). *Motivational management: Inspiring your people for maximum performance.* New York, NY: AMACOM.

Somov, P. G. (2010). Present perfect: *A mindfulness approach to letting go of perfectionism and the need for control.* Oakland, CA: New Harbinger Publications, Inc.

Thomas, K. W. (2009). *Intrinsic motivation at work: What really drives employee engagement* (2nd ed.). San Francisco, CA: Berrett-Koehler Publishers.

Deep dive learning resource links

Ancowitz, N. (2009, September 18). Introverts: Manage your perfectionism and reduce your agita! *Psychology Today.* Retrieved from http://www.psychologytoday.com/blog/self-promotion-introverts/200909/introverts-manage-your-perfectionism-and-reduce-your-agita

AsapScience. (2012, December 12). The science of productivity [YouTube]. AsapScience. Retrieved from https://www.youtube.com/watch?v=lHfjvYzr-3g

Branson, R. (2011, September 27). Richard Branson on time management. *Entrepreneur.* Retrieved from http://www.entrepreneur.com/article/220418

Editor in Chief, Pick the Brain. (2007, October 3). *7 Ways to overcome the fear of failure.* Pick the Brain. Retrieved from http://www.pickthebrain.com/blog/overcome-fear-of-failure/

Klein, P. (2012, June 6). How to find work with purpose. *Forbes.* Retrieved from http://www.forbes.com/sites/csr/2012/06/06/how-to-find-work-with-purpose/

Litt, M. (2012). Why you have to fail to have a great career: Michael Litt at TEDxUW [YouTube]. TED. Retrieved from https://www.youtube.com/watch?v=hNQRRsL3R4A

Pink, D. (2009, August 25). Dan Pink: The puzzle of motivation [YouTube]. TED. Retrieved from https://www.youtube.com/watch?v=rrkrvAUbU9Y

22 |

Shellenbarger, S. (2009, November 18). No time to read this? Read this. *The Wall Street Journal*. Retrieved from http://online.wsj.com/news/articles/SB10001424052748704538404574541590534797908

Taylor, J. (2012, January 2). Personal growth: Motivation: The drive to change. *Psychology Today*. Retrieved from http://www.psychologytoday.com/blog/the-power-prime/201201/personal-growth-motivation-the-drive-change

Recommended search terms

If you'd like to explore Action oriented further, try searching online using the following terms:

- Effective time management.
- Finding your motivation.
- Learning from failure.
- Overcoming fear of failure.
- Reducing perfectionism.

(i) More help...

Go to www.kornferry.com/fyi-resources and link directly to the deep dive resources in this chapter. Visit the site often to see the additional resources that are uploaded on a regular basis.

3. *Manages* ambiguity

Operating effectively, even when things are not certain or the way forward is not clear.

Whether at work or off work, people constantly face situations that are ambiguous or uncertain—where it's not clear what the problem is or what the solution is. Where the unknown outweighs the known by a wide margin. Some studies estimate that 90% of what managers deal with is at least somewhat ambiguous. New demands, new technology, new marching orders, new processes. Nothing lasts very long. In an era when clarity is scarce and certainty is fleeting, relying on solutions that have worked in the past may seem safe, but it's actually risky. New times require new solutions. Solving problems and getting things done in this volatile context means being willing to forge ahead when the path is foggy, at best. It means adjusting your approach—to both problems and people—to match changing conditions. To surrender the need to be sure. The world is getting less and less predictable. By having a mindset geared to viewing uncertainty as the new normal, you'll be better prepared when the next unknown appears. And better prepared to view that unknown as an opportunity to capitalize on.

*" Take advantage of the ambiguity in the world.
Look at something and think what else it might be. "*

Roger von Oech – American speaker, conference organizer, and author

***Manages* ambiguity** is in the **Self** factor (IV) in the Korn Ferry Leadership Architect™. It is part of Cluster L, **Being flexible and adaptable,** along with Nimble learning (22), *Being* resilient (26), and Situational adaptability (31). You may find it helpful to also take a look at some of the tips included in those chapters to supplement your learning.

Skilled

Deals comfortably with the uncertainty of change.

Effectively handles risk.

Can decide and act without the total picture.

Is calm and productive, even when things are up in the air.

Deals constructively with problems that do not have clear solutions or outcomes.

Less skilled

- Struggles to make progress when facing ambiguous or uncertain situations.

- Delays moving forward until all the details are known.

- Appears stressed when things are uncertain.

- Operates best when things are structured and predictable.

Talented

- Is energized when faced with ambiguity and uncertainty.

- Makes significant progress and remains calm and composed, even when things are uncertain.

- Manages the risk that comes with moving forward when the outcome isn't certain.

- Adapts quickly to changing conditions.

Overused skill

- May move to conclusions or action without enough data.

- May err toward the new and risky at the expense of proven solutions.

- Doesn't honor others' need for some level of clarity before acting.

26 |

Some possible causes of lower skill

Causes help explain *why* a person may have trouble with *Manages* ambiguity. When seeking to increase skill, it's helpful to consider how these might play out in certain situations. And remember that all of these can be addressed if you are motivated to do so.

- Prefers maintaining control.
- Easily overwhelmed.
- Cautious; avoids risk.
- Likes things to be predictable.
- Dislikes change.
- Negative bias; focuses on the downsides.
- Freezes without a clear plan.
- High need to be right.
- Too inflexible.
- Perfection oriented.

Brain booster

Your brain likes certainty. It is designed to predict and anticipate what will happen next. You look for patterns or scripts that make it easy to see what comes next. When patterns play out the way you expect, your brain experiences a reward. When patterns do not play out the way you expect, your brain experiences a threat. Ambiguity is distressing because it means we cannot rely on patterns, we can't predict what will happen next. This gives us a sense of a lack of control or autonomy. When uncertainty is beyond our control, we experience high levels of stress. When uncertainty is within our control (we need to make a decision about something), the stress feels more manageable. To manage ambiguity and uncertainty, take stock of what control you have in the situation. What choices can you make. What routes might you take, given different possible outcomes. The more you can feel like an agent in the situation, the lower your stress levels will be.[3]

Tips to develop *Manages* ambiguity

1. **Holding too tightly to the past? Just let go.** Dealing comfortably with uncertainty and ambiguity means letting go of sureness. Like letting go of one trapeze in the air to catch the next one. For a small amount of time, you have nothing to hold on to. If you cling to the first trapeze, afraid you will fall, you'll always return to the same old platform—safe but not new or different. Staying put means it's more likely your safe platform will keep getting smaller and smaller until it disappears completely. Taking that leap gets you to a new platform and a new place. Manage the uncertainty around you by being proactive. Keep informed about business/technological advances. Keep alert to trends and what entrepreneurs are inventing in their garages. Visualize different pathways and different outcomes. Talk about it. Invite ideas. The more you do this, the more comfortable you'll feel because you'll be part of the next wave.

2. **Don't know where to begin? Experiment with small steps.** Imagine all the lights suddenly go out. Or you wake up in the middle of the night in a strange location. What do you do? You feel your way around until your eyes adjust. You reach for a light. Embarking on a new venture or acting on an ambiguous problem with no precedents to follow is similar. Work to make the unknown known. Break a large issue into manageable pieces. Take small steps and see what happens. Get instant feedback, correct the course, then move forward a little more. Don't try to get it all right the first time. The more uncertain the situation is, the more likely mistakes will be made. Expect it—bumping into things while looking for the light is common. Think of mistakes as valuable feedback steering you in the right direction. Make it safe to talk about them. Build curiosity while undertaking risk—this will decrease stress and increase creativity. Experiment, prototype, conduct soft launches. Engage stakeholders to make sense of what emerges and evolves. If criticism follows flawed results, accept it while pointing out how you'll apply what's been learned in the next iteration.

3. **Think you need to have all the answers? Convey your overall intention.** Many feel shaky without a concrete plan. It's understandable—how can you lead when you're not sure where you're going? How can you assess progress without clear targets to measure against? Moving through transitions or into any new turf, people want to know where they stand. What to do when they go to work each day. More importantly, why those things matter. So speak honestly about what's going on. Explain what you know and don't know. If you don't have a game plan with firm time lines, share the

overall intention instead—what you're aiming toward and how that supports the mission. Change expert Peggy Holman asserts that intentions are "powerful shapers of action." They energize and align self-directed people in complex situations. They fuel a sense of purpose. So co-create your intentions with invested colleagues, communicate with them often, and watch what emerges. Make sense of patterns and reinforce what's working, adjusting along the way. Expressed with confidence, intentions convey certainty in the midst of uncertainty.

Want to learn more? Take a deep dive...

Doheny, K. (2008). *Strategies to reduce perfectionism.*
   Psych Central.

Schwartz, T. (2012, May 1). Turning 60: The twelve most
   important lessons I've learned so far. *Harvard Business Review
   Blog Network.*

Thomke, S. (2011, June 6). *How business experimentation fuels
   innovation.* Chief Executive.net.

3

4. **Losing your cool? Manage uncertainty-driven stress.** It's not uncommon to get stressed when dealing with increased ambiguity. We lose our anchor. Stress increases the chances that you'll respond to conditions and people more emotionally. Maybe you lash out. Close down. Berate yourself. Go into panic mode. However you react, remember that your reactions probably don't just affect you. So take charge of it. Get familiar with what triggers your reactions. Is it when you don't know what to do, don't want to make a mistake, are afraid of the consequences, lack the confidence to act? Pause. Observe your patterns and label your emotions—this will provide some perspective and reduce escalation. Do some research, then try different ways to regain your equilibrium until you find what works best for you. There are lots of resources available online, from breathing and mindfulness exercises to tips on tackling underlying issues. When a situation seems overwhelming, drop the problem for a while. Go do something else. Return to it after you've had time to decompress and reflect. Practice responding more consistently in ways that will best serve you and your colleagues.

5. **Tentative about entering the unknown? Shift gears and welcome it.** Are you the type that dips a toe in the water before diving in? Tries your best to avoid all surprises? Makes a habit of never changing a habit? There's nothing wrong with being cautious—to an extent. But

taken to an extreme, that tendency could keep you stuck in a bygone era. Wake up to now. Learn to dive in and see what happens. Start with the easy stuff: order new things from the menu, take a new route to work, go on a mini-vacation without an itinerary. Try things that seem fun and a little scary. Like taking a class in improvisation where you'll be forced to wing it and work with what shows up. Spend time with people who are energized by adventure. Find out how they approach risk and forge new ground, then try it out for yourself. Remind yourself that the unknown isn't the enemy, fear is. So ask, "What's the worst thing that could happen?" Play out the scenario and notice how resourceful you can be when put to the test. Still feel queasy? Jump in anyway. It may be uncomfortable at first but be rewarding in the long run.

6. **Daunted by an ambiguous challenge? Gain some perspective.** Start by defining the challenge—what it is and what it isn't. Visualize it as if you're seeing it from above. From the bird's eye view, what are the various components? How do they relate? Use mapping techniques or concept mapping software to cluster what's connected and explore links with the larger ecosystem. Then look below the surface of the challenge. What underlying issues are causing problems? Keep drilling down, asking why something is happening, until you get to the root causes. For a different take on what's at play, generate discussion using one or more useful frameworks. For example, examine organizational issues using McKinsey's 7S model: strategy, structure, systems, shared values, skills, style, and staff. Or explore challenges using 9 building blocks identified in *Business Model Generation*. (*For more information, visit* www.businessmodelgeneration.com.) Whatever framework you use, look for patterns and interconnections to gain perspective and inform solutions.

7. **Negativity taking over? Counter closed-door thinking.** When there are a lot of unknowns, people sometimes fill in the blanks with doom and gloom forecasts. This can block the ability to be optimistic—to see the advantages of change. Through years of research, psychologist Martin Seligman has found that optimism can be developed in specific ways. (*For more information, visit* www.ppc.sas.upenn.edu.) Identify what *can* be done in the midst of uncertainty. At minimum, a shift in attitude is always possible. Research shows that there are more optimists in the senior levels of leadership. It's unclear whether they're promoted partly because they're optimistic or if they become that way once they've arrived. What is clear is that optimism is influential. Although tied to one's natural disposition, it can be developed through consistent effort.

Want to learn more? Take a deep dive...

Laufenberg, D. (2010, December). Diana Laufenberg: How to learn? From mistakes [Video file]. TED.

Sidhu, I. (2011, January 24). Overcoming ambiguity: Three steps that every business can take. *Forbes.*

Wilkinson, A., & Kupers, R. (2013, May). Living in the futures. *Harvard Business Review.*

8. **Want to be 100% sure? Balance thinking with action.** Lots of us want all the data in and all our ducks in a row before we act. Perfectionism is tough to let go of, especially when past success can be traced back to getting it right with zero defects. Recognize your perfectionism for what it might be—collecting more information to improve your confidence in making a fault-free decision, thereby avoiding risk and criticism. Try to decrease your need for complete information and your need to be right all the time. Decrease it slightly every week until you reach a more reasonable balance between thinking it through and taking action. Try making some small decisions on little or no data. Anyone with 100% of the data can make good decisions. The real test in the marketplace is who can act the soonest with a reasonable amount—but not all—of the data.

9. **Prefer to check things off your list? Redefine what progress means.** Do you have a high need to complete tasks? Wrap things up in nice neat packages? Working well with ambiguity often means moving from incomplete task to incomplete task. Some projects may be put on hold, some may never be finished. You'll constantly have to edit your actions and decisions. It's the way things typically go with emerging realities or new initiatives. When going through transitions, it's common to put temporary structures in place—temporary teams, org chart, systems. After one thing ends and before something new begins, scaffolding gets erected, torn down, then replaced. Life in flux means it's time to change your internal reward system. Instead of just feeling good when you finish a project, it's about moving things forward incrementally. Think progress over perfection. Recognize it. People always need appreciation for a job well done—so do you.

10. **Need inspiration? Learn from others who thrived during uncertainty.** There are examples throughout history of people who have done well when the environment around them was highly ambiguous. People like Steve Jobs, Nelson Mandela, Winston Churchill, or Aung San Suu Kyi. There are those who were energized by quests into the unknown—Lewis and Clark, Leonardo da Vinci, Jane Goodall. Learn about them through biography.com or other sources. Then take your search closer to home. Interview trailblazers in your own company or industry—people who took risks and paved new terrain. Find out how they dealt with similar concerns you have. Did they think the journey was worth it? If your team or organization is facing ambiguity (market shifts, new regulations, geo-political crisis, you name it), find case studies of other companies that have addressed similar challenges.

Want to learn more? Take a deep dive...

Biography.com

Bregman, P. (2012, January 4). Your problem isn't motivation. *Harvard Business Review Blog Network*.

The Staff of the Corporate Executive Board. (2011, December 20). Preventing 'Analysis Paralysis.' *Bloomberg Businessweek*.

Job assignments

• Lead an organizational transition such as an acquisition or merger, handling ambiguous factors involving structure, systems, people, or processes.

• Start something from scratch for your company or customers (e.g., a new product, service, department). Manage the unknowns that accompany all start-ups.

• Be part of an initiative around entering a new or emerging market, with accountability for results despite no clear path to follow.

• Manage a group through a tough crisis with no easy answers. The tension may escalate, giving you a chance to practice keeping your emotions in check.

• Increase the scope or complexity of what you are currently doing, which will take you out of your comfort zone while needing to make decisions and effectively contribute.

Take time to reflect...

If you feel more anxious than energized when things are uncertain...

> ...then try to identify the source of your anxiety. If you understand what you're specifically concerned about, it will be easier for you to overcome your worries.

If you tend to move slowly for fear of making mistakes...

> ...then consider whether it's necessary caution or needless worry that's holding you back. Be prudent, but be persistent. Errors are inevitable. If you stumble and stray, view these as learning opportunities.

If you feel overwhelmed when things are not crystal clear...

> ...then recognize that ambiguity is inevitable. Things change. Accept ambiguity as the new normal. Embracing it will help you become comfortable with it.

"*Neurosis is the inability to tolerate ambiguity.***"**

Sigmund Freud - Austrian neurologist and founding father of psychoanalysis

3

Learn more about *Manages* ambiguity

Hodgson, P., & White, R. (2001). *Relax, it's only uncertainty: Lead the way when the way is changing.* London, England: Pearson Education Limited.

Johri, V. (2010, March 9). Leaders today have to be comfortable with ambiguity. *Business Standard.*

Keough, D. R. (2008). *The ten commandments for business failure.* New York, NY: Penguin Group.

Osterwalder, A., & Pigneur, Y. (2010). *Business model generation: A handbook for visionaries, game changers, and challengers.* Hoboken, NJ: John Wiley & Sons.

Schlesinger, L. A., Kiefer, C. F., & Brown, P. B. (2012). *Just start: Take action, embrace uncertainty, create the future.* Boston, MA: Harvard Business School Publishing.

Seligman, M. E. P. (2006) *Learned optimism: How to change your mind and your life.* London, England: Vintage.

Wilkinson, D. J. (2006). *The ambiguity advantage: What great leaders are great at.* Hampshire, England: Palgrave MacMillan.

 Deep dive learning resource links

Biography.com

Bregman, P. (2012, January 4). Your problem isn't motivation. *Harvard Business Review Blog Network.* Retrieved from http://blogs.hbr.org/2012/01/your-problem-isnt-motivation/

Doheny, K. (2008). *Strategies to reduce perfectionism.* Psych Central. Retrieved from http://psychcentral.com/lib/strategies-to-reduce-perfectionism/0001526

Laufenberg, D. (2010, December). Diana Laufenberg: How to learn? From mistakes [Video file]. TED. Retrieved from http://www.ted.com/talks/diana_laufenberg_3_ways_to_teach.html

Schwartz, T. (2012, May 1). Turning 60: The twelve most important lessons I've learned so far. *Harvard Business Review Blog Network.* Retrieved from http://blogs.hbr.org/2012/05/turning-60-the-twelve-most/

Sidhu, I. (2011, January 24). Overcoming ambiguity: Three steps that every business can take. *Forbes.* Retrieved from http://www.forbes.com/sites/indersidhu/2011/01/24/133/

34 |

The Staff of the Corporate Executive Board. (2011, December 20). Preventing 'Analysis Paralysis.' *Bloomberg Businessweek.* Retrieved from http://www.businessweek.com/management/preventing-analysis-paralysis-12202011.html

Thomke, S. (2011, June 6). *How business experimentation fuels innovation.* Chief Executive.net. Retrieved from http://chiefexecutive.net/how-business-experimentation-fuels-innovation

Wilkinson, A., & Kupers, R. (2013, May). Living in the futures. *Harvard Business Review.* Retrieved from http://hbr.org/2013/05/living-in-the-futures/ar/1

Recommended search terms

If you'd like to explore *Manages* ambiguity further, try searching online using the following terms:

* Dealing with ambiguity/ambiguity tolerance.
* Managing uncertainty.
* Preventing analysis paralysis.
* Reducing perfectionism.
* Succeeding through failure.

More help...

Go to www.kornferry.com/fyi-resources and link directly to the deep dive resources in this chapter. Visit the site often to see the additional resources that are uploaded on a regular basis.

4. Attracts top talent

Attracting and selecting the best talent to meet current and future business needs.

Organizations need to be filled with talent. For many organizations, it's the single biggest driver of organizational performance. Achieving goals is easier when there are enough of the right people with the right skills in the right place at the right time. When there is a full and flowing pipeline of diverse talent ready to take on the next challenge. Success relies on understanding what the organization, unit, or team is trying to achieve and making the right hiring and staffing decisions in line with that. There is very little out in plain sight when it comes to evaluating people. Spotting talent may seem like it comes from instinct. What is more likely is that instinct is actually an intuitive sense that's developed from much careful study of human behavior. To evaluate people well, you need to be a master observer. Accurately assessing strengths and weaknesses and having the courage to act on that assessment. Knowing that the talent decisions you make impact every part of your organization—from creating a workforce that brings to life the company values and brand, to one that is ready to take on the challenges of today and tomorrow. You'll be most effective when you know how to assess and select talent. When you're able to build a quality pipeline of talent that strengthens the resilience of the organization and its ability to innovate, adapt, and survive.

"If you hire the best and brightest, you will solve whatever issues arise in the future."

Lee Kun-hee – South Korean business magnate and chairman of Samsung Group

4

Factor III: People
Cluster H: Optimizing diverse talent
Competency 4: Attracts top talent

Attracts top talent is in the **People** factor (III) in the Korn Ferry Leadership Architect™. It is part of Cluster H, **Optimizing diverse talent,** along with Develops talent (13), *Values* differences (14), and *Builds effective* teams (34). You may find it helpful to also take a look at some of the tips included in those chapters to supplement your learning.

Skilled

Attracts and selects diverse and high caliber talent.

Finds the right talent to meet the group's needs.

Closes talent gaps with the right balance of internal and external candidates.

Is a good judge of talent.

Less skilled

- Haphazardly selects talent into the organization.
- Takes little action to match the talent to the role or organization.
- Is unclear about selection criteria or how to evaluate others' skills.
- Selects people that are very similar to self.

Talented

- Actively seeks and secures the best talent available.
- Creates pipelines of talent for the future from both internal and external talent pools.
- Evaluates talent using a thorough and consistent process.

Overused skill

- Overanalyzes and fails to get people into roles quickly enough to meet the needs of the business.
- May overlook slow starters and quiet, less expressive talent.

Factor III: People
Cluster H: Optimizing diverse talent
Competency 4: Attracts top talent

4

Some possible causes of lower skill

Causes help explain *why* a person may have trouble with Attracts top talent. When seeking to increase skill, it's helpful to consider how these might play out in certain situations. And remember that all of these can be addressed if you are motivated to do so.

- Lacks experience hiring people.

- Lacks courage to do something different.

- Narrow perspective on what talent looks like.

- Fears being shown up by a better person.

- Too impatient or afraid to let a mediocre candidate go in order to search for a better one.

- Doesn't understand what the company needs; no knowledge of talent gaps.

- Unclear on selection criteria for hiring or staffing.

- Overreliance on undeveloped intuition.

- Selects candidates similar to current staff or self.

- Thinks anyone can pick up the skills on the job.

 Does it best

Since the first Google search in 1998, the Google organization has grown to become one of the most well-respected and innovative companies in the world. And how many organizations can take credit for their name generating a new verb? In 16 years, Google's market valuation has grown to an estimated US$46 billion. Not only is the company known for its innovation, it has also built a reputation for attracting and retaining the brightest and most driven talent available. So much so, that they have hit the number one spot on Fortune's 100 Best Companies to Work For® list three years running—2012, 2013, and 2014. So, what attracts people to work for Google? The organization figures out what's important to their Googlers, as employees are called, and they deliver it. Google is famous for their employee-friendly perks such as on-site free cafes, dry cleaners, bowling alleys, and nap pods—all designed to encourage collaboration and help Googlers work around the clock. Google encourages autonomy and open, creative dialogue, and offers one of the best compensation packages in the tech industry. It's an attractive proposition for top talent.[4, 5]

| 39

4

Factor III: People
Cluster H: Optimizing diverse talent
Competency 4: Attracts top talent

Tips to develop Attracts top talent

1. **Don't know if you've got the right talent? Start with the end in mind.**
    When you know where you're headed, you can define the kind of
    talent needed to get there. Articulate, as clearly as you can, the
    critical priorities to be delivered by your team, unit, or organization.
    What is it that you need to achieve? What does success look like?
    Short-term and long-term. Define what kind of talent you need.
    What skills will be critical to delivering success, now and in the
    future? Where is deep expertise and knowledge needed? What
    critical roles need to be in place? What experience is needed from
    critical role holders? Involve others in the discussion where you need
    to. Review what comes out and make a comparison with the talent
    already in place. How does it compare? You may find you have the
    right skills, knowledge, expertise, and experience in place. You may
    find there are gaps to fill. Either way, you'll have the clarity you need
    to take appropriate action.

2. **Not hiring the right people? Look beyond the resume.** A great
    resume is attractive and often the first contact we have with a
    potential hire. You can see their skills, experience, work history, and
    education. What you might call their can-do qualities. So how come
    those with the best resumes don't always turn out to be right for the
    role? Research shows that many new hires fail because of factors
    beyond any lack of skill or can-do quality. More likely, they find
    themselves at odds with motivational factors such as the culture,
    values, compensation structures, promotion opportunities, etc.
    Don't rely solely on the resume when you evaluate someone. Treat it
    like an advertisement—a small (and not always dependable) part of
    the equation. Find out what motivates and drives the person. Ask
    about values and what's important to them. What do they want
    from a role and an employer? Pay attention to patterns and themes
    in their responses. What's their mindset? Will they fit the culture?
    Maybe have them complete a formal biodata inventory, which
    contains factual questions about life and work experiences as well
    as finding out about opinions, values, beliefs, and attitudes. Biodata
    instruments can capture the past behavior of a person and thus help
    predict how they're likely to act in the future. Use this additional
    information to complement the resume. To make an all-round
    assessment of suitability.

3. **Losing talent as quickly as you find it? Understand why.** You can be
    great at attracting and hiring talent, but it all goes to waste if you
    can't keep it. The first few months after hiring are critical. Half or
    more new employees quit within the first seven months. The major

4

Factor III: People
Cluster H: Optimizing diverse talent
Competency 4: Attracts top talent

4

reasons people quit are because they feel isolated socially, left out of the stream of information, or stuck in depressing working conditions. Get in the habit of conducting exit interviews. They'll help you understand what's causing people to leave. Find out specifically what they liked and disliked about the job and the organization. People tend to be more honest in providing their feedback when they are leaving the organization. You might discover some common themes. An exit interview is a chance to show that you value the individual and their opinion. A chance to leave a positive impression. When you understand what's causing your talent to leave, you can work on fixing the problem. Establish a better employee value proposition and do a better job in attracting and retaining the right talent.

4. **Can't seem to attract talent? Work on your brand image and reputation.** Research shows that employers with a positive brand image and reputation attract more potential hires than those who don't. Thus allowing them to be more selective on top talent. Not only that, it shows that having a positive reputation can influence applicant behavior. Cable and Turban (2003) demonstrated that participants would accept a 7% smaller salary as a result of joining an employer with a highly favorable reputation. Build your brand identity. Make it clear what you stand for. Tell a compelling story that brings to life what it would be like to work for you. Showcase what's on offer (compensation structures, benefits, promotion opportunities, etc.). Promote your employee value proposition (EVP). This is the value or benefit an employee can expect to feel as a member of the organization. Invite employees to share their stories; help get the word out. Nothing is more captivating than real experiences. Use internal and external professional media to promote your brand. Received any recognition or awards relating to your employee proposition? Tell people. Working in a global context? Pay attention to cultural difference. Do all that you can to capture the attention of prospective candidates. Hold their interest long enough for them to want to take action, want to come and work with you.

Want to learn more? Take a deep dive...

James, G. (2013, October 22). Hiring: 6 Secrets to attracting top talent. *Inc.*

Tjan, A. K. (2011, February 9). Three ways to recognize a talent magnet. *Harvard Business Review Blog Network.*

Weiss, T. (2008, March 25). Exit right. *Forbes.*

4

Factor III: People
Cluster H: Optimizing diverse talent
Competency 4: Attracts top talent

5. **Hiring people like you? Seek diversity.** Clone yourself too much? Have a preference for people who think and act as you do? Believe you'll communicate more effectively? Have a better working relationship? Maybe so, but it can be dangerous to place too much value on certain characteristics. They'll become the first thing you look for when evaluating others' talent potential. And that means you're likely to make marginal people decisions. You could be ignoring weaknesses and downsides. At worst, you could be excluding people because they're different. In the extreme, this could be discriminatory, which could result in legal trouble. It's a common human tendency to want to clone yourself. But, long-term, in most organizations, variety and diversity almost always outperform clones. Those not like you may seem to be missing something. The reality is that they probably have something you need. Actively look for positive difference in others. Consciously create a team of people who complement each other. Can challenge each other. Who bring different skills and perspectives. Make it your aim to surround yourself with people who are not like you. Learn to sit comfortably among them.

6. **Worried you'll be shown up? Be an "A" player.** "A" players know what they don't know. They do not pretend they know when they don't. They're aware of their weaknesses and accept them. "A" players aren't threatened by people who are better than they are. Who can do things they can't. Consequently, they hire "A" players. In contrast, "B" players are threatened by "A" players. They hire "C" players to avoid being shown up. No one has all possible strengths. Chances are everyone in your unit is better at something than you are. The key is to take this natural fear and turn it into a positive gain. Hire the "A" players who have areas of strength you don't. Who can bridge talent gaps you can't. Study how they think, watch how they go about exercising their strengths, and use this knowledge to improve yourself. When you hire to complement your weaknesses, you'll have more time to focus on your strengths.

7. **Can't tell great from good? Look for learning agility.** To be good at anything requires some knowledge, skills, and technical know-how. What separates the great from the good is the ability to perform well under first-time, challenging conditions. These "high potential" people are known as learning agile. They can take lessons from the past and fit them into new and different challenges they are facing. They know what to do when they don't know what to do. Look for people who find it easy to learn new tasks and functions. People who are excellent critical thinkers who enjoy and deal well with ambiguity and complexity. People who don't accept the status quo,

Factor III: People
Cluster H: Optimizing diverse talent
Competency 4: Attracts top talent

4

are impatient. They are curious, like to try new things, take different approaches. They will be the ones who tend to push the envelope and are willing to take the heat when things fail. Learning agile people are self-aware. They exhibit the sort of presence that builds confidence in themselves and others. When it comes to talent and potential, learning agility separates the best from the rest.

Want to learn more? Take a deep dive...

Cohan, P. S. (2013, September 25). Your secret to hiring a kick-ass team. *Entrepreneur.*

Krakovsky, M. (2007, March/April). The effort effect. *Stanford Magazine.*

Stillman, J. (2012, February 28). The case against hiring people just like you. *Inc.*

8. **Evaluation a bit haphazard? Follow a fair and consistent process.** When selection criteria are unclear or out of date and processes inconsistent, the evaluation of talent can become haphazard. People rely more on their gut instinct. On their perceptions of what's needed. Perceptions that are subjective and can be wrong as often as they are right. What feels like a well-rounded assessment may actually be incomplete. No more reliable than flipping a coin. Have a consistent framework for hiring. Establish objective selection criteria. Review the job description; make sure it's accurate. What level of skill and experience is needed for the role? Which criteria are essential and which are desirable? What formal qualifications are required? How will you measure, rate, or score each candidate against the defined criteria? How will you use those metrics to differentiate? Make sure any formal testing is valid and relevant to the role. Document the end-to-end process each candidate will go through—references process, interview, assessment center, psychological assessments, biodata testing to understand more about the values and beliefs of the person and as a predictor of how they'll act, etc. Include how you'll give feedback. Treat candidates fairly, with honesty and respect. Your recruitment efforts are more likely to be effective and you'll project a great brand image.

9. **Interview on autopilot? Sharpen your skills.** A great interview takes time, planning, and focus. It's your biggest opportunity to connect with your potential hire. To get to know them. Spot any red flags. It's easy to get lazy. Rush into the interview, clutching a barely read resume. Switch to autopilot, asking the same predictable questions

4

Factor III: People
Cluster H: Optimizing diverse talent
Competency 4: Attracts top talent

and not really listening to the response. Results become vague and lack any real insight. Not what you need to make accurate decisions. Dedicate time to planning your interviews. Take a thorough look at the resume and results of other formal assessments. Look at the role you're filling. Decide what questions you need to ask; have a legitimate reason for each one. During the interview, listen carefully to the candidate's responses. Not satisfied that you've heard enough? Ask another question to tease out more information. Invite the candidate to ask questions. Get a colleague to interview with you. They can offer a different perspective or act as a note taker, leaving you free to concentrate on the conversation. Remember, the interview is also a chance for the candidate to evaluate you. If the process isn't delivered well, they may reject your offer.

10. **Want to see your short list in action? Run a practical assessment.** It's a great way of differentiating candidates in the final stages of recruitment. Especially where candidates seem very similar on paper and performed equally well during the interview. Run well, it'll put them through their paces and give you an opportunity to see them in action. Invite small groups of candidates (6–20) to participate in group exercises, role plays, and other activities (in-tray, presentation, case study, problem solving, etc.) that simulate the challenges and situations they'll face if successful. Use the job profile and competencies to focus and develop relevant activities. Observe the candidates in action. How are they performing? How are they behaving? Are they working well with the group? What does this tell you about their ability to do the job? Record and rank each candidate against agreed-upon criteria. Invite colleagues trained in assessment to help. This ensures everyone has equal opportunity to shine and be noticed. Give feedback to all candidates on their performance, successful or not. Ask them for feedback too. Have the activities made them reassess their own suitability for the role? Do they have any feedback that could help improve future practical assessments?

11. **Overlooking red flags? Complete a thorough background check.** As an employer, you have a right to verify the reliability of an application. A background check will validate that an applicant has the credentials they claim. It demonstrates your commitment to safety and security by protecting against potential criminal acts such as theft, workplace violence, and other legal issues that could damage your organization. Quality applicants will understand and appreciate this. You may need to outsource the checks to people expert in criminal investigation and who know how employers are protected from liability. They can often persuade a reluctant former employer to give out legally acceptable information. Completing a thorough

Factor III: People
Cluster H: Optimizing diverse talent
Competency 4: Attracts top talent

4

background check before you hire could save you time and money later.

Want to learn more? Take a deep dive...

Barker, E. (2011, July 19). *Scientific, time-tested methods for hiring the best people*. Business Insider.

Haun, L. (2013, January 14). Don't hire the perfect candidate. *Harvard Business Review Blog Network.*

Moore, D. (2012, February 7). Stop being deceived by interviews when you're hiring. *Forbes.*

12. **Always wait for a vacancy? Recruit ahead of the curve.** Finding the right people can be difficult when it is done on an "as needed" basis. When recruitment is vacancy led. A more successful strategy involves continually searching for talent—succession planning. Identifying the talent needed for long-term success and finding it before you need it. Creating an internal pipeline of people ready and willing to take on the next opportunity. An external pipeline of people waiting to join. What talent do you need to line up for the future? Where will it come from? Do you have a replacement plan for yourself? Who has, or will have, the ability to take your job or another key role? Who are you sponsoring for promotion? It's OK to state up front, "We're not currently hiring, but I'm always on the lookout for great people." Keep in touch with people; keep them interested. Maximize opportunities to onboard people early to prepare them for a future role. This strategy not only builds a database of resumes, it increases your own personal network of contacts (providing referrals will generally be reciprocated). Never stop looking for talent.

13. **Hire too quickly or too slowly? Slow down or speed up.** Either tendency will probably get you and the organization in trouble. Do you hire too quickly? Think anyone can learn the job? Worry you won't fill the vacancy, so you hire the first candidate that comes along? Slow down. Don't be afraid to let a mediocre candidate go in order to search for a better one. It might take more time now, but it will save you time later. Maybe you take too long? Fear making a bad hire? Wait for the perfect candidate? Learn to moderate yourself. Always try to wait long enough to have choices but not so long that you lose a very good candidate while waiting for perfection. There's a risk that your idea of perfection doesn't exist. But you can hire someone who comes pretty close.

4

Factor III: People
Cluster H: Optimizing diverse talent
Competency 4: Attracts top talent

14. **Overly reliant on a single source of talent? Cast the net far and wide.** Prefer to fish for talent in the internal pond? Or do you only look outside to bring in new talent? Either way, you're limiting the pool of talent you have exposure to. And limiting the diversity of culture and strengths and weaknesses you have to choose from. Widen your search. Give equal consideration to internal and external talent pools. Involve others who can cast the net wider—in-house recruiters, headhunters, temporary staffing agencies. Make the most of employee referral programs, campus recruiting. Advertise—use the web and appropriate professional social media. Working in a global context? Look outside your own backyard. Embrace the concept of a global talent pool. Best-in-class companies scour the world in search of the best and the brightest.

15. **Made a mistake? Act quickly.** Sometimes, despite your best efforts, you'll hire the wrong person. It usually shows up in the first 90 days. But before you think about letting them go, be sure the problem isn't fixable. Maybe they have not been onboarded effectively? Perhaps they were given too much responsibility too soon. Or was it that they weren't given enough and have gone off the boil? Have interpersonal issues with certain team members hampered their progress? Look beneath the surface to find out what's gone wrong. But when it can't be fixed and you need to let them go, act quickly. Avoiding the situation will only make it worse. Be respectful. Let the person know that this role is not playing to their strengths. Remind them that another environment or role may be a better match for their talents, allow them to shine. Support their transition out of the role. Can you help them find another position inside the organization? Offer a reference? If you are exiting them from the organization, do it gracefully and in line with due process. Always address your hire mistakes. It's important to remember that you made the offer. Don't beat yourself up; instead, learn what you can from the experience and move forward.

Want to learn more? Take a deep dive...

Entrepreneur. (n.d.). How to recruit top talent. *Entrepreneur.*

Kerpen, C. (2013, February 25). Why "hire slow, fire fast" is a better idea than you think. *Fast Company.*

Quast, L. (2012, May 21). Recruiting, reinvented: How companies are using social media in the hiring process. *Forbes.*

Vlachoutsicos, C. (2013, July 24). How to fix the bad employee syndrome. *Harvard Business Review Blog Network.*

Factor III: People
Cluster H: Optimizing diverse talent
Competency 4: Attracts top talent

4

Job assignments

- Volunteer to work as an assessor in an assessment center for a team outside your unit. If possible, double up with another assessor to learn from their experience.

- Work on a team that's deciding which talent to keep and which to let go in a layoff, shutdown, delayering, or merger. Adopt a thorough, objective decision-making process to address the talent the organization needs going forward.

- Offer to review and recommend improvements to the way your organization attracts and recruits talent. Talk to people who have used the current hiring process. Find out what works well and what needs improvement.

- Lead a project that's unfamiliar territory for you. Choose one that requires you to hire and manage experts in a field you are not used to working in.

- Offer to support someone whose current role is not a great match for their talent. Coach them through their transition to a role that better suits their talents and strengths.

Take time to reflect...

If you focus more on what the organization delivers than on the people it hires...

...then understand that without strong talent, none of the organization's goals will be achieved. Getting the right people on board is the first step to making great things happen.

4

If you never change your routine when it comes to hiring talent...

...then stop and think about your approach. Each situation is different, so put the need ahead of the process.

If your gut instinct is strong and has never failed you yet...

...then consider that this time it easily could. Your "good feeling" could turn out to be a very bad mistake.

" *The employer generally gets the employees he deserves.* **"**

Sir Walter Gilbey – English merchant and philanthropist

4

Factor III: People
Cluster H: Optimizing diverse talent
Competency 4: Attracts top talent

 Learn more about Attracts top talent

Adler, L. (2007). *Hire with your head: Using performance-based hiring to build great teams* (3rd ed.). Hoboken, NJ: John Wiley & Sons.

The Best Practice Institute, Goldsmith, M., & Carter, L. (Eds.). (2010). *Best practices in talent management: How the world's leading corporations manage, develop, and retain top talent.* San Francisco, CA: Pfeiffer.

Davila, L., & King, M. (2007). *Perfect phrases for perfect hiring: Hundreds of ready-to-use phrases for interviewing and hiring the best employees every time.* New York, NY: McGraw-Hill.

Hallenbeck, G. S., Jr., & Eichinger, R. W. (2006). *Interviewing right: How science can sharpen your interviewing accuracy.* Minneapolis, MN: Lominger International: A Korn Ferry Company.

Lawler, E. E., III. (2008). *Talent: Making people your competitive advantage.* San Francisco, CA: Jossey-Bass.

 Deep dive learning resource links

Barker, E. (2011, July 19). *Scientific, time-tested methods for hiring the best people.* Business Insider. Retrieved from http://www.businessinsider.com/what-are-the-scientific-time-tested-methods-for-hiring-the-best-people-2011-7

Cohan, P. S. (2013, September 25). Your secret to hiring a kick-ass team. *Entrepreneur.* Retrieved from http://www.entrepreneur.com/article/228564#

Entrepreneur. (n.d.). How to recruit top talent. *Entrepreneur.* Retrieved from http://www.entrepreneur.com/article/78598#

Haun, L. (2013, January 14). Don't hire the perfect candidate. *Harvard Business Review Blog Network.* Retrieved from http://blogs.hbr.org/2013/01/dont-hire-the-perfect-candidat/

James, G. (2013, October 22). Hiring: 6 Secrets to attracting top talent. *Inc.* Retrieved from http://www.inc.com/geoffrey-james/6-secrets-for-hiring-great-people.html

Kerpen, C. (2013, February 25). Why "hire slow, fire fast" is a better idea than you think. *Fast Company.* Retrieved from http://www.fastcompany.com/3006206/why-hire-slow-fire-fast-better-idea-you-think

Krakovsky, M. (2007, March/April). The effort effect. *Stanford Magazine.* Retrieved from http://alumni.stanford.edu/get/page/magazine/article/?article_id=32124

|

Factor III: People
Cluster H: Optimizing diverse talent
Competency 4: Attracts top talent

4

Moore, D. (2012, February 7). Stop being deceived by interviews when you're hiring. *Forbes*. Retrieved from http://www.forbes.com/sites/forbesleadershipforum/2012/02/07/stop-being-deceived-by-interviews-when-youre-hiring/

Quast, L. (2012, May 21). Recruiting, reinvented: How companies are using social media in the hiring process. *Forbes*. Retrieved from http://www.forbes.com/sites/lisaquast/2012/05/21/recruiting-reinvented-how-companies-are-using-social-media-in-the-hiring-process/

Stillman, J. (2012, February 28). The case against hiring people just like you. *Inc.* Retrieved from http://www.inc.com/jessica-stillman/the-case-against-hiring-someone-similar-to-yourself.html

Tjan, A. K. (2011, February 9). Three ways to recognize a talent magnet. *Harvard Business Review Blog Network*. Retrieved from http://blogs.hbr.org/2011/02/three-ways-to-recognize-a-tale/

Vlachoutsicos, C. (2013, July 24). How to fix the bad employee syndrome. *Harvard Business Review Blog Network*. Retrieved from http://blogs.hbr.org/2013/07/how-to-fix-the-bad-employee-sy/

Weiss, T. (2008, March 25). Exit right. *Forbes*. Retrieved from http://www.forbes.com/2008/03/25/exit-interview-management-lead-careers-cx_tw_0325bizbasics.html

References

Cable, D. M., & Turban, D. B. (2003). The value of organizational image in the recruitment context: A brand equity perspective. *Journal of Applied Social Psychology, 33,* 2244-2266.

4

Recommended search terms

If you'd like to explore Attracts top talent further, try searching online using the following terms:

- Best practices for hiring employee talent.
- Employer interview best practices.
- Employer recruiting best practices.
- Importance of employee culture fit.
- Practical selection assessments.

4

Factor III: People
Cluster H: Optimizing diverse talent
Competency 4: Attracts top talent

 More help...

Go to www.kornferry.com/fyi-resources and link directly to the deep dive resources in this chapter. Visit the site often to see the additional resources that are uploaded on a regular basis.

4

50 |

5. Business insight

Applying knowledge of business and the marketplace to advance the organization's goals.

You gotta know the territory! Nothing beats knowing what's going on, and it can be essential to developing credibility. This means people developing insight through two routes. First, they pay attention to their own industry. Build expertise in their functional discipline. Understand how the departments and drivers of their organization relate to and work with each other. Understand the agenda, issues, and concerns of the people they work with inside their organization. See things as others do. Walk a mile in their shoes. Second, they look outside. Learn about their competition and customers. Identify trends. Spot potential opportunities and threats that could come their way. When you know what's going on, you can maximize your contribution. Be better able to put forward ideas and suggestions that pass the business practicality test. Make it your business to learn about the business.

“Business, more than any other occupation, is a continual dealing with the future; it is a continual calculation, an instinctive exercise in foresight.”

Henry R. Luce – American media mogul

Business insight is in the **Thought** factor (I) in the Korn Ferry Leadership Architect™. It is part of Cluster A, **Understanding the business,** along with Customer focus (11), Financial acumen (17), and Tech savvy (35). You may find it helpful to also take a look at some of the tips included in those chapters to supplement your learning.

Skilled

Knows how businesses work and how organizations make money.

Keeps up with current and possible future policies, practices, and trends in the organization, with the competition, and in the marketplace.

Uses knowledge of business drivers and how strategies and tactics play out in the market to guide actions.

Less skilled

- Doesn't understand how businesses work.

- Is not up-to-date on current and future policies, trends, and information affecting the organization.

- Is unaware of how strategies and tactics work in the marketplace.

- Doesn't take business drivers into account when planning and executing own work.

Talented

- Has an in-depth understanding of how businesses work and make money.

- Is the first to spot possible future policies, practices, and trends in the organization, with the competition, and in the marketplace.

- Consistently applies a business driver and marketplace focus when prioritizing actions.

Overused skill

- Overdevelops or depends upon industry and business knowledge and skills at the expense of personal, interpersonal, managerial, and leadership skills.

52 |

Some possible causes of lower skill

Causes help explain *why* a person may have trouble with Business insight. When seeking to increase skill, it's helpful to consider how these might play out in certain situations. And remember that all of these can be addressed if you are motivated to do so.

- Inexperienced; new to the organization.
- Lacks interest in general business.
- Lacks interest in financial matters.
- Narrow perspective.
- No exposure outside the function.
- Overly dedicated to a profession, not the organization.
- Very tactical and here-and-now oriented.
- Focuses only on own agenda.

(?) Did you know?

Research carried out by the Perth Leadership Institute in 2008 found there to be no correlation between high levels of intelligence (measured by IQ) and business acumen. It also revealed that having a business education is unrelated to level of business acumen. Or, in some cases, can lead to worse-than-average performance if a person overestimates their business know-how. It turns out that developing true business insight is mostly about absorbing and understanding what's around you—your industry, your organization, your customers, your competitors.[6]

5

Tips to develop Business insight

1. **Need to be better informed? Read more.** As well as business books, pick up publications such as *Fast Company, Harvard Business Review, The Wall Street Journal, Bloomberg Businessweek, Forbes, Fortune,* or *Inc.* magazine. Pay attention to business social media and blogs. Read across a range of topics: marketing, finance, customer service. Focus on content that will educate you about your industry and the business environment as a whole. Look for information on new and emergent thinking. Interpret what you read into information that is relevant for you. Make notes on why and how it may be useful. Subscribe to Soundview Executive Book Summaries. They summarize in a few pages all the major business books that are on the best-seller lists.

2. **Not up to speed? Watch the right sources.** Watch the news and business channels. They often have interviews with business leaders and reviews by industry experts, as well as general reviews of companies. Watch online business presentations and TED Talks. Begin to watch one or two programs a week until you can zero in on what you specifically need to know.

3. **Baffled by buzzwords? Learn the lingo.** Listen for and learn the meaning of common business terms, acronyms, and abbreviations. Like the accounting term EBITDA, which is actually an acronym but most business people say it as a noun. Ask for more information when you hear something you are not familiar with. Figure out the settings where the use of jargon is helpful or where straight talk will get the message across better. For your message to be engaging and have impact, it needs to be understood.

Want to learn more? Take a deep dive...

Perrine, J. (2011, April 23). *Developing your business acumen: You must read to succeed.* All Things Admin.

Zezima, K. (2010, January 6). A program helps sharpen the business acumen of those on the rise. *The New York Times.*

4. **Need access to expertise? Join a professional industry network or association.** Join the professional networks or associations for your industry. Join one of their special interest groups to get a close-in look. Sign up for newsletters and publications. Attend conferences and seminars. Connect with the people you meet. Share ideas. Join

business-related communities using social media. Not only will you benefit from hearing the latest information and thinking in your sector, you will develop your professional network.

5. **Ready to continue your education? Take a class.** Formal education classes provide a supportive and structured approach to learning about business. They offer the opportunity to come together with a group of like-minded people learning together. Research the business courses that are offered online and by your local college or university. You'll find that you don't have to take on a full-time degree or MBA program to further your business education. There will be ways for you to take it one lesson at a time.

6. **Want to learn from the pros? Surround yourself with wise counsel.** Find a business mentor. Look inside and outside your organization. Consult someone whose business skills you admire and want to emulate. A long-tenured individual who has navigated events such as recessions, booms, unemployment, mergers, acquisitions, product or service shifts, and reorganizations. Someone who will take an interest in your career and help you think. Spend time with them. Ask them to share experiences and give you advice on the best way to learn about different areas of expertise. Do more listening than talking. Take your ideas and problems to them for discussion and guidance. Write down what you learn, when you learned it, and from whom. Test what you learn and use your mentor conversations to review your successes and failures. Read up on some of the benchmark names in business, for example: Muhammad Yunus (Grameen Bank), Indra Nooyi (PepsiCo), Katsuaki Watanabe (Toyota), Steve Jobs (Apple), Richard Branson (Virgin), Sheryl Sandberg (Facebook).

Want to learn more? Take a deep dive...

Broder, L. (2013, September 18). *Networking tips for novices*. Fox Business.

Chowdhury, R. (2011, May 26). *The importance of networking*. Business Insider.

Hannon, K. (2011, October 31). How to find a mentor. *Forbes*.

5

7. **Stuck in tactical mode? Engage with the strategy.** Successful organizations have well-thought-out strategies. They know where they are, where they are heading, and how they are going to get there. They understand their competition. They know where they

have competitive advantage. For a strategy to be successful, individuals need to understand it at a local level. Actions and decisions that are taken need to be aligned to it. Ask for lunch or just a meeting with the person who is in charge of the strategic planning process in your company. Have them explain the strategic plan for the organization. Particularly, have them point out the mission-critical functions and capabilities the organization needs to be on the leading edge of to win.

8. **Superficial understanding of your business? Think like an executive.** Read what you can about the organization as a whole. Study your annual report and other important communications, including financial reports. Learn about the structure, systems, functions, and processes. How do the moving parts work together? What is your value proposition? What are your key performance indicators? How do you go to market? What makes you different? Who are your competitors? Build up your understanding enough to be able to articulate clearly how your business operates, how it makes money, and how you contribute to that.

9. **Narrow insight? Broaden your perspective.** Analyze the business from multiple sources. The big three angles are finance, marketing, and customer service. There is a tendency to favor one source of information over others. This is natural and consistent with education, training, and experience, but to truly understand the business, all three of these broad perspectives need to be taken into consideration. Don't understand the financials? Talk to someone who does. Read and understand the implications of balance sheets, income statements. Learn about return on investment (ROI) and what it looks like for your organization. Is marketing a mystery? Find out how your organization goes to market. What's the value proposition? What makes the organization stand out against the competition. Unclear on customer service? Identify your key customer groups. Look internally and externally. Find out how products and services are sold and delivered to them. Understand what they want and need from you.

Want to learn more? Take a deep dive...

Cope, K. (2012, February 29). *How to see the big picture, without losing sight of the details*. Chief Executive.net.

Kurtz, R. (2008, September 5). Analyzing your company's strengths and weaknesses. *Bloomberg Businessweek*.

10. **Want fresh insights? Get close to your customers.** Studies show that there is significant correlation between indicators of financial health—such as increased sales, growth margins, and shareholder return—and how customers rate service. Meet with a counterpart in customer service. Have them explain the function to you. Listen in to customer service calls or, even better, handle a couple yourself. Look for ways to gather feedback from some customers and strengthen the organization's relationship with them. What do customers expect from your products or services? What is the biggest customer complaint? What delights them? Track their changing needs and expectations. Include the customer perspective in your decision-making process.

11. **Want to stay ahead in the game? Become a student of the competition.** Part of knowing your business is knowing how you stack up against other players in the marketplace. Use the same online sources that you use to gain intel on your own business and the customer's business to learn about your competitors. Analyze their websites. Read up on customer reviews of their products or services. Start a spreadsheet with columns listing their key features and how they stack up to yours. If it's a brick and mortar business or otherwise open to the public, go into stealth mode. Blind shop to get a sense of their price points, customer service, and operational norms. See who is attending the same trade association events as you. Grab brochures from their booth. When possible, audit sponsored workshops or receptions. See how they position their business with customers.

Want to learn more? Take a deep dive...

Handley, A. (2013, August 7). Build a better understanding of customers, get a competitive advantage. *Entrepreneur*.

Schoemaker, P. J. (2013). 5 Ways to know what your customers want before they do. *Inc.*

Zaltman, G. (2008, June 29). Understanding your customers' minds [Video file]. *Harvard Business Publishing*.

5

12. **Feeling pigeonholed? Go on a company tour.** Knowledge is embedded (and oftentimes hidden) in the social fabric of your organization. Branch out from your day-to-day activities to get to that knowledge. Volunteer for cross-functional assignments, committees, projects, or task forces that include people outside your function and topics outside your area of expertise. Work in an

office setting? Visit the shop floor and talk to frontline workers. Not in a customer-facing role? Do a ride-along on a sales call to a client. Different employees and different customers will offer different perspectives on your business. Talk to one new person a week. Ask them about what they do. Learn from them. Your coworkers and customers are the biggest free training and development resource you have.

13. **Think only about your part of the business? Consider the integration points.** In order to be a well-running business, all of the pieces and parts need to work together. A business is a closed system. Success is dependent on the coordinated efforts of everyone. What happens in one area always affects everything else. Identify your key stakeholders. Recognize their priorities and the implications of your actions on them. Clearly communicate the rationale behind decisions you make. Let others know the part they play. Explain their roles and responsibilities. The rewards of success and risks of failure. Demonstrate how the impact of your decision contributes to the achievement of company objectives.

14. **Struggle to recommend ways forward? Deconstruct your thinking.** Questions can help you think things through. Help shape and test ideas. Break complex problems down into smaller, more manageable chunks. Ask yourself: What's happening now in the organization? Positive or negative? What's causing it? Is it resulting from external forces (i.e., market conditions, consumer preference/choice) or internal influences (i.e., management style, product or service emphasis)? What other forces are at play? Is it an issue? What are the consequences (positive and negative) of doing nothing? What outcome does the organization need? What's my challenge? What actions can I take to resolve problems or issues? What do I have control and influence over? Who else needs to be consulted? What is the logical next step? While you may not always come up with the perfect recommendations, working through your thinking is a great way to gain insight into how the business works.

Want to learn more? Take a deep dive...

Capozzi, C. (n.d.). How to become more business-minded. *Chron.*

Hill, B. (n.d.). What is a strong general business acumen? *Chron.*

Kelly-Detwiler, P. (2013, September 30). How Walmart and G.E. are leading a transformation in the energy market. *Forbes.*

Job assignments

- Volunteer to participate in the budget setting and monitoring process. Use this as an opportunity to dig beneath the surface of the business and broaden your understanding.

- Offer to take new starters on a company tour. Introducing them to different parts of the business can be a great way to hone your own knowledge of how the business operates.

- Work short rotations in other units, functions, or geographies you've not been exposed to before. Select areas you know least about.

- Do a customer-satisfaction survey in person or by phone, and present the results to key stakeholders. Use the customer feedback to help you understand what the business is doing right and what needs to change. Make recommendations for improvement.

- Do a competitive analysis of your organization's products or services or position in the marketplace, and present it to the people involved. What can you learn from other organizations? What does the analysis teach you about business as a whole?

Take time to reflect...

If you think understanding the business doesn't apply to you

> ...then remember that being part of the organization involves understanding how it works. Break down the complexities. Demystify the concepts. Develop a comprehensive picture of how the business operates.

If you make your decisions without considering the business context...

> ...then take a step back to think through the business implications of your choices. Even logical decisions can sometimes be at odds with strategy. Think holistically. Think context. Think organizational goals.

If you're too busy to learn about the industry and market...

> ...then understand the importance of developing greater insight. Taking time to look more broadly will open your eyes. It will help you anticipate what's coming your way.

5

" *There is nothing so terrible as activity without insight.* **"**

Johann Wolfgang von Goethe – German poet, scientist, and diplomat

5

Learn more about Business insight

Berman, K., Case, J., & Knight, J. (2006). *Financial intelligence: A manager's guide to knowing what the numbers really mean*. Boston, MA: Harvard Business School Publishing.

Buffet, W., & Cunningham, L. (2013). *The essays of Warren Buffett: Lessons for corporate America* (3rd ed.). Durham, NC: Carolina Academic Press.

Cope, K. (2012). *Seeing the big picture: Business acumen to build your credibility, career, and company*. Austin, TX: Greenleaf Book Group.

Ensher, E. A., & Murphy, S. E. (2005). *Power mentoring: How successful mentors and protégés get the most out of their relationships*. New York, NY: John Wiley & Sons.

Kahneman, D. (2011). *Thinking, fast and slow*. New York, NY: MacMillan.

 ## Deep dive learning resource links

Broder, L. (2013, September 18). *Networking tips for novices*. Fox Business. Retrieved from http://www.foxbusiness.com/personal-finance/2013/09/18/networking-tips-for-novices/

Capozzi, C. (n.d.). How to become more business minded. *Chron*. Retrieved from http://smallbusiness.chron.com/become-businessminded-23904.html

Chowdhury, R. (2011, May 26). *The importance of networking*. Business Insider. Retrieved from http://www.businessinsider.com/the-importance-of-networking-2011-5

Cope, K. (2012, February 29). *How to see the big picture, without losing sight of the details*. Chief Executive.net. Retrieved from http://chiefexecutive.net/how-to-see-the-big-picture-without-losing-sight-of-the-details

Handley, A. (2013, August 7). Build a better understanding of customers, get a competitive advantage. *Entrepreneur*. Retrieved from http://www.entrepreneur.com/article/227100

Hannon, K. (2011, October 31). How to find a mentor. *Forbes*. Retrieved from http://www.forbes.com/sites/kerryhannon/2011/10/31/how-to-find-a-mentor/

Hill, B. (n.d.). What is a strong general business acumen? *Chron*. Retrieved from http://smallbusiness.chron.com/strong-general-business-acumen-21849.html

5

Kelly-Detwiler, P. (2013, September 30). How Walmart and G.E. are leading a transformation in the energy market. *Forbes*. Retrieved from http://www.forbes.com/sites/peterdetwiler/2013/09/30/walmart-ge-and-lighting-a-case-study-in-market-transformation/

Kurtz, R. (2008, September 5). Analyzing your company's strengths and weaknesses. *Bloomberg Businessweek*. Retrieved from http://www.businessweek.com/smallbiz/tips/archives/2008/09/analyzing_your_companys_strengths_and_weaknesses.html

Perrine, J. (2011, April 23). *Developing your business acumen: You must read to succeed*. All Things Admin. Retrieved from http://allthingsadmin.com/administrative-professionals/developing-business-acumen-read/

Schoemaker, P. J. (2013). 5 Ways to know what your customers want before they do. *Inc*. Retrieved from http://www.inc.com/paul-schoemaker/5-ways-to-know-what-your-customer-wants.html

Zaltman, G. (2008, June 29). Understanding your customers' minds [Video file]. *Harvard Business Publishing*. Retrieved from http://hbr.org/video/2226586964001/understanding-your-customers-minds

Zezima, K. (2010, January 6). A program helps sharpen the business acumen of those on the rise. *The New York Times*. Retrieved from http://www.nytimes.com/2010/01/07/business/smallbusiness/07sbiz.html?_r=0

Recommended search terms

If you'd like to explore Business insight further, try searching online using the following terms:

- Business savvy.
- Business strategy alignment.
- Corporate finance and strategy.
- Developing business acumen.
- Importance of mentoring.

(i) More help...

Go to www.kornferry.com/fyi-resources and link directly to the deep dive resources in this chapter. Visit the site often to see the additional resources that are uploaded on a regular basis.

62 |

6. Collaborates

Building partnerships and working collaboratively with others to meet shared objectives.

Inside and outside of work today, it's hard to find examples where anything of value gets done without collaboration. Collaboration is the art of bringing people together to leverage their skills, talents, and knowledge to achieve a common purpose. Collaborating creates synergy—resulting in a combined effort with greater results than those achieved by individuals. It breaks down barriers. Increases mutual respect and recognition. Helps overcome issues of poor communication, lack of cooperation, suspicion, and a myriad of dysfunctional behaviors. Collaborative relationships must be managed so the friction is removed and the power of those relationships can be realized. Good collaboration is all about reciprocity. Mutual openness and idea sharing. Mutual accountability and commitment. The most effective collaborators know when it's the right time to bring people together. What has to be achieved and why? Who has what's needed to reach the goal? How should people be brought together? Collaboration leads to more efficient use of time and resources and the easy exchange of ideas and talent. Things get done quicker. Ideas are built upon. There is less duplication of effort. People are more likely to be committed rather than just compliant.

> " No member of a crew is praised for the rugged individuality of his rowing. "

Ralph Waldo Emerson – American essayist, lecturer, and poet

|

Collaborates is in the **People** factor (III) in the Korn Ferry Leadership Architect™. It is part of Cluster G, **Building collaborative relationships,** along with *Manages* conflict (9), Interpersonal savvy (20), and *Builds* networks (21). You may find it helpful to also take a look at some of the tips included in those chapters to supplement your learning.

Skilled

Works cooperatively with others across the organization to achieve shared objectives.

Represents own interests while being fair to others and their areas.

Partners with others to get work done.

Credits others for their contributions and accomplishments.

Gains trust and support of others.

Less skilled

- Overlooks opportunities to work collaboratively with others.

- Values own interests above others'.

- Shuts down lines of communication across groups.

- Prefers to work alone and be accountable for individual contributions.

Talented

- Models collaboration across the organization.

- Facilitates an open dialogue with a wide variety of contributors and stakeholders.

- Balances own interests with others'.

- Promotes high visibility of shared contributions to goals.

Overused skill

- Is overly consensus-driven and struggles to make decisions in a timely manner.

- Risks being perceived as lacking courage and failing to stand up for own beliefs.

- May be too accommodating.

- May prioritize collaboration at the expense of making tough decisions.

6

64 |

Some possible causes of lower skill

Causes help explain *why* a person may have trouble with Collaborates. When seeking to increase skill, it's helpful to consider how these might play out in certain situations. And remember that all of these can be addressed if you are motivated to do so.

- Overly formal in relationships.
- Competitive with peers.
- Doesn't respect other groups.
- Impersonal style.
- Isn't a team player.
- Isn't forthcoming with information.
- Poor collegial skills.
- Doesn't communicate well.
- Poor time management.
- Possessive.

Brain booster

For better or worse, our brains are set to a default position when it comes to people we don't know. Strangers are foes until proven otherwise. At the heart of collaboration lies relationship. Relying on others. Sharing ideas and being vulnerable. Sharing resources. These all go more smoothly when your brain sees your collaborators as friends, not foes. Fortunately, the brain is wired to read social cues and pick up on people's intent behind their actions. Our brains have neurons that mirror in our minds the actions we see others taking. That is how we are so good at determining positive or negative intent—in our minds we are mirroring the action we're observing. When the brain interprets positive intent, it adds more points to the "friend" column. And once our brains categorize someone as a friend (or not a threat), our bodies release oxytocin, a chemical that denotes and promotes a feeling of trust, safety, and connectivity. Show positive intent. Give time for teams and partnerships to build trust. Facilitate more opportunities for positive social cues to be exchanged between strangers. These efforts will pay off when it comes time to collaborate.[7]

6

Tips to develop Collaborates

1. **Have a decision to make? Think collaboration.** People are more likely to be motivated to support a decision that they have helped make. When a decision is required, first think about whether it can be made in a collaborative manner. That's not always the case. The need for speed may override involvement. But, in most cases, inclusive decision making drives more effective solutions. Deeper analysis. More creative ideas. Buy-in from those involved. Who needs to be involved? Who has a stake in the decision? Who needs to buy in? Consult with others and share information. Ask people what they want to know. Make sure you give them a sense of the big picture and relevant information. Invite input and feedback. Then, listen. What do they think is the core issue? What ideas do they have? Brainstorm to work out a decision that has the greatest benefit.

2. **Not clear on where others are coming from? Work to make connections.** Collaboration is not just creating dialogue. It is about making connections with others. Research suggests that the best collaborators are connectors. They connect ideas outside of the organization with internal challenges. They help build bridges throughout the organization. Ultimately they link people, ideas, and resources that would not normally connect with one another. The key is to connect. Build trust. Build relationships. Connect your priorities to those of others. In each situation where you are working with other people, it is important to think about their perspective. Where are your viewpoints similar? Where are they different? Relate your goals to theirs. Are there interdependencies? What initiatives or projects do you have in common? How do your values align? Bring similarities to the forefront. Look for ways that you can bring external ideas into the discussion. Link resources. Shine a light on alignment between groups and individuals. Don't think there are connection points? Watch and observe. Ask questions. Get to know others. Chances are the more you listen and become aware, the more likely you are to find ways to connect.

3. **Need help but don't know how to ask? Clarify your needs.** Others can't read your mind. When you need help from others, the best thing you can do is ask for it. Before talking to the person, think about your key messages. What is it that you really want to accomplish? Do you need extra resources? Ideas? Time? Are there ways for your groups to work together more effectively? Be very specific around your need and what you are requesting from the

other person. Ask plainly. Don't beat around the bush. What do they have that you need? What support do you think they can provide? What difference will this make to you? If you don't know, explain your situation and ask for their input. What suggestions do they have? How might they be able to help? If they can't help, whom can they suggest? In turn, think about how you can help them. Collaboration is about give-and-take. Where can you find synergies that benefit the organization and get better results?

4. **Lack position power? Be an influencer.** Peers generally do not have authority over each other. That means that influence skills, understanding, and trading are the currencies to use in collaboration. Don't just ask for things. Find some common ground where you can provide help. What do the peers you're contacting need? Do you really know how they see the issue? Is it even important to them? How does what you're working on affect them? If it affects them negatively, can you trade something, appeal to the common good, figure out some way to minimize the work (volunteering staff help, for example)? Try to connect your messages to what is important to the other person or their area of the organization. People are more likely to buy into something, even if it doesn't help them, if they can see the broader organizational benefit.

5. **Overwhelmed by the complexity of the organization? Learn to maneuver** Wondering how to get things done across the complexity of the organization? Who are the movers and shakers in the organization? How do they get things done? Who do they rely on for expediting things through the maze? Who are the major gatekeepers. Who controls the flow of resources, information, and decisions? Who are the guides and the helpers? Get to know them better. Who are the major resisters and stoppers? Learn to watch people and observe behavior before you need to collaborate. Build relationships with others before you need help. You will have a much better sense of who you are dealing with and who to trust when the time comes to work together. In a virtual world, you may need to use different approaches. Face-to-face is usually best. But you may need to be creative in how to best connect with others outside of your immediate location. Think about cultural norms, values, and differences before you reach out to others across the organization. Be prepared. Be observant. Know who you are dealing with before you initiate a conversation.

6

Want to learn more? Take a deep dive...

Anderson, K. (2013, February 2). What makes collaboration actually work in a company? *Forbes.*

Cohen, G. B. (2009, September 29). Leadership: How to ask the right questions. *Bloomberg Businessweek.*

Harvard Management Update. (2008, February 28). Exerting influence without authority. *Harvard Business Review Blog Network.*

Richardson, A. (2011, May 31). Collaboration is a team sport, and you need to warm up. *Harvard Business Review Blog Network.*

6. **Not sure what others want? Listen.** It's easy to assume you understand someone's position. Do you walk into meetings with preconceived notions of their views? Do you finish people's sentences and not hear what they think? Do you really know what is going on in their heads? The only way to truly understand what's important to them is to ask questions and listen. Use open-ended questions. Questions that cannot be answered with a one-word answer. "Tell me more about..." "How did you...?" "What do you think about...?" Show through your non-verbals that you are paying attention. Nod in response to what they're saying. Maintain good eye contact. Ensure your posture is open (no folded arms). Make notes on key points. Summarize what you are hearing. Paraphrase your understanding of what they say—"So what you're saying is..." Ask clarifying questions if you're unsure. Demonstrate that you care and want to understand. This builds bridges with others. Digest what you're hearing. Does it make sense? Do you have a clear picture of what's important to them? If not, ask for more information.

7. **Having trouble building trust? Make your intentions clear.** People are less likely to want to work with you when they are not sure of your intentions or actions. When you begin a project, consult with others and provide information. Share your plans for dealing with an issue and invite input and feedback from others. Do something with what you have heard. Link their views to other aspects of the plan. Validate their input through making connections. Communicate freely and encourage others to do the same. If appropriate, conduct a town hall or a Q&A session. Be transparent and candid about decisions and plans. Be clear on your priorities. Paint a clear picture of the goal. What does success look like? Don't just talk about your values, live them. Let others know when things are not going well.

Ask for their ideas on turning things around. Can't deliver on a commitment? Keep all relevant people informed. Not just about the problem, but also steps you are taking to correct it.

8. **Collaborate only so far, then stop? Include others in executing on decisions.** "Coming together is a beginning. Keeping together is progress. Working together is success." Henry Ford got it right. Collaboration does not stop with the decision. It is just the beginning. Make sure you involve others in the action plan moving forward. Share responsibility. Clarify who is accountable for different aspects of the project. Be clear. When working with your team, delegate as much accountability as you can. Responsibility helps to drive ownership. Be clear on expectations and milestones. Have a plan to check in with each other. Follow your plan. When you need to adjust the plan, do so together. Share information freely and encourage others to do the same. Be quick to let people know if there are external changes affecting the initiative. Keep people in the loop and ask them to do the same.

9. **Making the wrong impression? Pay attention to your personal style.** Many times, negative personal styles get in the way of effective relationships. People who leave positive impressions get more things done with others than those who leave cold, insensitive, or impersonal negative impressions. Collaboration is easier when people are positive about each other. Convey warmth. Ask questions. Listen. Show your concern. Use humor. Offer your help. Be a person whom others want to be around. Still not sure how you are perceived? Ask for feedback about your personal style. From multiple sources (boss, peers, colleagues). Use various methods. In person. Via a 360 survey. Listen. Make a plan. Show them that you can handle criticism and that you are willing to work on the issues they see as important.

Want to learn more? Take a deep dive...

Charan, R. (2012, June 21). The discipline of listening. *Harvard Business Review Blog Network*.

Gallo, C. (2007, April 25). Rules for making a good impression. *Bloomberg Businessweek*.

Russell, N. S. (2012, August 20). 10 Ways effective leaders build trust. *Psychology Today*.

Smith, J. (2013, October 3). 10 Tips for getting your colleagues to work with you better. *Forbes*.

6

| 69

10. **One-sided in your interactions? Be more cooperative.** If others see you as excessively competitive, they will cut you out of the loop and may sabotage your collaboration attempts. To be seen as more cooperative, explain your thinking and invite them to explain theirs. Generate a variety of possibilities first rather than stake out positions. Be tentative, allowing them room to customize the situation. Focus on common goals, priorities, and problems. Invite criticism of your ideas. Be helpful to others. Someone struggling with an issue? Read up on the subject. Offer them some suggestions. Know someone who's an expert in that area? Connect them. Someone stuck for ideas? Offer to brainstorm with them. See them making mistakes you've made? Offer to mentor. Have knowledge they don't? Share information. Look for ways to reach out and help others be successful. Be proactive. Look for ways to cooperate and support before you need to collaborate.

11. **Getting competitive? Know the difference between healthy and unhealthy competition.** Research shows that organizations that encourage people to offer help and ask for help are more successful than companies that create unnecessary competition and a "taker" mentality. It is one of the strongest predictors of team success. One-upmanship, pride, ego, and "not invented here" mentality all get in the way of success. Working well with peers over the long-term helps everyone, makes sense for the organization, and builds a capacity for the organization to do greater things. It encourages collaboration. Often the least-used resource in an organization is lateral exchanges of information and resources. Share the wealth. Don't be afraid to help your peers. Shift your thinking from the needs of your area to what is best for the organization. Thinking at this higher level will help you avoid unhealthy internal competition. Review the performance metrics and measures you are using as a team. Consider whether they are detrimental to collaboration. If you gain, does someone else lose? Does your success create costs elsewhere? Are you competing for the same resources? Adjust where you need to, to encourage collaboration and teamwork.

12. **Lacking self-awareness in conflicts? Monitor yourself in tough situations.** What's the first thing you attend to? How often do you take a stand vs. make an accommodating gesture? What proportion of your comments deal with relationships vs. the issue to be addressed? Mentally rehearse for worst-case scenarios/hard-to-deal-with people. Anticipate what the person might say and have responses prepared so as not to be caught off guard. Tend to think battle and justification? Think resolution and progress instead.

Collaboration isn't caving to others' opinions. Rather, know where you stand and be able to communicate your perspective and needs in a direct, concise, and clear manner. Support your viewpoint with specific background and explanation. Tie your views back to the organizational goals and priorities. Focus on solving the problem rather than winning the argument.

13. **Are you taking all the credit? Pass along the praise.** When others have helped you achieve a goal, share the credit both privately and publically. Tell others about cross-organizational collaboration. Talk about it with your team. With your boss. With your peers. When collaboration works, celebrate it. Show appreciation for the work of others. The more you talk about collaboration, the more people see its benefits. This helps generate more teamwork in the future. Celebrate accomplishments with your collaborators. Go out for lunch. Bring in dessert. Write personal thank you notes. Make sure that people know that you appreciate their work. When people feel recognized and feel that their contributions were noted, they are much more likely to want to work with you again in the future.

Want to learn more? Take a deep dive...

Ashkenas, R. (2011, August 2). Learning not to compete. *Harvard Business Review Blog Network*.

Frost, S. (n.d.). How to cooperate as a team member in a workplace. *Chron*

Lipman, V. (2013, February 9). In praise of praise. *Forbes*.

Mind Tools. (n.d.). *Managing your emotions at work: Controlling your feelings...before they control you*. Mind Tools.

Job assignments

• Work on a project with someone you've disagreed with in the past so you can practice give-and-take dialogue, working through conflict, and finding shared goals and values.

• Volunteer to make a presentation on a group project. Ask everyone who participated on the project to help with the presentation and then debrief the situation after you are done.

6

• Resolve an issue in conflict between two people, units, geographies, functions. Help them share their perspectives, build understanding, and bring the issue to resolution.

- Manage a cost-cutting exercise or a project where there are various perspectives and inherent conflict, where you need to solve the problem and keep all parties satisfied.

- Take on a project that is too large for one person and requires cross-organizational collaboration in order to achieve results and solve the problem.

Take time to reflect...

If you have a tough goal that you're not sure how to reach...

...then others likely hold the key. You don't have to do it all yourself. You don't need to have all the answers. Partnering with people can make the path clearer and make solutions stronger.

If you'd rather do it yourself than collaborate with others...

...then realize that there are many risks to going it alone. Isolation. Overwork. Independence is great, but a soloist can't make a symphony.

If you focus more on your own victories than on shared success...

...then recognize that your talents, however great, are only part of the whole. Many heads are often better than one, and the overall result far greater.

" *It's the group sound that's important, even when you're playing a solo.* **"**

Oscar Peterson – Canadian jazz pianist and composer

|

Learn more about Collaborates

Bateman, T., & Snell, S. (2012). *Management: Leading & collaborating in the competitive world*. New York, NY: McGraw-Hill.

Covey, S. M. R. (2006). *The speed of trust: The one thing that changes everything*. New York, NY: Free Press.

Hoppe, M. H. (2007). *Active listening: Improve your ability to listen and lead*. Greensboro, NC: Center for Creative Leadership.

Katz, J. H., & Miller, F. A. (2013). *Opening doors to teamwork and collaboration: 4 Keys that change everything*. San Francisco, CA: Berrett-Koehler.

Sawyer, K. (2008). *Group genius: The creative power of collaboration*. New York, NY: Basic Books.

Vivona, J. M. (2009). Leaping from brain to mind: A critique of mirror neuron explanations of countertransference. *Journal of the American Psychoanalytic Association, 57*(3), 525-550.

 Deep dive learning resource links

Anderson, K. (2013, February 2). What makes collaboration actually work in a company? *Forbes*. Retrieved from http://www.forbes.com/sites/kareanderson/2013/02/02/what-makes-collaboration-actually-work-in-a-company/

Ashkenas, R. (2011, August 2). Learning not to compete. *Harvard Business Review Blog Network*. Retrieved from http://blogs.hbr.org/2011/08/learning-not-to-compete/

Charan, R. (2012, June 21). The discipline of listening. *Harvard Business Review Blog Network*. Retrieved from http://blogs.hbr.org/2012/06/the-discipline-of-listening/

Cohen, G. B. (2009, September 29). Leadership: How to ask the right questions. *Bloomberg Businessweek*. Retrieved from http://www.businessweek.com/managing/content/sep2009/ca20090929_639660.htm

Frost, S. (n.d.). How to cooperate as a team member in a workplace. *Chron*. Retrieved from http://smallbusiness.chron.com/cooperate-team-member-workplace-11347.html

Gallo, C. (2007, April 25). Rules for making a good impression. *Bloomberg Businessweek*. Retrieved from http://www.businessweek.com/stories/2007-04-25/rules-for-making-a-good-impressionbusinessweek-business-news-stock-market-and-financial-advice

6

Harvard Management Update. (2008, February 28). Exerting influence without authority. *Harvard Business Review Blog Network.* Retrieved from http://blogs.hbr.org/2008/02/exerting-influence-without-aut/

Lipman, V. (2013, February 9). In praise of praise. *Forbes.* Retrieved from http://www.forbes.com/sites/victorlipman/2013/02/09/in-praise-of-praise/

Mind Tools. (n.d.). *Managing your emotions at work: Controlling your feelings...before they control you.* Mind Tools. Retrieved from http://www.mindtools.com/pages/article/newCDV_41.htm

Richardson, A. (2011, May 31). Collaboration is a team sport, and you need to warm up. *Harvard Business Review Blog Network.* Retrieved from http://blogs.hbr.org/2011/05/collaboration-is-a-team-sport/

Russell, N. S. (2012, August 20). 10 Ways effective leaders build trust. *Psychology Today.* Retrieved from http://www.psychologytoday.com/blog/trust-the-new-workplace-currency/201208/10-ways-effective-leaders-build-trust-0

Smith, J. (2013, October 3). 10 Tips for getting your colleagues to work with you better. *Forbes.* Retrieved from http://www.forbes.com/sites/jacquelynsmith/2013/10/03/10-tips-for-getting-your-colleagues-to-work-with-you-better/

Recommended search terms

If you'd like to explore Collaborates further, try searching online using the following terms:

- Building trust at work.
- Developing listening skills.
- Effective collaboration.
- Leaving a good impression on others.
- Monitoring your emotions at work.
- Working through informal work channels.

(i) More help...

Go to www.kornferry.com/fyi-resources and link directly to the deep dive resources in this chapter. Visit the site often to see the additional resources that are uploaded on a regular basis.

74 |

7. Communicates effectively

Developing and delivering multi-mode communications that convey a clear understanding of the unique needs of different audiences.

Organizations thrive when the flow of information and ideas is timely and accurate. When quality of communication is a consistent high priority. Good communication results in mutual understanding, harmony, and action. Poor communication wastes time and resources, hinders goal accomplishment, and sours relationships. Leaders communicate to inform, persuade, coach, and inspire. People at all levels share ideas, learn from each other, and keep each other informed about problems, opportunities, progress, and solutions. Effective communicators provide a clear message that is understood by everyone in the audience. They are attentive listeners who are open to others' ideas. They deliver a message that is consistent but fine-tuned for a particular audience. It has just the right tone. The perfect pacing. The best possible wording. The audience finds the message to be crisp. Relevant. Impactful. Effective communication, whether written or verbal, enables you to convey your vision, to point the way forward, and to energize others to work together and pull in the same direction.

" Think like a wise man but communicate in the language of the people. "

William Butler Yeats – Irish poet

Communicates effectively is in the **People** factor (III) in the Korn Ferry Leadership Architect™. It is part of Cluster I, **Influencing people,** along with *Drives* engagement (16), Organizational savvy (23), Persuades (24), and *Drives* vision and purpose (37). You may find it helpful to also take a look at some of the tips included in those chapters to supplement your learning.

Skilled

Is effective in a variety of communication settings: one-on-one, small and large groups, or among diverse styles and position levels.

Attentively listens to others.

Adjusts to fit the audience and the message.

Provides timely and helpful information to others across the organization.

Encourages the open expression of diverse ideas and opinions.

Less skilled

- Has difficulty communicating clear written and verbal messages.

- Tends to always communicate the same way without adjusting to diverse audiences.

- Doesn't take the time to listen or understand others' viewpoints.

- Doesn't consistently share information others need to do their jobs.

Talented

- Delivers messages in a clear, compelling, and concise manner.

- Actively listens and checks for understanding.

- Articulates messages in a way that is broadly understandable.

- Adjusts communication content and style to meet the needs of diverse stakeholders.

- Models and encourages the expression of diverse ideas and opinions.

Overused skill

- May overinform, giving out information that isn't helpful or harms productivity.

- May try to win with style and communication skills over fact and substance.

- May invest too much time crafting communications.

Some possible causes of lower skill

Causes help explain *why* a person may have trouble with Communicates effectively. When seeking to increase skill, it's helpful to consider how these might play out in certain situations. And remember that all of these can be addressed if you are motivated to do so.

- Dominates discussions.
- Messages lack focus.
- Doesn't listen.
- Shy.
- Doesn't write or use visual tools well.
- Doesn't connect to the audience.
- Avoids difficult conversations.
- Prepares poorly or not at all.
- Discourages the flow of ideas.

Does it best

Mention Martin Luther King Jr. and most people immediately think of his "I have a dream" speech. This 1963 speech has been ranked one of the greatest of the 20th century. One of the things that made his speech truly great was his ability to deviate from prepared notes and adapt his message based on what would best resonate with his audience. When a good friend in the audience shouted, "Tell 'em about the dream," King put his notes aside and improvised much of the second half of the speech, including the familiar refrain, "I have a dream." King told his story with the authenticity and conviction that moved people to act.[8, 9]

Tips to develop Communicates effectively

1. **Tend to be quiet? Push yourself to connect.** Each of us is wired differently. Extraverts get their energy from interactions with others. They may speak more easily, enjoy gatherings, and develop ideas out loud. Introverts may hold back more. They want to get more information before they speak. They prefer writing to speaking. If you are this quieter, more reserved type, recognize that others want to hear from you. They want to know your thoughts and perspective. So push yourself to be part of the conversation. Want more information before you speak? Show interest by asking questions. Feeling great about something? Let people know. Have a better idea? Follow up after the meeting ends. Like a book or helpful website? Send an enthusiastic e-mail. Let yourself pause when you need to think. Find quiet moments to gather your thoughts. But remember to join the conversation. You have a lot to add.

2. **Like to ensure you're heard? Quiet down and listen.** Energy can be engaging. But if you're too loud or talkative, you may alienate more quiet or task-focused colleagues. Maybe others can't get their work done when you're around. Meetings can't start on time because you are busy with side conversations. Or others aren't heard because you dominate discussions. If you're naturally outgoing, practice a little self-observation to see if your behavior is a problem. Or ask others what they see. Then learn to quiet yourself down so that others can speak. Find other, appropriate outlets for your energy. At work, learn to respect others' space and time. Balance speaking with listening. Do you tend to speak more in meetings than anyone else? Are you always the first to answer a question or offer an opinion? Hold back. Let others speak first. Listen to what they have to say and then comment. Pace yourself. For every instance that you chime in to the conversation, don't speak again until two other participants have had a say. Occasionally, try saying nothing.

3. **Not open to others' ideas? Solicit input and discussion.** In love with your own ideas? Like to figure things out and do your own planning? Issue orders and give instructions? Effective communicators see the value of different perspectives. They listen to others, brainstorm ideas, and collaborate on plans. They are open to what they can learn. To improve as a communicator, set aside the need to know it all. Ask what others can contribute. Welcome divergent views. Put yourself in learning mode. Even when ideas conflict, new and better solutions can emerge. If you are closed to new ideas or think you already know everything there is to know, then you are not a great communicator. Period.

4. **Sending the wrong signals? Watch your non-verbals.** Pride yourself on preparing for meetings? Have all of your messages lined up and ready to deliver? Your preparation can be derailed by a few unconscious mannerisms or non-verbal habits. Non-verbals can cause distractions or send unintended signals like impatience, disinterest, or nervousness. To clean up your non-verbals, give others your full attention. Turn away from your computer, shut off your cell phone, and set distractions aside. Keep your facial expressions open and friendly. Watch out for habits like glancing at your watch, checking for incoming messages, or giving an impatient "I'm busy" look when people need more time. Avoid fidgeting. Don't let your eyes "glaze over." Stay focused and have good eye contact. Ask a few trusted friends what they've observed. Work on eliminating mannerisms that suggest you're disinterested.

Want to learn more? Take a deep dive...

Adams, S. (2013, November 19). How to communicate effectively at work. *Forbes*.

Charan, R. (2012, June 21). The discipline of listening. *Harvard Business Review Blog Network*.

Cherry, K. (n.d.). *Types of nonverbal communication: 8 Major nonverbal behaviors*. About.com Psychology.

5. **Using jargon or acronyms? Choose clear language.** Every group has a lexicon of its own. Teenagers. Politicians. Technical groups such as systems engineers. Functional groups such as finance and human resources. They use acronyms specific to their function or sector—ROIC for "return on invested capital" or OPEC instead of "Organization of the Petroleum Exporting Countries." They fall back on jargon, choose an abstract term, or string too many nouns together. Like writing "visual pattern identification depiction" when "map" would do. If you are writing or speaking for an insider group, you may not need to translate anything. In fact, it can make you sound more credible when you speak their insider lingo. But to reach a wider audience, you need to state things as simply as you can. Watch out for jargon, acronyms, and insider terms. Translate slang—especially if you are writing for an international audience. Watch out for spelling and usage errors. If you're a regular texter, you may have fallen into some bad habits. Ask someone from your target audience to review your work for clarity. Use grammar check in Word to flag any unusual constructions. Use a thesaurus to find the best vocabulary. Use a style guide—such as Strunk and White's *The Elements of Style*—for ideas on how to make things clear.

6. **Communications missing the mark? Adjust for individual differences.** Do people sometimes not understand you? What you are saying seems perfectly clear to you. But others ask, "What exactly do you mean?" A lot of miscommunication occurs because people process information differently. Some get the picture without a lot of detail. Others need more explanation or examples to understand clearly. Some need an illustration or a case study. Others ignore the diagrams. Some like to take notes. Others retain most of what they hear. Don't assume that everyone processes information as you do. Get to know the communication styles of the people around you. Investigate what's worked before. What they relate to and what they don't. What pace is appropriate? What techniques they like? What holds their interest? What approaches have they rejected? What level of detail they've asked for from others? How do they provide information to others? (People often deliver as they like to receive.) Research your audience and tailor your approach.

7. **Don't know where to start? Create a plan and an outline.** Plenty of ideas to share, but find it hard to get started? Whether you are writing or presenting, whether your message is targeted for a large group or for a one-to-one dialogue, start by planning. Who is your audience? What is the main message? What is your main objective in communication? To inform? Entertain? Influence? Motivate? How much time or how many pages will you fill? Once you've identified these parameters, move on to the outline. State your message or purpose in one or two lead sentences. What in the introduction will grab the reader or the audience? Then outline three to five chunks of your argument to support your thesis. What are your priority points and how will you explain them? Organize the detail under the main points. Some points are made better by example, some by the logic of the argument, some by facts or stories. Check your facts and assertions for accuracy. Finally, how will you close? Do you want to move others to action? Or inspire them with a final, powerful message? Or maybe you just want to give them more resources for learning. Use your outline as you actually create the document or presentation. Change it only when there is a good reason to do so.

8. **Messages not flowing? Create a first draft—and then edit.** When you write, any sentence that does not relate to your main message should not be there. When you speak, everything you communicate needs to keep the audience engaged. Great writers and speakers seem to do this effortlessly. Their thoughts flow. Their words have rhythm and cadence. Their messages have immediate impact. You want to be great. But if you aim for perfection the first time, you can get stuck. Whether you are writing an article or creating a

presentation, free up your writing by letting it all flow before you edit. Don't worry about grammar or the fine details of PowerPoint until you get your thoughts out. Get the words down first, then go back to make changes. Set your draft aside for 24 hours and then go back to it. You will see it with fresh eyes and have a better perspective on what needs to be changed. Read what you've written out loud to hear the places you can make changes. You will find new ways to make your writing or your presentation flow.

Want to learn more? Take a deep dive...

Belena, R. (2010, February 17). *Communication tips for avoiding the use of business jargon.* Inside Business 360.

Cohan, P. (2012, December 4). 5 Ways to communicate more clearly. *Inc.*

Nierenberg, A. (2005, February 17). *Adapting to different communication styles.* Small Business Advocate.

9. **Lack impact? Amp up your personal power.** When you look your best, it makes an impression. Your posture, choice of wardrobe, and other factors send important signals. Look confident and approachable. Observe the people around you. Who consistently looks great? Who attracts you so that you want to work with them? Do they dress formally or informally? On-trend or conservatively? How about the people above you? What does "dress for success" look like in your organization? Now do an honest appraisal of yourself and your wardrobe. Toss out anything shabby, ill-fitting, or unflattering. Invest in a few new items that help you shine. Like suits or jackets for when you need to be more formal and some good-looking pieces for casual situations. Ask friends for some input and do the same for them. Consider your physical presence. Can you become more fit and energetic? Maybe you could get more sleep or eat better. Maybe you need a lunch-hour walking group or regular trips to the gym. The idea is not to become a clone of anyone else— but to present your best self. Have fun with this.

10. **Need to hold attention? Ramp up the visuals.** We live in a visual age. Information comes in pictures and sound, via e-mail and video link. People scan documents rather than read them. They use an electronic newsletter to share information. They multi-task during dull conference calls. Cut through the clutter. People will listen and read—but they need shorter, more succinct messages and visual cues that tell them what is important. Remember that everyone is

suffering from information overload. If an e-mail doesn't grab the reader in less than 10 seconds, your whole message will be ignored. They need to see immediately why your presentation or document is worth their time and attention. Support conference calls with a few short slides. Break up a long document with call-outs and illustrations. Create section heads and use fonts effectively to keep the eye moving through long text. Great graphics are not a substitute for great thought—but they go a long way toward keeping the audience engaged.

11.   **Addressing multiple audiences? Adjust your message.** Unfortunately, one presentation or document generally does not play equally well across differing audiences. Whether you are writing or speaking, you will have to adjust the length, tone, pace, style, and even the message and how you couch it for different audiences. Writing for high-level management? Use an executive summary. At the end, tell them what decision you are asking for. If they indicate interest, follow up with the longer document. In formal presentations, keep the supporting visuals short and offer to send supporting data later. Adjust the supporting information to the needs of the audience. Need to keep the legal group informed? Supply them with the why, the history, parallels in the marketplace, legal potholes. Direct reports? They need implementation detail. You may need to write one long document and then break it up and move elements around for various audiences. Don't try to make one document stretch. If you have time, run your speech or writing past someone who represents this group. If they understand your message, you have a better chance of reaching everyone.

12.   **Losing your audience? Check in with them.** You've identified your target audience. You're pretty sure you understand their challenges. You're speaking their language. You know why they would want to listen to you. Then 10 minutes into your presentation you're seeing puzzled looks. Closed faces. People are fidgeting or checking their messages. This doesn't mean your presentation is a failure—but it's important to check in to find out what's going on. If you're losing your audience, stop what you're doing and ask what's going on. Are there any questions so far? Are you going too fast or too slow? Do people need a break? Maybe the room is too hot. Or it's the end of the week and people are just tired. Or they want to stop listening and discuss something you've said. Consider the audience as an important participant in your presentation. Change your pace or language. Move more quickly or slowly through the material. Be flexible in meeting their needs.

7

Want to learn more? Take a deep dive...

Harrison, C. (2007, December). *Who's your audience? Ways to win your audience through inclusion.* Toastmasters International.

Mind Tools. (n.d.). *Creating effective presentation visuals: Connecting people with your message.* Mind Tools.

Tardanico, S. (2012, May 29). Want to be a better public speaker? Do what the pros do. *Forbes.*

13. **E-mail rhetoric heating up? Talk directly.** E-mail is essential to organizational communication. It's a great way to send info, set up meetings, convey documents, and make requests. But it's a poor way to convey emotion or discuss really complex matters. There's no tone of voice, body language, or facial cues to help the recipient interpret your mood. Taken out of context, "thank you" can sound grateful—or dismissive and sarcastic. Research shows that we lose half of our communication power when not face-to-face and an even higher percentage when not voice-to-voice. To avoid misunderstanding, soften your messages with greetings and appropriate personable comments, as you would in an informal letter or a phone call. Don't use e-mail to conduct an argument, convey hurt feelings, issue brusque orders, or justify your position to others. When an e-mail exchange is especially contentious, don't hit send until you've had time and space to reflect. Better still, when things get heated or emotional, reach for the phone instead. If you're in the same office, go and see the other person. Apologize for anything that has been misconstrued. Offer to have a full conversation and repair the damage before it starts.

14. **Difficult conversation? Acknowledge emotions.** Emotional conversations are the most difficult. When you need to convey bad news. Deliver a poor performance review. Discuss conflict or a misunderstanding. If you are faced with a meeting like this, don't make the mistake of ignoring or avoiding emotions. Start by asking questions of yourself. What is it about this conversation that makes it difficult for you? What emotions or worries does it create? What emotional reactions might the other person (or group) have? Once you have acknowledged this, it will be easier to think about what information you need to communicate and the best way to do it. Process emotion, but don't get stuck there. Move on to what needs to be discussed. Focus on your main message and make sure it doesn't get buried by other information. Focus on a good outcome and create an understanding of next steps.

15. **Driving a strategic message? Plan carefully and follow the plan.** There may be times when you need to lead or be part of a strategic communication. When strategy and timing are crucial. When confidentiality is paramount. Whether you're the CEO making an announcement, the head of a function or department, or a manager of a small team, determine which internal and external audiences you need to reach. When and how messages need to be communicated. Is this a crisis, a positive development, or the rollout of a new process? An internal message only or external as well? What media—including social media—will you use? Who will speak? When will they speak? How will you balance the "need to know" with confidentiality issues? What role will managers and supervisors play in informing their staff? How will you handle leaks and rumors, both internally and externally? Whether you are a leader of the strategy or a communicator in the chain, respect the plan and process. Pull in resources from marketing, communications, HR, and/or legal to advise you.

Want to learn more? Take a deep dive...

Everse, G. (2011, August 22). Eight ways to communicate your strategy more effectively. *Harvard Business Review Blog Network*.

Federer, D. (2014, January 10). Have the difficult conversation. *Business Observer*.

Hughes, S. (2012, October 25). I banned all internal e-mails at my company for a week. *Forbes*.

Job assignments

- Lead or join a team charged with communicating a major change initiative in your function. Think carefully about the challenging messages that need to be conveyed and plan how you will cover them clearly and succinctly.

- Create and deliver a presentation on a new technological development that could revolutionize your business area. Think carefully about how you tailor the presentation to suit the audience.

- Write a report justifying a major capital investment in new production equipment. Communicate the financial information clearly to engage and inform the reader.

84 |

- Collect ideas to improve a critical process in your function and write a synopsis discussing the merits of each.

- Lead a team discussion on how to improve their accountability and commitment to each other. Use this as an opportunity to involve everyone. Draw them into the conversation and make them feel involved.

Take time to reflect...

If you assume communication is simple to get right...

> ...then understand that it's just as simple to get it wrong. Take time to consider the feedback you receive. Make changes to hone your technique.

If you're lacking in confidence when you have to communicate...

> ...then allocate time for preparation. It often requires several "takes" to get the content and the style right. Planning and practice will give your confidence the boost it needs.

If your message doesn't land with the impact you want...

> ...then recognize that communication is far more than just getting the right words out. Whether through speaking or writing, having only one approach is too limiting. Planning the "how" is just as important as preparing the "what."

" *Yes, in all my research, the greatest leaders looked inward and were able to tell a good story with authenticity and passion.* **"**

Deepak Chopra – Indian-American physician and writer

Learn more about Communicates effectively

Bailey, E. P., Jr. (2007). *Writing and speaking at work* (4th ed.). Upper Saddle River, NJ: Prentice Hall.

Bough, B., & Condrill, J. (2005). *101 Ways to improve your communication skills instantly* (4th ed.). San Antonio, TX: GoalMinds, Inc.

Garcia, H. F. (2012). *The power of communication: Skills to build trust, inspire loyalty, and lead effectively*. Upper Saddle River, NJ: FT Press.

Hamilton, C. (2013). *Communicating for results: A guide for business and the professions*. Boston, MA: Cengage Learning.

Weeks, H. (2008). *Failure to communicate: How conversations go wrong and what you can do to right them*. Boston, MA: Harvard Business School Press.

Deep dive learning resource links

Adams, S. (2013, November 19). How to communicate effectively at work. *Forbes*. Retrieved from http://www.forbes.com/sites/susanadams/2013/11/19/how-to-communicate-effectively-at-work-3/

Belena, R. (2010, February 17). *Communication tips for avoiding the use of business jargon*. Inside Business 360. Retrieved from http://www.insidebusiness360.com/index.php/communication-tips-for-avoiding-the-use-of-business-jargon-and-acronyms-14169/

Charan, R. (2012, June 21). The discipline of listening. *Harvard Business Review Blog Network*. Retrieved from http://blogs.hbr.org/2012/06/the-discipline-of-listening/

Cherry, K. (n.d.). *Types of nonverbal communication: 8 Major nonverbal behaviors*. About.com Psychology. Retrieved from http://psychology.about.com/od/nonverbalcommunication/a/nonverbaltypes.htm

Cohan, P. (2012, December 4). 5 Ways to communicate more clearly. *Inc*. Retrieved from http://www.inc.com/peter-cohan/five-ways-to-improve-your-communication-success.html

Everse, G. (2011, August 22). Eight ways to communicate your strategy more effectively. *Harvard Business Review Blog Network*. Retrieved from http://blogs.hbr.org/2011/08/eight-ways-to-energize-your-te/

Federer, D. (2014, January 10). Have the difficult conversation. *Business Observer*. Retrieved from http://www.businessobserverfl.com/section/detail/have-the-difficult-conversation/

Harrison, C. (2007, December). *Who's your audience? Ways to win your audience through inclusion*. Toastmasters International. Retrieved from http://www.toastmasters.org/ToastmastersMagazine/ToastmasterArchive/2007/December/WhosYourAudience.aspx

Hughes, S. (2012, October 25). I banned all internal e-mails at my company for a week. *Forbes*. Retrieved from http://www.forbes.com/sites/forbesleadershipforum/2012/10/25/i-banned-all-internal-e-mails-at-my-company-for-a-week/

Mind Tools. (n.d.). *Creating effective presentation visuals: Connecting people with your message*. Mind Tools. Retrieved from http://www.mindtools.com/pages/article/creating-presentation-visuals.htm

Nierenberg, A. (2005, February 17). *Adapting to different communication styles*. Small Business Advocate. Retrieved from http://www.smallbusinessadvocate.com/small-business-articles/adapting-to-different-communication-styles-1427

Tardanico, S. (2012, May 29). Want to be a better public speaker? Do what the pros do. *Forbes*. Retrieved from http://www.forbes.com/sites/susantardanico/2012/05/29/want-to-be-a-better-public-speaker-do-what-the-pros-do/

Recommended search terms

If you'd like to explore Communicates effectively further, try searching online using the following terms:

- Adjust your presentation for the audience.
- Dealing effectively with difficult conversations.
- Effective two-way communication.
- How to adapt to different communication styles.
- Knowing your audience during presentations.
- Strategic communication.

 More help...

Go to www.kornferry.com/fyi-resources and link directly to the deep dive resources in this chapter. Visit the site often to see the additional resources that are uploaded on a regular basis.

| 87

|

8. *Manages* complexity

Making sense of complex, high quantity, and sometimes contradictory information to effectively solve problems.

Problems are getting more complex all the time. Success today depends on figuring out the best solution to difficult, high-stakes issues. Issues that have so many moving parts that it's hard to make sense of it all. Most people are smart enough to solve problems effectively, but they don't always go about it the right way. They don't define the problem carefully or rush to conclusions. Or they go to the other extreme and analyze it to death without trying anything out. They may also rely too much on themselves, when multiple people usually have a better chance of arriving at the best solution. It's tempting to skim the surface of a thorny issue. But skim-the-surface solutions will yield superficial results at best and be flat out wrong at worst. You need to drill down, gather data from diverse sources, sort through it, and then distill it into simpler, understandable themes. Evaluate the pros and cons of potential solutions. Test out the best options. Learn and share lessons along the way. And stay alert for future problems that may arise.

"Fools ignore complexity. Pragmatists suffer it. Some can avoid it. Geniuses remove it. "

Alan Perlis – American computer scientist

***Manages* complexity** is in the **Thought** factor (I) in the Korn Ferry Leadership Architect™. It is part of Cluster B, **Making complex decisions,** along with Decision quality (12) and *Balances* stakeholders (32). You may find it helpful to also take a look at some of the tips included in those chapters to supplement your learning.

Skilled

Asks the right questions to accurately analyze situations.

Acquires data from multiple and diverse sources when solving problems.

Uncovers root causes to difficult problems.

Evaluates pros and cons, risks and benefits of different solution options.

Less skilled

- Misses the complexity of issues and force fits solutions.
- Doesn't gather sufficient information to assess situations completely.
- Relies solely on intuition, even when contrary information exists.
- Is caught off guard when problems surface without an obvious solution.

Talented

- Readily distinguishes between what's relevant and what's unimportant to make sense of complex situations.
- Looks beyond the obvious and doesn't stop at the first answers.
- Analyzes multiple and diverse sources of information to define problems accurately before moving to solutions.

Overused skill

- May tend toward analysis paralysis.
- May wait too long to come to a conclusion.
- May get caught up in the process and miss the big picture.
- May make things more complex than needed.

Some possible causes of lower skill

Causes help explain *why* a person may have trouble with *Manages* complexity. When seeking to increase skill, it's helpful to consider how these might play out in certain situations. And remember that all of these can be addressed if you are motivated to do so.

- Disorganized.
- Impatient.
- Jumps to conclusions.
- Overly self-reliant.
- Gets overwhelmed.
- Perfectionist, needs too much data.
- Oversimplifies.
- Doesn't think ahead.
- Limited problem-solving toolkit.

 Brain booster

Your brain has tremendous capacity to handle complex challenges. But dealing with complexity uses up more fuel more quickly than routine activities. There is such a thing as "brain food." Your brain needs glucose and oxygen when it works hard to make sense, make decisions, commit things to memory, and analyze tough problems. This is why you may feel depleted after significant mental exertion. Give your brain time to refuel. Plan to take a walk, have a brain-healthy snack such as fruit or nuts. Do your most challenging work when you are well rested. Stay fresh and alert for critical tasks by setting aside other things that may require your attention. The less a complex problem has to compete for brain resources, the more likely you will see clearly, be able to simplify, and see the way forward.[10]

Tips to develop *Manages* complexity

1. **Not sure where to start? Define the problem.** For at least half the time allotted to deal with a problem, shut off your solution machine and get clear about what needs fixing. You'd be in good company—Einstein once said that if he had one hour to save the world, he'd spend 55 minutes defining the problem and only 5 minutes finding the solution. Experts agree that rigor in problem definition pays off in better solutions. So start by defining what the problem is and what it isn't. Be as clear and succinct as possible. Why is it important to solve? How would customers, stakeholders, your organization benefit? Make a goal or write a desired outcome statement that describes what will be better when the problem is solved. Keep in mind problem definition may not be a once-and-done proposition. Complex issues evolve quickly, so revisit the problem definition over time to be sure you're still solving the right problem.

2. **Things too vague? Gather relevant information.** First, get organized. What information already exists? What else do you need? Gather data on who, what, when, where, why, and how the problem occurs. Is it sporadic or chronic? Mild or severe? Shine a light on the "FOG" by differentiating Facts, Opinions, and Guesses. The team charged with finding a solution and those who will fund it need something solid to go on. Be willing to hunt for useful information. It's often scattered—in someone's head, in random spreadsheets, archived virtually. Some information is relevant and reliable, some is noise. Sift through and find the good stuff, then supplement it with surveys, analytics, or field studies. Whenever possible, observe the problem where it lives so you can see firsthand what's at play. How much is the right amount of information to gather? Weigh the potential benefit of knowing something against the cost of finding it out. Learn to discern when enough really is enough.

3. **Trouble getting at what's under the surface? Drill down to root causes.** A typical error in problem-solving is to mistake a symptom (what shows up) for a cause (the underlying factor that triggered it). Try root cause analysis tools like cause-and-effect diagrams to get some clarity. Or the "5 Whys" that is prevalent in Lean manufacturing and in companies that use Six Sigma methods. First, describe the problem statement. Then ask, "Why does this occur?" After the first answer, ask "Why" again for a total of five times. See how many underlying causes you can come up with and how many categories you can put them in. Then ask what they have in common and how they are different. This increases the chance of a more creative solution because you can see more connections. Look for

patterns in the data, don't just collect it. Put it in categories that make sense to you and your colleagues.

4. **Have difficulty finding the answer? Ask more questions.** Get curious and explore all angles of the challenge. What are the must-have criteria that need to be met? What would be nice to have but not essential? What solutions have already been tried and what were the results? What are the forces that perpetuate the problem? What's the ideal time line for a solution to be in place? What will happen if no action is taken? What resources exist for finding, testing, and implementing a solution? What constraints? What's the full scope of the issue? Is the entire process broken or just one part? What is the least likely thing it could be? What's related to it and what's not? How will you know if a solution does or doesn't work? Create a checklist of questions that will be useful when solving a myriad of problems. Add to it with each new case to build in-demand, problem-solving expertise.

5. **Prefer solving it on your own? Consult diverse resources.** Many try to do too much by themselves. Even if you think you have a decent solution, ask other people for input just to make sure. Tackle sticky problems with a diverse task force—people with different experiences and perspectives. Access networks across the organization and beyond so you have the right information to begin with and a steady stream flowing in. A key way to ensure that others share information with you is to make it a habit to share yours with them. Tap into experts and novices. Ask experts how they approach new, complex problems. What golden nuggets might work with your current issue? Ask new team members to share ideas. They may bring a fresh perspective to tough issues you and your colleagues have tried to untangle for years. Get diverse input through internal or external crowdsourcing. Make it a competition to see who provides the best solution to your problem. You may find that it's the people who aren't direct experts in the topic that offer the most innovative solution.

Want to learn more? Take a deep dive...

Baer, D. (2013, March 26). Einstein's problem-solving formula, and why you're doing it all wrong. *Fast Company*.

Dann, J. (2009, July 14). *Darden prof: Tap outside resources to rev your innovation engine*. CBS News.

Llopis, G. (2013, November 4). The 4 most effective ways leaders solve problems. *Forbes*.

6. **Stuck in default solution mode? Don't rush to judgment.** When it comes to tackling complex problems, people sometimes move to solutioning at breakneck speed. Some are action-oriented, fire-ready-aim types. A lot of mistakes would be prevented just by taking more time to think things through. Then there are chronically impatient people who give answers too soon as a way of being. Gather data? Who has time. Try out a new solution? Why bother when there's a tried-and-true solution that worked in the past. Favoring historical solutions is tempting but risky. Instead of giving new options your full attention, you may be looking for corroborating evidence that supports the solution you've already decided to take. Make use of the pause button for better problem solving. Go through a mental checklist to see if you've considered how all the possible outcomes of the current challenge might play out. Study the relevant information with fresh eyes. Research has shown that the first solution you think of is seldom the best choice. Keep digging to come up with more, and probably better, alternatives.

7. **Looking for clues? Study successes for principles to apply.** If you can find three times that something worked, ask why it worked despite differences in the situations. What was common to each success, or what was present in each failure but never present in a success? Focus most on learning from the successes—it will yield more information about underlying principles you can replicate. Look for patterns about the people involved, the work processes, or the larger ecosystem. Reduce your insights to rules of thumb you can repeat or tailor to the current situation. Also, hunt for similar underlying issues in other organizations, including those totally outside your field. For example, who has to manage to razor-thin profit margins (grocery stores, airlines)?

8. **Overwhelmed by complexity? Break it down.** This is the era of organizational and market uncertainties. With this as the norm, it's likely that the problems you face daily are becoming more and more complex. One way to deal with complex problems is to turn something that looms large into a series of smaller problems. People who are good at this are incrementalists. They make a series of smaller decisions, get instant feedback, correct the course, get a little more data, then move forward a little more until the bigger problem is under control. They don't try to get it all right the first time. Going a little at a time means that glitches or unintended consequences will be more manageable too. Another trick if you're overwhelmed by complexity is to put all like elements into conceptual

buckets (e.g., everything to do with costs in one bucket, people in another). Analyze how the buckets can work in sync or in opposition. Be careful not to overcomplexify. If a solution is obvious or elegantly simple, let it be.

Want to learn more? Take a deep dive...

Goodman, N. (2013, February 28). Creative problem-solving strategies to test your business idea. *Entrepreneur.*

Wooden, J. (2009, March). John Wooden: The difference between winning and succeeding [Video file]. TED.

Zwilling, M. (2011, July 19). *Nine steps to effective business problem solving.* Business Insider.

9. **Perfectionist? Balance perfection with action.** Want to wait for all of the information to come in? Need to be 100% sure you have the right solution? Many of us would prefer that. Perfectionism is tough to let go of because most people see it as a positive trait—one that's helped them succeed so far. It's understandable that you want to collect more information to boost your confidence in making a fault-free decision, which will reduce risk or criticism. But face it: numerous studies show that more data may increase confidence but doesn't necessarily increase decision accuracy. The problem may be getting worse while you keep gathering more information. It's about finding the right balance. Listen to your trusted colleagues. If they think you tend to overanalyze, start taking action sooner so you can land on a workable solution.

10. **Overloaded with information? Learn to discern.** Information overload is indeed a reality. In fact, the Institute for the Future has named Signal/Noise Management as an imperative leadership skill. Having this skill means you are able to filter meaningful information, finding the useful parts from the massive streams of data produced and received. When effectively distilled, categorized, and integrated, data provides a road map to many best-possible solutions. A road map that helps alert you to signals that trouble may be brewing or that opportunities are ripe. Work with leadership to craft a big data plan for your organization. Find ways to get it to work for you, not against you—anticipating problems, mining fresh insights, tracking progress, and making better predictions.

11. **Need a new approach? Use more problem-solving tools.** There are all kinds of tools and techniques you can use by yourself or (even better) in collaboration with others:

    • Depict a complex problem visually. Separate its components and cluster similar aspects. Use flowcharts, mind maps, or sticky notes to show relationships or to see if a different order would help make sense of things.

    • Use a pictorial chart, called a storyboard, where a problem is conveyed in a sequence of events through images or metaphors.

    • Try storytelling to illustrate how the problem manifests, how stakeholders think or feel about the current reality, and what their hopes are for the future state.

    • Devise worst-case scenarios—going to extremes sometimes suggests a different solution. Take the present state of affairs and project it into the future to reveal how and where the system may break down.

    • Create an evaluation matrix to assess potential solutions. List the options along the side in rows; across the top in columns put the requirements that must be met.

    • Use online collaboration software and apps for productive group and virtual work. Vision boards, ways to organize data, voting tools—they're all out there.

12. **Unsure how to choose? Test and weigh your options.** Wherever possible, create prototypes, experiment, or run some tests. Anticipate glitches as best you can and have contingencies in place to address them. Gather data so you can make rational comparisons. Weigh the options against specific criteria that need to be met (e.g., cost, speed, quality, customer satisfaction). Identify the pros/cons and costs/benefits of all possible solutions, then work to make the best ones even stronger. The Creative Problem Solving Institute recommends a tool for evaluating and strengthening solutions called PPCO. First, state the solution's Pluses or clear strengths. Next, discuss its Potential. What Concerns do you have, including any risks? Finally, how might you Overcome the concerns and mitigate risks? Be sure to consider how other areas of the ecosystem will be impacted—not just your own team or unit. Look at potential long-term effects. What unintended consequences might surface, good and bad? Use the data you generated to get buy-in and the go-ahead from key stakeholders.

96 |

13. **Wondering if you have a winner? Measure solution effectiveness.** A solution isn't a winner until it has held up when fully put into action. What before-and-after metrics does it make sense to collect? Think through what matters most to your stakeholders and will validate the solution once a baseline is established. How will you monitor and document results (e.g., in higher revenue, fewer complaints, better safety records)? Also, be alert to capture outcomes you didn't expect. Create feedback loops to flag issues and alert the right team members. Determine how you'll track success of the solution over time so that when you want to make the business case for continued resources or amplification, you're ready. Use the diagnostic and analytical tools your organization has to support your efforts. Celebrate short- and long-term wins, and share what you and your team have learned in order to grow your collective problem-solving skills.

Want to learn more? Take a deep dive...

Hershfield, H. (2013, June). You make better decisions if you 'see' your senior self. *Harvard Business Review*.

Neville, A. (2013, May 10). Perfectionism is the enemy of everything. *Forbes*.

Weber, L. (2012, December 24). How to be a creative problem solver. *The Wall Street Journal*.

Job assignments

- Collaborate with others to troubleshoot a performance or quality problem with a product or service that is receiving many customer or stakeholder complaints.

- Take on an assignment where you will be charting new ground, collecting and analyzing lots of data, and making recommendations to senior leaders.

- Tackle a tough problem that others have previously failed to solve. Besides analyzing the why behind the failure, think about applying principles from similar situations that had successful solutions.

- Assemble a team of experts to solve a complex issue with potentially serious implications for employees, customers, the public, or your organization's reputation (health, safety, etc.).

- Work with colleagues across the enterprise to determine the root causes of a talent-related problem (e.g., increase in turnover, decline in engagement) and recommend steps to address it.

Take time to reflect...

If you rely on experience to address challenging new problems...

> ...then realize that what you already know won't always lead you to where you need to be. Sometimes it pays to play the naive card.

If you don't know where to start with a complex issue...

> ...then avoid focusing too much on the unknown. Follow the facts and see where they lead you. Building the puzzle piece by piece will help you see the whole picture.

If you don't have the facts to reach the solution...

> ...then get out there and find them. Plunge into a wide variety of sources. Ask questions of the experts. Draw on resources you already have and explore those you don't.

"*The eye sees only what the mind is prepared to comprehend.***"**

Henri Bergson – French philosopher

|

Learn more about *Manages* complexity

Davidson, J. E., & Sternberg, R. J. (Eds.). (2003). *The psychology of problem solving*. New York, NY: Cambridge University Press.

Gharajedaghi, J. (2011). *Systems thinking: Managing chaos and complexity: A platform for designing business architecture* (3rd ed.). Burlington, MA: Morgan Kaufmann.

Hoenig, C. (2000). *The problem-solving journey: Your guide for making decisions and getting results*. Cambridge, MA: Perseus Publishing.

Rock, D. (2009). *Your brain at work: Strategies for overcoming distraction, regaining focus, and working smarter all day long*. New York, NY: HarperCollins Publishers.

Rosenhead, J., & Mingers, J. (2001). *Rational analysis for a problematic world: Problem structuring methods for complexity, uncertainty and conflict*. West Sussex, England: John Wiley & Sons, Ltd.

Watanabe, K. (2009). *Problem solving 101: A simple book for smart people*. New York, NY: Portfolio Hardcover.

 # Deep dive learning resource links

Baer, D. (2013, March 26). Einstein's problem-solving formula, and why you're doing it all wrong. *Fast Company*. Retrieved from http://www.fastcompany.com/3007430/einsteins-problem-solving-formula-and-why-youre-doing-it-all-wrong

Dann, J. (2009, July 14). *Darden prof: Tap outside resources to rev your innovation engine*. CBS News. Retrieved from http://www.cbsnews.com/news/darden-prof-tap-outside-resources-to-rev-your-innovation-engine/

Goodman, N. (2013, February 28). Creative problem-solving strategies to test your business idea. *Entrepreneur*. Retrieved from http://www.entrepreneur.com/article/225923

Hershfield, H. (2013, June). You make better decisions if you 'see' your senior self. *Harvard Business Review*. Retrieved from http://hbr.org/2013/06/you-make-better-decisions-if-you-see-your-senior-self/ar/1

Llopis, G. (2013, November 4). The 4 most effective ways leaders solve problems. *Forbes*. Retrieved from http://www.forbes.com/sites/glennllopis/2013/11/04/the-4-most-effective-ways-leaders-solve-problems/

Neville, A. (2013, May 10). Perfectionism is the enemy of everything. *Forbes*. Retrieved from http://www.forbes.com/sites/amandaneville/2013/05/10/perfectionism-is-the-enemy-of-everything/

Weber, L. (2012, December 24). How to be a creative problem solver. *The Wall Street Journal*. Retrieved from http://blogs.wsj.com/atwork/2012/12/24/how-to-be-a-creative-problem-solver/

Wooden, J. (2009, March). John Wooden: The difference between winning and succeeding [Video file]. TED. Retrieved from http://www.ted.com/talks/john_wooden_on_the_difference_between_winning_and_success.html

Zwilling, M. (2011, July 19). *Nine steps to effective business problem solving*. Business Insider. Retrieved from http://www.businessinsider.com/nine-steps-to-effective-business-problem-solving-2011-7

8

Recommended search terms

If you'd like to explore *Manages* complexity further, try searching online using the following terms:

- Dealing with complex problems in the workplace.
- Effective problem solving.
- Incremental problem solving in business.
- Problem solving tools/models.
- Reducing/managing perfectionism in the workplace.

 More help...

Go to www.kornferry.com/fyi-resources and link directly to the deep dive resources in this chapter. Visit the site often to see the additional resources that are uploaded on a regular basis.

---

9. *Manages* conflict

Handling conflict situations effectively, with a minimum of noise.

Conflict is a natural part of organizational life. Organizations are made up of diverse people with differing opinions and competing interests, making conflict inevitable. There is conflict over information, resources, opinions, territory, position. If it's important to someone, it has the potential to cause conflict. Handled badly, conflict can entrench. Disrupt productivity. Damage relationships. But conflict isn't always a bad thing. Conflict surfaces previous undiscussables. Highlights not just the disconnects but also the intersection of ideas. Managed well, conflict provides a forum for finding better alternatives, even breakthroughs, in building relationships and solving problems. But only when the people involved treat each other constructively and respectfully. When you manage conflict effectively, you begin to see conflicts less as headaches and more as opportunities. Issues get resolved. Collaboration improves. Solution focus replaces negativity and recrimination. Things progress in a positive direction.

"*In the middle of difficulty lies opportunity.***"**

Albert Einstein – German-born Nobel Prize-winning physicist

Manages conflict is in the **People** factor (III) in the Korn Ferry Leadership Architect™. It is part of Cluster G, **Building collaborative relationships,** along with Collaborates (6), Interpersonal savvy (20), and *Builds* networks (21). You may find it helpful to also take a look at some of the tips included in those chapters to supplement your learning.

Skilled

Steps up to conflicts, seeing them as opportunities.

Works out tough agreements and settles disputes equitably.

Facilitates breakthroughs by integrating diverse views and finding common ground or acceptable alternatives.

Settles differences in productive ways with minimum noise.

Less skilled

- Avoids conflict.
- Struggles to make progress when working through disagreements.
- Takes sides without digging deeply enough to fully understand the issues.
- Allows conflicts to cause massive disruption in the organization.
- Puts people on the defensive.
- May accommodate, wanting everyone to get along.

Talented

- Anticipates conflicts before they happen, based on knowledge of interpersonal and group dynamics.
- Asks questions and listens closely to all issues presented by stakeholders.
- Finds common ground and drives to consensus, ensuring that all feel heard.
- Defuses high-tension situations effectively.

Overused skill

- May be seen as meddling in others' issues.
- Is too eager to engage others in debate.
- Pushes for resolution before others are ready.

Some possible causes of lower skill

Causes help explain *why* a person may have trouble with *Manages* conflict. When seeking to increase skill, it's helpful to consider how these might play out in certain situations. And remember that all of these can be addressed if you are motivated to do so.

- Avoids conflict.
- Defensive.
- Inflexible or rigid.
- Gets too emotional.
- Takes things too personally.
- Too sensitive.
- Strong viewpoints on everything.
- Impatient.
- Poor communicator.
- Prioritizes own interests over others'.
- Doesn't gauge impact on others well.

Brain booster

At its core, conflict is perceived by the brain as a threat. Conflict and threat activate the limbic, or emotional, system of the brain and very quickly you may feel your heart rate, breathing, or temperature change. Those are the signs that stress hormones like cortisol have been released into your system. There is a chain reaction effect in play once your fight, flight, or freeze response is engaged. If the amygdala, or emotional response center, becomes "hijacked," your prefrontal cortex (center of rational thinking and decision making) is impaired. You might not hear things correctly or you might misinterpret what people say. Based on how the brain works, it's easy to see why conflicts get so heated so quickly. Why arguments take illogical turns for the worse. But as emotional intelligence expert Daniel Goleman explains, you don't have to surrender to an amygdala hijack. When you are aware of what's happening and name it, you begin to regain control—of your emotions, your decisions, your responses. The old "count to 10" trick still stands. Take the time you need to get your prefrontal cortex back in the driver's seat.

Tips to develop *Manages* conflict

1. **Too much peace and harmony? Encourage healthy conflict.** A perfectly peaceful and harmonious workplace isn't always a good thing. When people are focused on keeping the peace, they can become too agreeable, afraid to rock the boat, complacent. Research shows that the single greatest predictor of poor company performance is complacency. Every organization needs a healthy dose of dissent. Encourage others to challenge the status quo and vocalize where things aren't working. To put their views on the table. Engage in debate. To fight for things they truly believe in, things that could be game changing. Ignite their imagination. Encourage them to think about bold and wide-reaching possibilities. Support them to let go of the past, resist apportioning blame, and focus their energy on looking at the road ahead. To use conflict productively. Don't allow them to fight dirty or behave destructively. Look for signs that others are trying to avoid conflict. Do they continually change the subject? Put off the conversation until a later date. Remind them that productive conflict is a necessary step in the journey toward a better future. That working through rough patches helps to reinforce the collective effort and commitment of everyone.

2. **Not getting your message through? Deliver clear, problem-focused communication.** Follow the rule of equity: Explain your thinking and ask them to explain theirs. Be able to state their position as clearly as they do whether you agree or not; give it legitimacy. Separate facts from opinions and assumptions. Generate a variety of possibilities first rather than stake out positions. Keep your speaking to 30–60 second bursts. Don't give the other side the impression you're lecturing or criticizing them. Explain objectively why you hold a view; ask the other side to do the same. Ask lots of questions, make fewer statements. Identify interests behind positions; ask them why they hold them or why they wouldn't want to do something. Always restate their position to their satisfaction before offering a response.

3. **Unsure of the culture? Watch and do as the locals do.** Most cultures have a unique way of handling difficult situations. In some cultures, direct confrontation is a no-no, while in others, confrontation is expected and accepted. In some cultures, an intermediary is used to deliver tough messages. It is important to know and understand local practices as well as understand that individuals also react according to general cultural norms for conflict situations. Watch and learn. As a rule of thumb, move with caution until there is full understanding of what locals do and what the cultural context may be. Don't criticize the practices of other cultures. Fully understand the implications of your remarks.

104 |

Want to learn more? Take a deep dive...

Davis, M. P. (2013, January 18). Want your team to work together? Start a fight. *Inc.*

Hallett, T. (n.d.). T*he 7 Cs of communication: A checklist for clear communication*. Mind Tools.

Martin, J. (2014, January 17). For senior leaders, fit matters more than skill. *Harvard Business Review Blog Network.*

Myatt, M. (2012, February 22). 5 Keys of dealing with workplace conflict. *Forbes.*

4. **Causing unnecessary conflict? Choose words appropriately.** Words are powerful. Language and timing set the tone and can cause unnecessary conflict that has to be managed before you can move on to the real issues. Self-check your language. Do you use terms and phrases that may be perceived as challenging or demeaning to others? Use negative or aggressive humor? Offer conclusions, solutions, statements, dictates, or answers early in the transaction? When you give solutions first, people often directly challenge the solutions instead of defining the problem. Slow down. Give reasons first, solutions last. Pick words that are neutral. That don't challenge or sound one-sided. Use tentative rather than definitive language; give others a chance to maneuver and save face. Phrase your comments so they're about the problem and not the person. Avoid direct blaming remarks; describe the problem and its impact.

5. **Judgmental? Stay neutral.** Rather than judging, focus on observing what's going on with other people. People can sense your judgment, disdain, lack of interest. If you can't stay neutral, constructive, and solution oriented, you can't expect others to either. Stay in tune with what others are experiencing and how they are reacting. If they're confused, state your point differently. Angry? Stop and find out what's going on. Quiet? Ask a question to get them engaged. Disinterested? Figure out what's in it for them. Watch the reactions of people to what you are doing or saying. Be ready to adjust.

6. **Tensions escalating? Turn it around.** Being attacked? Let the other side vent frustration and blow off steam but don't react directly. Listen. Nod. Ask open-ended questions: "What's bothering you most?" "What could I do to help?" Restate the person's position periodically to signal you have understood: "What I think you're saying is..." "So you think I need to..." Don't judge. Allow the person

to keep talking until they run out of venom. When the other side takes a rigid position, don't reject it. Explore the principles behind the position—what's the theory of the case, what brought this about? People will usually respond by saying more, coming off their position a bit, or at least revealing their true interests. Always separate the people from the problem. When someone attacks you, rephrase it as an attack on the problem. Many times, with unlimited venting and your understanding, the actual conflict shrinks.

7. **Too emotional? Keep your cool.** Sometimes our emotional reactions lead others to think we have problems with conflict. What emotional reactions do you have? Impatience? Non-verbals like flushing or drumming your pen or fingers? Learn to recognize them as soon as they start and substitute something more neutral. Most emotional responses to conflict come from personalizing the issue. Separate people issues from the problem at hand and deal with them separately. Always return to facts and the problem before the group; stay away from personal clashes. Try on their views for size—the emotion as well as the content. Ask yourself if you understand their feelings. Ask what they would do if they were in your shoes. Take time out to restate each other's position. Show that you recognize that's how they see things. If you get emotional, pause and collect yourself. You are not your best when you get emotional. Then return to the problem.

8. **Easily provoked? Watch for triggers.** Most of us have certain things that trigger a reaction. What pushes your buttons? Do specific people, issues, styles, or groups set you off? Think about the last several times you handled conflict poorly. What was common in the situations? Are there three to five common themes? Are the same people involved? Different people but the same style? Certain kinds of issues? Once you have isolated the cause, mentally rehearse a better way of handling it when it comes up next time. Try role playing it. Often the first few sentences are the hardest. Work with someone you trust and practice how you'll start the conversation the next time the situation arises. Test out different approaches. Identify one you're most comfortable with.

Want to learn more? Take a deep dive...

Eisaguirre, L. (2008, April). *Communicating effectively during conflict*. Mediate.com.

Harper, J. (2012, July 18). 10 Tips for tackling the toughest workplace conflicts: A guide to resolving on-the-job disputes. *U.S. News & World Report*.

Heffernan, M. (2012, August). Margaret Heffernan: Dare to disagree [Video file]. TED.

Trikha, R. (2012, May 15). How to manage your emotions in the workplace: Tips for expressing your feelings in the workplace. *U.S. News & World Report*.

9. **Too focused on differences? Seize on common points of agreement.** Almost all conflicts have common points that get lost in the heat of the battle. After a conflict has been presented and understood, start by saying that it might be helpful to see if we agree on anything. Write them down. If it's difficult to find common ground, start by going back to the most basic principles: "We both want this program to succeed." "We both want the right outcome for our customers." Then write down the areas left open. Keep the open conflicts as small as possible and concrete. Address the problem by focusing on common goals, priorities, and problems, not people and their positions. Allow others to save face by conceding small points that are not central to the issue; don't try to hit a home run every time. If you can't agree on a solution, agree on a process to move forward. Collect more data. Appeal to a higher power. Get a third-party arbitrator. Something. This creates some positive motion and breaks stalemates.

10. **Each possesses something the other wants? Give in order to get.** Since you can't absolutely win all conflicts (unless you keep pulling rank), you have to learn to bargain and trade. Relationships don't last unless you provide something and so does the other person. Find out what they want and tell them what you want. What do they need that you have? What do you need that they have? What could you do for them outside this conflict that could allow them to give up something you need now in return? How can you turn this into a win for both of you? Adopt a positive attitude; strike a bargain.

11. **Committing blunders? Navigate the political terrain.** Organizations are a complex maze of constituencies, politics, issues, and rivalries. They're peopled by strong egos, sensitive personalities, and empire protectors. Most are decentralized and compartmentalized, which in itself sets up natural conflict. Avoid causing unnecessary conflict by working to understand the politics of the organization. Who are the movers and shakers in the organization? Who are the major gatekeepers who control the flow of resources, information, and decisions? Who are the guides and the helpers? Get to know them better. Do lunch. Who are the major resisters and stoppers? Either avoid them or sidestep them or make peace with them. Consider the level of the people you're dealing with. What will they respond positively to? What are the potential pitfalls? How do you need to adapt your approach?

12. **Caught in a win/lose predicament? Seek cooperative relationships.** The opposite of conflict is cooperation. Developing cooperative relationships involves demonstrating real and perceived equity. Focus on ensuring that the other side feels understood and respected. Take a solution-oriented viewpoint and approach. Don't try to win every battle and take all the spoils; focus on finding some common ground. Look for opportunities to collaborate. Find wins on both sides. Give in on small points. Avoid starting with an entrenched position; show respect for the other person and their position. Work to reduce any remaining conflicts as much as possible.

13. **Standing firm on your position? Be open to changing your mind.** When it comes to finding solutions, generating a variety of possibilities is more useful than staking out a rigid position. When you're framing a disagreement, state your position and explain your thinking, but stay open to possibilities you hadn't considered. Encourage dialogue. It may surface opposing rationale, counterevidence, or ideas that you wouldn't be able to spot alone. Engaging in disagreements or conflicts where you show willingness to change your mind is not a point of weakness. It's part of being a reasonable, level-headed person. Your willingness to concede on certain things builds a climate of cooperation and trust. And cooperative, trusting relationships are less likely to experience a stalemate.

14. **Hopelessly stuck? Go to arbitration.** When there is a true impasse, suggest an equal-power third party to resolve the conflict. Use a third party to write up each side's interests and keep suggesting solutions until you can agree. Or, if time is an issue, pass it on to a

higher authority. Present both sides calmly and objectively and let the chips fall where they may.

Want to learn more? Take a deep dive...

Ashe-Edmunds, S. (n.d.). Conflict & cooperation in the workplace. *Chron*.

Gallo, A. (2010, May 12). The right way to fight. *Harvard Business Review Blog Network*.

Glaser, J. E. (2013, February 28). Your brain is hooked on being right. *Harvard Business Review Blog Network*.

Manktelow, J. (n.d.). *Resolving team conflict: Building stronger teams by facing your differences*. Mind Tools.

Job assignments

- Make peace with an enemy, someone you've disappointed or don't get along with. Apologize for you part in the conflict, encourage dialogue, and listen to find a solution for the greater good.

- Resolve a conflict between two people or two departments. Get clear on the values and positions of each individual and gauge how that will play out during resolution efforts.

- Assemble a team of diverse people to accomplish a difficult task. Anticipate the natural conflicts this will bring about and prepare to work through, rather than avoid, them.

- Enroll as a member of a union-negotiating or grievance-handling team. You'll be exposed to opportunities to practice staying calm and neutral when tensions escalate.

- Manage a group through a significant international crisis or conflict that is outside your home country. Research and be clear on the cultural norms for dealing with conflict before stepping in.

9

Take time to reflect...

If you often get bogged down when disagreement arises...

> ...then understand that the end point doesn't have to be win/lose. There are lots of other potential outcomes. A conflict well handled can bring about great ideas and new possibilities.

If you often have firm views that lead you into conflict with others...

> ...then appreciate that your way is not the only way. Others may also have strong opinions. You don't have to agree with these views, but you will need to listen if you want to make any progress.

If you tend to get emotional when conflict is looming...

> ...then consider that emotions can turn a spark into an inferno. The last thing you want to do is fan the flames. Keep your emotions in check. Manage conflict; don't let it manage you.

9

❝ *You only find complete unanimity in a cemetery.* **❞**

Abel Aganbegyan – Russian economist

Learn more about *Manages* conflict

Freeley, A. J., & Steinberg, D. L. (2013). *Argumentation and debate: Critical thinking for reasoned decision making*. Boston, MA: Cengage Learning.

Gerzon, M. (2006). *Leading through conflict: How successful leaders transform differences into opportunities*. Boston, MA: Harvard Business School Press.

Joni, S., & Beyer, D. (2010). *The right fight: How great leaders use healthy conflict to drive performance, innovation, and value*. New York, NY: HarperCollins Publishers.

Raines, S. S. (2013). *Conflict management for managers: Resolving workplace, client, and policy disputes*. San Francisco, CA: Jossey-Bass.

Runde, C. E., & Flanagan, T. A. (2008). *Building conflict competent teams*. San Francisco, CA: Jossey-Bass.

Deep dive learning resource links

Ashe-Edmunds, S. (n.d.). Conflict & cooperation in the workplace. *Chron.* Retrieved from http://work.chron.com/conflict-cooperation-workplace-19238.html

Davis, M. P. (2013, January 18). Want your team to work together? Start a fight. *Inc.* Retrieved from http://www.inc.com/mark-peter-davis/leadership-encourage-constructive-disagreement.html

Eisaguirre, L. (2008, April). *Communicating effectively during conflict*. Mediate.com. Retrieved from http://www.mediate.com/articles/eisaguirreL3.cfm

Gallo, A. (2010, May 12). The right way to fight. *Harvard Business Review Blog Network*. Retrieved from http://blogs.hbr.org/2010/05/the-right-way-to-fight/

Glaser, J. E. (2013, February 28). Your brain is hooked on being right. *Harvard Business Review Blog Network*. Retrieved from http://blogs.hbr.org/2013/02/break-your-addiction-to-being/

Hallett, T. (n.d.). *The 7 Cs of communication: A checklist for clear communication*. Mind Tools. Retrieved from http://www.mindtools.com/pages/article/newCS_85.htm

Harper, J. (2012, July 18). 10 Tips for tackling the toughest workplace conflicts: A guide to resolving on-the-job disputes. *U.S. News & World Report*. Retrieved from http://money.usnews.com/money/careers/articles/2012/07/18/10-tips-for-tackling-the-toughest-workplace-conflicts

Heffernan, M. (2012, August). Margaret Heffernan: Dare to disagree [Video file]. TED. Retrieved from http://www.ted.com/talks/margaret_heffernan_dare_to_disagree.html

Manktelow, J. (n.d.). *Resolving team conflict: Building stronger teams by facing your differences*. Mind Tools. Retrieved from http://www.mindtools.com/pages/article/newTMM_79.htm

Martin, J. (2014, January 17). For senior leaders, fit matters more than skill. *Harvard Business Review Blog Network*. Retrieved from http://blogs.hbr.org/2014/01/for-senior-leaders-fit-matters-more-than-skill/

Myatt, M. (2012, February 22). 5 Keys of dealing with workplace conflict. *Forbes*. Retrieved from http://www.forbes.com/sites/mikemyatt/2012/02/22/5-keys-to-dealing-with-workplace-conflict/

Trikha, R. (2012, May 15). How to manage your emotions in the workplace: Tips for expressing your feelings in the workplace. *U.S. News & World Report*. Retrieved from http://money.usnews.com/money/blogs/outside-voices-careers/2012/05/15/how-to-manage-your-emotions-in-the-workplace

Recommended search terms

9

If you'd like to explore *Manages* conflict further, try searching online using the following terms:

• Benefits of hearing both sides of the argument.

• Encouraging healthy conflict/debate.

• Finding common ground during a disagreement.

• Listening skills and workplace conflict.

• Maintaining your composure in conflict.

• Organizational conflict and culture fit.

(i) More help...

Go to www.kornferry.com/fyi-resources and link directly to the deep dive resources in this chapter. Visit the site often to see the additional resources that are uploaded on a regular basis.

112 |

10. Courage

Stepping up to address difficult issues, saying what needs to be said.

Leading is a courageous act. It's being out front, ushering in change, and challenging the status quo. Courage involves being comfortable with the conflict that is inherent to being a champion of an idea or course of action. It sometimes means staking out tough and lonely positions. Politically risky positions. Effective leaders meet tough situations head-on to constructively resolve them. They say what needs to be said at the right time, to the right person, in the right manner to effect change. Many times it's not positive. Something went wrong. Something is being covered up or over. Something is not being done right. Someone isn't performing well. Someone is holding something back. Someone is going off on the wrong track. Courage involves letting people know where you stand. Having difficult conversations. Standing alone. Being courageous requires your brain to balance fight/flight instincts with logical analysis. To weigh the benefits and drawbacks of addressing tough issues. Courage does not mean you are not afraid. Courage means you overcome the fear to do what is right.

" *You must never be fearful about what you are doing when it is right.* **"**

Rosa Parks – American civil rights activist

Courage is in the **Self** factor (IV) in the Korn Ferry Leadership Architect™. It is part of Cluster J, **Being authentic,** along with *Instills* trust (36). You may find it helpful to also take a look at some of the tips included in that chapter to supplement your learning.

Skilled

Readily tackles tough assignments.

Faces difficult issues and supports others who do the same.

Provides direct and actionable feedback.

Is willing to champion an idea or position despite dissent or political risk.

Less skilled

- Shies away from difficult issues or challenging assignments.
- Expresses point of view in an indirect manner.
- Avoids giving corrective feedback.
- Fails to take a stand on important issues.

Talented

- Tackles difficult issues with optimism and confidence.
- Shares sensitive messages or unpopular points of view in a motivating manner.
- Lets people know where they stand, honestly and sensitively.
- Volunteers to tackle and lead tough assignments.

Overused skill

- Struggles to identify which battles to take on and when to back down.
- Shares point of view on everything and could be seen as intimidating or a "know-it-all."
- Communicates bluntly and fails to recognize the impact on relationships with others.
- Neglects own work in favor of getting involved in multiple difficult issues.

Some possible causes of lower skill

Causes help explain *why* a person may have trouble with Courage. When seeking to increase skill, it's helpful to consider how these might play out in certain situations. And remember that all of these can be addressed if you are motivated to do so.

- Avoids conflict.
- Can't take the heat.
- Fears being wrong.
- Fears losing.
- Gets emotional.
- Doesn't like to be out in front.
- Doesn't identify strongly with any issue.
- Isn't self-confident.

Brain booster

It's OK to be afraid of something. In fact, fear is a normal response to danger in the environment. When your brain detects something that could potentially threaten your survival, your limbic (or emotional) system automatically becomes activated. The amygdala and thalamus prepare the body for fight or flight by increasing your heart rate and blood pressure. The limbic system fires up far more intensely when it perceives a danger than a reward due to the inherent negativity bias of the human brain. Bad news sticks longer in memory than good news. Unpleasant experiences impact the brain more powerfully than pleasant ones. In uncertain situations, people tend to overestimate risk but underestimate potential reward. So what does this mean? The threat may be exaggerated or imaginary instead of being real. Recognize that your fear may be irrational. Then reflect on questions like these: How would others effectively respond in your situation? What's the worst that could happen? What skills do you already possess that could help you through it? What growth or development could you derive from it? By considering these questions, you activate the ventrolateral prefrontal cortex, which inhibits limbic system arousal. Result? Your fear subsides.[11]

Tips to develop Courage

1. **Facing a challenging issue? Prepare for tough stands against the grain.** Taking a tough stand demands confidence in what you're saying along with the humility that you might be wrong—one of life's paradoxes. To prepare to take the lead on a tough issue, work on your stand through mental interrogation until you can clearly state in a few sentences what your stand is and why you hold it. Build the business case. How do others win? Ask others for advice. Scope the problem, consider options, pick one, develop a rationale, then go with it until proven wrong. Consider the opposing view. Develop a strong case against your stand. Prepare responses to it. Expect pushback.

2. **Laid back? Step into the fray.** None of your business? Tend to shy away from courage situations? Why? What's getting in your way? Are you prone to give up in tough situations, fear exposing yourself, don't like conflict? Ask yourself—what's the downside of delivering a message you think is right and will eventually help the organization but may cause someone short-term pain? What if it turns out you were wrong? Treat any misinterpretations as chances to learn. What if you were the target person or group? Even though it might hurt, would you appreciate it if someone brought the data to your attention in time for you to fix it with minimal damage? What would you think of a person you later found out knew about it and didn't come forward, and you had to spend inordinate amounts of time and political currency to fix it? Follow your convictions. Follow due process. Step up to the plate and be responsible, win or lose. People will think better of you in the long-term.

3. **Not being heard? Go up the chain if you must.** Sometimes the seriousness of the situation calls for more drastic action. Keeping in mind you are doing this for the collective benefit of the organization and that personal gain or vengeance is not at stake, be prepared to go all the way. Even if it pits you against a colleague or even a boss. If your initial message is rejected, covered, denied, hidden, or glossed over and you are still convinced of its accuracy, go up the chain. Continue until it's dealt with or someone in power two levels or more above the event or person asks you to stop. If you have a mentor, seek their counsel along the way. A caution: In a study of whistle-blowers, 100% of the failures spoke in general terms, tying their message to lofty values such as integrity. All the successes dealt with the specific issue as it was—problem and consequences. They didn't generalize at all.

4. **Talking to the wrong people? Provide information to the right person.** The basic rule is to deliver it to the person who can do the most with it. Limit your passing of the information to one or as few people as possible. Consider telling the actual person involved and give them the opportunity to fix it without any further exposure to risk. If that's not possible, move up the chain of command. Don't pass indirect messages via messengers.

Want to learn more? Take a deep dive...

Davey, L. (2013, December 25). Conflict strategies for nice people. *Harvard Business Review Blog Network.*

Guthrie, D. (2012, June 1). Creative leadership: Humility and being wrong. *Forbes.*

Mills Scofield, D. (2011, August 3). Paradox of innovation and status quo. *Forbes.*

Richardson, E. J. (2011, April 11). *So you want to become a whistleblower? 5 Things to consider before doing so.* Corporate Compliance Insights.

5. **Not comfortable being out front? Face criticism with courage.** Leading is riskier than following. While there are a lot of personal rewards for taking tough stands, it puts you in the limelight. Look at what happens to political leaders and the scrutiny they face. People who choose to stand alone have to be internally secure. Do you feel good about yourself? Can you defend to a critical and impartial audience the wisdom of what you're doing? They have to please themselves first that they are on the right track. They have to accept lightning bolts from detractors. Can you take the heat? People will always say it should have been done differently. Even great leaders are wrong sometimes. They accept personal responsibility for errors and move on to lead some more. Don't let criticism prevent you from taking a stand. Build up your heat shield. If you know you're right, standing alone is well worth the heat. If it turns out you're wrong, admit it and move on.

6. **Scared? Expect and manage emotion.** Even the most well-trained military members or emergency responders who go into life-threatening situations feel fear. Courage does not mean being fearless or anxiety free. Rather, people who are courageous manage their emotional reaction. How? By training and preparing. By becoming so skilled in the work that needs to be accomplished that

they can perform the task without getting stuck on the potentially crippling emotion. Practice and repetition help overcome the emotional aspect of the challenge. Another way? Find a role model. Observe a person who demonstrates courage. What do they do? What emotions do they show or not show? How can you emulate their actions? Envision yourself acting with courage before you take action. Last, do something. Often, it is the inactivity before taking action when we feel the most fear. Take action and the courage will follow.

7. **Unsure of the consequences? Analyze the impact.** Sometimes irrational fears can get in the way of the ability to act with courage. The best way to overcome irrational fear is to critically analyze the potential impact of the action. Courage requires calculation and logic. Think about the potential consequences if you take action one way or another. What is the worst that can happen? Failure? Embarrassment? What is the best potential outcome? Resolving a problem. Helping a colleague. Standing up for what is right. How do your values enter into the equation? Even if there are no clear business outcomes of your potential action, what is the value of following your personal ethics? Alternatively, think about the implications if you don't take any action. Do a cost-benefit analysis. This can help you move forward with assurance. Once you have really thought through the impact, you can overcome the emotion of the situation and have a clear line of sight to potential outcomes.

8. **Shy away from tough assignments? Start small.** You don't have to volunteer to go start up an office in a new region/culture or lead a downsizing effort where you have to make tough decisions. Instead, raise your hand for something close to your subject-matter expertise or known expertise. Volunteer to train someone new. Visit a client site. Learn a new skill. Raise the bar on the new or challenging tasks as you develop a comfort level with the unknown. What's the worst you can do? Fail? Courage involves pushing the envelope, taking chances, and suggesting bold new initiatives. Doing those things leads to more misfires and mistakes. Treat any mistakes or failures as chances to learn. Nothing ventured, nothing gained. Research says that successful general managers have made more mistakes in their careers than the people they were promoted over. They got promoted because they had the guts to try, not because they were always right. Other studies suggest really good general managers are right about 65% of the time. Put errors, mistakes, and failures on your menu. Everyone has to have some spinach for a balanced diet. Don't let the possibility of being wrong hold you back from standing alone when you believe it's right.

118 |

9. **Holding back while others push forward? Support others who stand up.** Do you have a peer or colleague who is standing up for something important? Do you support their position? Then get up there with them. Show solidarity. Don't just tell this person in secret that you think they are right. Demonstrate your support. Talk to your boss or other leaders to show your support. Campaign. Lobby key influencers. Talk to those who are in a position to make a difference. Communicate. Act. Follow through.

Want to learn more? Take a deep dive...

Fernandez-Araoz, C. (2012, March 27). Position yourself for a stretch assignment. *Harvard Business Review Blog Network*.

Heffernan, M. (2013, August). Margaret Heffernan: The dangers of "willful blindness" [Video file]. TED.

Lava, S. (n.d.). Voicing your opinion in the workplace. *Chron*.

Warrell, M. (2013, April 5). 7 Ways to push back without being pushy. *Forbes*.

---

10. **Not making your point effectively? Deliver a direct message.** Be succinct. You have limited attention span in tough feedback situations. Don't waste time with a long preamble, particularly if the feedback is negative. If your feedback is negative and the recipient is likely to know it, go ahead and say it directly. They won't hear anything positive you have to say anyway. Don't overwhelm the person/group, even if you have a lot to say. Go from specific to general points. Keep it to the facts. Don't embellish to make your point. No passion or inflammatory language. Don't do it to harm or out of vengeance. Don't do it in anger. If feelings are involved for you, wait until you can describe them, not show them. People with courage take action to find a better outcome, not to destroy others. Stay calm and cool. If others are not composed, don't respond. Just return to the message.

11. **Is it personal? Focus on the behavior, not the person.** If you are personally involved and you are delivering a message to someone who didn't meet your expectations, stick to the facts and the consequences for you. Do it in a timely manner. Don't wait for a formal development interaction. The closer the feedback is to the event, the more helpful it is. Separate the event from the person. It's OK to be upset with the behavior, less so with the person, unless it's a repetitive transgression. Most of the time they won't accept it the

first time you deliver the message. "I'm not happy with the way you presented my position in the staff meeting." Many people are defensive. Don't go for the close in every delivery situation. Just deliver the message enough so you are sure they understood it. Give them time to absorb it. Be prepared for their emotion. Allow the time for them to process the emotion. Don't seek instant acceptance. Just deliver the message clearly and firmly. Don't threaten.

12. **Not clear on what you want? Let others know your expectations.** Giving feedback demands courage. Often, people stop there and think they are done. Feedback isn't helpful if you only call out the behavior and don't say what you want. Clearly state the corrective action you expect from the person. Make sure it is specific, actionable, and behavioral so they know exactly what they need to do to change. You can't expect someone to make a change if you don't tell them how.

13. **Catching others off guard? Choose the appropriate time and place.** Effectively giving direct and actionable feedback involves delivering negative messages with the minimum of noise and the maximum effect. Tread boldly but carefully. Deliver messages in private. Cue the person what you are coming to talk about: "I have a concern over the way X is being treated and I would like to talk to you about it." Give the person a road map for the conversation. Consider but don't be deterred by political considerations. Pick the right timing. A relaxed setting. With time to spare. Don't try to fit it into an uncomfortable elevator conversation. If possible, let the person pick the timing and the setting.

14. **Focusing on the negative? Bring a solution if you can.** Nobody likes a critic. Everybody appreciates a problem solver. Give people ways to improve; don't just dump and leave. Tell others what you think would be better—paint a different outcome. Help others see the consequences. You can ask them what they think. Also, you can tell them what the consequences are from your side if you are personally involved ("I'd be reluctant to work with you on X again").

Want to learn more? Take a deep dive...

Ashkenas, R. (2012, January 10). In presentations, learn to say less. *Harvard Business Review Blog Network*.

DiSalvo, D. (2012, July 8). 10 Dumb things I've learned from brilliant people. *Forbes*.

James, G. (2012, August 21). 10 Smart rules for giving negative feedback. *Inc*.

Zenger, J., & Folkman, J. (2014, January 15). Your employees want the negative feedback you hate to give. *Harvard Business Review Blog Network*.

Job assignments

- Manage a group through a significant business crisis that requires quick action and difficult decisions.

- Manage a cost-cutting project where you need to reduce inventory, resources, or realign the organization, such as shutting down a plant, regional office, product line, business, or operation.

- Do a postmortem on a failed project, identifying what went well, what didn't go well, what could have been done differently, and your suggestions for the future. Present it to the people involved.

- Work on a team looking at a reorganization plan where there will be more people than positions and requires courageous decisions and clear communication.

- Write a proposal for a new policy, process, mission, charter, product, service, or system, and present and sell it to top management.

10

Take time to reflect...

If you find it easier to go along with the status quo...

> ...then recognize that just drifting in the stream won't prepare you for possible turbulent rapids ahead. There are times when you need to steer against the current. Remember that convictions only have an impact if you act on them.

If you're worried your views will turn people against you...

> ...then focus on your reason for taking a stand. If something's wrong, it needs to be right. If there's a better way, it needs to be found. Show resolve. You don't have to be popular to be respected.

If you're worried that what you say will just rock the boat...

> ...then ask yourself if holding back is in the best interests of the organization. It might be time to shake things up. You might take some heat today, but tomorrow people may thank you for having the courage to speak up.

" *Courage is what it takes to stand up and speak; courage is also what it takes to sit down and listen.* **"**

Winston Churchill – Former Prime Minister of the U.K. and Nobel Prize-winning writer

10

Learn more about Courage

Chaleff, I. (2003). *The courageous follower: Standing up to and for our leaders*. San Francisco, CA: Berrett-Koehler Publishers.

Freeley, A. J., & Steinberg, D. L. (2013). *Argumentation and debate: Critical thinking for reasoned decision making*. Boston, MA: Cengage Learning.

Hayman, S. (2010). *Be more assertive: Teach yourself*. New York, NY: McGraw-Hill.

Joni, S., & Beyer, D. (2010). *The right fight: How great leaders use healthy conflict to drive performance, innovation, and value*. New York, NY: HarperCollins Publishers.

Lee, G., & Elliott-Lee, D. (2006). *Courage: The backbone of leadership*. San Francisco, CA: Jossey-Bass.

Deep dive learning resource links

Ashkenas, R. (2012, January 10). In presentations, learn to say less. *Harvard Business Review Blog Network*. Retrieved from http://blogs.hbr.org/2012/01/in-presentations-learn-to-say/

Davey, L. (2013, December 25). Conflict strategies for nice people. *Harvard Business Review Blog Network*. Retrieved from http://blogs.hbr.org/2013/12/conflict-strategies-for-nice-people/

DiSalvo, D. (2012, July 8). 10 Dumb things I've learned from brilliant people. *Forbes*. Retrieved from http://www.forbes.com/sites/daviddisalvo/2012/07/08/10-dumb-things-ive-learned-from-brilliant-people/

Fernandez-Araoz, C. (2012, March 27). Position yourself for a stretch assignment. *Harvard Business Review Blog Network*. Retrieved from http://blogs.hbr.org/2012/03/position-yourself-for-a-stretc/

Guthrie, D. (2012, June 1). Creative leadership: Humility and being wrong. *Forbes*. Retrieved from http://www.forbes.com/sites/dougguthrie/2012/06/01/creative-leadership-humility-and-being-wrong/

Heffernan, M. (2013, August). Margaret Heffernan: The dangers of "willful blindness" [Video file]. TED. Retrieved from http://www.ted.com/talks/margaret_heffernan_the_dangers_of_willful_blindness.html

James, G. (2012, August 21). 10 Smart rules for giving negative feedback. *Inc*. Retrieved from http://www.inc.com/geoffrey-james/how-to-give-negative-feedback-10-rules.html

Lava, S. (n.d.). Voicing your opinion in the workplace. *Chron*. Retrieved from http://work.chron.com/voicing-opinion-workplace-4397.html

Mills Scofield, D. (2011, August 3). Paradox of innovation and status quo. *Forbes*. Retrieved from http://www.forbes.com/sites/work-in-progress/2011/08/03/paradox-of-innovation-status-quo/

Richardson, E. J. (2011, April 11). *So you want to become a whistleblower? 5 Things to consider before doing so*. Corporate Compliance Insights. Retrieved from http://www.corporatecomplianceinsights.com/so-you-want-to-become-a-whistleblower-5-things-to-consider-before-doing-so/

Warrell, M. (2013, April 5). 7 Ways to push back without being pushy. *Forbes*. Retrieved from http://www.forbes.com/sites/margiewarrell/2013/04/05/7-ways-to-push-back-without-being-pushy/

Zenger, J., & Folkman, J. (2014, January 15). Your employees want the negative feedback you hate to give. *Harvard Business Review Blog Network*. Retrieved from http://blogs.hbr.org/2014/01/your-employees-want-the-negative-feedback-you-hate-to-give/

Recommended search terms

If you'd like to explore Courage further, try searching online using the following terms:

- Assertiveness at work.
- Avoid shying away from conflict.
- Challenging the status quo at work.
- How to have an unpopular opinion at work.
- Voicing your opinions at work.
- When and how to give negative feedback.

(i) More help...

Go to www.kornferry.com/fyi-resources and link directly to the deep dive resources in this chapter. Visit the site often to see the additional resources that are uploaded on a regular basis.

124 |

11. Customer focus

Building strong customer relationships and delivering customer-centric solutions.

The most important people in any organization are customers. Whether for profit or non-profit, community-based, social serving, or governmental agency, there is always a customer of some kind at the heart of most every action. Without customers, it's likely your organization would not exist. In some roles, there is a direct link to external customers and in others the connection is more indirect. Or the customer you primarily serve is inside the organization. Bottom line—those who please customers the most will win. Winning organizations are always customer oriented and responsive. Winning strategies always include a customer-facing lens. Being successful means continuously paying attention to customer needs and adapting as these evolve. You need to evaluate and flex, understand and respond. A focus on customers opens up thinking, drives innovation, and creates a responsive and agile organization. Internal or external— they're equally important. It's hard to develop a high level of customer satisfaction externally if those within the organization are disengaged.

" *A satisfied customer is the best business strategy of all.* **"**

Michael LeBoeuf – American business author

Customer focus is in the **Thought** factor (I) in the Korn Ferry Leadership Architect™. It is part of Cluster A, **Understanding the business,** along with Business insight (5), Financial acumen (17), and Tech savvy (35). You may find it helpful to also take a look at some of the tips included in those chapters to supplement your learning.

Skilled

Gains insight into customer needs.

Identifies opportunities that benefit the customer.

Builds and delivers solutions that meet customer expectations.

Establishes and maintains effective customer relationships.

Less skilled

- Is unaware of customer expectations.

- Acts on incomplete or inaccurate understanding of customer needs.

- Conducts work activities from an internal, operational standpoint.

- Fails to build effective relationships with key customers.

Talented

- Anticipates customer needs and provides services that are beyond customer expectations.

- Uses customer insights to drive and guide the development of new offerings.

- Serves as a strategic partner to build, grow, and maintain profitable and long-lasting relationships with key accounts.

Overused skill

- Prioritizes information about customers over other important business realities.

- In the efforts to satisfy customers, takes liberties with the organization's policies and procedures.

- Becomes too close to customers; makes promises to customers that the organization is unable to keep.

Some possible causes of lower skill

Causes help explain *why* a person may have trouble with Customer focus. When seeking to increase skill, it's helpful to consider how these might play out in certain situations. And remember that all of these can be addressed if you are motivated to do so.

- Self-centered.
- Shy, afraid of transacting with new people.
- Lacks self-confidence.
- Doesn't hear feedback.
- Poor listener.
- Defensive in the face of criticism.
- Poor time management; too busy.

Does it best

Since 1994, Amazon has grown to become one of the most widely respected online retailers. What sets the company apart? Relentless customer focus. CEO, Jeff Bezos, believes customers will always be interested in low costs, big selection, and fast delivery. Everything is designed to address those customer interests. Amazon creates the ultimate customer experience with a website that is clear, simple, and easy to navigate. Filters help customers quickly find the products they are looking for. And as they shop, through intricate algorithms, they provide data that will inform suggestions for future customers. Amazon is able to recommend products to customers that they had never even thought of purchasing. So committed is Bezos to customer satisfaction, that approximately 80% of the measurable goals used to track performance relate specifically to the customer, including focus on what customers *don't* want to happen— delays, products out of stock, defects. Measures are in place to make them as rare as possible. The result? Amazon has been the top online retailer in customer satisfaction for years and is repeatedly in the top 10 among all companies. Since its initial public offering in 1997, the company's stock price has risen from a modest US$18 per share to US$300+ per share in 2014.[12, 13, 14]

11

Tips to develop Customer focus

1. **Looking to delight the customer? Anticipate customer needs.** Get in the habit of meeting with your internal or external customers on a regular basis. Set up a dialogue. Customers need assurance they can contact you about problems or ideas to improve service. Create open, explicit lines of communication. The more personal you can make your interactions, the clearer it is to customers that you want to meet their needs. Instead of anonymous market research, create personal connections. Ask customers for feedback. Solicit their ideas. When you roll out a new product or service, connect it back to how it addresses their feedback. Try to anticipate their need for your products and services before they even know about them. A new technology update that can improve their experience. Or a different service option for upcoming needs as their business grows. Surprise them in the best way. Features they weren't expecting. Delivery in a shorter time. Added value to what they ordered. Show your customer you're in it for the long run. Show that your primary interest is their success. Period. Everything else follows from this.

2. **Not sure what customers want or expect? Put yourself in your customers' shoes.** If you were a customer of your organization, what would you expect? What kind of turnaround time would you tolerate? What price would you be willing to pay for the quality of your product or service? What would be the top three things you would complain about? What would delight you? Design your processes, products, services, and the overall customer experience with the answers to these questions in mind.

3. **Disconnected from customers? Keep in high-quality touch.** Satisfying the reasonable needs of customers is fairly straightforward. First you need to know what they want and expect. The best way to do that is to ask them. Then deliver on their suggestions in a timely way at a price/value that's justified. Find ways to keep in touch with a broad spectrum of your customers to get a balanced view. Face-to-face. Online or phone surveys. Questionnaires. Social media. Response cards with your products and services. To keep in high-quality touch, recognize the difference between convenience for the customer and convenience for you. Telephony (voice activated technology) and other telecommunications innovations work when the customer experience is top of mind. What customer hasn't experienced the frustration of endless computer routing, only to get no answer or get to the wrong person? High-quality touch with your customers means getting them to the right person in the minimum number of steps.

4. **Get defensive? Be prepared for customer complaints.** Be ready for the good news and the bad news. Don't be defensive. Just listen and respond to legitimate criticisms. Vocal customers will usually complain more than compliment. Listen to what the customer is saying. Make sense of it by looking for themes. Are there consistent messages you are hearing from various customers? Where do you see opportunities to develop? Don't get overwhelmed by the negative comments. People who have positive opinions speak up less. When you get a complaint that is justified, put a plan in place. Work with the customer to identify the goal. Then monitor progress against that goal to ensure resolution of the problem. Check in with the customer to see if they are satisfied with the solution. Change your mental frame about customer complaints. Studies show that customers who complain are still engaged, which means you still have a chance to turn them around. It's the dissatisfied customer who doesn't complain that ends up going to the competition.

Want to learn more? Take a deep dive...

Di Fiore, A. (2011, November 30). How to get past your customers' lies. *Harvard Business Review Blog Network*.

Hall, A. (2013, May 17). Listening to customers yields success. *Forbes*.

Kalb, I. (2012, January 19). *Here's what happens when you don't listen to your customers' complaints*. Business Insider.

Spiegelman, P. (2010, January 18). Connect with your customers. *Entrepreneur*.

---

5. **Want to know why customers leave? Think of yourself as a dissatisfied customer.** Write down all of the unsatisfactory things that have happened to you as a customer during the past month. Things like delays. Orders not right. Costs not as promised. Phone calls not returned. Cold food. Bad service. Inattentive employees. Out-of-stock items. Are any of these things happening to your customers? Then do a study of your lost customers. Find out what the three key problems were and see how quickly you can eliminate 50% of the difficulties that caused them to depart. Study your competitors' foul-ups and see what you can do to both eliminate those and make your organization more attractive. And keep at it. Make this an ongoing aspect of your customer focus. Make it your business to understand what you're not doing right for your customers and correct it. Apply that learning to help you spot issues before they cause a problem.

11

6. **Want to know why customers stay? Think of yourself as a satisfied customer.** Write down all of the satisfactory things that have happened to you as a customer during the past month. What pleased you the most as a customer? Good value? On-time service? Courtesy? Returned phone calls? Are any of your customers experiencing any of these satisfactory transactions with you and your business? Study your successful customer transactions so they can be institutionalized. Then study what your competitors do well and see what you can also do to improve customer service. Be a learner. Constantly look to identify ways to enhance the level of quality and service your customers are enjoying. The best customer is the customer you already have.

7. **Looking for opportunities to see customer service in action? Play detective.** Be a student of the workflows and processes around you at airports, restaurants, hotels, supermarkets, government services, etc. What do you see? What do you hear? What are customers saying out of earshot of the staff? How can you relate the service approaches in those industries to your own environment? What processes could be adapted? As a customer, how would you design those things differently to make them more effective and efficient? What difference will this make to your customers? How can you improve on this even further?

8. **Want to create stronger customer loyalty? Build the relationship.** Let's face it. It is about customer loyalty, but it is also about repeat business. The number one way to maintain loyalty is to build and maintain a relationship with your key customers. Come up with a plan. How are you going to regularly interact with your customers? Customers are less likely to think about you if they don't hear from you. Then, add value. How are your products or services helping your customers? Use real-life case studies of wins with key customers as a way of demonstrating your value. Think beyond simply selling your products or services. How can you help your customers be more successful? Offer a suggestion for a way to streamline processes. Help cut costs. Recommend a person for an open position. Refer a potential customer to your customer. Go beyond the traditional sales cycle. Provide additional value for your customers in unexpected ways.

9. **Just looking externally? Delight your internal customers.** Not all customers are external. Internal customers are all those people who work every day to make the organization a success. There's a complex web of customer relationships and interdependencies

across the organization. For example, a sales person who does not work well with dispatch can cause service issues for the external customer. A glitch in the relationship between a designer and production can delay speed to market. First, identify your key internal customers. Who do you interact with on a regular basis? Who reviews your work? Who is impacted by the quality of your product? Second, ask for feedback. How are you doing? What would they like to change? Continue doing? Lastly, take action to improve your internal customer experience. Think outside the box. Consider issues from their perspective. What can you do to make their job easier? How can you help them be more successful? What information do you need to supply? Shift your thinking and look for ways to create internal customer delight.

Want to learn more? Take a deep dive...

Merholz, P. (2009, March 6). The best way to understand your customers. *Harvard Business Review Blog Network*.

Nauert, R. (2011, June 2). *Employee satisfaction key for customer satisfaction*. Psych Central.

Steinkirchner, S. (2012, August 22). 5 Ways to improve your customer service. *Forbes*.

Young Entrepreneur Council. (2013, December 4). 4 Ways to turn an angry customer into a satisfied one at your startup. *Upstart Business Journal*.

10. **Need a customer service process? Think "customer-in."** Always design your work and manage your time from the customer in, not from you out. Your best will always be determined by your customers, not you. Research suggests that companies that have restructured themselves around customer needs are often more nimble and agile. These companies are able to respond quickly and effectively to the needs of the customer. Try not to design and arrange what you do only from your own view. The best innovation comes from the outside-in—your customers tell you what they need and you respond by making improvements to products, services, or processes. Your customers know what they want. All you need to do is ask them. Create an organization that listens to and then builds on customer needs and requests. One of the most important aspects of great service is anticipation. See what the customer needs even before they do. Try to always know and take the viewpoint of your customer first. You will always win following that rule. Can you sell an experience, not just a product or service.

11

11. **Stuck in a customer service rut? Create an environment for experimentation and learning.** One principle of these techniques is to drive for continuous improvement. Never be satisfied. Always drive to improve all work processes so they deliver zero-defect goods and services. Don't be afraid to try and fail. Give your team members opportunities to experiment and try new things. Reward creative thinking. Set up customer service brainstorming sessions. Think outside the box and come up with new ways to serve your customers. Recognize the most innovative ideas and encourage more. If things haven't gone well, get people to think through why. What was the root cause? How could things have been different? What was the customer expecting that wasn't delivered? What's the plan for next time? How will you continue to monitor and improve the customer experience?

12. **Disconnect between employee and customer satisfaction? Construct a service-profit chain.** It's well known that employee satisfaction is linked to customer loyalty, satisfaction, and profits. The employees closest to the customer will have the biggest impact on customer service. In a bank, it's the tellers. A restaurant, the servers. A tech company, the customer service representatives. Pay attention to these employees. Support what they do. Help them make their work more efficient. Provide development opportunities. Show appreciation. Empower your people to serve the customers. Provide them with the tools and the training they need. Reward exceptional customer service. A recent study suggests that employee commitment and engagement has a direct impact on customer satisfaction and business performance. Example? A fast food chain set up a crew system without a manager. Working in teams proved to be more challenging and motivating. They learned they could get better results for their customers working in this way. Happier employees—happier customers.

13. **Not focusing on the right customers? Nurture your most profitable customers.** Some customers may be unprofitable because of excess service requirements. You can require them to order in larger quantities. Forego certain services, or charge for them. Use activity-based accounting. This method links purchasing data with cost data. It costs between 5 and 20 times as much to get a new customer than to keep an existing one. Old customers cost less over time and bring more revenue. How can you go from being a 20% supplier to a 50% one? Sometimes customers are simply not a good fit for the business. You may need to divest the business. But do it right. A study in the *Harvard Business Review* suggests that the best way to manage unprofitable customers is to take your time. Think about

the impact. Look for alternatives to make the relationship more profitable. Take appropriate action. Divesting customers is sometimes the best move. But, be careful. Think strategically.

Want to learn more? Take a deep dive...

Conner, C. (2013, August 16). Why every organization needs a standard response time policy. *Forbes*.

DeRose, C., & Tichy, N. (2013, July 1). Here's how to actually empower customer service employees. *Harvard Business Review Blog Network*.

Rosenbaum, M. (2012, March 20). *Engage your customers, don't just satisfy them*. Fox Business.

Stark, K., & Stewart, B. (2013, January 10). Nurture your most profitable customers. *Inc*.

Job assignments

- Manage a dissatisfied internal or external customer; troubleshoot a performance or quality problem with a product or service.

- Train customers in the use of the organization's products or services. Collaborate with them. Make them feel involved.

- Work a few shifts in the telemarketing or customer service department, handling complaints and inquiries from customers. Experience your customers firsthand.

- Spend time with internal or external customers. Write a report on your observations, and present it to the people involved.

- Do a customer satisfaction survey in person or by phone, and present the results to the people involved.

11

Take time to reflect...

If you don't think customers figure into your role...

...then remember that, whatever your job description, customers are part of it. Frontline or internally facing, you have a responsibility to customers in some way—recognize it and act upon it.

If you view customers as statistics rather than stakeholders to be served...

...then recognize the danger of thinking of them in this cold, impersonal way. You probably need them more than they need you. Give them a reason to come to you. Give them better reasons for staying.

If you know there are barriers to customers being happy...

...then take steps to break them down. Find a way through them. Explore options for getting over them. A blocker to customer delight is a blocker to the organization's success.

" *Whatever you do, do it well.*
Do it so well that when people see you do it,
they will want to come back and see you do it again,
and they will want to bring others. **"**

Walt Disney – American cartoonist and entrepreneur

11

134 |

Learn more about Customer focus

Aun, M. A. (2011). *It's the customer, stupid! 34 Wake-up calls to help you stay client-focused*. Hoboken, NJ: John Wiley & Sons, Inc.

Barlow, J., & Moller, C. (2008). *A complaint is a gift: Recovering customer loyalty when things go wrong* (2nd ed.). San Francisco, CA: Berrett-Koehler Publishers.

Cockerell, L. (2013). *The customer rules: The 39 essential rules for delivering sensational service*. New York, NY: Crown Publishing Group.

Curtin, S. (2013). *Delight your customers: 7 Simple ways to raise your customer service from ordinary to extraordinary*. New York, NY: AMACOM.

Zaltman, G. (2003). *How customers think: Essential insights into the mind of the market*. Boston, MA: Harvard Business School Publishing.

 ## Deep dive learning resource links

Conner, C. (2013, August 16). Why every organization needs a standard response time policy. *Forbes*. Retrieved from http://www.forbes.com/sites/cherylsnappconner/2013/08/16/why-every-organization-needs-a-standard-response-time-policy/

DeRose, C., & Tichy, N. (2013, July 1). Here's how to actually empower customer service employees. *Harvard Business Review Blog Network*. Retrieved from http://blogs.hbr.org/2013/07/heres-how-to-actually-empower-customer/

Di Fiore, A. (2011, November 30). How to get past your customers' lies. *Harvard Business Review Blog Network*. Retrieved from http://blogs.hbr.org/2011/11/how-to-get-past-your-customers/

Hall, A. (2013, May 17). Listening to customers yields success. *Forbes*. Retrieved from http://www.forbes.com/sites/alanhall/2013/05/17/listening-to-customers-yields-success/

Kalb, I. (2012, January 19). *Here's what happens when you don't listen to your customers' complaints*. Business Insider. Retrieved from http://www.businessinsider.com/heres-what-happens-when-you-dont-listen-to-your-customers-compiants-2012-1

Merholz, P. (2009, March 6). The best way to understand your customers. *Harvard Business Review Blog Network*. Retrieved from http://blogs.hbr.org/2009/03/the-best-way-to-understand-you/

Nauert, R. (2011, June 2). *Employee satisfaction key for customer satisfaction*. Psych Central. Retrieved from http://psychcentral.com/news/2011/06/02/employee-satisfaction-key-for-customer-satisfaction/26623.html

Rosenbaum, M. (2012, March 20). *Engage your customers, don't just satisfy them*. Fox Business. Retrieved from http://smallbusiness.foxbusiness.com/marketing-sales/2012/03/20/engage-your-customers-dont-just-satisfy-them/

Spiegelman, P. (2010, January 18). Connect with your customers. *Entrepreneur*. Retrieved from http://www.entrepreneur.com/article/204690

Stark, K., & Stewart, B. (2013, January 10). Nurture your most profitable customers. *Inc.* Retrieved from http://www.inc.com/karl-and-bill/nurture-your-most-profitable-customers.html

Steinkirchner, S. (2012, August 22). 5 Ways to improve your customer service. *Forbes*. Retrieved from http://www.forbes.com/sites/sundaysteinkirchner/2012/08/22/5-ways-to-improve-your-customer-service/

Young Entrepreneur Council. (2013, December 4). 4 Ways to turn an angry customer into a satisfied one at your startup. *Upstart Business Journal*. Retrieved from http://upstart.bizjournals.com/resources/advice/2013/12/04/keeping-startup-customers-happy.html?page=all

Recommended search terms

If you'd like to explore Customer focus further, try searching online using the following terms:

- Empowering employees for customer service.
- Engaging your customers.
- Learning more about your customer service.
- Learning from customer feedback.
- Nurturing your most profitable customers.
- Understanding your customers.

(i) More help...

Go to www.kornferry.com/fyi-resources and link directly to the deep dive resources in this chapter. Visit the site often to see the additional resources that are uploaded on a regular basis.

136 |

12. Decision quality

Making good and timely decisions that keep the organization moving forward.

Making good decisions can be challenging: Short time frames. Limited information. Impatient people waiting for answers in the face of difficult trade-offs. Good decisions are based upon a mixture of analysis, wisdom, experience, and judgment. Trouble is, people are not all that good at making decisions. They tend to overestimate their ability to make good judgments and are overconfident in forecasting outcomes. Making quality decisions in organizations today means working in an environment where ambiguity and uncertainty are the norm. Where considering whom to engage, what information to gather, and when to apply helpful tools are all considerations to take into account. Sound decisions come from a balance between speed and quality. Being totally correct all the time isn't a realistic goal. Instead, it's about being correct *enough* on decisions to move ahead and allow adequate time for effective execution.

> **"** *An expert is someone who has succeeded in making decisions and judgments simpler through knowing what to pay attention to and what to ignore.* **"**
>
> Edward De Bono – Maltese physician, author, and inventor

Decision quality is in the **Thought** factor (I) in the Korn Ferry Leadership Architect™. It is part of Cluster B, **Making complex decisions,** along with *Manages* complexity (8) and *Balances* stakeholders (32). You may find it helpful to also take a look at some of the tips included in those chapters to supplement your learning.

Skilled

Makes sound decisions, even in the absence of complete information.

Relies on a mixture of analysis, wisdom, experience, and judgment when making decisions.

Considers all relevant factors and uses appropriate decision-making criteria and principles.

Recognizes when a quick 80% solution will suffice.

Less skilled

- Approaches decisions haphazardly or delays decision making.

- Makes decisions based on incomplete data or inaccurate assumptions.

- Ignores different points of view or makes decisions that impact short-term results at the expense of longer-term goals.

Talented

- Decisively makes high-quality decisions, even when based on incomplete information or in the face of uncertainty.

- Actively seeks input from pertinent sources to make timely and well-informed decisions.

- Skillfully separates opinions from facts.

- Is respected by others for displaying superior judgment.

Overused skill

- Applies an overly rigorous or methodological decision process to all issues, even where experience and intuition can work equally well.

- Is overly confident about own decision-making capability; reluctant to delegate decision making to others or hesitant to involve others when generating solutions.

138 |

12

Some possible causes of lower skill

Causes help explain *why* a person may have trouble with Decision quality. When seeking to increase skill, it's helpful to consider how these might play out in certain situations. And remember that all of these can be addressed if you are motivated to do so.

* Undervalues relevant data.
* Goes too fast or too slow.
* Avoids including others.
* Unaware of own biases.
* Not objective.
* Limited use of analytic tools.
* Conflict averse.
* Doesn't consider consequences.
* Seeks perfection.

 Brain booster

Even if you're certain that your decision is the right one, pause. What beliefs, opinions, personal interests, favoritism, or prejudices may be influencing you? Our brains have developed numerous shortcuts that help us expend less energy, pay less attention, and make decisions more efficiently (though not necessarily more effectively). Unconscious biases may also be at play, for example: Confirmation bias: where you only see what you already believe to be true. Frequency bias: where you're more likely to believe something you hear or see repeatedly over time. Recency bias: where what you've learned most recently carries more weight. Negative bias: where stored negative emotional memories of similar situations or people cloud your judgment. Attachment bias: holding on to a status quo you helped shape. To mitigate against biases, work to surface any red flags—a third party can help. The point is not to let biases affect you or your team's ability to be objective. Take an extra moment to question your conclusions. What assumptions are you making? What might be making you biased or partial to one solution versus another? What alternatives did you not explore? Are there observations you made that contradict your overall impression of the situation? Are you ignoring contrary evidence? Turning your decisions over in your mind and evaluating them from all angles may prompt you to think differently or come to a different conclusion. At the very least, you can stick with your first decision with more confidence.[15]

Tips to develop Decision quality

1. **Not sure where to begin? Define the issue and map out a process.** A consistent finding is that most groups don't take enough time up front to define the situation—they jump to a conclusion or a solution. Rigor pays off. Establish what's at play and at stake—the context, parameters, scope. Next, define the intended outcome of the decision. How will you know if you made the right call? The clearer the criteria for determining success, the better. Gather all the relevant data. Analyze it, interpret it, test your assumptions. Generate alternatives and evaluate them based upon what you want to accomplish. Invite open dialogue and healthy debate if that will help you determine the best course of action. Monitor what was intended against what actually happens so you can learn from the decision and make corrections where needed.

2. **Just going through the motions? Apply more rigor.** Avoid imprecise thinking when analyzing data and evaluating options. Do you state things as facts when they are really opinions or assumptions? Do you attribute cause and effect to relationships when you don't know if one really causes the other? Are you relying on decisions you made in the past rather than seeing the current situation with fresh eyes? Don't just collect data, figure out what it means for the short- and long-term. Write down your assumptions. Challenge them. Don't simply inform stakeholders of your progress, engage them in the process. When weighing alternatives, make rational comparisons against specific criteria (e.g., revenue, speed, customer retention). Anticipate potential glitches as best you can. Identify the pros/cons and costs/benefits of all possible solutions, then work to make the best ones even stronger before making a final decision.

3. **Want to analyze more data in less time? Turn to technology and tools.** It's impossible to eliminate all risks, but your chances of making good decisions will improve by using the right decision-making tools. An abundance of them exist. Analytic tools can help you explore the implications of potential scenarios. Make decisions about what to invest in or fund. Aggregate and synthesize data to gain insights from the past and better forecast the future. The latest technology is more precise than before and can help you analyze data in less time. Conventional capital budgeting tools work well too. Don't throw out tried-and-true decision trees, cost-benefit analysis, and plus-minus methods. Instead, add to them selectively. The choice of tools may seem overwhelming at first. Having too many options—even good ones—can cause "decision paralysis," as Dan and Chip Heath describe in *Switch*. Decision paralysis happens

when people freeze and don't pick anything at all when they're overloaded. So get some recommendations. Ask experts to help you select the best decision tools for your specific situation.

Want to learn more? Take a deep dive...

Teepe, T. (2009). Problem solving ideas that work [YouTube].

Wolf, R. F. (2012, September 24). How to minimize your biases when making decisions. *Harvard Business Review*.

Zwilling, M. (2011, July 19). *Nine steps to effective business problem solving*. Business Insider.

---

4. **Wonder who to include? Let the demands of the situation guide you.** You want to make the best decision you can. How you arrive at what *best* means will vary. Sometimes it's appropriate to make the call alone, other times it's best to engage others. Consider complexity, expertise, execution, and timing. The more complex the situation is, the more you'll need multiple perspectives. When people hold different pieces of the information puzzle, you need to bring them together. The more that commitment is required for follow through, the more you should involve the people responsible for execution. If you want to develop people's leadership skills, push decisions down to the lowest possible level. If a decision needs to happen fast (like in a crisis) and you are the expert, make it yourself. Be up front about what decision process you'll use. If you want someone's advice but know they won't have a say in the final decision, just tell them. Trust can erode if you ask for someone's opinion but don't use it. In all cases, explain to stakeholders how the decision came about.

5. **Too much agreement in the group? Encourage open dialogue and debate.** When all heads nod and people see issues similarly, the decision-making process goes faster. But faster doesn't necessarily lead to better. To reach optimum decisions, all angles of an issue need to be discussed. Don't stop when the first acceptable solution is presented. Welcome dissenting voices—they enhance decision quality by forcing people to expand their perspectives. Separate the facts from the opinions. Spark debate through questioning. What are our assumptions? What's missing? What's another way to interpret the data? What other alternatives could work? What's the best possible end result? What might go wrong? Another approach is to assign someone to play devil's advocate—to poke holes in the current logic. Do whatever you can to reduce groupthink, which is conformity of opinion. Pressure to conform can cause people to

12

|

censor their views and ignore vital data. Whether you're the decision owner or contributor, insist on candid dialogue.

6. **Virtual teams need decision-making assistance? Use collaboration tools.** There are many benefits to virtual teaming, but one drawback is the loss of communication horsepower due to limited face-to-face communication. Language barriers and the lack of non-verbal cues can at times strain mutual understanding, which is needed for making quality decisions. However, research shows that there are also advantages to asynchronous communication when instant decisions aren't required. By using virtual collaboration tools, people have more time to carefully write or illustrate their point of view. More time to reflect on others' ideas or data presented before responding. There's less a chance of hasty judgment. Of missing what someone said. Of a strong personality taking over a conversation. In addition, relevant information can be stored and retrieved in the future.

Want to learn more? Take a deep dive...

Harvard Business Review. (2013). The management tip: Tips on decision making. *Harvard Business Review*.

John, C. (2013). How to establish open communication at work. *Chron*.

Shaughnessy, H. (2013, December 9). 15 Ways to make much better decisions. *Forbes*.

---

7. **Need to speed things up? Counter overthinking with action.** Lots of us want all the data in and all our ducks in a row before we decide. We want to be 100% sure. Nice in theory, but that slows you down. Perfectionism is tough to let go of because many people see it as a positive trait for themselves. Recognize your perfectionism for what it might be—collecting more information to improve your confidence to make a fault-free decision, thereby avoiding risk and criticism. Try to reach a more reasonable balance between thinking it through and making the call. Try making some small decisions on little or no data, using expertise or past experience as a guide. Anyone with 100% of the data can make good decisions. The real test is who can act the soonest with a reasonable amount—but not all—of the data. Give yourself a deadline and stick to it.

8. **Not sure the timing is right? Listen to your own clock.** How do you know if it's important to decide now or if it may be better to wait? When urgency is the new normal, it can be tempting to charge ahead, even when evidence—or lack of evidence—suggests otherwise. Recent information may have shifted the success criteria. New data may reveal additional risks. A deadline may not really be firm—especially in ambiguous or rapidly changing industries, or when cutting-edge differentiation is key. Some of the most respected leaders have put quality, safety, or innovation ahead of a predetermined timetable. Pulling the plug or testing things further before making a decision may serve the best interests of your stakeholders in the long run. Keep your strategic priorities top of mind and be willing to adjust the timing.

9. **Tempted to bend the rules? Do the right thing.** Wise decision making requires you to be ethical—to uphold standards of right and wrong. People rarely start their careers planning to be unethical. More often it comes about slowly, little by little. Here are some justifications people give for making unethical decisions: *Everyone else is doing it. Nobody will find out. My boss told me to. The end justifies the means. It's not exactly illegal. We didn't have time to check. It won't hurt anybody.* See these rationales for what they really are: excuses. Read your organization's ethical guidelines and principles. Discuss them with your team. What would small and large ethical breaches look like? What consequences might occur? What do you do if you find yourself in a gray zone? Ask difficult questions. Don't hedge the truth. Make it safe to disclose mistakes. Recognize when greed, ambition, or needing to cover one's hide creeps in. It's everyone's job to uphold high standards of professional responsibility in decision making.

10. **Want to best ensure a quality decision? Keep things in balance.** When a quality decision is what you're after, you need to find the right balance among many factors. There's the need for divergence— so you consider differing views and options with an open mind. And the need for convergence—so you make a timely decision and people unite prior to implementation. There's the need to balance advocacy (making convincing arguments) alongside inquiry (asking powerful questions). There's having the courage to make tough calls. And having courage to let go, letting others decide. There's balancing facts and logical reasoning with intuition. There's quality versus speed. The desire to get it right at odds with the need to move on to other things. Review your decisions over time. Which ways do you tend to lean? What's been your track record? Aim to strike the right balance.

12

Want to learn more? Take a deep dive...

Batista, E. (2013, November 8). Stop worrying about making the right decision. *Harvard Business Review*.

Denning, S. (2012, April 24). How are really great decisions actually made? *Forbes*.

The Staff of the Corporate Executive Board. (2011, December 12). Preventing 'Analysis Paralysis.' *Bloomberg Businessweek*.

Job assignments

- Join a task force making decisions on an important issue, where you will need to share information and consider the long- and short-term implications for the business.

- Make a strategic decision on where to invest future resources (new markets, new products/services, etc.). Evaluate alternatives using the best-suited analytical tools combined with the judgment of experienced stakeholders.

- Be part of a talent review or hiring process, making people decisions for the department or unit as objectively and unbiased as possible.

- Manage the procurement of important services, equipment, supplies, systems, etc., gathering diverse input from stakeholders and analyzing the data before making the call.

- Handle a crisis for the organization, requiring you to make a timely decision where all parties will not be pleased with the outcome.

12

Take time to reflect...

If you tend to be impulsive and plunge right in...

> ...then consider that investing time up front can save time later on. If you rush now, you might have to revise or repair later. Stop. Consider. Choose your direction more wisely.

If your personal views often seem to take precedence...

> ...then recognize that stepping back from your own views may improve the quality of your decisions. Gathering the facts and analyzing the information available will help you be far more objective.

If you worry about not having the answers required...

> ...then understand that it doesn't all have to be down to you. Inviting other people's input can add a new dimension to the decision-making process with the added benefit of taking some pressure off you.

" *Whenever you see a successful business,*
someone once made a courageous decision. **"**

Peter F. Drucker   Austrian-born American writer and management consultant

Learn more about Decision quality

Davidson, J. E., & Sternberg, R. J. (Eds.). (2003). *The psychology of problem solving*. New York, NY: Cambridge University Press.

Haines, S. G. (2006). *The top 10 everyday tools for daily problem solving: Strategic thinking handbook #1*. San Diego, CA: Systems Thinking Press.

Harvard Business Essentials. (2006). *Decision making: 5 Steps to better results*. Boston, MA: Harvard Business School Press.

Janis, I. L. (1982). *Groupthink: Psychological studies of policy decisions and fiascoes*. Boston, MA: Cengage Learning.

Kahneman, D. (2011). *Thinking, fast and slow*. New York, NY: Farrar, Straus and Giroux.

Kourdi, J. (2007). *Think on your feet: 10 Steps to better decision making and problem solving at work*. London, England: Cyan Communications.

Deep dive learning resource links

Batista, E. (2013, November 8). Stop worrying about making the right decision. *Harvard Business Review*. Retrieved from http://blogs.hbr.org/2013/11/stop-worrying-about-making-the-right-decision/

Denning, S. (2012, April 24). How are really great decisions actually made? *Forbes*. Retrieved from http://www.forbes.com/sites/stevedenning/2012/04/24/how-are-really-great-decisions-actually-made/

Harvard Business Review. (2013). The management tip: Tips on decision making. *Harvard Business Review*. Retrieved fromhttp://hbr.org/web/management-tip/tips-on-decision-making

John, C. (2013). How to establish open communication at work. *Chron*. Retrieved from http://smallbusiness.chron.com/establish-open-communication-work-25071.html

Shaughnessy, H. (2013, December 9). 15 Ways to make much better decisions. *Forbes.* Retrieved from http://www.forbes.com/sites/haydnshaughnessy/2013/12/09/15-ways-to-make-much-better-decisions/

Teepe, T. (2009). Problem solving ideas that work [YouTube]. Retrieved from https://www.youtube.com/watch?v=t2ZlEk5oHzo

The Staff of the Corporate Executive Board. (2011, December 12). Preventing 'Analysis Paralysis.' *Bloomberg Businessweek*. Retrieved from http://www.businessweek.com/management/preventing-analysis-paralysis-12202011.html

Wolf, R. F. (2012, September 24). How to minimize your biases when making decisions. *Harvard Business Review*. Retrieved from http://blogs.hbr.org/2012/09/how-to-minimize-your-biases-when/

Zwilling, M. (2011, July 19). *Nine steps to effective business problem solving*. Business Insider. Retrieved from http://www.businessinsider.com/nine-steps-to-effective-business-problem-solving-2011-7

Recommended search terms

If you'd like to explore Decision quality further, try searching online using the following terms:

- Avoiding groupthink.
- Effective decision making.
- Effective problem solving.
- Encouraging open dialogue at work.
- Making smart decisions.
- Reducing (confirmation, frequency, recency, negative, attachment) bias.

(i) More help...

Go to www.kornferry.com/fyi-resources and link directly to the deep dive resources in this chapter. Visit the site often to see the additional resources that are uploaded on a regular basis.

12

13. Develops talent

Developing people to meet both their career goals and the organization's goals.

Most people want to grow and develop. To be as effective as possible and able to take on bigger, more significant challenges. Organizations need people to develop as the nature of their role, and the organization, changes. Talent development is about creating pools of people ready and willing to take on new challenges and step up when needed. It's a continuous process of building skill and capability at an individual and organizational level. It works best as a three-part harmony. First, the person needs to be ambitious and willing to do what's required to grow and progress. People won't grow if they don't want to. Second, the organization has to have a process in place to help those who want to grow. People won't grow if the organization shows no interest and offers no support. And third, those with responsibility for developing others have to be prepared to play an active part. People won't grow if you don't make it a priority. Without your time, interest, and effort, people won't develop to their full potential. People need support. Get it right and you'll develop a more effective, efficient, productive, and motivated workforce.

> " *The mediocre teacher tells.*
> *The good teacher explains.*
> *The superior teacher demonstrates.*
> *The great teacher inspires.* "

William Arthur Ward – American writer

Develops talent is in the **People** factor (III) in the Korn Ferry Leadership Architect™. It is part of Cluster H, **Optimizing diverse talent,** along with Attracts top talent (4), *Values* differences (14), and *Builds effective* teams (34). You may find it helpful to also take a look at some of the tips included in those chapters to supplement your learning.

Skilled

Places a high priority on developing others.

Develops others through coaching, feedback, exposure, and stretch assignments.

Aligns employee career development goals with organizational objectives.

Encourages people to accept developmental moves.

13

Less skilled

- Doesn't take time to work on development of others.

- Is a check-the-box developer; goes with the easiest option to fulfill talent development obligations.

- Doesn't make use of available organization resources and systems to develop others.

- Has difficulty identifying developmental moves or assignments.

Talented

- Views talent development as an organizational imperative.

- Consistently uses multiple methods to develop others.

- Stays alert for developmental assignments both inside and outside own workgroup.

- Readily articulates the value and benefit of stretch assignments to others.

Overused skill

- Concentrates on the development of a few at the expense of many.

- Overestimates people's capacity for growth.

- May be too quick to adopt faddish development approaches.

Some possible causes of lower skill

Causes help explain *why* a person may have trouble with Develops talent. When seeking to increase skill, it's helpful to consider how these might play out in certain situations. And remember that all of these can be addressed if you are motivated to do so.

- Doesn't believe people really want to develop.
- Thinks development is someone else's responsibility.
- Doesn't have the time for it.
- Doesn't know how to develop people.
- Reluctant to share the spotlight.
- Poor coaching skills.
- Shies away from giving developmental feedback.
- Lacks patience.
- Has a one-dimensional view of how people develop.

13

(?) Did you know?

Providing the career development your team members need is critical if you are to retain your top talent. It's not surprising, then, that failing to deliver on this is likely to be one of the strongest drivers for your high-potential employees to seek their development somewhere else. A survey of over 1,200 high achievers, averaging 30 years old, revealed that 95% of them regularly engaged in job-search activities. Dissatisfaction with the development available to them featured strongly in their decision to leave their organization. On the whole, they were satisfied with their on-the-job development, which included being placed in high-visibility positions, increased responsibility, etc. But one of the most significant factors fueling early exit was lack of *formal* development to support them in those high-visibility positions. Formal development like mentoring, coaching, and training courses. While the research is clear that 70% of development comes from job experiences, importance of the 20% they gain through learning from other people and the 10% through formal learning programs shouldn't be ignored. Offer a balanced menu of development opportunities to ensure you retain your talent.[16, 17]

Tips to develop Develops talent

1. **Never have career conversations? Start talking.** While it's not your responsibility to own and drive another's career, you do play an essential role in supporting them to do this for themselves. That's where career conversations come in. Take time to have these future-focused, one-on-one conversations at least once a year. Prepare for the conversation by reflecting on what you see as the person's potential. What's the highest level you believe they can reach? What do you see as their strengths? Key development needs? Potential next assignment? Ask them to share their thoughts on where their career is headed. What they want to achieve short- and long-term. Do they have the desire (and potential) to reach a senior-level leadership position? Or are they focused on deepening their technical expertise? Listen to what you hear and let them know where they stand. Be honest. Use what you hear to differentiate talent and the way you develop it. Remember, if you don't know where a person is headed, you can't help them get there. And one-size-fits-all development is rarely effective.

2. **Too busy? Prioritize the time.** Do you try to focus on developing others but find that other activities have higher priority? For most people, time is what they have the least of to give. But to help others develop beyond today's job, you need to prioritize, on average, eight hours per year per person. Two hours are for an annual appraisal of the person in terms of current strengths, weaknesses, and competencies they need to develop. Two hours are for an in-depth career discussion with each person. Two are for creating a development plan with the person. And the last two hours are there should you need to present findings and recommendations in a succession planning process or arrange for developmental events to take place. Start scheduling in time for developing others. Make it a priority to help people grow. You, your team, and the organization will benefit from increased performance and people feeling happier in their jobs.

3. **Could your experience help others? Be a mentor.** Mentors play a critical role in supporting career development through the offer of experience-based insight and guidance. Before you agree to mentor someone, check that they're following a career path that is similar to yours. To mentor well, you need to have already "walked the path" of the mentee. Spend time with them on a regular basis. Find out what specifically they would like support with. Focus on being a positive guiding influence. On encouraging them to look at situations from different perspectives. On offering non-threatening critique and

challenge. Work on building their confidence. Share knowledge, experiences, and perspectives that can help them find creative solutions to problems, make decisions, and shape their career. If your organization has a mentoring program, find out how it works. If it doesn't, set one up within your unit or function.

4. **One-dimensional view of development? Think 70:20:10.** Research tells us that around 70% of learning comes from practice—from on-the-job experience. From completing assignments and tasks that are challenging. About 20% comes from the feedback, coaching, and mentoring we get from others. And 10% comes from formal, instructional activities such as training programs, reading books, etc. Help others create development plans that are three-dimensional. For example, if someone is looking to develop leadership capability, you might encourage them to read a biography, attend a course. Offer to support them finding a mentor, someone whose leadership they admire. Someone they could study, spend time with, listen to, and learn from. And help them find opportunities to apply their learning in real situations and reflect on what they learned from it. Why is this three-dimensional approach so important? Research indicates that the learning that occurs outside formal classes and courses is generally more frequent and effective than its formal counterpart.

Want to learn more? Take a deep dive...

Fast Company Staff. (2005, May 2). Learn more now. *Fast Company*.

Gallo, A. (2011, February 1). Demystifying mentoring. *Harvard Business Review Blog Network*.

Gallo, C. (2013, June 21). Seven ways to inspire employees to love their jobs. *Forbes*.

Gardner, J. (2011, August 31). *Keep your team by keeping them learning*. Business Insider.

5. **Want to encourage self-awareness? Give and facilitate feedback.** Most people are motivated by feedback for three reasons. First, it helps them understand how they're doing against their goals, what they're doing well, what they need to improve, and how they're impacting others. It enables them to make midcourse corrections. Second, it shows them what they are doing is important and that you're there to help. Third, it's not the "gotcha" game of negative

and critical feedback after the fact. If there are negatives, they need to know them as soon as possible. Encourage people to get feedback from multiple sources, including you, on what matters for success in their job. Formal 360 feedback is a great place to start. If they have direct reports and peers, recommend asking their associates for comments on what they should stop, start, and continue doing to be more successful. Be straight with your people. Give as much real-time, accurate, and balanced feedback as you can.

6. **Want to encourage personal responsibility? Coach.** Coaching puts an individual firmly in the driver's seat of their own development. And, it requires your letting go of control and resisting the urge to "tell" them what and how to develop. As a coach, your role isn't to know the right answers, it's to know the right questions. Questions that are thoughtfully constructed with the aim of facilitating a person's thinking around their development. Questions that help them gain clarity on where they're heading, "What's *your* goal?" That encourage them to explore where they are in relation to their goal, "Where are *you* right now?" "What else do *you* need to do to get there?" Questions that encourage action-oriented thinking, "What alternative courses of action could help *you* move forward?" "What might help or hinder *your* progress?" Questions that commit them to ownership and action, "What will *you* do now?" "By when?" "How will *you* measure progress and success?" Be specific with the use of *you/your* in the questions—it reinforces that the responsibility sits with them.

7. **People getting too comfy? Challenge and support them.** Remember, real development is not cozy or safe—it comes from varied, stressful, and adverse tasks that require us to learn to do something new or different, or fail. It involves real work. It's rewarding but scary. Be open with your people about this. Work with them to identify challenges that force them out of their comfort zone. Consider tasks that are no longer developmental for you but would be for others and delegate them. Trade tasks and assignments between two people—have them do each other's work. Assign a task that the person hasn't done before. Provide support. It sends a message that there's safety on the other side. It helps people cope with the pain of developing while maintaining a positive view of themselves as a capable, worthy, valuable person who can learn and grow. Without support, the developmental experience may overwhelm them rather than foster learning. Cheer from the sidelines and celebrate their accomplishments, even the smallest.

8. **Underperformers? Take action.** Few people come to work with the intention of doing a bad job. Find out the cause and take action to address it. Perhaps they haven't had adequate opportunity, support, and time to achieve the required performance level? If you can offer more, and the role is achievable for them, create a development plan for them that focuses on lifting performance. Maybe the role isn't suited to their talents. You may need to support them in moving on, either to a more suitable role at the same level within the organization or one with less responsibility. In some cases, it may be more appropriate to initiate a process to exit them from the organization. Demoting or exiting a person is a tough thing to do. But, longer-term, it may be the most effective action for the future performance of both your workgroup and the individual.

Want to learn more? Take a deep dive...

Colan, L. (2013, July 29). 4 Keys to coaching underperforming employees. *Inc.*

Coutu, D. (2008, December 29). What coaches can do for you. *Harvard Business Review Blog Network.*

Joseph, C. (n.d.). The ways to challenge employees. *Chron.*

Murphy Paul, A. (2013, March 18). Four ways to give good feedback. *Time.*

---

9. **Focused on developing skills for today? Look to the future.** Take a longer-term view of developing talent. Of creating a workforce that can meet the demands of today while rising to the challenges of tomorrow. Start with the current state. Where is the organization now? What skills and capabilities does it have in place? What does it need? Then look to the future. Where is the organization moving to? What skills and capabilities will be critical to future success? What's the gap between the current and future state? You may have the right level of skill and capability in place. You may find there are gaps. Either way, you'll have the clarity you need to create and implement a longer-term strategy for talent development. Involve others in the creation of the strategic plan where you need to. Share the vision and purpose of the development effort. Tell them why it's important and what they and others stand to gain.

10. **Development happening in silos? Work as a collective.** Make collaborative development conversations a regular part of your people agenda. Seek out HR partners and talent managers beyond

your unit. Get together regularly for the sole purpose of talking about people and talent development. Discuss what each of you is doing. Share best practices and review talent pools (high potentials, new recruits, graduates, etc.) and succession plans. Identify development opportunities (vacancies, assignment moves, coaching, training courses, etc.) that are coming up. How can you best offer them to people? What can you do collectively to help people gain the right skills and experience to meet the needs of the business now and in the future? Commit to action and hold each other accountable for following through. Let people know you're having these conversations. Show you're taking development seriously.

11. **Limited opportunity to promote people? Encourage lateral moves.**
You can't create promotion opportunities that don't exist. For those ready to step up, this can be a cause of frustration. Lateral moves are a great alternative to keep people motivated and challenged while they wait for that promotion opportunity. Besides, advancement may be more likely if they've developed broader skills and experience. Find out what skills they would benefit from developing. What new responsibilities they could take on. What experience they'd like to gain. Help them look for a temporary or permanent assignment that fits their need, moves them forward developmentally, and increases their visibility in the organization. Visibility is vital when it comes to being considered for new opportunities. Support their transition. They may not be moving up, but they could be going from knowing the most to learning the most, which is daunting. Give others outside your team/unit the opportunity to make a lateral move into your team/unit where you can. Global context? Look at opportunities for international moves.

12. **Want a strong succession pipeline? Focus on developing leaders.**
Make the development of leaders, from first level to senior executive, a core part of your people strategy. Don't know who the leaders of the future are? Identify them. Focus on developing them through a range of techniques. Go beyond traditional programs. Use conferences or leadership summits as development opportunities. Devise a curriculum that focuses on supporting people through key leadership transition points. Raise the profile of high potentials through board breakfasts or similar meetings. Offer internal or external coaching and mentoring. Find specialized development assignments that focus on leadership. Encourage action- and experience-based learning by bringing people together to work on solving real business problems. Research shows that the best

organizations for leaders are typically twice as likely to use a variety of developmental techniques for their best and brightest.

13. **Frustrated when others don't want to progress? Value depth of expertise.** Not everyone is pushing to be promoted or to be the next CEO. Some are satisfied to focus on what they do to the best of their ability, even if it limits their career options. While you should advise them of the consequences, all organizations need strong performers dedicated to skill-building in their current area only. Don't imply that someone who likes to execute must become a strategist to be valued. Instead, create more ways for people to excel and get status recognition. If a person wants to be a customer service representative for life, recognize that as critical and help the person develop in every way possible within that area.

Want to learn more? Take a deep dive...

Bregman, P. (2013, September 3). Four areas where senior leaders should focus their attention. *Harvard Business Review Blog Network*.

McGregor, J. (2011, October 13). How to make a smart lateral career move. *Fortune*.

Myatt, M. (2012, December 19). The #1 reason leadership development fails. *Forbes*.

The Wall Street Journal. (n.d.). How to develop future leaders. *The Wall Street Journal*.

Job assignments

- Volunteer to mentor someone outside your unit. Understand their goals and expectations and make sure you're tailoring your approach to meet their needs.

- Offer to lead the creation of a two- to five-year capability development plan for your unit. Focus on the organization's strategy and the skills and abilities required to achieve it.

- Manage a team of inexperienced people. Work with each individual to create a 70:20:10 development plan to build the skills they need. Review and appraise progress regularly.

- Take responsibility for developing an underperformer. Start by giving them a fair and accurate appraisal of their current strengths and weaknesses and clarify the performance gap.

- Lead the setup of a people development forum across your unit/ organization. Showcase best practices, break down silos, and share talent more effectively.

Take time to reflect...

If you think helping others develop isn't your job...

...then recognize that it's potentially part of everyone's role. Develop the habit of providing support and guidance. Help people when they're stuck. Become a spontaneous coach. Do a little every day.

If you expect that people should learn on their own time...

...then understand that most learning comes from ongoing experience. Helping people see the learning opportunities in everything they do is helping them to develop.

If you're focused on the skills that are needed today...

...then ask yourself what will be needed tomorrow. Starting to build these capabilities now will give you a head start for the future.

"*I never teach my pupils,
I only attempt to provide the conditions
in which they can learn.* **"**

Albert Einstein – German-born Nobel Prize-winning physicist

Learn more about Develops talent

The Best Practice Institute, Goldsmith, M., & Carter, L. (Eds.). (2010). *Best practices in talent management: How the world's leading corporations manage, develop, and retain top talent*. San Francisco, CA: Pfeiffer.

Harvard Business School Press. (2009). *Harvard Business Review on developing high-potential leaders*. Boston, MA: Harvard Business School Press.

Hunt, J. M., & Weintraub, J. R. (2010). *The coaching manager: Developing top talent in business* (2nd ed.). Thousand Oaks, CA: Sage.

Lawler, E. E., III. (2008). *Talent: Making people your competitive advantage*. San Francisco, CA: Jossey-Bass.

Smilansky, J. (2007). *Developing executive talent: Best practices from global leaders*. Chichester, West Sussex, England: John Wiley & Sons.

 ## Deep dive learning resource links

Bregman, P. (2013, September 3). Four areas where senior leaders should focus their attention. *Harvard Business Review Blog Network*. Retrieved from http://blogs.hbr.org/2013/09/four-areas-where-senior-leader/

Colan, L. (2013, July 29). 4 Keys to coaching underperforming employees. *Inc*. Retrieved from http://www.inc.com/lee-colan/4-keys-to-coaching-underperforming-employees.html

Coutu, D. (2008, December 29). What coaches can do for you. *Harvard Business Review Blog Network*. Retrieved from http://blogs.hbr.org/2008/12/what-coaches-can-do-for-you/

Fast Company Staff. (2005, May 2). Learn more now. *Fast Company*. Retrieved from http://www.fastcompany.com/919020/learn-more-now

Gallo, A. (2011, February 1). Demystifying mentoring. *Harvard Business Review Blog Network*. Retrieved from http://blogs.hbr.org/2011/02/demystifying-mentoring/

Gallo, C. (2013, June 21). Seven ways to inspire employees to love their jobs. *Forbes*. Retrieved from http://www.forbes.com/sites/carminegallo/2013/06/21/seven-ways-to-inspire-employees-to-love-their-jobs/

Gardner, J. (2011, August 31). *Keep your team by keeping them learning.* Business Insider. Retrieved from http://www.businessinsider.com/keep-your-team-by-keeping-them-learning-2011-8

Joseph, C. (n.d.). The ways to challenge employees. *Chron.* Retrieved from http://smallbusiness.chron.com/ways-challenge-employees-11946.html

McGregor, J. (2011, October 13). How to make a smart lateral career move. *Fortune.* Retrieved from http://management.fortune.cnn.com/2011/10/13/career-lateral-move/

Murphy Paul, A. (2013, March 18). Four ways to give good feedback. *Time.* Retrieved from http://ideas.time.com/2013/03/18/four-ways-to-give-good-feedback/

Myatt, M. (2012, December 19). The #1 reason leadership development fails. *Forbes.* Retrieved from http://www.forbes.com/sites/mikemyatt/2012/12/19/the-1-reason-leadership-development-fails/

The Wall Street Journal. (n.d.). How to develop future leaders. *The Wall Street Journal.* Retrieved from http://guides.wsj.com/management/managing-your-people/how-to-develop-future-leaders/

Recommended search terms

If you'd like to explore Develops talent further, try searching online using the following terms:

- Coaching employees.
- Dealing with underperforming employees.
- Developing employees for future success.
- Focusing on leadership development.
- Mentoring employees.
- Ways to challenge your employees.

(i) More help...

Go to www.kornferry.com/fyi-resources and link directly to the deep dive resources in this chapter. Visit the site often to see the additional resources that are uploaded on a regular basis.

---

160 |

14. *Values* differences

Recognizing the value that different perspectives and cultures bring to an organization.

Valuing differences creates a work environment where people can and want to do their best. As the economy becomes increasingly global, our workforce has become more diverse. The typical definition of diversity—race, ethnicity, culture—now includes perspectives, styles, and thought. Savvy organizations recognize that success is increasingly dependent on those who can interact effectively and respectfully with all types. Research shows that employee engagement, innovation, teamwork, and the bottom line can be improved by truly valuing each other. Working effectively in this diverse world starts with self-awareness. Knowing how you react to others. Recognizing the biases you have. Knowing how your behavior is perceived. Understanding your attitude toward others with a diverse point of view. After awareness comes action. Considering how you handle bias, poor treatment, and conflict. Demonstrating that you value others. To be effective, you won't ignore the differences. You'll understand and embrace them. You'll accommodate and encourage them. Valuing differences will help you learn and benefit from the wealth of knowledge and experience that diversity brings. It opens doors to new ways of thinking and new opportunities for building the success of the organization.

" *The goal is to work toward a world where expectations are not set by the stereotypes that hold us back, but by our personal passion, talents, and interests.* "

Sheryl Sandberg – American technology executive and COO of Facebook

***Values* differences** is in the **People** factor (III) in the Korn Ferry Leadership Architect™. It is part of Cluster H, **Optimizing diverse talent,** along with Attracts top talent (4), Develops talent (13), and *Builds effective* teams (34). You may find it helpful to also take a look at some of the tips included in those chapters to supplement your learning.

Skilled

Seeks to understand different perspectives and cultures.

Contributes to a work climate where differences are valued and supported.

Applies others' diverse experiences, styles, backgrounds, and perspectives to get results.

Is sensitive to cultural norms, expectations, and ways of communicating.

Less skilled

- Lacks awareness of other cultures.
- Treats everybody the same without regard to their differences.
- Expects everyone to adapt to his/her way of thinking and communicating.
- Lacks curiosity and interest in different people's backgrounds and perspectives.

Talented

- Actively seeks out information about a wide variety of cultures and viewpoints.
- Promotes a team environment that values, encourages, and supports differences.
- Ensures that different experiences, styles, backgrounds, and perspectives are leveraged appropriately.
- Senses how differences will play out in terms of needs, values, and motivators.

Overused skill

- May prioritize valuing difference over achieving results.
- May make too many allowances for members of a particular group.
- Is overly sensitive to different groups when delivering tough messages.

Some possible causes of lower skill

Causes help explain *why* a person may have trouble with *Values* differences. When seeking to increase skill, it's helpful to consider how these might play out in certain situations. And remember that all of these can be addressed if you are motivated to do so.

- Unaware of biases.
- Resistant to feedback.
- Poor communication skills.
- Not attuned to others' needs.
- Weak at building relationships.
- Avoids conflict.
- Narrow perspective.
- Uncomfortable with differences.
- Prefers familiarity.
- Lacks curiosity.

Brain booster

Most people have stereotypes—simplified and generalized views of people from a particular group. They're often based on gender, race, religion, or geography. Due to social norms and political correctness, these tend to lie under the surface and people may not even be aware of them. But they still influence behavior. The process is automatic and very fast. In neuroscientific terms, making the connection between a person and a stereotype occurs within 300 milliseconds (less than a typical blink of an eye) of encountering that person. Because the *conscious* control is not there, responses can be prejudiced and socially inappropriate. How do you overcome unconscious prejudice? Recognize there are more differences within one group than there are between groups. Unlearn the stereotypes. This is called disassociation. Consider several people from a specific group. Compare each with what you think you know about that group. Recognize how they are inconsistent with your stereotypical view. Create a new categorization not based on social demographics. Focus on how people are similar instead of different to form a new, favorable perception that will override any underlying prejudice.[18]

Tips to develop *Values* differences

1. **Tend to go with your gut reaction? Check your response.** Gut reactions are human nature. They can range from appreciation, to tolerance, to avoidance. It's what we do with these reactions that's important. They can dictate the direction and nature of our relationships. This direction can be unproductive. Examine your reactions to different people. Do you show appreciation by valuing their perspective, talent, or experience? Do you tolerate them because you have to? Or do you avoid them altogether and completely disengage? Identify the characteristics in others that cause you to react this way—whether you appreciate, tolerate, or avoid. How are these reactions impacting your relationships? Work to go beyond your gut responses. Make an effort to seek out additional information about people you may simply tolerate or perhaps avoid. Ask questions. Go beyond tolerating. Tolerating is not good enough to create a productive, harmonious work environment.

2. **Treat people differently? Examine your biases.** Anyone who is living has biases and makes assumptions. This is part of being human. Biases may be conscious or unconscious. Recognize your biases and how they impact workplace interactions and judgments. Do you treat one person differently than another? What is it about that person that causes you to treat them differently? Go beyond your initial assumptions. Ask questions. Be curious. Surround yourself with people about whom you have formed preconceived notions. Work with them on teams. Go out to lunch. Get to know them. Understand them. Look beyond your preconceptions. Find ways to ensure that your behavior fully supports all of those around you, not just those you are most comfortable with.

3. **Tunnel vision? Seek out different perspectives.** It's easy to develop a one-track mind when you're working on a challenging project with tight deadlines. You probably go full steam ahead toward successful completion. You likely seek out your usual go-to people who have helped you in the past and whom you trust. That's the way you've always done it. This can be limiting. You're relying on the same people, same perspectives, same experience. It excludes others and doesn't give them exciting development opportunities. Get others involved. Reach out to those you might not tap into regularly. Ask for their input and perspective. Innovation arises from multiple perspectives. Inclusion happens when all are invited to contribute.

4. **Fixed viewpoint? Develop a capacity-building mindset.** Think that a person can only learn and grow so much? Research shows that some believe people are born with a fixed set of job-related abilities and that's it. This fixed-capacity mindset is restrictive. It limits what we believe people can achieve. Managers with this mindset may assign projects based on a belief that some people have it and some don't. Develop a capacity-building mindset. Believe that people, with dedicated effort and feedback, can learn whatever is necessary to do their jobs. That they can keep up with change and contribute to building and sustaining competitive advantage. This outlook opens the door to what we are able to achieve and what we expect others can achieve. Invite someone with a different skill set to work with you on a project. Give someone who has struggled another chance.

5. **Not sure how you are perceived? Get feedback.** Feedback is a navigational tool that can tell you whether you are on or off course. Perception is reality in the eyes of the beholder. You need to know how people perceive you in order to work more effectively with them. Ask for feedback. Are you demonstrating bias? Do your interactions show mere tolerance rather than appreciation? The feedback you get may uncover some blind spots. You may be treating someone differently because they are not like you and you're uncomfortable. You may not even know it. Get feedback from your manager. Your coworkers. Your customers. View feedback from a learning orientation rather than a proving orientation. A learning orientation welcomes feedback as a natural part of improvement rather than having to prove your worth and ability. Be open and work on a nugget or two. After you've tried out some new behaviors, ask for more feedback.

Want to learn more? Take a deep dive...

Hastings, R. R. (2012, November 8). *Awareness of biases helps leaders adapt to diversity.* Society for Human Resource Management.

Musselwhite, C. (2007, October 1). Self-awareness and the effective leader. *Inc.*

Walter, E. (2014, January 14). Reaping the benefits of diversity for modern business innovation. *Forbes.*

6. **Not always considerate? Show that you value others.** Do you value and respect others? You may think you are valuing others, but it may be hidden. Bring it to the forefront through your words and actions. Use skills that send the message that you respect and appreciate others. Convey empathy—"I see that you've worked hard to make this a success." Accept that a person's perspective is their truth— "This appears to be something that is important to you." Demonstrate that you understand their emotion—"I can see that this is frustrating for you." Show that you hear their perspective, idea, or concern—"So your idea is to..." Express encouragement by accepting rather than interrogating—"I want to learn more about how you see this...could you help me understand...?" Try out one of these skills each day. You'll get more comfortable and confident. And your relationships and productivity will flourish.

7. **Stuck in your style? Flex your communication approach.** Different communication styles originate from culture, upbringing, and past experiences. Valuing differences includes valuing the nuances of our styles and perspectives, not just the obvious. You may be a person of few words or a person of many. Or you prefer details over free-form idea generation. Don't know your style? Use a profiling tool to uncover your style preferences. Gauge the effectiveness of your style. Is it working? In what situations and with whom? Does it turn others off? Make sure to monitor your body language. Dr. Albert Mehrabian's research on trust and believability found that body language has great impact on the message. Communication can be sabotaged when body language does not align with words. Use strong body language such as posture and eye contact to show confidence. Gesture and smile to display enthusiasm. Once you've identified your style, encourage others to do the same. Discuss each other's styles. Leverage each style. And remember, when there's conflict, it could be a style issue rather than personal.

8. **Trouble connecting with people from different cultures? Hone your cross-cultural interaction skills.** Cultural background influences what people see as appropriate and inappropriate behavior. Consider the various dimensions of culture when interacting with others. For example, what is the power structure of the culture? Is it more hierarchical or egalitarian? In cultures with a more collectivistic or interdependent style (where "saving face" may be important), avoid surprises that might catch people off guard and embarrass them. Give them information beforehand so they can prepare and feel comfortable. Does the culture place more importance on the task or the relationship? If it is relationship focused, do more rapport building rather than jumping into the task. Are emotions more

controlled or expressive? If controlled, don't interpret limited reaction as uncaring. Assess where you fall within these cultural dimensions. Plan how you will adapt to the cultural gaps. Don't assume your style is better and impose it. Adapt without mimicking others or changing your natural self. Let others know you are trying to better understand them.

Want to learn more? Take a deep dive...

Fuld, L. (2012, August 1). Cross-cultural communication takes more than manners. *Harvard Business Review Blog Network*.

Nierenberg, A. (2005, February 17). *Adapting to different communication styles*. Small Business Advocate.

Vanderkam, L. (2014, January 24). 4 Soft skills that you need to learn. *Fast Company*.

14

9. **Struggle to see the value of diversity and inclusion? Explore the business case.** Research shows that people's intentions to leave an organization were associated with their perceptions of the organization's diversity climate. Catalyst, a research organization focusing on women and work, found that companies that achieve diversity in their management and on their corporate boards attain better financial results, on average, than other companies. What is your organization doing to promote diversity and inclusion? What are the objectives? How can you help meet these objectives in your daily work? Remember, diversity and inclusion are not just a "nice to do." They are a "need to do."

10. **Lack understanding of different cultures? Develop cultural competence.** Cultural competence is the ability and knowledge to interact with different cultures, languages, styles, and experiences. It's the ability to get results across cultural differences. It's recognizing all people as unique individuals. Realizing that their experiences, beliefs, values, and language affect their perceptions. Start small. Don't expect to master knowledge of every culture. View developing your cultural competence as a process of discovery, adaptation, and skill building. Learn about other cultures through books, movies, travel, and cultural events. Walk through ethnic markets. Visit various neighborhoods in your local city. Try restaurants with food from a different culture. Attend a religious service unlike your own. Ask questions to learn about others' backgrounds. Be open when you interact with someone different from you. The more open you are, the more open they'll be. Be curious.

11. **Want to know more about dealing with differences? Participate in diversity initiatives.** Naive about people different from you? Unsure about how to work with people who have a different background, culture, ethnicity? Take advantage of your organization's efforts to promote diversity and inclusion. These may be formal programs or they may be informal such as all-company get-togethers. These efforts will build your awareness of your biases, reactions, and how they play out in the workplace and beyond. They'll give you ideas and skills for working with others effectively. And your participation will signal to others that you are committed to learning more. Join your company's mentoring program. Partner with someone who is different from you. A positive mentoring relationship is safe ground where you can ask questions that you may not be able to ask others. A mentor can help you practice difficult conversations and interactions before you try them out.

12. **Want to make a difference? Become a diversity change agent.** Being a change agent means commitment to things being different. Recognizing what's not right. Identifying what needs to change. Taking preemptive action to get things where they need to be. For diversity, this means recognizing personal biases and assumptions. Understanding the negative impact of acting on those biases. Hear something inappropriate? Take that person aside and say, "I'm not sure you are aware of what you said, but I found that comment to be offensive." If you feel you can't make a difference alone, remember, change has to start somewhere. Set an example for others to follow and be the catalyst for change. Address issues head-on as you encounter them. Don't let intolerant or biased behavior pass. Help others understand the importance of appreciating diversity. Encourage them to follow your lead. Build a team of diversity change agents with a mission to build a culture of valuing differences.

Want to learn more? Take a deep dive...

Conant, D. R. (2011, July 28). How to make diversity and inclusion real. *Harvard Business Review Blog Network*.

DeloitteLLP. (2012, July 25). Insights: The business case for diversity and inclusion [YouTube].

Hewlett, S. A., Marshall, M., & Sherbin, L. (2013, December). How diversity can drive innovation. *Harvard Business Review*.

13. **Experiencing bad behavior? Speak out against poor treatment.** Have you witnessed others being treated poorly? Have you noticed

stereotyping, exclusion, condescension, lack of respect, or low expectations? Treating others poorly can be conscious or subconscious. It can occur due to bias, assumptions, and gut reactions. It is often unintentional. However, it can result in a loss of confidence, isolation, reduced motivation, and decreased engagement. Take a close look at the interactions around you. Look for any behavior that could undermine the confidence and effort of others. Notice the experience of those who seem withdrawn or disengaged. Is there something going on that contributes to their behavior? Have a conversation. Plan what you are going to say. Describe what you saw or heard and what is working or not working. Stick to facts and be descriptive. Offer specific suggestions for improvement. Focus on one issue at a time. Giving feedback on several issues at a time might feel like an attack. Be timely. Conversations of this type don't mean that everyone will be happy afterwards. Just do it. Show that you're trying to create a respectful, open, honest work environment.

14. **Struggle with disagreement? Handle conflict caused by differences respectfully and skillfully.** Disagreement is inevitable when people have different perspectives, experiences, styles, cultures. One person may think one way, due to their background, and another person may think differently. But conflict is not a bad thing. Resolved effectively, it can lead to greater awareness and understanding of different perspectives and cultures. It can help you handle differences more productively and openly next time. Handled poorly, it can be damaging. It can lead to negative feelings and continued bias toward those who are different from you. Try the FREAS approach when dealing with conflict:

- **F**ace up to your role, if any, in the conflict and the impact on the team and your relationship with them. Take accountability.

- **R**eframe the issue in terms of a business need and a development opportunity, rather than about personal issues.

- **E**xplore the other person's perspective by asking questions, gathering information, and actively listening.

- **A**gree to a solution or strategy.

- **S**upport each other to live up to the agreement.

15. **Unsure what to do next? Create an action plan.** It's easy to say, "I'm going to start valuing differences in others." But it's harder to do. Create an action plan. Pick an action that will address an issue in your work environment. Resolving a conflict between two team members. Asking for input from a team member who's often ignored.

|

Putting together a team with different perspectives. Write down why this issue is important to you, what might keep you from addressing it, and how this action will benefit you. Then, think about how this action will help others and your organization. Identify specific opportunities or situations you can use to apply your action. Think about what support/resources you might need to implement it. Be as detailed as possible. Set a clear time frame. Share your action plan with a trusted coworker. This will increase the accountability and likelihood that you'll follow through.

Want to learn more? Take a deep dive...

Belak, T. (2004, February). *How to handle difficult behavior in the workplace*. Mediate.com.

Frost, S. (n.d.). How to deal with bad behavior in the workplace. *Chron*.

Myatt, M. (2012, February 22). 5 Keys of dealing with workplace conflict. *Forbes*.

Job assignments

- Participate in a project with people who have different backgrounds, perspectives, and experiences than you. Tap into their knowledge and experience.

- Take on a task working with global team members or customers that requires you to communicate regularly across borders, time zones, and cultures.

- Get a mentor who is different from you. Learn about their unique perspective based on their culture, background, ethnicity.

- Volunteer to join a team with a history of conflicted relationships where you can practice conflict-resolution skills with people who have different points of view or work styles.

- Work on a project that requires overseas travel. Immerse yourself in the culture.

Take time to reflect...

If you surround yourself with people who are similar to you...

> ...then recognize the value of a wider circle. Embrace difference. Respect diversity. Open the door to new ideas and possibilities.

If you sense a resistance to diversity in your team...

> ...then step in to turn things around. Everyone has a responsibility to create an environment where all are valued, listened to, and learned from.

If you tolerate differences but don't embrace their value...

> ...then you're probably missing the point. Diversity brings benefits that sameness can't. Recognize the need for differences and you help ensure the organization excels in an increasingly diverse world.

14

" *We owe almost all our knowledge*
not to those who have agreed,
but to those who have differed. **"**

Charles Caleb Colton – English cleric and author

Learn more about *Values* differences

Bates-Ballard, P., & Smith, G. (2008). *Navigating diversity: An advocate's guide through the maze of race, gender, religion, and more*. Charleston, SC: BookSurge.

Hofner Saphiere, D., Kappler Mikk, B., & Ibrahim Devries, B. (2005). *Communication highwire: Leveraging the power of diverse communication styles*. Yarmouth, ME: Intercultural Press.

Hyter, M. C., & Turnock, J. L. (2005). *The power of inclusion: Unlock the potential and productivity of your workforce*. Mississauga, ON, Canada: John Wiley & Sons Canada, Ltd.

Olver, K., & Baugh, S. (2006). *Leveraging diversity at work: How to hire, retain, and inspire a diverse workforce for peak performance and profit*. Country Club Hills, IL: Inside Out Press.

Thiederman, S. (2008). *Making diversity work: 7 Steps for defeating bias in the workplace*. New York, NY: Kaplan Publishing.

Deep dive learning resource links

Belak, T. (2004, February). *How to handle difficult behavior in the workplace*. Mediate.com. Retrieved from http://www.mediate.com/articles/belak4.cfm

Conant, D. R. (2011, July 28). How to make diversity and inclusion real. *Harvard Business Review Blog Network*. Retrieved from http://blogs.hbr.org/2011/07/how-to-make-diversity-and-incl/

DeloitteLLP. (2012, July 25). Insights: The business case for diversity and inclusion [YouTube]. Retrieved from http://www.youtube.com/watch?v=w1D7-cn3v-s

Frost, S. (n.d.). How to deal with bad behavior in the workplace. *Chron*. Retrieved from http://smallbusiness.chron.com/deal-bad-behavior-workplace-12304.html

Fuld, L. (2012, August 1). Cross-cultural communication takes more than manners. *Harvard Business Review Blog Network*. Retrieved from http://blogs.hbr.org/2012/08/cross-cultural-communication-takes-more/

Hastings, R. R. (2012, November 8). *Awareness of biases helps leaders adapt to diversity*. Society for Human Resource Management. Retrieved from https://www.shrm.org/hrdisciplines/Diversity/Articles/Pages/Awareness-Biases-Leaders-Diversity.aspx

Hewlett, S. A., Marshall, M., & Sherbin, L. (2013, December). How diversity can drive innovation. *Harvard Business Review*. Retrieved from http://hbr.org/2013/12/how-diversity-can-drive-innovation/ar/1

Musselwhite, C. (2007, October 1). Self-awareness and the effective leader. *Inc.* Retrieved from http://www.inc.com/resources/leadership/articles/20071001/musselwhite.html

Myatt, M. (2012, February 22). 5 Keys of dealing with workplace conflict. *Forbes.* Retrieved from http://www.forbes.com/sites/mikemyatt/2012/02/22/5-keys-to-dealing-with-workplace-conflict/

Nierenberg, A. (2005, February 17). *Adapting to different communication styles.* Small Business Advocate. Retrieved from http://www.smallbusinessadvocate.com/small-business-articles/adapting-to-different-communication-styles-1427

Vanderkam, L. (2014, January 24). 4 Soft skills that you need to learn. *Fast Company.* Retrieved from http://www.fastcompany.com/3025282/how-to-be-a-success-at-everything/4-soft-skills-that-you-need-to-learn

Walter, E. (2014, January 14). Reaping the benefits of diversity for modern business innovation. *Forbes.* Retrieved from http://www.forbes.com/sites/ekaterinawalter/2014/01/14/reaping-the-benefits-of-diversity-for-modern-business-innovation/

Recommended search terms

If you'd like to explore *Values* differences further, try searching online using the following terms:

- Appreciating diverse communication styles.
- Being more inclusive at work.
- Cross-cultural diversity management.
- Dealing with difficult and disrespectful behavior.
- Handling workplace conflict.
- Respecting others' opinions.

(i) More help...

Go to www.kornferry.com/fyi-resources and link directly to the deep dive resources in this chapter. Visit the site often to see the additional resources that are uploaded on a regular basis.

15. Directs work

Providing direction, delegating, and removing obstacles to get work done.

There is a major career transition point when a person needs to shift from doing the work to getting work done through others. The transition is difficult for many. It means giving up direct control over the work, which involves more risk. More need to trust and equip others to get the work done. And a shift in focus from personal achievement to enabling and empowering others. Another major transition happens when a leader stops *being* the expert in a particular function, area, discipline, and instead starts *leading* the experts. A tough transition again—to give up being the person most in-the-know. Leaders who succeed at these transitions start developing new skills and know when it's time to stop relying on the old. They learn to set clear expectations, to track progress, and to communicate information that people need to do their jobs. Their focus shifts to helping others develop their skills and gain confidence. Guide. Delegate. And trust. Navigate these leadership rites of passage and you'll not only help other people be successful in their roles, you'll be on your way to becoming more successful in yours.

" *Never tell people how to do things.*
Tell them what to do and they will surprise you
with their ingenuity. "

George S. Patton – United States Army general

Directs work is in the **Results** factor (II) in the Korn Ferry Leadership Architect™. It is part of Cluster E, **Managing execution,** along with Plans and aligns (25) and *Optimizes* work processes (38). You may find it helpful to also take a look at some of the tips included in those chapters to supplement your learning.

Skilled

Provides clear direction and accountabilities.

Delegates and distributes assignments and decisions appropriately.

Monitors progress by maintaining dialogue on work and results.

Provides appropriate guidance and direction based on people's capabilities.

Intervenes as needed to remove obstacles.

Less skilled

- Provides incomplete, vague, or disorganized instructions.
- Delegates work to people without giving them sufficient guidance.
- Sets goals and objectives so easy to achieve that people are demotivated in the process.
- Saves high-profile tasks for self.

Talented

- Masterfully matches people to assignments.
- Conveys clear performance expectations and follows up consistently.
- Sets stretch goals and objectives, pushing individuals or teams to perform at higher levels.
- Delegates work in a way that empowers ownership.
- Tracks how work is progressing without meddling.

Overused skill

- May be overly directive and stifle creativity and initiative.
- Pushes people too hard by asking them to work at their upper limits.
- May overdelegate without providing enough direction or help.
- Gives people authority that they shouldn't have.

Some possible causes of lower skill

Causes help explain *why* a person may have trouble with Directs work. When seeking to increase skill, it's helpful to consider how these might play out in certain situations. And remember that all of these can be addressed if you are motivated to do so.

- Doesn't trust others.
- Poor judgment of people's skill and ability.
- Fear of letting go of control or power.
- Micromanages.
- Doesn't delegate well.
- Has unrealistic expectations of others.
- Low risk tolerance.
- Impatient.

 Culture card

As organizations become increasingly global, it's important to understand that how leaders direct work varies significantly in different parts of the world. In their research on the leadership styles of different countries, Bersin by Deloitte found that in India, leaders place emphasis on execution, operational effectiveness, and careful planning. In Denmark, Sweden, and the Netherlands, the style is more visionary and transformational, executed through innovation and persuasive communication. Where you are responsible for directing the work of people in other cultures, you need to adjust your approach to get the best results. A highly results-focused leader in the United States may frustrate colleagues in China who prefer to build relationships before committing to the task and who are accustomed to a more unstructured and flexible approach. One size definitely does not fit all.[19, 20]

15

Tips to develop Directs work

1. **Uncomfortable directing others? Give yourself permission.** Do you feel guilty telling others what to do? Worry about giving people work? Don't want to be thought of as pushy? Being a leader requires you to exercise authority and provide direction. When you do it well, people respect you for it. Give yourself permission to be directive, to assert appropriate authority, and to delegate assignments. Know that without directing work, you will make life harder for the team— leaving them to guess what it is you want from them. Remind yourself of the positive outcomes you'll cause. You're developing them, empowering them, putting them on the right path, setting them up for success. Still have concerns? Directing others isn't for everyone. Examine whether this path is the right one for you. Maybe you'd be more suited to a role that allows you to be an individual contributor.

2. **Prefer to do things yourself? Trust other people.** Most people prefer to depend on themselves to get things done. Especially the important things. You trust your own expertise. You got to where you are because you're good at what you do—right? It's scary to think about letting someone else take over. What if they don't do it right? What if the outcome isn't up to your standard? A belief that others can't be trusted to deliver only leads to your hanging on to the work. You're training them to be dependent on you. They'll take less initiative, feel less motivated, and stop putting in extra effort. You'll continue to be unimpressed with their results, confirming your belief that you need to do it yourself. It becomes a self-reinforcing cycle. Worse, you'll end up with less time to do what you need to do and they'll have less opportunity to develop. Challenge the beliefs that get in the way of trusting others. Think they're not qualified or motivated to do a great job? Ask them; find out. Don't assume this is the case. Remember, they might also be where they are because they're good at what they do.

3. **Holding on to too much? Delegate.** As jobs get bigger, the requirements for success change. You can't do everything yourself. You need to let go. Successful delegation is a win all round. It frees up your time, allowing you to direct attention toward bigger, more important issues, while enabling others to grow. Unsure what to delegate? A simple and effective way of deciding is to ask people, "What do I do that you could help me with? What do I do that you could do with a little help from me? What do I do that you could do by yourself?" You probably won't agree to everything, but try to pick one or a few things to delegate each time. Delegate a balance

of routine and important tasks. Delegate whole tasks rather than parts. People tend to be more motivated when they have responsibility for the whole. Add the larger context. Tell them why this task needs to be done, where it fits in the grander scheme, and its importance to the goals and objectives of the unit. Give people the appropriate level of authority required to carry out the task. Fail to do that and you render them powerless. Give them too much and you risk inappropriate decisions being made. Delegate things that others do well or better than you. Delegate tactical; keep strategic. Delegate short-term; keep long-term. You'll get more work done when you delegate than you ever will alone.

4. **Struggling to get people motivated? Set stretching goals.** Most people prefer to do things that stretch them rather than things they could do in their sleep. Setting easy goals may seem like a good thing to them and you in the short-term. But it won't motivate people to move out of their comfort zone. To push performance beyond their current best. Research indicates that having a challenging goal actively encourages a person to achieve more. To work hard toward higher standards of performance. To have more confidence in their ability to rise to tough challenges. Facilitate growth in others by assigning tasks that contain stretching elements they've not done before. Start by understanding their current level of skill and asking, "What task or goal can I assign them that requires a step beyond what they're doing today. That makes the most of the skills they have but is slightly bigger than their current capabilities?" Make sure that the task will stretch them, not break them. If they think it's far beyond their capacity, they will be less engaged and not motivated to try.

15

Want to learn more? Take a deep dive...

Chinn, D. (n.d.). How to motivate employees using E. A. Locke's goal-setting theory. *Chron.*

Mind Tools. (n.d.). *Successful delegation.* Mind Tools.

Saunders, E. G. (2012, October 30). Stop being a people-pleaser. *Harvard Business Review Blog Network.*

Zwilling, M. (2013, October 2). How to delegate more effectively in your business. *Forbes.*

5. **Leaving people confused? Give clear direction and accountability.** Are people unclear about what's expected of them? Are you just too busy? Do you communicate to some and not to others? Or think they'd know what to do if they were any good. Whatever the reason, leaving people without clear direction and accountability will lead to frustration, low engagement, a job poorly done, and rework. People need to know which direction to go and what you expect to happen. What does the outcome look like? When do you need it by? What's the budget? What resources do they get? What are they accountable for? Not accountable for? What decisions can they make? What are the checkpoints along the way? How will success be measured? What role will you take? What are the rewards and consequences of success and failure? Reflect on recent projects or tasks that have required you to direct others. How well did you communicate direction and accountability? Ask those you're communicating with to reflect their understanding of what you've said. Checking for understanding gives you opportunity to clarify any misunderstandings and ensure everyone sets off in the right direction.

6. **Losing track of what's going on? Monitor progress appropriately.** It's important to strike a balance between keeping track of progress and constantly looking over someone's shoulder. Do you need to monitor the progress of a task? There may be times when a well-communicated and delegated task doesn't need to be routinely monitored by you. Where it is important that you stay connected with progress, agree to the approach up front. For example, set checkpoints: every Monday; after each 10% is complete; by milestones such as completion of a first draft. Monitor progress to support better performance, not to control.

7. **Micromanaging? Give people freedom to perform.** Immerse yourself in others' work? Always correcting tiny details? Take over tasks before they're finished? Like to be in control? Insist that people go through you for decisions? These are all signals that you could be micromanaging. Disempowering people. Slowing progress. Hampering creativity and innovation. It's OK (and important) to give people clear direction on what needs to be achieved and by when. But then step aside and give them the freedom to perform. Invite them to figure out how to achieve the result in their own way. People are more motivated when they can determine the how for themselves. Micromanagers include the how, which turns people into task automatons instead of empowered and energized staff. Give them leeway. Encourage them to try things, correct their own mistakes. Resist jumping in and taking over just because things aren't being done the way you'd do

them. Be approachable, but not intrusive. Intervene only when agreed-upon criteria are not being followed or expectations are not being met. Let people finish their work. Your role in directing work is to get results through people, not for people.

8. **Overwhelming others? Help them take control.** When you're directing work through others, be conscious of not pushing people so hard that they feel out of control. This can lead to stress and anxiety. If you sense that someone is feeling overwhelmed, talk to them. Find the cause. Volume of work, pressure to get things right, lack of confidence, or something else? Whatever the cause, it's important to support the person to take control rather than overstretch them, which can make them feel even more overwhelmed. If they have too much, take something away. If they lack confidence or don't know where to start, work with them. Express confidence in their ability. Describe the skills that led you to assign them the task. Encourage them to focus on what they can do and eliminate negative self-talk. Help them see how they can break down whole tasks into a series of smaller chunks. Support them in finding and achieving some quick wins. Don't micromanage. Stay on the sidelines, but be there to support and guide. Give lots of praise and recognition as well as consistent feedback as they make progress. Do all you can to help them take control and do a great job.

9. **Expect others to completely go it alone? Intervene appropriately.** There are all sorts of obstacles that can get in the way of people making progress. Red tape, organizational politics, hierarchy, disagreements, being overloaded. Sometimes they'll be able to overcome the obstacles without your intervening and sometimes they won't. Don't let your people sink or swim by being too hands-off. Judge when it is appropriate to step in. Not sure how? Foster regular two-way communication with people. This will help you detect early warning signs of problems before they become serious. Ask them how they plan to clear the obstacle. If they have the resources, great—encourage them. If they don't and the obstacle is slowing down or impeding effectiveness, it's time for you to step in. Respond quickly. This may mean using your positional power to get what's needed from the organization, negotiating for resources, redistributing work. Let people know that you consider it your job to remove obstacles to performance and be available for troubleshooting.

Want to learn more? Take a deep dive...

Ashkenas, R. (2011, November 15). Why people micromanage. *Harvard Business Review Blog Network*.

Corley, J. (2012, April 20). *10 Ways to help employees feel less overwhelmed*. Business Management Daily.

Reh, F. J. (n.d.). *Employee coaching: When to step in*. About Management.

Wile, E. (n.d.). How to give orders to your employees. *Chron*.

10. **Giving too much or too little direction? Flex your approach.** Different people need and want different levels of direction. You can judge what's appropriate by understanding their current levels of capability and confidence. Think of people as broadly being in one of three categories. First, there are those who are highly capable of doing the task and confident in their ability. These are the people to delegate to. Overdirect these people and you'll stifle them. Second are those who are capable of doing the work but perhaps lack confidence in their ability. Provide more support. Give a little more direction on how to approach the task while encouraging them to come up with suggestions themselves. Ask questions to facilitate their thinking. Reinforce good suggestions. Third are the people who are highly motivated to do a great job but lack capability to do so independently. They come across as confident because they don't yet know what they don't know. These people need lots of direction. Without it, they are at risk of going off in the wrong direction, making unnecessary mistakes. Neglect to give these people direction and you set them up to fail. Talk to your people. Find out what they need, then give it to them.

11. **Playing favorites? Match people to work.** Be candid with yourself. Do you have a favored few people to whom you always assign work? People you trust with the important stuff? Or you don't really stop to consider—is this the best person for the job? Do you avoid working with people not like you or who make you uncomfortable? If so, you're unlikely to be treating people fairly or getting the most from them. Those you're excluding will become demotivated and those you favor will become overloaded. Either way, you're not distributing the work as effectively as you could be. Turn off your judgment program. Get to know people based on their level of skill, ability, and areas of expertise. Use what you know about them at this level to assign work. Balance the size and complexity of the task(s) with the

capability of the person. Include everyone in the process so you can be sure you get the best possible fit. Become a master at matching people to work.

12. **Things go off track when you're away? Empower others.** Give others enough information, direction, and authority to get work done in your absence. Who is acting as your deputy when you're unavailable? Who has decision-making authority? To what level? Where do people go for support? Make sure everyone involved in the work understands not only their individual responsibilities but also how they fit into the greater purpose. Edward Lawler (1992) suggests that an understanding of the organization's mission is critical for empowerment. The sense of meaning it creates enables people to align decisions with the goals and purpose of the organization. It keeps things on the right track. That people are pulling in the same direction. Work on creating a shared mindset—a climate that encourages team members to support each other while you're away. In the words of Lau Tzu, "When the best leader's work is done the people say, 'We did it ourselves.'"

Want to learn more? Take a deep dive...

Daum, K. (2013, September 30). 8 Tips for empowering employees. *Inc.*

Giang, V. (2013, October 10). *3 Ways to empower your employees to own their work*. Business Insider.

Reh, F. J. (n.d.). *Fairness is good management*. About Management.

Theriault, M. (2014, January 10). *Why managers shouldn't treat all employees the same*. Fox Business.

Job assignments

- Assemble and direct a team of diverse people to accomplish a difficult task. One where you can't go it alone and leveraging the skills of others is integral to success.

- Lead a group of people on a project that requires them to step up. Tap into their current skill and ability levels, then delegate responsibilities to stretch, challenge, build skill, and increase confidence.

- Offer to take over a failing project. Engage in real-time damage control, removing obstacles, negotiating for resources, redistributing work, etc., while keeping the team on task toward its goal.

- Manage a group of people who are towering experts and you are not. Give them a clear outcome, then stand back and allow them the freedom to perform. Let them take credit for success.

- Volunteer to manage a group of low-competence or low-performing people through a task they couldn't do by themselves.

Take time to reflect...

If you find it difficult to usher people to action...

...then make sure people understand what's important. Helping them see the goal will create energy and drive around achieving it. Using a "pull" strategy will likely be more effective than pushing others to act.

If letting go of control makes you nervous and tense...

...then consider that hanging onto it will hold you back. Letting go of the reins will be a huge step forward in getting more work done overall.

If you feel that your way is the only way to succeed...

...then open your mind to means untested. Directing work is more about providing focus and structure than dictating methods. Encourage ideas; stimulate commitment.

"Obstacles are those frightful things you see when you take your eyes off your goal. **"**

Henry Ford – American industrialist and founder of the Ford Motor Company

Learn more about Directs work

Baker, W. F., & O'Malley, M. (2008). *Leading with kindness: How good people consistently get superior results*. New York, NY: AMACOM.

Harvard Business School Press. (2006). *Leading teams: Expert solutions to everyday challenges*. Boston, MA: Harvard Business Review Press.

Harvard Business School Press. (2008). *Delegating work*. Boston, MA: Harvard Business Review Press.

Kurtzman, J. (2010). *Common purpose: How great leaders get organizations to achieve the extraordinary*. San Francisco, CA: Jossey-Bass.

Linsky, M., & Heifetz, R. A. (2002). *Leadership on the line: Staying alive through the dangers of leading*. Boston, MA: Harvard Business Review Press.

 Deep dive learning resource links

Ashkenas, R. (2011, November 15). Why people micromanage. *Harvard Business Review Blog Network*. Retrieved from http://blogs.hbr.org/2011/11/why-people-micromanage/

Chinn, D. (n.d.). How to motivate employees using E. A. Locke's goal-setting theory. *Chron*. Retrieved from http://smallbusiness.chron.com/motivate-employees-using-ea-lockes-goalsetting-theory-24176.html

Corley, J. (2012, April 20). *10 Ways to help employees feel less overwhelmed*. Business Management Daily. Retrieved from http://www.businessmanagementdaily.com/30433/10-ways-to-help-employees-feel-less-overwhelmed

Daum, K. (2013, September 30). 8 Tips for empowering employees. *Inc*. Retrieved from http://www.inc.com/kevin-daum/8-tips-for-empowering-employees.html

Giang, V. (2013, October 10). *3 Ways to empower your employees to own their work*. Business Insider. Retrieved from http://www.businessinsider.com/3-ways-to-empower-your-employees-2013-10

Mind Tools. (n.d.). *Successful delegation*. Mind Tools. Retrieved from http://www.mindtools.com/pages/article/newLDR_98.htm

Reh, F. J. (n.d.). *Employee coaching: When to step in*. About Management. Retrieved from http://management.about.com/od/coaching/a/coach_stepin905.htm

Reh, F. J. (n.d.). *Fairness is good management*. About Management.

Retrieved from http://management.about.com/od/
managementskills/a/Fairness-Is-Good-Management.htm

Saunders, E. G. (2012, October 30). Stop being a people-pleaser.
Harvard Business Review Blog Network. Retrieved from http://
blogs.hbr.org/2012/10/stop-being-a-people-pleaser/

Theriault, M. (2014, January 10). *Why managers shouldn't treat
all employees the same*. Fox Business. Retrieved from http://
smallbusiness.foxbusiness.com/legal-hr/2014/01/10/managers-
dont-treat-all-employees-same-way/

Wile, E. (n.d.). How to give orders to your employees. *Chron*.
Retrieved from http://smallbusiness.chron.com/give-orders-
employees-15942.html

Zwilling, M. (2013, October 2). How to delegate more effectively in
your business. *Forbes*. Retrieved from http://www.forbes.com
/sites/martinzwilling/2013/10/02/how-to-delegate-more-
effectively-in-your-business/

References

Lawler, E. E. (1992). *The ultimate advantage: Creating the high-
involvement organization*. San Francisco, CA: Jossey-Bass.

15

Recommended search terms

If you'd like to explore Directs work further, try searching online using
the following terms:

- Avoid overwhelming your employees.
- Delegating work effectively.
- Don't manage all employees the same way.
- Empowering your employees.
- Giving clear instructions to your employees.
- Lead others to lead themselves.

(i) More help...

Go to www.kornferry.com/fyi-resources and link directly to the deep
dive resources in this chapter. Visit the site often to see the additional
resources that are uploaded on a regular basis.

186 |

16. *Drives* engagement

Creating a climate where people are motivated to do their best to help the organization achieve its objectives.

Greater things can happen when people are engaged. Think of three accomplishments you're proud of, then ask yourself what was driving your engagement when you achieved them. If you can figure out what increases the engagement level of others and focus on building that, their accomplishments will be greater. Engaged employees are more productive because their work behavior is energized, focused, and more aligned to the needs of the organization. Retention rates are higher among engaged employees because they are challenged by their work in the context of a supportive environment with a caring, encouraging, and empowering boss. They feel appreciated, listened to, and supported. Multiple studies in a variety of industries have shown that increases in employee engagement result in improvements in profitability, quality, productivity, revenue, customer satisfaction, innovation, and retention. Engaged employees care about the right things—the things that best serve the organization. They view the organization's problems as their own. They take personal responsibility for the success of the organization and go the extra mile. But people are different. What triggers their engagement and keeps it high differs considerably. Engaging everyone takes a varied approach, so adapt to individuals. Find out what makes them tick so you can engage them and *keep* them engaged.

> **"** The simple act of paying positive attention to people has a great deal to do with productivity. **"**
>
> Tom Peters – American management consultant and author

***Drives* engagement** is in the **People** factor (III) in the Korn Ferry Leadership Architect™. It is part of Cluster I, **Influencing people,** along with Communicates effectively (7), Organizational savvy (23), Persuades (24), and *Drives* vision and purpose (37). You may find it helpful to also take a look at some of the tips included in those chapters to supplement your learning.

Skilled

Structures the work so it aligns with people's goals and motivators.

Empowers others.

Makes each person feel his/her contributions are important.

Invites input and shares ownership and visibility.

Shows a clear connection between people's motivators and the organizational goals.

Less skilled

- Has little insight into what motivates others.
- Doesn't give people enough flexibility and autonomy to do their work.
- Does little to create enthusiasm.
- Is unwilling to share ownership and give up control of assignments.

Talented

- Creates a positive and motivating working environment.
- Knows what motivates different people and aligns work accordingly.
- Gives others appropriate latitude to get work done.
- Invites input from others.
- Makes people feel that their contributions are visible and valued.

Overused skill

- May accommodate others' motivators at the expense of getting needed work done.
- May empower beyond people's capacity.
- May avoid giving constructive feedback if it could negatively impact engagement.

Some possible causes of lower skill

Causes help explain *why* a person may have trouble with *Drives engagement*. When seeking to increase skill, it's helpful to consider how these might play out in certain situations. And remember that all of these can be addressed if you are motivated to do so.

- Does not understand the importance of engagement.
- Believes everyone should be naturally engaged.
- Finds it difficult to relate to others with different preferences and drivers.
- Is unable to size people up.
- Fails to see the importance of strategic focus and clarity.
- Treats others unfairly or inequitably.
- Does not recognize others' efforts and contribution.
- Does not demonstrate trust in others.
- Avoids sharing information.
- Does not show an interest in others.
- Insecure about own contributions.
- Needs the spotlight.

Does it best

When it comes to engagement, William Rogers, CEO of British commercial radio operator UKRD Group, knows how to get it right. Rogers knows all 283 employees by name and makes a point of taking a personal interest in them. He has created an environment in which people never feel bored, they love their jobs, and feel proud to work for UKRD. With a mission "To change people's lives," UKRD is heavily involved in a variety of community projects, contributing to the confidence of 95% of employees that the organization is based on strong values. Six words guide the behaviors encouraged at UKRD: open, honest, fair, fun, professional, and unconventional. Staff operate with high levels of autonomy, unusual in local radio. They feel their ideas are always considered and encouraged. UKRD is not just a place where people turn up to work. They are emotionally invested in the organization. In 2009, UKRD acquired The Local Radio Company and within two years transformed it from losing £2.5m per annum to turning a profit in excess of £500,000. This

16

coincided with engagement levels helping UKRD to leap from being 27th in the Sunday Times 100 Best Companies to Work For poll in 2010 to number one in 2011. The organization has retained its top ranking for four consecutive years.[21, 22, 23, 24]

Tips to develop *Drives* engagement

1. **Not sharing the big picture? Nurture commitment to purpose and direction.** When people understand the organization beyond their own role, they can better appreciate the significance of what they do. They realize the importance of their cog in the wheel. Without that broader perspective, a job is just a job. They focus on their own role but not the overall goal it contributes to. It's the difference between "laying bricks and building a cathedral." Clearly communicate the strategy to them. Talk in their language. Help them see where their role fits in. How does what they deliver contribute to the achievement of the overall purpose of the organization? Use visuals that show their position in the structure. Let them see the connections that link them to the end user. Illustrate how their achievements impact other roles.

2. **Tend to be too directive? Make collaborative goal setting the norm.** Research shows that highly engaged employees are goal oriented. And disengaged team members are often unclear about what's expected of them. Shared goals benefit the organization because they get everyone on the same page and pulling in the same direction. Efforts are coordinated and aligned. Goals ensure clarity of purpose. They provide focus. They provide the basis for assessment of performance and enable more effective coaching. Collaborating with people to establish goals increases buy-in and motivation. Personal communication around goals fosters ownership and understanding. When people have a sense of personal accountability for achieving goals, engagement increases. Generally, they perform better with goals that can be realistically reached by putting forth significant effort. Stretch goals are especially helpful in pushing for new skills. Research shows that when goals are set appropriately and communicated clearly, engagement increases.

3. **Aware of roadblocks in the way? Remove barriers to success.** Constantly being stalled by things getting in the way of progress is frustrating. It's demotivating. When barriers present themselves, they slow things down. They create bottlenecks that stop things moving forward further down the line. People feel paralyzed by something that is often out of their control. Clear the way ahead. Be

relentless in identifying protected turf, sacred cows, bureaucratic processes, and resource constraints. Tear down walls built on "it's always been that way" foundations. Challenge thinking. Ask questions. Then ask some more. Come up with alternatives—and show the benefits.

Want to learn more? Take a deep dive...

Hill, L., & Lineback, K. (2011, June 28). Build your group into a true team. *Bloomberg Businessweek.*

Jackson, N. M. (2009, April 17). Team-building with a purpose. *Entrepreneur.*

4. **Not sure how people feel about things? Encourage them to open up.** Engaging others can be a challenge if you don't know what you're working with. If you want to make things better for people, you need to know the size of the gap you need to fill. Trouble is, people don't always want to talk about why they're disengaged. The trick is to find a way to encourage people to open up and lay their cards on the table. Let them know you'd like to help make things better for them. Ask questions, but be gentle. Be specific—ask them how they're feeling about something in particular rather than things in general. Don't rush them. Be patient. Listen attentively and actively. Use a survey to establish what people are happy about and what needs to improve. (Check with human resources to see how they can support you.) Take action to address issues that surface. In 2010, a UK police force did exactly this and in two years, sickness absences reduced by 25%—equivalent to 18,600 sick days. Financial savings? Nearly £1,500,000 (Robertson & Cooper, 2010).

16

5. **Not showing your appreciation? Recognize and reward other people's efforts.** It's hard to imagine anyone's level of engagement being increased by having their hard work and achievements ignored. People like to be recognized in very different ways, but get it right, and most people will feel good knowing they are appreciated. They'll feel proud that they have made a difference. It's hard to beat the value of spontaneous, in-the-moment, recognition. That moment of catching someone doing something well. A report, hot off the press, that compels you to compliment the author on their excellent recommendations. That innovative idea that you can tell its creator led to the rescue of a failing project. Look for opportunities to recognize achievement and give credit.

6. **All work and no play? Have some fun.** When the pressure is on and the pace is fast, it's easy to forget to relax, to let off steam, to breathe. There's a time and a place for everything and having a bit of fun is no exception. Free your spirit of adventure. Cast aside the serious business of work for a little while. Create the opportunity for people to get to know each other on a personal level. What do they have in common? How are they different? Who are they beyond their day job? What do they really care about? What makes them tick? All these things surface more readily when people step out of a role and become themselves. Learning about people means learning how to engage them. And fun is not just a frivolous waste of time if it helps increase people's engagement. When people are highly engaged, their commitment to achieve increases—the organization benefits. Research shows that companies with high employee engagement levels have 3.9 times the earnings per share when compared to those in the same industry with lower engagement levels (Arruda, 2013). It pays to have fun!

Want to learn more? Take a deep dive...

David, S. (2013, July 15). Disengaged employees? Do something about it. *Harvard Business Review Blog Network.*

Vorhauser-Smith, S. (2013, August 14). How the best places to work are nailing employee engagement. *Forbes.*

7. **Play your cards too close to your chest? Be transparent with people.** Information is power. Lack of information can be demotivating for people. If they feel you have a hidden agenda, they will draw up their own. Sometimes what they imagine is worse than the truth. If you have bad news, come clean as soon as you are able. Give them reasons (if you can) to help them understand. Ask for their help. Make decision-making processes as transparent and inclusive as possible. Of course, sometimes conditions and context restrict decisions to a small number of decision makers. You'll need to respect that, but share what you can and keep people informed. Anticipate their questions and answer those you can ahead of being asked. Make transparency your standard way of operating.

8. **Losing people and don't know why? Find out and fix it.** How often do people leave the team or the organization and you don't truly understand the reason? There will always be some departures you do not see coming and that cannot be avoided. But there are also people who leave whom you could have kept if only you'd known

they were unhappy. When people move on, they may not always be honest about why. Encourage them to share with you their reason for leaving: Great opportunity? Why is it better than the role they currently have? More prospects? What are they looking for that they don't currently see? More money? How much more? Better work environment? What's missing that's important to them? Learn from those who leave so you can keep those who are staying. Research shows that engaged employees are five times less likely to leave an organization (Arruda, 2013). Conduct exit interviews. Ask people to complete questionnaires. Welcome their feedback and use it to build engagement in others.

9. Live by "no news is good news"? Build a feedback-rich environment. In organizations that have created a culture steeped in candor and straight talk, giving and receiving feedback is as natural as breathing. Feedback is given frequently and usually in real time—during or immediately following performance. This helps people adjust what they're doing along the way and allows them to make midcourse corrections. Feedback, delivered correctly, shows people that what they're doing is important and you care enough to help them get it right. Supplement your feedback with coaching and mentoring to help people grow and progress. Encourage them to reciprocate by giving you feedback. Welcome it. Learn from it. Apply it appropriately. Be a feedback role model.

Want to learn more? Take a deep dive...

Huhman, H. R. (2013, January 23). *3 Essential rules to workplace honesty*. Business Insider.

Marks, S. (2013, May 8). *7 Ways to build trust in a team*. Recruiter.com.

16

10. Not engaged yourself? Get committed. It's hard to drive levels of engagement that are higher than your own. If you're lacking commitment, it shows in your face. It's apparent in the way you hold yourself. It affects your pace, your demeanor, even the way you communicate. If your "get up and go" has "got up and gone," people will see right through you. So get your own house in order. What's turning you off? Turn it back on. Lost interest? Figure out what will excite you again and get involved. Something niggling away at you? Confront it. Bring it out into the open and get it resolved. Frustrated? Talk to the person who can make a difference in the situation. Find your commitment again and bring people with you.

11. **Tend to see the gloomy side? Develop and project a can-do attitude.** If you look on the downside, before you know it, you're surrounded by people agreeing with your point of view. That's the bad news. The good news is that while negativity is infectious, so is positivity. But it needs to be sincere. If you feel downcast about something but try to sell the fact you feel great about it, people will see right through you. So get your own head in order first. If you're disengaged about something, what's causing you to feel that way? What don't you understand? Find out who has more information. Don't see how something can be done? Talk to those who do. Been there, done it, and it failed? Find out what's different this time. Once you believe in it, you can bring others on board too.

Want to learn more? Take a deep dive...

Biro, M. M. (2012, October 14). Your employees are engaged... REALLY? *Forbes*.

Roth, T. (2013, January 18). Engagement starts with your leaders. *Training Magazine*.

---

12. **Not getting the most out of people? Show confidence in their abilities by empowering them.** The proverb gets it right: Give a person a fish and they will eat for a day. Teach a person to fish and they will eat for a lifetime. The trick with empowerment is framing it so it's not interpreted as, "Fantastic...more work to do at the same salary." The team member who truly experiences the positive effects of empowerment (1) believes they can accomplish the task, (2) believes the task will result in a positive outcome (i.e., it will work), and (3) believes that the extra responsibilities that come along with the task are personally "worth it." When empowering others, focus on developing and cultivating the three elements above. If any of the three are missing, the person is not ready to take ownership of something by themselves.

13. **Known for being a tough taskmaster? Remove the fear of failure.** Failures are going to occur—the very thought of failure, however, can be crippling to many individuals. Frame failure as an expected part of the larger picture of progress. We tend to learn more from our failures than our successes—innovation and experimentation will be best realized if people are allowed to fail. They won't feel comfortable with short-term setbacks if you do not communicate that such setbacks are expected and provide long-term benefits. Share a failure that you experienced and what you learned/how you

overcame the failure. You will be more respected if you open up and disclose failures as well as successes, and hopefully others will learn from the lessons learned in your failures. An important component in disclosing personal setbacks is communicating how those setbacks were ultimately overcome or otherwise ended in a positive way (e.g., "We ended up losing that client, but the lessons learned allowed us to land our next big client.").

14. **Tend to treat everyone the same? Deal with people fairly, but not equally.** Equal is not fair. Fair is what's appropriate, what's fitting. Individuals and teams vary in capabilities, motivation, interests, contribution, and many other dimensions. It follows, then, that to be fair about it, they should be treated differently. Different levels of support. Different development. Different rewards. Different, but fair. Preventing problems depends on decisions being made in an informed and carefully calculated way, with the best intentions in mind for the organization and for individuals. Those intentions should be out in the open and clearly communicated. When one project team learns it is not getting the same level of resources that another is, it's tough to swallow if the intentions are concealed or suspect. On the other hand, the straightforward disclosure of intentions behind the decision makes it more acceptable. Even if the shortchanged team disagrees with the decision, they will appreciate understanding the intent behind it. And trust in the leadership will be preserved, even strengthened.

Want to learn more? Take a deep dive...

Anderson, A. R. (2013, April 17). Good employees make mistakes. Great leaders allow them to. *Forbes.*

Goldsmith, M. (2010, April 23). Empowering your employees to empower themselves. *Harvard Business Review Blog Network.*

16

Job assignments

- Pull together a creative-thinking group, inviting people from all functions, at all levels, to share their ideas on overcoming key business challenges.

- Volunteer to lead a group through a change where there is a high level of resistance. Take time to understand what's causing people to feel as they do about the change and help them work through it.

- Lead an engagement task force to identify what needs to be done to increase levels of engagement across the organization. Report findings and recommendations back to senior management.

- Take on a failing project and rally a team to turn it around. Involve everyone fully in generating ideas for making the project a success and give them accountability.

- Identify the number one barrier to success across the organization. Present a proposal to senior management on what must be done to eliminate the barrier.

Take time to reflect...

If you're self-motivated, pumped, and raring to go...

> ...then recognize that everyone might not be. What engages one may disengage another. Take time to find out what makes people tick.

If you demand great results and give nothing back...

> ...then be aware that burnout could be just around the corner. Even those most committed to their work need some recognition and stimulation to keep them going.

If you think you've "done" engagement and have checked it off your list...

> ....then remember that engagement is not a "once and done." It can take a long time to build and seconds to crumble. Keeping it strong requires constant maintenance and repair work.

16

" *Speaking roughly, by leadership we mean the art of getting someone else to do something that you want done because he wants to do it.* **"**

Dwight D. Eisenhower – World War II Allied Commander
and 34th President of the United States

196 |

Learn more about *Drives* engagement

Boverie, P., & Kroth, M. (2001). *Transforming work: The five keys to achieving trust, commitment & passion in the workplace.* Cambridge, MA: Perseus Publishing.

Covey, S. M. R. (2006). *The speed of trust: The one thing that changes everything.* New York, NY: Free Press.

Katz, J. H., & Miller, F. A. (2013). *Opening doors to teamwork and collaboration: 4 Keys that change everything.* San Francisco, CA: Berrett-Koehler Publishers.

Loehr, J., & Schwartz, T. (2003). *The power of full engagement: Managing energy, not time, is the key to high performance and personal renewal.* New York, NY: Free Press.

Thomas, K. W. (2009). *Intrinsic motivation at work. What really drives employee engagement* (2nd ed.). San Francisco, CA: Berrett-Koehler Publishers.

 Deep dive learning resource links

Anderson, A. R. (2013, April 17). Good employees make mistakes. Great leaders allow them to. *Forbes.* Retrieved from http://www.forbes.com/sites/amyanderson/2013/04/17/good-employees-make-mistakes-great-leaders-allow-them-to/

Biro, M. M. (2012, October 14). Your employees are engaged... REALLY? *Forbes.* Retrieved from http://www.forbes.com/sites/meghanbiro/2012/10/14/your-employees-are-engaged-really/

David, S. (2013, July 15). Disengaged employees? Do something about it. *Harvard Business Review Blog Network.* Retrieved from http://blogs.hbr.org/2013/07/disengaged-employees-do-someth/

Goldsmith, M. (2010, April 23). Empowering your employees to empower themselves. *Harvard Business Review Blog Network.* Retrieved from http://blogs.hbr.org/2010/04/empowering-your-employees-to-e/

Hill, L., & Lineback, K. (2011, June 28). Build your group into a true team. *Bloomberg Businessweek.* Retrieved from http://www.businessweek.com/management/build-your-group-into-a-true-team-06282011.html

Huhman, H. R. (2013, January 23). 3 *Essential rules to workplace honesty.* Business Insider. Retrieved from http://www.businessinsider.com/3-essential-rules-to-workplace-honesty-2013-1

16

Jackson, N. M. (2009, April 17). Team-building with a purpose. *Entrepreneur*. Retrieved from http://www.entrepreneur.com/article/201322

Marks, S. (2013, May 8). *7 Ways to build trust in a team*. Recruiter.com. Retrieved from http://www.recruiter.com/i/7-ways-to-build-trust-in-a-team/

Roth, T. (2013, January 18). Engagement starts with your leaders. *Training Magazine*. Retrieved from http://www.trainingmag.com/content/engagement-starts-your-leaders

Vorhauser-Smith, S. (2013, August 14). How the best places to work are nailing employee engagement. *Forbes*. Retrieved from http://www.forbes.com/sites/sylviavorhausersmith/2013/08/14/how-the-best-places-to-work-are-nailing-employee-engagement/

References

Arruda, W. (2013, October, 8). Three steps for transforming employees into brand ambassadors. *Forbes*. Retrieved from http://www.forbes.com/sites/williamarruda/2013/10/08/three-steps-for-transforming-employees-into-brand-ambassadors/

Robertson, I. T., & Cooper, C. L. (2010). Full engagement: The integration of employee engagement and psychological well-being. *Leadership & Organization, 31*(4), 324–336.

Recommended search terms

If you'd like to explore *Drives* engagement further, try searching online using the following terms:

- Allowing employees to fail.
- Allowing an open dialogue on a team.
- Building team trust.
- Creating a shared purpose on a team.
- Empowering employees.

(i) More help...

Go to www.kornferry.com/fyi-resources and link directly to the deep dive resources in this chapter. Visit the site often to see the additional resources that are uploaded on a regular basis.

198 |

17. Financial acumen

Interpreting and applying understanding of key financial indicators to make better business decisions.

Finance is about how organizations generate, preserve, account for, spend, manage, and move money. Every organization needs to be concerned with its financial health. Failure to keep a laser focus on financial matters will ultimately doom most any enterprise. Every part of an organization, whether for profit or not, is impacted directly or indirectly by financial results. Finance is at the core of business activities. It affects how an organization raises capital, analyzes and values investments, develops and executes plans, pays for improvements, and pays its taxes. As central and important as finance is, studies show it is not well understood outside of the specific domains of finance, accounting, and audit functions. You don't need to be a finance expert, but you do need acumen on the fundamentals, at minimum. People at all levels need to understand the financial information that is relevant to them so that they can act on it. To be successful as a leader, you need to not only understand finance, but also know how to incorporate a financial thinking lens into every major decision you make.

> " *'Know your numbers' is a fundamental precept of business.* "
>
> Bill Gates – American businessman and philanthropist

Financial acumen is in the **Thought** factor (I) in the Korn Ferry Leadership Architect™. It is part of Cluster A, **Understanding the business,** along with Business insight (5), Customer focus (11), and Tech savvy (35). You may find it helpful to also take a look at some of the tips included in those chapters to supplement your learning.

Skilled

Understands the meaning and implications of key financial indicators.

Uses financial analysis to generate, evaluate, and act on strategic options and opportunities.

Integrates quantitative and qualitative information to draw accurate conclusions.

Less skilled

- Is unfamiliar with financial terms.

- Is unclear about the cause-and-effect relationships among different business functions and overall financial performance.

- Pays little attention to financial impact when drawing conclusions.

Talented

- Transforms financial information into business intelligence through analysis and integration of quantitative and qualitative information.

- Identifies and monitors key financial indicators to gauge performance, identify trends, and suggest strategies that can impact results.

Overused skill

- Uses financial indicators as the only decision criteria, leading to an unbalanced view of organizational performance that is narrowly focused on financial outcomes.

- May sacrifice long-term business objectives for short-term financial gains.

Some possible causes of lower skill

Causes help explain *why* a person may have trouble with Financial acumen. When seeking to increase skill, it's helpful to consider how these might play out in certain situations. And remember that all of these can be addressed if you are motivated to do so.

- Overwhelmed by data.
- Not curious.
- Ignores financial information.
- Doesn't think strategically.
- Lacks basic financial skills.
- Unaware of how finance drives the business.
- Makes emotional decisions.
- Leaves finance to others.
- Doesn't dig for root causes.

(?) **Did you know?**

Developing financial acumen early in your career works in your favor, especially if your goal is to attain the top job at an organization. Roughly 30% of Fortune 500 CEOs spent the first few years of their careers developing a strong foundation in finance. But that doesn't mean financial acumen alone will get you to the head of the table. Of those Fortune 500 CEOs who started early in finance, only 5% were promoted directly from CFO positions. Most of them came from broader COO or president positions. So, the message? Build your financial acumen early. Keep developing it. Combine it with a broader working knowledge of the business. Breadth of knowledge and experience built on a solid financial foundation could be your ticket to the top.[25, 26]

17

Tips to develop Financial acumen

1. **Don't know the basics? Get training.** Finance can feel like a strange terrain where people speak a foreign tongue. According to a 2009 article in *Harvard Business Review*, a sample of US managers scored an average of 38% on a test of financial literacy. Most didn't know the difference between "profit" and "cash." Or between an income statement and a balance sheet. Two-thirds did not understand that discounting prices affects gross margins. Financial information is critical to your decisions. So if you're at a loss, learn what you need to know. Get an explanation of basic techniques and the language of financial analysis. Trends. Benchmarks. Common size. Percentage change. Ask an analyst to explain the business models and tools used in your organization. What do they measure and why? Where does the data come from? What else do we need to know? Find out how an auditor looks at your operations. Learn to use budgeting and planning software. Find a book or search online to become familiar with terms like Economic Value Added (EVA) or value-based management. Assemble a study group or ask if your organization or a local college provides training in the basics of finance. A course like Basics of Budget Management or Finance for Non-Financial Managers can be invaluable in helping you think about the business in the right way.

2. **Think finance is not your responsibility? Get involved.** It's easy to consider finance the responsibility of the CFO and strategic thinking something that happens only in the C-suite. If you're more junior, you might not think much about how your decisions affect the overall organization. If you lead a function like human resources or marketing, you might tune out when financial questions are raised. But it is in everyone's interest to include cost, investment, and other financial considerations in decisions. Regardless of which department you're in, you can't be an effective strategic partner without demonstrating a solid understanding of finance. Apply your own function's lens to financial matters. In human resources, how do staffing considerations, retirement benefits, or health care costs affect the bottom line? If you are in engineering, what is the financial contribution of better design or processes? In product or service development, how do economies of scale affect pricing and profitability? Even in a non-profit, costs, funding, and the economic benefit of best practices are critical factors for success. Challenge your own thinking as well as others'. Ask questions. Explore "what if" scenarios. Work with analysts to run financial models. Find ways to constantly upgrade your skills and thinking.

3. **Focus too narrow? Expand your perspective.** Do you lead a business unit, manufacturing facility, or other operational unit? In charge of a

functional group such as IT, legal, or distribution? If so, you may focus your financial leadership solely on your department or operation. Step outside of your silo and consider the wider picture. Get a full perspective of how your unit contributes to the whole. Understand how the business works—how it functions within its industry. Start by subscribing to great publications such as the *Wall Street Journal, Fortune, Inc., Barron's,* the *Economist, Harvard Business Review*. Scan them regularly for events and trends that affect your business now. Sign up on sites like Hoover's, LinkedIn, or Dun & Bradstreet to receive updates on companies you want to follow. Read annual reports and business blogs. Download business/industry/future-oriented articles on your tablet to read when you are traveling. Join or form an executive networking group. Get their take on the economy and what is happening in their industries. Talk to other executives. Engage your CEO or CFO in a broad conversation about the business. Build out your sources of information so that you have a pulse on the different levers that drive business. Challenge yourself to explore a new idea every month.

4. **Emotional about decisions? Ground yourself in data.** Depending on the issue, you may feel very strongly about the outcome. Or maybe there is a great deal at stake and the wrong decision could have serious consequences. Emotions fuel our passion. They provide energy for decisions. But we can't operate on emotion alone. Numbers aren't everything but they are a good way to stay grounded when tough decisions are needed. Acknowledge feelings, then turn to the numbers. Pull together a team to share the decision making. Get your CFO or financial analyst involved. Ask: What can good financial modeling tell us about the future? What does accounting tell us about the past? What is at risk? Based on these facts, how do we make the best decision—now—to assure the long-term prosperity of the organization? Make your decision only after you consider all sides of the equation.

Want to learn more? Take a deep dive...

Berman, K., & Knight, J. (2009, October 7). The dismal financial IQ of US managers. *Harvard Business Review Blog Network*.

Campbell, D. H. (2011, July 26). Financial literacy is every business's responsibility. *Forbes*.

Mind Tools. (n.d.). *Understanding accounts: Basic finance for non-financial managers*. Mind Tools.

Schulman, N. H. (2013, March). *Use your financial data to make business decisions*. Citibank.

17

| 203

5. **Overwhelmed by data? Select and focus on a few key metrics.** Finance deals with all aspects of the organization—revenues, costs, taxes, losses, profits, market projections, investment analysis. It provides historical data. Forecasts and projections. Accounting for cost control. Analysis to understand customer trends. It deals with macroeconomics and specific quarterly variables. To make wise financial decisions, you need to start with good information. Data to create a credible picture that you can act on. Look for three to five key metrics you can use as the bellwether data point for your planning and decision making. What is the key factor that will drive the situation? What numbers provide a green light or signal caution? Bring the data into context. Is the organization focused on reducing expenses? Expanding service? Supporting growth? Are you concerned about financial outcomes compared to forecasts? Run your numbers past some colleagues—especially in finance—and ask if they agree with your assumptions. Understanding how these numbers promote or hinder future financial performance will allow you to make strong strategic and tactical decisions.

6. **Make spending decisions? Proceed wisely.** Whether you're developing a five-figure project budget or just submitting an expense report, it's easy to lose perspective on the money. You may see yourself in a tug of war to secure resources. You may feel constrained by controls that you don't agree with. Wise spending balances short-term needs with long-term effects. If you're writing a budget, understand the full picture, then drill down into the details. Look for savings in equipment, travel, or staff that can be more wisely spent in another area. Set policies that meet goals while protecting funds. Review expense reports to keep expenditures under control. Review vendor contracts for savings opportunities. Renegotiate whenever you can. Talk to peers about what they are doing to support the business while reining in costs. Talk with your purchasing department about other ideas to reduce costs. Some spending is pure cost and should be eliminated. Some is a necessary price of doing business. Other spending is an investment in morale, learning, or productivity and should be well funded and wisely managed. Build buy-in and compliance by sharing the decision-making process with the team. While certain details of the budget are confidential, the team will benefit from knowing how expenditures are allocated. Share the decisions. Give your team some budget parameters; pass some discretionary power for budgeting and spending down to them. Treat the organization's money as your own.

204 |

7. **Need to write a forecast? Look beyond existing data.** Accounting data primarily tells us what has occurred to date. But sometimes you need to leap into the future to make a recommendation. Decisions to invest in products, to add to or cut staff, to buy or divest a business—all require you to make educated guesses about the future. To forecast the future, use grounded processes. Create best-case and worst-case scenarios. Look at three years of data to spot trends that might continue. Look inside and outside the organization—what could alter prevailing trends? Share your assumptions with a few colleagues. Ask them to challenge your thinking. Recognize that there is no crystal ball. Financial projections are developed from solid knowledge of how the business operates and a willingness to identify extraneous factors that may impact the business in the near future. At its best, a forecast is an educated guess about what the future will hold based on current conditions and sometimes-hazy projections. But it is an essential tool for planning spending, borrowing, and investment decisions.

8. **Presenting financial information? Tailor your message to the audience.** At any level of the organization, you may be asked to present financial information. This could be part of budget planning, capital purchasing, or reporting on final fiscal results. You need to consider your audience in planning both the content and your approach. First, find a key metric and use consistent messaging. What is most relevant to this group? If you regularly communicate financial results, find key performance metrics that you can use as the bellwether data point for others to cue in on. Second, if the data suggests certain actions need to be taken—such as cutting costs, raising pricing, etc. let the audience know. Then use the data to support your recommendation. Third, use visuals effectively. Present information in a way that others can see and comprehend quickly. Columns of grey print are a good way to bury information. Great graphics help you tell a story and illuminate trends. Study annual reports and other financials for formats that are easy to use and comprehend. Fourth, be concise. Don't drown the audience or reader—only include what's essential to understanding your message. Put additional data in an appendix for those who want it. Finally, be careful what you share. There can be serious compliance implications for insider data that seeps into the marketplace. Know your audience and make sure that you present only the data that they need in order to hear your message.

17

Want to learn more? Take a deep dive...

Ashe-Edmunds, S. (n.d.). Budget forecasting techniques. *Chron*.

Black, T. (2010, September 27). 12 Best tools for budgeting. *Inc*.

Hannabarger, C., Buchman, F., & Economy, P. (n.d.). *Presenting financial reports: Turning numbers into information*. For Dummies: A Wiley Brand.

Tjan, A. K. (2009, June 8). The fallacy of financial metrics. *Harvard Business Review Blog Network*.

9. **Want to improve operations? Understand audit.** While perhaps not the most glamorous of functions, audit serves a valuable purpose in any organization. By auditing the different facets of the operation, important information surfaces—both on what's going right and what needs fixing. Auditing helps organizations to minimize risk. Increase efficiency. Eliminate waste. Save resources. Avoid legal or regulatory trouble. And because they examine operating procedures in a detailed way, they provide an invaluable look at how the organization functions—from the inside out. So if you are new to the organization, or you want to make real improvements that will change the bottom line, or you just want to know more about how things happen, get to know your auditor or audit team. Study the reports they generate. Look for improvements you can make. If any area is of particular concern, consider requesting a special audit. Studies show that when you define the problem, action follows. Good audit information is a spur to decision making and improvement.

10. **Disappointed by results? Study data to make course corrections.** Organizations start the fiscal year with great intentions. They produce forecasts and annual operating plans. Create budgets to predict and control spending. Build marketing, sales, and staffing plans to drive growth. In a perfect world, results would roll in as predicted. But variances are a reality. Costs exceed budgets. Sales lag expectations. Investments fail to deliver as planned. You may not want to see these numbers, but they highlight areas for improvement. Delve into this information. Get access to monthly and quarterly reports and dig into the data. Where are variances occurring? How serious are they? What are the causes? What is the impact? Sales lagging? Could be due to a flaw in the pricing or marketing strategy. Costs too high? Could be external market conditions like rising labor rates or unforeseen developments affecting the commodities market. What can you change or control to bring results back in line

with projections? One large manufacturer studied how to better predict markets. They discovered that their own six-month leading sales number was the best predictor for economic forecasting. This insight allowed them to make the right staffing and production decisions to meet demand and stay in front of market changes. Get your team together to discuss what is happening. Mine the data for insight. Focus on underlying causes and make corrections.

11. **Obsessed with meeting goals? See the bigger picture.** Yes, goals are important. You want to realize a return. Build value. Turn in results. But to get the full picture, you need to look beyond the numbers to the bigger picture. Financial results are vital signposts and ways of measuring progress, not the ultimate reason the organization exists. If you are overly focused on hitting a number, you may miss something else important. You could control costs but strangle growth. Maintain a tight budget and miss an investment opportunity. When you're setting a financial goal, ask yourself why it is important. Consider what is at stake and what it will mean if you achieve that goal or fall short. Consider both qualitative and quantitative information about the business. Think long-term as well as short-term. Use financial goals as one measure—but not the only measure—of how you define success.

Want to learn more? Take a deep dive...

Lavinsky, D. (2013, June 12). Numbers you need to know to grow your business. *Entrepreneur.*

Loth, R. (2011, April 1). *12 Things you need to know about financial statements*. Investopedia.

Seach, P. (n.d.). *Learn the basics: Auditing 101*. New York State Society of CPAs.

U.S. Securities and Exchange Commission. (2007, February 5). *Beginners' guide to financial statements*. U.S. Securities and Exchange Commission.

17

Job assignments

• Work with an analyst to create a financial justification for the major purchase of equipment, materials, program, or system for your organization.

• Join an audit team examining your operations and present its findings and recommendations to your team. Anticipate the questions that are likely to come up and ensure you're equipped to answer them.

- Create an online financial skills training course for new employees. Teaching someone else can be a great way to embed your own learning.

- Attend a meeting of the finance committee of your organization's board and summarize the main issues on the agenda. Ask for input from a member of the committee following the meeting to help clarify anything you're unsure about.

- Lead your team in creating an annual budget, with full justification for all spending decisions. Build a robust business case and be prepared to talk through it.

Take time to reflect...

If finance seems like a foreign language to you...

> ...then find a good translator. Develop an ear for the language of finance. Become familiar with the interplay of figures and metrics. Learn what the numbers are saying and let them guide you.

If you're used to making decisions without considering the bottom line...

> ...then realize the risks you're taking. Making bold moves without studying the facts and implications is like a doctor treating patients without reading their lab results.

If you think understanding finance doesn't relate to you or your work...

> ...then start close to home and work outwards. Understanding your own team's contribution first will help you see the data in context. It will make the broader financial landscape more relevant and more interesting.

17

"*Money is a tool.*
Used properly it makes something beautiful –
used wrong, it makes a mess! **"**

Bradley Vinson – American financial educator and author

Learn more about Financial acumen

Berman, K., Case, J., & Knight, J. (2006). *Financial intelligence: A manager's guide to knowing what the numbers really mean.* Boston, MA: Harvard Business School Publishing.

Lambert, R. A. (2012). *Financial literacy for managers: Finance and accounting for better decision-making.* Philadelphia, PA: Wharton Digital Press.

Matias, A. J. (2012). *Budgeting and forecasting: The quick reference handbook.* Cambridge, MA: Matias & Associates.

Taillard, M. (2013). *Corporate finance for dummies.* Hoboken, NJ: John Wiley and Sons.

Wyatt, N. (2012). *The Financial Times essential guide to budgeting and forecasting: How to deliver accurate numbers.* Upper Saddle River, NJ: FT Press.

 Deep dive learning resource links

Ashe-Edmunds, S. (n.d.). Budget forecasting techniques. *Chron.* Retrieved from http://smallbusiness.chron.com/budget-forecasting-techniques-41843.html

Berman, K., & Knight, J. (2009, October 7). The dismal financial IQ of US managers. *Harvard Business Review Blog Network.* Retrieved from http://blogs.hbr.org/2009/10/us-managers-a-dismal-financial/

Black, T. (2010, September 27). 12 Best tools for budgeting. *Inc.* Retrieved from http://www.inc.com/guides/2010/09/12-best-tools-for-budgeting.html

Campbell, D. H. (2011, July 26). Financial literacy is every business's responsibility. *Forbes.* Retrieved from http://www.forbes.com/sites/forbesleadershipforum/2011/07/26/financial-literacy-is-every-businesss-responsibility/

Hannabarger, C., Buchman, F., & Economy, P. (n.d.). *Presenting financial reports: Turning numbers into information.* For Dummies: A Wiley Brand. Retrieved from http://www.dummies.com/how-to/content/presenting-financial-reports-turning-numbers-into-.html

Lavinsky, D. (2013, June 12). Numbers you need to know to grow your business. *Entrepreneur.* Retrieved from http://www.entrepreneur.com/article/226972

Loth, R. (2011, April 1). *12 Things you need to know about financial statements.* Investopedia. Retrieved from http://www.investopedia.com/articles/basics/06/financialreporting.asp

17

Mind Tools. (n.d.). *Understanding accounts: Basic finance for non-financial managers*. Mind Tools. Retrieved from http://www.mindtools.com/pages/article/newCDV_45.htm

Schulman, N. H. (2013, March). *Use your financial data to make business decisions*. Citibank. Retrieved from https://online.citibank.com/US/JRS/pands/detail.do?ID=CitiBizArticleFinancialDecisions

Seach, P. (n.d.). *Learn the basics: Auditing 101*. New York State Society of CPAs. Retrieved from http://www.nysscpa.org/sound_advice/basics.htm

Tjan, A. K. (2009, June 8). The fallacy of financial metrics. *Harvard Business Review Blog Network*. Retrieved from http://blogs.hbr.org/2009/06/the-fallacy-of-financial-metri/

U.S. Securities and Exchange Commission. (2007, February 5). *Beginners' guide to financial statements*. U.S. Securities and Exchange Commission. Retrieved from http://www.sec.gov/investor/pubs/begfinstmtguide.htm

Recommended search terms

If you'd like to explore Financial acumen further, try searching online using the following terms:

- Budgeting and forecasting.
- Economic value added.
- Financial auditing.
- Financial literacy.
- Understanding business finance.
- Value added management.

 More help...

Go to www.kornferry.com/fyi-resources and link directly to the deep dive resources in this chapter. Visit the site often to see the additional resources that are uploaded on a regular basis.

18. Global perspective

Taking a broad view when approaching issues, using a global lens.

Working in a global context is a likely permanent reality today, regardless of your home base. Whether it's managing cross-boundary business implications or collaborating with people of different cultural backgrounds in your own backyard, the work world is becoming more broad and more diverse. In the 21st century, having a global perspective is about more than geographic reach. Cultivating a broad, global perspective today starts with curiosity. Curiosity about people, events, problems, ideas, history, and the future. And it doesn't spring up overnight. It's developed over time. Through varied experiences. Exposure to a diverse set of international topics. Building relationships with people from different cultures and countries. Having a broad, global perspective is like viewing the world around you in wide-screen—you take in more and gain more resources to draw upon when tackling complex issues or scouting for opportunities. More chances to make unique connections that form into new ideas and strategies. Fresh solutions come more from a prepared mind than from raw intelligence or creativity. So start preparing. Zoom out and begin using a global lens.

" A man's feet must be planted in his country, but his eyes should survey the world. "

George Santayana – Spanish philosopher and writer

Global perspective is in the **Thought** factor (I) in the Korn Ferry Leadership Architect™. It is part of Cluster C, **Creating the new and different,** along with *Cultivates* innovation (19) and Strategic mindset (33). You may find it helpful to also take a look at some of the tips included in those chapters to supplement your learning.

Skilled

Looks toward the broadest possible view of an issue or challenge.

Thinks and talks in global terms.

Understands the position of the organization within a global context.

Knows the impact of global trends on the organization.

Less skilled

- Is narrow in thinking when solving problems.

- Seldom comes up with multiple options or scenarios when addressing global issues.

- Maintains a home region or local-only perspective.

- Focuses on the here and now; shows little interest in the future or global issues.

Talented

- Considers multiple and varied viewpoints when addressing problems and opportunities.

- Thinks globally; excels at viewing issues on a worldwide basis.

- Develops scenarios to deal with the global uncertainties the organization faces.

Overused skill

- Has a tendency to overreach or to call upon experience that doesn't apply to the current situation.

- Minimizes local needs, overemphasizing global issues.

- Pushes for opportunities on a global scale that the organization is not prepared for.

18

Some possible causes of lower skill

Causes help explain *why* a person may have trouble with Global perspective. When seeking to increase skill, it's helpful to consider how these might play out in certain situations. And remember that all of these can be addressed if you are motivated to do so.

- Low curiosity.
- Narrow upbringing.
- Limited global experience.
- Comfortable with what already is.
- Short-term thinker.
- Rigid ideas and beliefs.
- Believes own group or culture is better than others.
- Highly localized expertise.
- Unaware of own cultural biases.

Does it best

Lalit Ahuja, managing director and president of Target India, part of Target Corporation, had a global mindset from the very beginning of his career. He started out as an international manager setting up Indian operations for LG Electronics and News Corporation. When he was hired by Target to establish a second corporate headquarters in India, his strategy was influenced by his global perspective. Instead of immediately diving in to establish the Indian operation, Ahuja decided to spend his first six months at Target's US headquarters in Minneapolis, Minnesota. He knew his success in India would depend on fully understanding the organization's unique corporate culture. This meant gaining an appreciation of the Midwest American culture in which Target was founded before he applied this to the Indian context. He also knew his global reach needed to be expanded through building his network and influence internationally across Target Corporation. And Ahuja didn't stop there. Recognizing the importance of developing global perspective in his managers, he established an international exchange program—a key initiative in developing people to succeed in this increasingly global enterprise.[27]

18

|

Tips to develop Global perspective

1. **Narrow expertise? Learn broader aspects of your organization and industry.** Be a sponge for knowledge about your business, customers, and competitors around the globe. Study your company's various financial reports and dive into your intranet to learn about your offerings, alliances, and structure. Have someone explain the strategic plan—how is the organization addressing market forces like globalization, changing demographics, world financial uncertainties? Does your firm differentiate through customer intimacy, innovation, operational excellence? How is technology driving change? Is your company leading or lagging in emerging markets? Be sure you grasp the mission-critical functions and capabilities the organization needs to be on the leading edge. What resources is it investing in around innovation, infrastructure, talent? Talk with counterparts in other regions and functions of the organization and tell each other what you do. If you don't know much about customers, listen in on customer calls or shadow someone in sales. If you don't know what engineering does, go find out. Seek the broadest possible exposure inside the organization and then put your expanded outlook to work.

2. **Limited exposure? Read and watch broadly.** Read publications with global coverage like *Commentary,* the *Economist, Monocle,* or the *International New York Times*. Learn to connect what's out there to your own situation. Check out "we present all sides" journals like the *Atlantic* to get the broadest possible view. Keep a log of ideas you get from each. Delve into the backgrounds of leaders such as Brazilian-Lebanese-French businessman Carlos Ghosn. Why him? He runs successful auto firms on two continents and is well regarded for his cross-cultural management style. Learn about other cultures through films or compilations such as *Latino Boom: An Anthology of US Latino Literature* or *The Norton Anthology of African American Literature*. Pick a country and study it. Explore world events through the perspectives of other cultures. What's the Russian view of the Middle East? What drives the Japanese economy? Study history, learning from inventors and trailblazers from the past. You're likely to find common underlying principles that you can apply to what you're doing today and tomorrow.

3. **Don't know what's coming next? Be a global trend watcher.** Organizations don't want you to just manage in the moment—they expect you to anticipate and lead into the future. Tap into future-focused resources such as the World Future Society, Institute for the Future, or Faith Popcorn's TrendBank. Join the Future Trends group

in LinkedIn or go to events sponsored by the Institute for International Research. These groups and others like them raise questions such as what will be the global impact of projected talent shortages? How will personalized medicine change the way health care is provided? How might shifting demographics or economic patterns affect buying decisions? What does it mean that by 2020, 70% of global market growth is expected to come from emerging markets? Will excessive pollution curtail manufacturing in some urban zones? How will big data and nanotechnology alter things? Immigration? Extreme weather events? Become a student of global trends and leverage the insights to inform your decisions and strategy. Always keep one eye toward the horizon.

Want to learn more? Take a deep dive...

Beinhocker, E., Davis, I., & Mendonca, L. (2013). The 10 trends you have to watch. *Harvard Business Review*.

Edin, P., Lingqvist, O., & Tamsons, A. (2012, July 26). The best sales leaders are trend hunters. *Harvard Business Review Blog Network*.

Rubin, J. (2013, June 19). Top recruiter to CIOs: Time to broaden your background and show some charisma. *Forbes*.

4. **Personal biases blocking your ability to think globally? Explore your own beliefs and biases.** Just as it would be hard for a fish to understand the concept of water—because it has always lived in it—it's not always easy to see the confines of one's own perspectives. People grow up in a given culture and accept this as the natural (and possibly superior) way. The Hopi Indians in the southwestern United States have one word for snow. The Inuit of Alaska, on the other hand, have many different words for snow that reflect the many ways their lives interact with snow. A Hopi couldn't survive very well in Alaska with just one snow concept. How might your experience unwittingly influence or limit your take on things? Notice how your closely held beliefs affect the way you make decisions, engage people, or contribute to the workplace. How do they color what you expect from others? Practice challenging your biases. Think outside your normal parameters when you're working on projects that would benefit from a different or wider angle.

18

5. **Spend most of your time with like-minded people? Connect with diverse individuals.** Spend time socially or at work functions with those who are broad in viewpoint and diverse in background. Make

it a point to discover new information and exchange ideas. Volunteer to work with people you haven't had much one-to-one conversation with—senior citizens, the disabled, at-risk youth, immigrants. Host a foreign exchange student for a semester. Build empathy and mutual understanding with people not just like you. On the work front, assemble a team of people of varying perspectives and backgrounds for an important project. Studies show that teams of people with the widest diversity of backgrounds produce the most innovative solutions to problems. Go broad with people to help analyze and make sense of issues.

6. **Stick to the known when traveling abroad? Expand your horizons.** Many people opt for adventure "lite" when exposed to a new country or culture. Adventure lite means sticking to business hubs and mainstream tourist sites. Staying in high-rent spots or corporate housing that separates expats from the local culture. If you seek out what's familiar when traveling outside your home country, you are likely to miss prime opportunities to build diverse experiences. Transformative global experiences are crucial for developing effective global leaders. That means experiencing what the real norm is there. Find ways to get involved directly in the local scene. Work alongside local people. Participate. Open up. Show respect and genuine interest in their culture and lives. Don't be surprised if you're invited in for tea. Taste what they have to offer. Digest it over time.

Want to learn more? Take a deep dive...

Al Mayassa, S. (2012, February). Sheikha Al Mayassa: Globalizing the local, localizing the global [Video file]. TED.

Mind Tools. (2013). *Hofstede's cultural dimensions: Understanding workplace values around the world*. Mind Tools.

Moran, G. (2013, April 10). How to avoid cultural missteps when doing business with other countries. *Entrepreneur.*

7. **Confused about complex issues? Practice reframing.** There's usually more going on than first meets the eye. Systems involve multiple moving parts and interconnections. A cause doesn't merely have one effect. How do you figure complex things out without getting dizzy? Try applying Bolman and Deal's "four frame" model to better decipher complex issues and not leave out vital implications. (*For more information, visit* www.leebolman.com *or* http://www.slideshare.net/ PhilVincent1/fourframe-model.) A global perspective includes

awareness of the various factors in a system plus the ability to synthesize and determine what matters.

8. **Lacking international scope? Build know-how through global connections.** When possible, take a stretching international assignment or join a cross-border task force to boost knowledge. The next best thing to experiencing something yourself is hearing from someone who's been there. Ask those who have worked overseas about their victories and cultural missteps. Invite speakers in to spark dialogue on global issues affecting your company. Create a network of expats to share lessons learned about operating in specific markets. Take part in virtual brainstorming sessions where someone in Sydney might share an idea that could help a leader in Prague. Try to have meetings that are normally held at headquarters moved to different foreign locations, and ask that tours of manufacturing or distribution sites be put on the agenda so you can see things firsthand. Use social media to connect with other employees and customers around the globe. Learning from global colleagues will help push your thinking beyond your home base.

9. **Too home-centric? Build a climate of global awareness.** During staff meetings, spend time talking about what it means to have a global perspective. Have a world map on display. Discuss international news and how that may affect your business. Apply a global lens to key initiatives. How could existing plans be adapted to play better in other countries? How would you handle government regulators not responding to requests, or vendors who miss commitments? Discuss the balance of flexing to local conditions while following ethical guidelines and delivering results. Let people know how your beliefs and experiences on and off the job have shaped you. Encourage them to do the same. What does it mean to be a woman whose parents escaped Vietnam? An Egyptian scientist now working in Buenos Aires? What is true, and what is a stereotypical belief? Model the mindset that you want others to adopt.

10. **Unknown business landscape? Study your global customers and competitors.** Find out what customers in different countries or regions like or don't like about your company's products or services. How do the preferences change from culture to culture? Find ways to connect with the end users. If you sell pharmaceuticals, talk with patients and physicians. If you market consumer products, go into the local stores. If you deliver professional services, meet the decision makers on their own turf. Look at what competitors are doing and how they are similar, different, priced. Spend time understanding the big players in the different markets that you serve. What is your

18

competitive advantage? How does your strategy or position differ from that of your competitors? Stay in front of these key differentiators.

11. **Don't understand global business? Figure out the rules of the global business game.** Distill your understanding of how global business operates to personal rules of thumb or insights. Write them down in your own words. An example would be "What are the drivers in marketing across countries and cultures?" One executive had 25 such drivers that he continuously edited, scratched through, and replaced as more up-to-date thinking emerged. Use these rules of thumb to analyze a business you know something about. Then pick two organizations that have achieved clever global strategies, one related to yours and one not. Study what they did, talk to people who know what happened and see what you can learn. Pick a particular business function—such as foreign exchange hedging or product distribution—and develop an understanding of how these functions work internationally or impact the country in which you are interested.

Want to learn more? Take a deep dive...

Bersin, J. (2013, April 23). The world is not global, it's local. *Forbes*.

Farzad, R. (2013, August 29). Explaining the pain in emerging markets. *Bloomberg Businessweek*.

Maurer, R. (2013, August 22). *International assignments: Who's going where and why?* Society for Human Resource Management (SHRM).

Job assignments

• Study an international trend, product, service, or process, and report back on how it relates to current issues and impacts future possibilities for your organization.

• Work on a project that involves travel and study of a global issue, and then present strategic implications to management.

• Take an extended overseas assignment that will deepen your international knowledge and scope.

- Lead or work with a cross-functional project or action learning team made up of nationals from a number of countries, making global connections and seeing how the pieces fit together.

- Become a volunteer for six months or more for an outside global organization in which you'll collaborate and have direct communication with people from different backgrounds or cultures.

Take time to reflect...

If you don't know much about other parts of the world...

...then widen your horizons. In today's world, brilliant ideas and disruptive competition can come from everywhere. Step beyond your borders. Become a global citizen.

If your field of vision tends to be limited and narrow...

...then broaden your perspective and see the world through a wide-angle lens. Be curious. Explore. Expand your comfort zone.

If you're worried about uncertainties in the global arena...

...then ask questions rather than relying on the same old answers. Appreciate differences. Recognize similarities. Build relationships across borders based on shared goals.

" *The world is but a school of inquiry.* **"**

Michel de Montaigne – French philosopher and writer

18

Learn more about Global perspective

Bolman, L. G., & Deal, T. E. (2008). *Reframing organizations: Artistry, choice, and leadership* (4th ed.). San Francisco, CA: Jossey-Bass.

Dalton, M., Ernst, C., Deal, J. J., & Leslie, J. (2002). *Success for the new global manager: How to work across distances, countries, and cultures*. San Francisco, CA: Jossey-Bass.

Gundling, E., Hogan, T., & Cvitkovich, K. (2011). *What is global leadership? 10 Key behaviors that define great global leaders.* Boston, MA: Nicholas Brealey International.

Molinsky, A. (2013). Global dexterity: *How to adapt your behavior across cultures without losing yourself in the process*. Boston, MA: Harvard Business School Publishing.

Smilansky, J. (2007). *Developing executive talent: Best practices from global leaders*. Chichester, West Sussex, England: John Wiley & Sons.

Travis, T. (2007). *Doing business anywhere: The essential guide to going global*. Hoboken, NJ: John Wiley & Sons.

Wild, J. J., & Wild, K. L. (2011). *International business: The challenges of globalization* (6th ed.). Upper Saddle River, NJ: Prentice Hall.

 ## Deep dive learning resource links

Al Mayassa, S. (2012, February). Sheikha Al Mayassa: Globalizing the local, localizing the global [Video file]. TED. Retrieved from http://www.ted.com/talks/sheikha_al_mayassa_globalizing_the_local_localizing_the_global.html

Beinhocker, E., Davis, I., & Mendonca, L. (2013). The 10 trends you have to watch. *Harvard Business Review*. Retrieved from http://hbr.org/web/extras/insight-center/health-care/10-trends-you-have-to-watch

Bersin, J. (2013, April 23). The world is not global, it's local. *Forbes*. Retrieved from http://www.forbes.com/sites/joshbersin/2013/04/23/the-world-is-not-global-its-local/

Edin, P., Lingqvist, O., & Tamsons, A. (2012, July 26). The best sales leaders are trend hunters. *Harvard Business Review Blog Network*. Retrieved from http://blogs.hbr.org/2012/07/sales-is-all-about-hitting/

Farzad, R. (2013, August 29). Explaining the pain in emerging markets. *Bloomberg Businessweek*. Retrieved from http://www.businessweek.com/articles/2013-08-29/explaining-the-pain-in-emerging-markets

Maurer, R. (2013, August 22). *International assignments: Who's going where and why?* Society for Human Resource Management (SHRM). Retrieved from http://www.shrm.org/hrdisciplines/global/articles/pages/international-assignments-survey.aspx

Mind Tools. (2013). *Hofstede's cultural dimensions: Understanding workplace values around the world.* Mind Tools. Retrieved from http://www.mindtools.com/pages/article/newLDR_66.htm

Moran, G. (2013, April 10). How to avoid cultural missteps when doing business with other countries. *Entrepreneur.* Retrieved from http://www.entrepreneur.com/article/226286

Rubin, J. (2013, June 19). Top recruiter to CIOs: Time to broaden your background and show some charisma. *Forbes.* Retrieved from http://www.forbes.com/sites/forbesinsights/2013/06/19/top-recruiter-to-cios-time-to-broaden-your-background-and-show-some-charisma/

Recommended search terms

If you'd like to explore Global perspective further, try searching online using the following terms:

- Diverse business cultures.
- Global business assignments.
- Global business trends/dynamics.
- Think globally, act locally.
- Understanding emerging markets.

 More help...

Go to www.kornferry.com/fyi-resources and link directly to the deep dive resources in this chapter. Visit the site often to see the additional resources that are uploaded on a regular basis.

18

19. *Cultivates* innovation

Creating new and better ways for the organization to be successful.

Organizations need innovation to survive and thrive in the constantly changing competitive landscape. How can they stay ahead of the curve? A first step is to make innovation a priority. To enlist contributors and leaders at all levels to spearhead innovations, large and small. It requires paying attention to what customers want and need—new and improved products, services, solutions, and experiences. It means generating lots of ideas and nurturing the best ones while they're being transformed into something tangible. It means constantly improving operational processes—even replacing them altogether—harnessing the latest research and technology. Innovation also involves rethinking your organization's business model—the value proposition, markets, revenue streams. To be an effective innovator, you need to take initiative and collaborate with people who have diverse points of view. You need to get comfortable taking risks. To experiment and apply what you learned from mistakes and failures. Even if you don't consider yourself to be naturally creative, it can be awakened at any time. Learn about the process of innovation and the tools that support it. Embrace the mindset that you and your organization are never done, never satisfied, never standing still.

" To stay ahead, you must have your next idea waiting in the wings. "

Rosabeth Moss Kanter – American academic and author

***Cultivates* innovation** is in the **Thought** factor (I) in the Korn Ferry Leadership Architect™. It is part of Cluster C, **Creating the new and different,** along with Global perspective (18) and Strategic mindset (33). You may find it helpful to also take a look at some of the tips included in those chapters to supplement your learning.

Skilled

Comes up with useful ideas that are new, better, or unique.

Introduces new ways of looking at problems.

Can take a creative idea and put it into practice.

Encourages diverse thinking to promote and nurture innovation.

Less skilled

- Stays within comfort zone rather than experimenting with new ways of looking at things.

- Presents ideas that are ordinary, conventional, and from the past.

- Tends to be critical of others' original ideas.

- Has a style that discourages the creative initiatives of others.

Talented

- Moves beyond traditional ways of doing things; pushes past the status quo.

- Continually assesses the market potential of an innovative idea or solution.

- Finds and champions the best creative ideas and actively moves them into implementation.

- Tries multiple, varied approaches to innovative ideas.

- Builds excitement in others to explore creative options.

Overused skill

- Gravitates toward the new and rejects the old.

- Comes up with so many unusual ideas that it overwhelms others.

- Expends too much time and effort looking at creative alternatives instead of taking action.

- Relentlessly pursues change and innovation at the cost of efficiency and reliability.

Some possible causes of lower skill

Causes help explain *why* a person may have trouble with *Cultivates* innovation. When seeking to increase skill, it's helpful to consider how these might play out in certain situations. And remember that all of these can be addressed if you are motivated to do so.

- Cautious; risk averse.
- Not open to new ideas.
- Narrow perspective.
- Not market/customer savvy.
- Complacent with what is.
- Lacks knowledge about process.
- Doesn't value innovation.
- Not curious.
- Limited creativity toolbox.
- Slow to change and act.

Brain booster

Creativity and innovation happen when talented people are given the space and freedom to be inventive. Mihály Csíkszentmihályi describes the *flow* state that promotes creative thinking and innovative results. The flow experience happens when individuals are able to concentrate intensely, feel a sense of control, and lose themselves in something they find intrinsically rewarding. This state of mind can produce amazing works of art, music, literature, but also applies in the areas of science and business. In fact, Green Cargo, Patagonia, and Microsoft have all applied flow principles in the workplace with success. Set up a work environment that can function as a playground for ideas. Avoid distractions and obstacles as much as possible. Kathryn Britton, who studied flow at work, finds that "frequent experiences of flow at work lead to higher productivity, innovation, and employee development.[28, 29]

Tips to develop *Cultivates* innovation

1. **Wonder what role you can play? Innovation takes a village.** You don't have to be an Idea Generator to bring value to innovation. As Roger von Oech and other experts have pointed out, many roles are necessary. Mix and match based upon project needs, your skills, and motivation. An Explorer seeks out new information, perspectives, and resources. A Leader aligns innovation with strategy and nurtures the climate and process. An Evaluator determines the merits of options and decides which to pursue. A Champion influences others to try it, fund it, or buy in. An Advancer moves the innovation through necessary channels in the internal/external environment. An Implementer executes, putting the idea into practice. A Refiner makes improvements along the way. A Manager tracks the budget, metrics, and risks involved. A Marketer tells the story and socializes good news. A Knowledge Manager shares lessons learned from successes and mistakes. A Rewarder recognizes those who played a valuable part.

2. **Desire to enhance group creativity? Diversify.** During World War II, it was discovered that teams with the widest diversity of backgrounds produced the most creative solutions to problems. The teams included people who knew absolutely nothing about the area (i.e., an English major working on a costing problem). Current research reinforces these findings. So when attacking problems, pull together the broadest group you can—people from different functions, levels, and backgrounds. Practice "open innovation," gathering ideas from customers and suppliers. Invite people to act as "provocateurs" to shake up ingrained ways of thinking about the challenge. Gather input through internal or external crowdsourcing, from experts and novices. Go broad when looking for new and different perspectives.

3. **Don't perceive yourself to be creative? Remove the restraints.** What's preventing you from contributing to your organization's innovative efforts? Are you overly cautious? Being creative is about entering the unknown with curiosity and discovering what happens. Do you tend to be a perfectionist? Innovation is not about instantly getting it right—it's an iterative process that calls for making improvements over time. Are you worried about what people may think? Let it go—innovation requires putting risky and untested ideas up for critique. Do you prefer being practical? Creative ideas may seem impractical or far-flung at first, but with experiments and feedback, you can make them unique *and* workable. You don't have to change who you are, but you may need to think and act differently when more innovation is required.

|

4. **Lack a climate conducive to innovation? Take the lead.** Research identifies specific actions that leaders can take to cultivate a climate of innovation: Question the way things have always been done. Establish challenging goals that rally energy and commitment. Explain how projects align with the organization's strategy. Encourage reasonable risk taking. Recognize and reward creative efforts as well as outcomes. Secure resources for promising ideas (time, space, materials, funding, talent, sponsorship). Steer project teams but don't micromanage them—freedom and flexibility are crucial for creative work. Buffer people from administrative tasks that prevent them from focusing. Expect mistakes and learn from them. Champion ideas and highlight wins. Promote cross-fertilization of ideas and experimentation on an ongoing basis. Include innovation-oriented developmental assignments to grow the capability of your talent.

5. **Worried about making mistakes? Treat them as stepping stones.** Innovation involves pushing the envelope, taking chances, trying out something that is untested. Doing these things will inevitably lead to more misfires and mistakes in the short-term but will ultimately yield better results. Assess risks up front and determine how much you're willing to take. Reduce risks by funding pilots and prototypes to allow for testing without far-reaching consequences. Avoid blame—treat any mistakes or failures as chances to learn. Nothing ventured, nothing gained. American inventor Thomas Edison always viewed failures in the lab as mini-successes. In his view, each time an attempt didn't work, it got him closer to the solution that would.

Want to learn more? Take a deep dive...

Fries, A. (2010, February 9). Sparking creativity in the workplace. *Psychology Today*.

Linkner, J. (2011, June 16). 7 Steps to a culture of innovation. *Inc.*

Smith Bedford, G. (2013, October 28). 5 Ways to promote creativity in the workplace. *The Business Journals*.

6. **In a rut with business-as-usual? Disrupt "what is" with "what could be."** Disruptive innovators are known to enter niche markets undetected by organizations complacently going about their business. Before long, the innovation often transforms the industry it has entered. (Think online shopping, personal computers, digital cameras, retail health care clinics.) Disruption brings greater access, simplicity, convenience, and affordability—things customers want.

Collaborate with stakeholders and design new and better business models, products/services, and ways of working. Challenge your assumptions. Ask: What business are we currently in? What business should we be in? How can we deliver more for considerably less? How can we make our customers' lives easier? How can we redefine value? What could competitors or start-ups do to make us obsolete? A mantra to adopt is "disrupt or be disrupted."

7. **Ideas drying up? Capitalize on trends and opportunities.** Innovation isn't just about solving existing problems. It's also about shaping future opportunities. Entering new markets, meeting emerging needs, generating new revenue streams. Pay attention to the latest trends. Do shifts in demographics or technology suggest new opportunities? How about changes in manufacturing capabilities or distribution channels? New regulations (related to food, health, the environment, etc.) may seem like obstacles yet be ripe with opportunity. Study successful entrepreneurs. Where do they invest their energy and money? Become an expert on what's happening in your industry and beyond. What do customers want more or less of? How can you profitably provide it?

8. **Feel too distant from the situation? Engage frontline employees for input.** Creating new or better methods is difficult if you're far from the action. Engage associates closest to the customers, process, or product/service at play. Those with firsthand knowledge and experience. Train them to pay close attention to opportunities for innovation by using what Twyla Tharp calls "forensic intensity." Supply these frontline investigators with starter questions: How can things be streamlined, easier, more reliable, more energy efficient? What needs aren't being met? What new things can be tried? Have them watch and listen for clues that lead to better solutions and new offerings. Capture and collate their suggestions. Together, evaluate the ideas and try out the best ones. In addition to making things better, you'll boost employee engagement by involving them in initiatives that have an impact.

Want to learn more? Take a deep dive...

Brown, R. (2010, November 29). Is your status quo killing your business? *Entrepreneur.*

Gallo, C. (2012, August 30). Apple's secret employee training manual reinvents customer service in seven ways. *Forbes.*

Rayport, J. F. (2012, April 24). Free your frontline workers to innovate. *Harvard Business Review Blog Network.*

9. **Need a fresh idea? Immerse yourself and then let go.** To come up with creative ideas on your own, begin by immersing yourself in the challenge. Don't rush it—carve out dedicated time. Explore similarities in other organizations—those in and outside your field. Think out loud with someone who's a good sounding board—many people don't know what they know until they talk it out. Consult with experts and irreverent thinkers. Study the data. Find new patterns and pick out unusual facts that don't quite fit. What's missing? Dig deep to determine root causes. Break up complex issues into smaller parts. Draw pictures or flowcharts to make sense of things. View it from different angles. What would it look like from an economic or political perspective? What's the least likely thing the problem could be? Search for opportunities in what appear to be obstacles. After an extended period of immersion, take a break. Do something relaxing or different—like take a walk, drive, or nap. While you consciously turn off the challenge, your unconscious mind will continue to process it. The best ideas frequently surface during these times of incubation. Be ready to write or sketch it out when it appears.

10. **Need a structure you can count on? Use tried-and-true methods.** Creativity and innovation don't have to be soft and fuzzy. Inventions don't have to happen by accident or magic. You don't have to be Einstein or Steve Jobs. Try following a deliberate process with extensive research to back it up. Originally developed by Alex Osborn, creative problem solving consists of (1) Identifying the general challenge or wish. (2) Gathering information and insights. (3) Clarifying or redefining the problem once you have useful data. (4) Generating lots of ideas/options. (5) Selecting and strengthening solutions with the greatest potential. (6) Planning for action—tests, implementation, follow-up. Get some training and practice to effectively participate in or lead this process.

11. **Want creative ideas while brainstorming? Use multiple tools and techniques.** Generate ideas using divergent thinking, which is about being open and exploring possibilities. Strive for three things— fluency (high quantity), flexibility (different categories of ideas), and originality (unique and unusual). Establish classic brainstorming guidelines like deferring judgment and combining and building on ideas. After clearly defining the problem or challenge, generate ideas with the group using techniques such as:

   • Asking a lot of questions: What if? What else? Why not? What if the problem is turned upside down? What if the opposite of our assumptions is true? What if the worst-case scenario occurs?

   • Analogies, forced connections, and parallels. Show images/ objects and ask, "How does this picture or object relate to the challenge?" Or "How is the organization similar to what's found in nature (e.g., a river or an oak tree)?"

- Storytelling, storyboards, or collages. These convey the current or desired customer experience through stories and images.

- Mind mapping and affinity diagrams. These show how things associated with the challenge are linked or connected in a non-linear way.

- Brainwriting, where individuals write down their ideas in silence and then pass them to each other to stimulate further thoughts.

- Visualizations or guided imagery, which prompt ideas to surface when people are in a relaxed state.

Go online or take courses to build your repertoire. Some groups like to have team members take turns leading activities. Others prefer to engage a neutral facilitator. After you've generated ideas, you'll then shift gears to sort through and evaluate them.

12. **Ready to select a solution? Evaluate and strengthen options first.** To select the most promising ideas, go into "convergent thinking" or evaluation mode. If you have a large quantity, first do a quick vote to narrow the list. Weigh the remaining options against specific criteria that need to be met (e.g., cost, quality, time to completion, stakeholder satisfaction, appealing design). Discuss the positives, negatives, and interesting features of each remaining option. How can you make the best ideas even stronger? How can you overcome any concerns or mitigate risks? Pay special attention to outliers who voice contrary opinions. Recognize the value their unique perspective brings. Together, plan how you'll test the solution, measure results, and execute on time and within budget. Build in feedback loops with stakeholders to make sure the solution meets or exceeds your targets. Keep track of all data so you can course-correct when needed, replicate wins, and share outcomes with the enterprise.

13. **Eager to put things to the test? Experiment and learn.** Most innovations aren't created instantly. They're the result of a long road of trial and error, risk taking, mistakes, even accidents. The more you experiment, the more chances you have to discover and improve things. So instead of debating pros and cons endlessly, make ideas more concrete. Share rough concepts or mock-ups with stakeholders and incorporate their feedback in the next iteration. Conduct soft launches or pilots to gather input prior to a full-fledged release. Create idea zones where employees can interact with prototypes

and offer suggestions. Or build an in-house innovation lab to continuously experiment with new ideas. Typically, these innovation centers house interdisciplinary teams (designers, engineers, marketers, artists, statisticians). They often have physical sets that simulate day-in-the-life contexts (e.g., a kitchen or office) or kiosks that replicate user experiences (shopping in a retail outlet). Dedicate time and space to quickly vet and make ideas better.

14. Not sure innovation is taken seriously? Establish innovation metrics. Apply the same discipline around innovation initiatives that you would for other business projects. Establish goals and measure your results. A common metric is cumulative profits generated from new products (a variation of ROI—return on innovation). You can also look at return on invested capital (ROIC). But don't limit yourself to financial measures. What is the impact of innovation on customer satisfaction? Employee engagement? Patent applications? Brand reputation? Select the most appropriate metrics and make them visible. Revisit them often, modifying when required.

19

Want to learn more? Take a deep dive...

Anthony, S. (2013, July 30). Five ways to innovate faster. *Harvard Business Review Blog Network*.

Bass, C. (2012, February 27). TEDxBerkeley – Carl Bass – The new rules of innovation [Video file]. TED.

Liedtka, J. (2012, November 28). How to innovate – without a miracle. *Forbes*.

Job assignments

- Relaunch an existing product, service, or process that's not doing well by gathering input from end users and trying things not tried before.

- Facilitate a brainstorming session—define and clarify the problem/opportunity, generate ideas using various techniques, and narrow the list to solutions you want to strengthen, test, and implement.

- Benchmark innovative business models, practices, processes, products, or services that come from both well-known and non-traditional competitors/sources, and report your findings to colleagues.

|

- Take part in an entire innovation cycle for a new product/service—from research, design, concept refinement, and prototyping, through to its launch and use in the marketplace.

- Identify an unmet need and experiment with different ways to fill the gap. Practice seeing failures or mistakes as opportunities to learn.

Take time to reflect...

19

If you rely on the familiar rather than seeking out the new...

> ...then consider that breakthrough results often arise from unconventional thinking. Challenge yourself to be creative. Be bold. Have fun. Give yourself permission to try, and maybe fail.

If you're quick to provide most of the ideas yourself...

> ...then hold back. Discover the fertile minds around you. Unleashing the creative potential will lead to innovation you didn't realize possible.

If you feel a creative approach could never work out...

> ...then start thinking of what can be possible if it does. Innovation and risk go hand in hand. Be bold. Think "What if?" Ask "Why not?"

"*Innovation distinguishes between a leader and a follower.* **"**

Steve Jobs – American entrepreneur, inventor, and cofounder of Apple Inc.

Learn more about *Cultivates* innovation

Adair, J. (2009). *Leadership for innovation: How to organize team creativity and harvest ideas*. Philadelphia, PA: Kogan Page Limited.

Afuah, A. (2009). *Strategic innovation: New game strategies for competitive advantage*. New York, NY: Routledge.

Anthony, S. D., Johnson, M. W., Sinfield, J. V., & Altman, E. J. (2008). *The innovator's guide to growth: Putting disruptive innovation to work*. Boston, MA: Harvard Business Review Press.

Gertner, J. (2013). *The idea factory: Bell labs and the great age of American innovation*. New York, NY: Penguin Press.

Teece, D. J. (2009). *Dynamic capabilities and strategic management: Organizing for innovation and growth*. New York, NY: Oxford University Press.

 Deep dive learning resource links

Anthony, S. (2013, July 30). Five ways to innovate faster. *Harvard Business Review Blog Network*. Retrieved from http://blogs.hbr.org/2013/07/how-to-innovate-faster/

Bass, C. (2012, February 27). TEDxBerkeley – Carl Bass – The new rules of innovation [Video file]. TED. Retrieved from http://tedxtalks.ted.com/video/TEDxBerkeley-Carl-Bass-The-New

Brown, R. (2010, November 29). Is your status quo killing your business? *Entrepreneur*. Retrieved from http://www.entrepreneur.com/article/217581

Fries, A. (2010, February 9). Sparking creativity in the workplace. *Psychology Today*. Retrieved from http://www.psychologytoday.com/blog/the-power-daydreaming/201002/sparking-creativity-in-the-workplace

Gallo, C. (2012, August 30). Apple's secret employee training manual reinvents customer service in seven ways. *Forbes*. Retrieved from http://www.forbes.com/sites/carminegallo/2012/08/30/apples-secret-employee-training-manual-reinvents-customer-service-in-seven-ways/

Liedtka, J. (2012, November 28). How to innovate – without a miracle. *Forbes*. Retrieved from http://www.forbes.com/sites/darden/2012/11/28/how-to-innovate-without-a-miracle/

Linkner, J. (2011, June 16). 7 Steps to a culture of innovation. *Inc.* Retrieved from http://www.inc.com/articles/201106/josh-linkner-7-steps-to-a-culture-of-innovation.html

Rayport, J. F. (2012, April 24). Free your frontline workers to innovate. *Harvard Business Review Blog Network*. Retrieved from http://blogs.hbr.org/2012/04/unleash-innovation-on-the-fron/

Smith Bedford, G. (2013, October 28). 5 ways to promote creativity in the workplace. *The Business Journals*. Retrieved from http://www.bizjournals.com/bizjournals/feature/small-business/tip-of-the-month-creativity.html?page=all

Recommended search terms

19

If you'd like to explore *Cultivates* innovation further, try searching online using the following terms:

- Creating a culture of innovation.
- Going against the status quo in business.
- Learning how to innovate.
- Promoting innovation/creativity.
- Rules for innovation.

(i) More help...

Go to www.kornferry.com/fyi-resources and link directly to the deep dive resources in this chapter. Visit the site often to see the additional resources that are uploaded on a regular basis.

20. Interpersonal savvy

Relating openly and comfortably with diverse groups of people.

Interpersonal savvy is an essential part of getting things done within organizations. The key to getting along with all kinds of people is to hold back or neutralize personal reactions and focus on others first. Being savvy is working from the outside in. It involves having a range of interpersonal skills and approaches and knowing when to use what with whom. Customers. Senior leaders. Peers. External stakeholders. Direct reports. All of these relationships deserve respect, authenticity, and care. A welcoming demeanor puts other people at ease and sets the stage for smooth, productive interactions. Being warm. Pleasant. Gracious. Considerate and diplomatic. Approachable and friendly. Attentive to others' perspectives. All are qualities of relating effectively to fellow human beings. When relationships are approached in a flexible and "others-oriented" way, you accomplish results while establishing goodwill and leave others interested in working with you again.

> *"In organizations, real power and energy is generated through relationships. The patterns of relationships and the capacities to form them are more important than tasks, functions, roles, and positions."*
>
> Margaret Wheatley – American writer and management consultant

Interpersonal savvy is in the **People** factor (III) in the Korn Ferry Leadership Architect™. It is part of Cluster G, **Building collaborative relationships,** along with Collaborates (6), *Manages* conflict (9), and *Builds* networks (21). You may find it helpful to also take a look at some of the tips included in those chapters to supplement your learning.

Skilled

Relates comfortably with people across levels, functions, culture, and geography.

Acts with diplomacy and tact.

Builds rapport in an open, friendly, and accepting way.

Builds constructive relationships with people both similar and different to self.

Picks up on interpersonal and group dynamics.

Less skilled

- Builds few relationships.
- Engages with people in immediate work area only.
- Is uncomfortable when interacting with people different from self.
- Expresses points of view in a blunt or insensitive manner.
- Shows little interest in others' needs.

Talented

- Proactively develops relationships with a wide variety of people.
- Builds immediate rapport, even when facing difficult or tense situations.
- Understands interpersonal and group dynamics and reacts in an effective manner.
- Engages input from others constantly and listens with empathy and concern.

Overused skill

- Is focused on understanding group and interpersonal dynamics at the expense of getting results.
- Makes ineffective decisions due to a strong need to be liked.
- May be seen as lacking authenticity.

Some possible causes of lower skill

Causes help explain *why* a person may have trouble with Interpersonal savvy. When seeking to increase skill, it's helpful to consider how these might play out in certain situations. And remember that all of these can be addressed if you are motivated to do so.

- Can't handle disagreement and attacks.
- Defensive in the face of criticism.
- Doesn't know what to do.
- Judgmental, rigid.
- Arrogant.
- Insensitive to others.
- Poor listening skills.
- Poor time management; too busy.
- Shy; lacks self-confidence.
- Too intense; can't relax.
- Unsure of working with different types of people.
- Difficulties reading office politics or social cues.

Brain booster

Empathy helps us feel and understand the emotions, thoughts, and intentions of others. It's the social and emotional glue of good relationships. We're born with this skill, but as we grow up, our social learning gets in the way. In the workplace, emotions are often labeled as irrational or unprofessional, so we learn to control them. But developing empathy is simpler than you might think. The general belief used to be that to empathize, we had to first perceive the emotion of the other person, process it to understand it, and then determine our response. Neuroscience provides us with a simpler approach. Turns out, we just need to play chameleon. When someone expresses an emotion, it activates something in our brains called mirror neurons. These cause us to simulate the same emotional expression. Through this simulation, we understand the other person's emotion. Happy. Sad. Excited. Frustrated. So, others smile; we smile. Others frown; we frown. Through this natural imitation, we are able to feel what others feel. And here's the bonus—not only do mirror neurons help us empathize, they also lead to rapport-building. Research also reveals that when we behave similarly to others, there's more chance they'll like us and want to cooperate and connect.[30]

Tips to develop Interpersonal savvy

1. **Not tuned in to people's styles? Be interpersonally flexible.** People have different backgrounds, perspectives, attitudes, and approaches. The key is to listen and to understand them. Look to the obvious. What do they do first? What do they emphasize in their speech? How do they interact? People have different styles—pushy, tough, soft, matter-of-fact. To figure these out, listen for the values behind their words and note what they have passion and emotion around. Show your appreciation of different styles. Flex yours, within reason, to be more in tune. This can be essential when working in a global context or outside of your cultural comfort zone. Understanding and managing differences is essential. Basically, people respond favorably to transactions being simple. Make it easy by accepting their normal mode of doing things. Don't fight their style. Work with it. Tune in. Don't defend your own style. Welcome theirs.

2. **Unapproachable? Adjust your style.** Arrogant? Insensitive? Distant? Too busy to pay attention? Not listening? Instant output? Sharp reactions? A bully? Don't want to be that way? Read your audience. Do you know what people look like when they are uncomfortable with you? Do they back up? Stumble over words? Cringe? Stand at the door hoping not to get invited in? You should work doubly hard at observing others. Always select your interpersonal approach from the other person in, not from you out. Your best choice of approach will always be determined by the other person or group, not you. Think about each transaction as if the other person were a customer whose business you wanted to win. How would you craft an approach? What do you say or do that makes them look uncomfortable? Do less of it. What is it that makes them appear more at ease? Do more of it. What makes them retreat altogether? Stop doing it.

3. **Selective interpersonal skills? Accommodate differences.** Tend to relate more comfortably to certain people? Find yourself talking to the same people on a regular basis? Challenged talking with people at certain levels of the organization? Analyze your discomfort. Where do you avoid interacting with others? With whom are you hesitant? Push yourself to interact with a wider variety of individuals. Get to know people in other workgroups, levels of the organization, or functional areas. The principles of interpersonal savvy are the same regardless of the audience. Do what you do with the comfortable group with the uncomfortable groups. The results will generally be the same.

Want to learn more? Take a deep dive...

Burns, K. (2010, January 27). 10 Tips for playing well with others at work. *U.S. News and World Report*.

Chamorro-Premuzic, T. (2012, July 6). Less-confident people are more successful. *Harvard Business Review Blog Network*.

Lutz, A. (2012, May 18). *The secret to working with 4 different types of people*. Business Insider.

4. **In a hurry to get down to business? Manage the first three minutes.** Life moves fast. Decisions need to be made. Information needs to be shared. Action needs to happen. But can you take three minutes? The first three minutes are essential. The tone is set. First impressions are formed. Work on being open and approachable. Take in information during the beginning of a transaction. This means putting others at ease so that they feel OK about disclosing. It means initiating rapport, listening, sharing, understanding, and comforting. Approachable people get more information, know things earlier, and can get others to do more things. The more you can get them to initiate and say early in the transaction, the more you'll know about where they are coming from, and the better you can tailor your approach.

5. **Are you overly private? Share more.** There's a balance to be struck between being too private and appropriate sharing. When you share a little of yourself, you get more in return. Let people know what you are thinking on a business issue. Talk about what's important to you. Share snippets of your weekend, upcoming vacation, or family events. It's not about bragging or comparing. It's being real and opening up to others. Let people see into your world a little. Others are more likely to share with you when you take the first step and show a little bit about yourself. Reveal things people don't need to know to do their jobs, but which will be interesting to them and help them feel valued.

6. **Are you all business? Personalize.** Work to know and remember important things about the people who work with you. Know three things about each of your coworkers—their interests or their family or something you can chat about other than the business agenda. These need not be social; they could also be issues of current affairs, global events, market shifts. The point is to establish common ground and connections. Show your human side. Learn people's

names and use them. Remember dates that are important to them. Acknowledge big events in their lives. Interact because you want to, not just because you have to.

7. **Need to demonstrate more interest? Use attentive non-verbals.** Understand the critical role of non-verbal communications. It's easy to say one thing and send a completely different message with your body language. That's confusing. Even before you utter a word, the other person will start to interpret your gestures. They'll look for meaning in your facial expressions. What they take from the non-verbals can completely override the words. Appear and sound open and relaxed. Keep consistent eye contact. Nod while the other person is talking. Work to eliminate any disruptive habits such as fidgeting or frequently looking at your computer. Put down your phone. Watch out for signaling disinterest with actions like glancing at your watch, fiddling with paperwork, or giving your impatient "I'm busy" look. When possible, schedule face-to-face or web-based meetings instead of e-mail or phone interaction.

8. **Shy? Make the first move.** Lack self-confidence? Generally hold back and let others take the lead? Feelings of being too vulnerable? Afraid of how people will react? Not sure of your social skills? Want to appear confident even when you're shaking inside? Have consistent eye contact. Ask the first question. For low-risk practice, talk to strangers. Set a goal of meeting new people at every event you go to; find out what you have in common with them. Talk to people in various social settings and test the outcome. The only way people will know you are shy and nervous is if you tell them through your actions. Watch what non-shy people do that you don't do. Practice those behaviors.

Want to learn more? Take a deep dive...

Goldschein, E. (2011, September 9). *19 Ways to overcome shyness at work*. Business Insider.

Schwartz, T. (2013, January 23). What if you could truly be yourself at work? *Harvard Business Review Blog Network*.

Smith, J. (2013, March 11). 10 Non-verbal cues that convey confidence at work. *Forbes*.

9. **Quick to judge? Be a better listener.** Listening is an action, not a passive response. When you're quick to make a judgment or interrupt to make a point, you're not a good listener. Ask questions. Show

240 |

appropriate non-verbal behaviors. Listen and summarize what you are hearing. Restate what you've heard to confirm understanding. Show your curiosity about the other person and their perspective. Good listeners get good information. They do not pass judgment. They gain an understanding of the message the other person is trying to get across. Listeners get more data.

10. **Find some people challenging? Be savvy with people you don't like.** In every organization there are people who are more difficult to get along with than others. You'll have an easy rapport with some and feel tense around others. Is there someone who makes you want to hide round the corner when you see them coming? Do you dread being stuck in the elevator with them? What should you do about these people? First step, get to know them. There is rarely a person who is fully unlikeable. By getting to know them better, you may be able to make a connection. Don't let your previous feelings about them get in the way of building a fresh relationship with them. Draw a line in the sand. Start to see them as someone you are just getting to know. Do you have common interests? What are their strengths? What is important to them? Put your judgments on hold, open up your thinking, and take some time to understand who this individual is. A fly on the wall should not be able to tell whether you're talking to friend or foe. Talk less and ask more questions. Show that you care by dedicating some time to them. This builds goodwill and trust.

11. **Are you a target? Turn around tense transactions.** What if you're attacked? What if venom is flowing? What if someone doesn't like you very much? What if everyone is angry and upset? Listen first. Allow the other side to vent and blow off steam without reacting directly. Remember that it's the person who hits back who usually gets into the most trouble. When emotion is in the way, people cannot deal with facts. Let them talk. Keep your cool. Ask clarifying, open-ended questions. "Why is this particularly bothersome to you?" "What could I do to help?" Summarize what you are hearing to show you have understood their perspective. Recognize when you are feeling defensive and let it go. When the other side takes a rigid position, don't reject it. Ask why—what's behind the position, what's the theory of the case, what brought this about? Separate the people from the problem. When someone attacks you, rephrase it as an attack on a problem. Take a deep breath. Calm yourself down before responding. Refrain from justifying yourself or your behavior. You just may surprise the other individual enough to calm them down before you respond. Choose your response to an attack. Sometimes, if the attack is personal or unreasonable, the best initial

response is to do or say nothing. If all else fails, defuse the situation by asking for a break and schedule some time at a later date.

Want to learn more? Take a deep dive...

Davey, L. (2013, October 19). Can I be happy at work if I don't like my teammates? *Psychology Today*.

Wademan Dowling, D. (2009, March 11). 7 Tips for difficult conversations. *Harvard Business Review Blog Network*.

Whitmore, J. (2014, January 13). 5 Ways to be a better listener. *Entrepreneur*.

---

12. **Having trouble connecting? Be authentic.** People know when they're dealing with a fake. When you're real with yourself and others, you will find it easier to make authentic connections. Authenticity is not an act. You need to know yourself, who you are, and why you are who you are. Only when you have spent some time with yourself can you be real with others. Build genuine relationships by getting to know others more deeply. Not just at the surface level, but know what's important to them, their motivations, their goals, and their fears. Only by being true to who you are can you encourage others to open up to you. In our digital world, it's easy to put up a facade through social media and electronic communication. Authenticity happens face-to-face, over coffee, at a client site, through a firm handshake and eye-to-eye interactions.

13. **Don't have time for relationships? Make networking a priority.** You don't have to go to a conference or special event to get to know people. Find time in your daily interactions to build your internal network. Ask questions in the elevator. Chat in the line at the coffee shop. Get to know the people you see on a daily basis. Drawing on your network in a business context is much easier when you have honed it in an informal context. Utilize every opportunity to interact meaningfully with others.

14. **Skimming the surface? Be attuned to social cues.** Understanding the underlying dynamics of a conversation or a relationship helps you influence and connect with others. When others respond in an unusual manner, there may be more to it than meets the eye. Observe interactions. Watch how people respond. Try to understand the underlying interrelationships between workgroups and individuals. Listen for more than words. What are people saying and not saying? Who works well together? Who doesn't get along? What are the

unspoken expectations? What are the cultural norms? Make a guess. Use your analytical skills to understand the social and interpersonal dynamics of the situation and respond accordingly.

Want to learn more? Take a deep dive...

Huffpost Video. (n.d.). How to read social cues [Howcast]. *The Huffington Post*.

Sundheim, K. (2013, May 7). How much does networking work for business. *Forbes*.

Vlachoutsicos, C. (2012, December 7). What being an "authentic leader" really means. *Harvard Business Review Blog Network*.

Job assignments

20

- Attend informational meetings presented by other departments and functional areas. Use these as an opportunity to interact with people from other areas of the organization.

- Get to know people on an informal level in informal settings. Grab coffee. Set up a lunch meeting. Go for a walk with colleagues.

- Seek projects that require you to work with other workgroups. Try to select those which will introduce you to areas you have had little or no contact with previously.

- Manage a dissatisfied internal or external customer; troubleshoot a performance or quality problem with a product or service. Adapt your interpersonal style to the situation.

- Resolve an issue between two people, units, geographies, functions, etc. Practice using your interpersonal skills to keep things calm and resolve the issues.

Take time to reflect...

If the prospect of interacting with others makes you want to turn and run...

> ...then turn and face it instead. Take the first step. Start the conversation. Share a little. Listen plenty. Learn a lot.

If you focus more on facts than on people and relationships...

> ...then be sure to find a balance. Creating and strengthening connections can make it easier for you to achieve your goals.

If you're savvy with some and awkward with others...

...then think carefully about what's different. Why are you less comfortable with some people? Recognize your blocker. Be OK with discomfort. Set yourself the goal of working through it.

"*I don't like that man.
I must get to know him better.***"**

Abraham Lincoln – 16th President of the United States

Learn more about Interpersonal savvy

Carnegie, D. (2009). *How to win friends and influence people* (Reissue ed.). New York, NY: Simon and Schuster.

Dimitrius, J., & Mazzarella, W. P. (2008). *Reading people: How to understand people and predict their behavior—Anytime, anyplace.* New York, NY: Ballantine Books.

Hayes, J. (2002). *Interpersonal skills at work.* New York, NY: Routledge.

Navarro, J., & Karlins, M. (2008). *What every body is saying: An ex-FBI agent's guide to speed-reading people.* New York, NY: Harper-Collins Publishers.

Silberman, M. L., (with Hansburg, F.). (2000). *PeopleSmart: Developing your interpersonal intelligence.* Hoboken, NJ: John Wiley & Sons.

 Deep dive learning resource links

Burns, K. (2010, January 27). 10 Tips for playing well with others at work. *U.S. News and World Report.* Retrieved from http://money.usnews.com/money/blogs/outside-voices-careers/2010/01/27/10-tips-for-playing-well-with-others-at-work

Chamorro-Premuzic, T. (2012, July 6). Less-confident people are more successful. *Harvard Business Review Blog Network.* Retrieved from http://blogs.hbr.org/2012/07/less-confident-people-are-more-su/

Davey, L. (2013, October 19). Can I be happy at work if I don't like my teammates? *Psychology Today.* Retrieved from http://www.psychologytoday.com/blog/making-your-team-work/201310/can-i-be-happy-work-if-i-dont-my-teammates

Goldschein, E. (2011, September 9). *19 Ways to overcome shyness at work.* Business Insider. Retrieved from http://www.businessinsider.com/ways-to-overcome-shyness-2011-9

Huffpost Video (n.d.). How to read social cues [Howcast]. *The Huffington Post.* Retrieved from http://videos.huffingtonpost.com/business/how-to-read-social-cues-517295650

Lutz, A. (2012, May 18). *The secret to working with 4 different types of people.* Business Insider. Retrieved from http://www.businessinsider.com/kate-wards-the-secret-to-working-with-almost-anyone-2012-5?op=1

Schwartz, T. (2013, January 23). What if you could truly be yourself at work? *Harvard Business Review Blog Network.* Retrieved from http://blogs.hbr.org/2013/01/what-if-you-could-truly-be-you/

| 245

Smith, J. (2013, March 11). 10 Non-verbal cues that convey confidence at work. *Forbes*. Retrieved from http://www.forbes.com/sites/jacquelynsmith/2013/03/11/10-nonverbal-cues-that-convey-confidence-at-work/

Sundheim, K. (2013, May 7). How much does networking work for business. *Forbes*. Retrieved from http://www.forbes.com/sites/kensundheim/2013/05/07/how-much-does-networking-work-for-business/

Vlachoutsicos, C. (2012, December 7). What being an "authentic leader" really means. *Harvard Business Review Blog Network*. Retrieved from http://blogs.hbr.org/2012/12/what-being-an-authentic-leader-really-means/

Wademan Dowling, D. (2009, March 11). 7 Tips for difficult conversations. *Harvard Business Review Blog Network*. Retrieved from http://blogs.hbr.org/2009/03/7-tips-for-difficult-conversat/

Whitmore, J. (2014, January 13). 5 Ways to be a better listener. *Entrepreneur*. Retrieved from http://www.entrepreneur.com/article/230722

Recommended search terms

If you'd like to explore Interpersonal savvy further, try searching online using the following terms:

- Active listening.
- Authentic leadership.
- Becoming more approachable at work.
- Dealing with difficult conversations.
- Overcoming shyness in the workplace.
- Working with different personalities.

(i) More help...

Go to www.kornferry.com/fyi-resources and link directly to the deep dive resources in this chapter. Visit the site often to see the additional resources that are uploaded on a regular basis.

---

21. *Builds* networks

Effectively building formal and informal relationship networks inside and outside the organization.

Most organizations have experienced tremendous change since the dawn of the 21st century. Flatter and more matrixed. Virtual teams and offices. Cross-functional ad hoc teams. Global operations. 24/7 connection. Shared services. Centralized and decentralized functions. This is how work gets done now. Decisions are made in teams, with input from multiple functions. Meetings are held on the web, crossing time zones and involving multiple geographies. It's no longer enough to go to work, meet with local colleagues, make a few phone calls, close your door and go home. Connections need to be made with support staff, idea generators, resource managers, and decision makers across the country or around the world. It's not only how work gets done—it's how ideas are spread and careers advanced. This is an exciting world for those who are both open to connecting and focused in forging relationships. But if you are dismayed by ambiguity or shy about reaching out, navigating the network may be a challenge for you. To be successful, you need to know who people are and what they do. How to collaborate, share resources, and maintain productive relationships. You need to be focused yet fluid. Willing to participate and ask for help.

" *Virtue in obscurity is rewarded only in heaven. To succeed in this world you have to be known to people.* **"**

Sonia Sotomayor – American Supreme Court Justice

***Builds* networks** is in the **People** factor (III) in the Korn Ferry Leadership Architect™. It is part of Cluster G, **Building collaborative relationships,** along with Collaborates (6), *Manages* conflict (9), and Interpersonal savvy (20). You may find it helpful to also take a look at some of the tips included in those chapters to supplement your learning.

Skilled

Builds strong formal and informal networks.

Maintains relationships across a variety of functions and locations.

Draws upon multiple relationships to exchange ideas, resources, and know-how.

Less skilled

- Builds limited relationships with different groups.
- Has difficulty determining who to contact for resources or knowledge.
- Doesn't tap into networks beyond own immediate area to exchange ideas or get things done.

Talented

- Consults with a wide network of internal and external connections.
- Connects the right people to accomplish goals.
- Works through formal and informal channels to build broad-based relationships and support.

Overused skill

- Relies on networking at the expense of other skills and work priorities.
- May be perceived as a one-sided networker, using networks solely for own advantage.

Some possible causes of lower skill

Causes help explain *why* a person may have trouble with *Builds* networks. When seeking to increase skill, it's helpful to consider how these might play out in certain situations. And remember that all of these can be addressed if you are motivated to do so.

- Lacks focus.
- Intimidated by complexity.
- Dislikes or avoids politics.
- Dislikes visibility.
- Lacks ambition.
- Clings to the familiar.
- Prefers linear processes.
- Not open to other ways of doing things.
- Not organized.
- Prefers defined roles and relationships.

Brain booster

21

Many of us build networks for practical reasons. Our network can serve as a platform for helping us achieve our work goals. It provides a coalition force. An information channel. A source of collective capabilities. But networking is also an end in itself. Our brains are wired to connect with others. We have a fundamental need for social interaction, more so than other physiological needs. Recall when you were rejected by others or isolated at school or in the workplace. Feel painful? Don't be surprised if it does. Our biology is built to require social connections. When we meet this need, we feel good. When we feel good, dopamine is released. Release of dopamine enables us to process thoughts more effectively. It helps us become more productive. Tap into this processing boost by making the most of networking opportunities. Before you meet someone, take a time-out. Close your eyes. Think about that person. What do you know about them? Have you interacted in the past? What is unique or special about them? How are you different from or similar to them? As you think through these points, you activate the regions in the brain (dorsomedial prefrontal cortex and temporal-parietal junction) related to social thinking. This activation prepares you for more productive social interaction. You'll feel good and the chain reaction is stimulated.[31]

Tips to develop *Builds* networks

1. **Not sure where to start? Create a relationship map.** New to the organization? The relationships you establish in the first few months on the job will be a critical factor in your success. If you're just starting to reach out, begin by creating a relationship map. Use an org chart to put names with titles and locations. Who is a good contact in other functions? Who are the major vendor reps or contract plant managers you need to connect with? Start local and then move further afield. Sit down with your boss and colleagues and ask them who you should know. Understand why these people would be good to connect with. Get some insight into how they like to work and what their concerns are. Then create a plan to introduce yourself. Use e-mail or phone to send a short introductory message. Tell them who you are, where you are, and what you hope to accomplish by working with them. Then plan to meet them face-to-face. The map you create now will become the hub of your productive network.

2. **Clinging to the familiar? Learn to let go.** Networks are, by their nature, open-ended, changeable, and ambiguous. There is no GPS to tell you which moves to make, or when. They are "navigated" in the way early explorers crossed the Atlantic. With a generally understood destination. A handful of information. A few tools and stars to steer by. Maybe you, on the other hand, like certainty. Routine. Structure. Linear process. Working with people who share your experience. But you will need to loosen up your old ways of doing things if you are going to successfully navigate the network. To become more flexible and accustomed to change, engage in activities that require new ways of thinking. Start small and then move on to bigger challenges. Take a new route to work. Eat lunch in a new locale and talk with new people. Read a book that challenges your thinking. Teach your language to immigrant adults. Plan a trip to a new country with your family. Then go. Design a new way of working and teach it to your team. Changing your approach will help you step into the moving stream of the network.

3. **Find it difficult to connect? Understand what's important to other people.** Building a productive relationship is far easier when you understand the world of the other person. The challenges they experience. What their priorities are. Opportunities they see in the near future. And what's going on for them on a day-to-day basis. So make it your business to dig beneath the surface. Put yourself in their shoes. Learn to talk their language. See life from their point of view. What is life like at their level of the organization? What's going

on in their business unit or function? Recognize that sometimes people have personal or professional challenges that affect their ability to work with you—even if they don't tell you about them. When you are tapping into your network, anticipate a good response but don't get discouraged if things don't happen as you would like. When you understand others' challenges, you will gain perspective on when and how to reach out to them.

4. **Not included? Be visible and approachable.** Relationships grow when people like each other, respect each other's competence, and trust each other to perform as promised. Accomplished networkers get things done because people remember them and want to work with them. You can be knowledgeable and accomplished. But if you are rude, not helpful, too busy to listen, or just not friendly, you'll be bypassed. Walking around like a curmudgeon? Be someone others want to know and work with. In meetings—smile and put others at ease. Convey openness with phrases like "I don't think we've met" or "I heard you speak this morning and wanted to introduce myself." Smile when you are speaking on the phone—it will create a more personal connection with the listener. Warm up your e-mails with friendly salutations "Good morning, Joe!" and signatures "Regards". Wish people a happy weekend or a happy holiday. When they're facing a personal or professional challenge, say, "Let me know how I can help." Be sure your e-mail signature includes your title and contact information so they can find you easily. Be enthusiastic. Be personable.

5. **Going global? Understand cultures—but don't stereotype.** The larger and more far-flung your organization, the more important effective networking becomes. And the more likely that you will be interacting with people of diverse nationalities located around the world. Virtual teams can include people from many countries. You want to make good contacts and work together in the best way possible. So prepare yourself. And open yourself to learning. If you are traveling, study the regional and national business culture. Learn how business is conducted. How meetings are run. How the culture views relationship vs. task. Formality vs. informality. Punctuality vs. a relaxed time frame. Put yourself in learning mode. Ask someone who has been there. When you work across geographies, you can appreciate differences—but don't stereotype. Be open and respectful. Get to know people as individuals.

Want to learn more? Take a deep dive...

Debaise, C. (2012, May 3). 7 Tips for networking. *Entrepreneur.*

Fitzgerald, J. (2014, January 12). Fine-tune your networking skills. *The Boston Globe.*

Hauer, C. (2012, June 14). Networking tips: Win friends, influence others [Video file]. *Bloomberg Businessweek.*

6. **Need help or information? Ask around.** Information is the life's blood of an organization. And information on who can help you get things done is crucial. Need a resource? Work it like a scavenger hunt. Send an e-mail to relevant people or groups. Wondering about best practices in customer service? Need the latest thinking on a new tracking system? Get ideas across the enterprise. Asked to work with colleagues in another country? Find someone who has been there. People love to share their travel tips! Ask personally and send out an e-mail to your contacts to find that key person or piece of missing information. Follow up on whatever comes your way and send a thank you to the person who made the referral. Always be willing to return the favor when requests come your way.

7. **Forming a team? Know who does what.** If you're tasked with forming a new team or workgroup, let your network help. Start by laying out your idea. Then create a chart of your needs. Treat this like a staffing challenge. What levels of seniority do you need? What kinds of skills or experience? What other criteria are important? Consider functions and geographies. How will you meet? Can you do a face-to-face or will this have to be virtual? Do you know someone who has led similar groups? Ask your peers about people they know and recommend. If you're asking for people from someone else's team, consider whether you should ask permission to "borrow" resources.

8. **Misplacing information? Use systems to organize.** Ever meet someone helpful and forget their name two days later? Get a business card and wonder why you had it? Promise to follow up and forget to do it? Strong performers spend about 80% of their days in transactions. Making connections. Accomplishing tasks. Getting things done. To stay on top of critical tasks, choose a few systems that work for you and act immediately on new information. Use internal organizational systems, where they exist, to find colleagues. Enter important to-dos on your calendar or other task-tracking system. Store cell phone numbers on your own phone. Move

information from business cards into your contact database. When you're out and about, set up next meetings immediately on your smartphone—don't wait until you get back to the office. Scan e-mail. Trash the ones you don't need to respond to. Respond to or file the rest for later action. Find small pockets of time to stay on top of the detail. Take 15 minutes at the end of the day to tie up loose ends.

9. **Reluctant to reach out to senior management? Ask for support.** It is critical to include more senior management people in your networks. They tend to have a broader range of relationships. After all, they've had more time to meet others, gain influence, and drive decisions. By including higher-level individuals in your network, you will build your own visibility. You will gain a higher-level perspective and important information. And potential support for your initiatives. To network with senior management, you can sometimes reach out to them directly. Especially if you have worked with them in the past or if it is a fairly close relationship on the org chart. Maybe all you need to do is ask an assistant to set up a meeting. If you are more comfortable being introduced, start with people you already know. They will often be happy to broaden your networks, if you ask. Tell them what you'd like to accomplish in your networking and ask for introductions. Outside the organization, send a message through LinkedIn. Or plan to introduce yourself at conference meetings or other events. If you worry about taking up someone's time, remember that the best leaders like to share their knowledge. They are valuable catalysts for making things happen. Talk with your boss and/or a trusted mentor or legacy leader to start making these important connections.

21

Want to learn more? Take a deep dive...

Clark, D. (2014, January 9). How networking can become your competitive advantage. *Forbes*.

HBR IdeaCast. (2011, July 21). Getting networking right [Podcast]. *Harvard Business Review Blog Network*.

Misner, I. (2012, September 6). 5 Ways to use your network to grow your business. *Entrepreneur*.

10. **Hate "politics"? Think about it in a new way.** Organizational politics can have a bad name. To some, it denotes hidden agendas, turf battles, and decisions made for the "wrong" reasons. In this view, politics is just another word for conflict. Painful conflict. But to ignore the political give-and-take means giving up influence over decisions.

|

To be part of the political landscape, recognize it for what it is—a web of relationships, opinions, positions, and perspectives. A complex of discussions and agreements that affects everyone in the organization. Including you. It's to your advantage to observe what's happening. To understand the perspectives of groups and their leaders. To be aware of others' concerns and agendas. To participate in discussions. To ask questions. To hold and express an opinion. The most successful networkers are tuned in. They understand how business trends, stock prices, personal opinions, and territorial responses affect decisions. Get your boss's perspective and consult your peers about what is going on. Read messages from the CEO and the board. By studying others' positions, you can learn to embrace the political landscape.

11. **Perceived as too ambitious? Network at *all* levels.** Networking inside your organization is not only a great way to get work done, it's also good for your personal visibility and career. It's a good idea to be known—especially to those who can help you advance. But if you sense that people think you're too ambitious, better adjust your approach a bit. You may be too eager to connect with higher-ups and ignoring other important relationships. Remember that the primary intention of building an internal network is to advance the work of the organization. Not to provide you as an individual with opportunities to look good or pursue a promotion. To avoid looking like a "me firster," reconnect with peers on your immediate team. Set up meetings with your reports. Follow up on anything you need to deliver to your boss. Then refocus your network to include people in your peer groups and colleagues in other functions. Whose name comes up as a great colleague? Whom might you be working with in the near future? And don't ignore subordinates, assistants, and people who support the projects you work on. They are potentially powerful allies when it's time to get things done. Treat people at all levels with respect.

12. **Spread too thin? Focus on best relationships.** You may be a natural networker—someone who meets people easily and loves making connections. You're happy to attend meetings, shake hands, and extend invitations on social media. You may know a lot of people, but in networking, it's important not to confuse quantity with the quality of your connections. A productive network—whose members can be called upon for information, resources, and referrals—has a focus and a set of shared interests. And a productive network is one you maintain. Whose members you interact with and whose names you recognize. Before you attend another event, set some criteria for making new contacts. Before you accept another social media

254 |

connection, ask yourself why making this connection can be important to your overall goals and direction. Before you join another LinkedIn group, consider how and when you can interact with its members. Look for shared interests and the potential for productive interaction. Consider going through your contact lists and deleting anyone whose name you don't recognize.

13. **Using social networks? Proceed carefully.** Social networks have become a fact of life. They keep us connected to friends and colleagues across time and geographies. But you can also lose your job or, derail your career there. There are two ways to think of networking sites: Professional. Personal. Use LinkedIn as a place to maintain a professional profile. Join groups and discussions. Find people in related functions and companies. Connect with former colleagues and new acquaintances. Use the rest primarily as personal sites. And then be careful. Even on a personal site, you represent your organization. Using Twitter? No tweeting opinions on your company, its competitors, products, or policies. No remarks about being bored at work. Or upset with something someone said. Posting photos on Facebook or Instagram? On the Internet, the whole world becomes a very big small town. Take down anything you would have to apologize for—or don't put it up in the first place. Check with HR, Legal, or Communications to get a copy of your organization's social media policy, and follow it scrupulously.

21

Want to learn more? Take a deep dive...

Dishman, L. (2013, November 22). How the most productive people grow their network while still getting it all done. *Fast Company.*

Ryan, L. (2010, April 7). Ten things that are not networking: Consulting edition. *The Huffington Post.*

Sharma, G. (2013, February 28). How to start networking – and succeed. *Forbes.*

Job assignments
• Join or lead a virtual team deploying a new system, process, or procedure across decentralized and/or dispersed units. Note what tools and processes are most effective in helping members of the team connect.

- Create and introduce a system for mapping important relationships for new employees. Test it out with the next few people to join the team.

- Interview six people in six different areas and write a report on what you learned about their perspectives on the business. Consider how you will be able to use this information to help build your network. Keep a record of the new relationships you develop at all levels.

- Lead a team that creates a multi-functional onboarding or mentoring program involving senior management.

- Join a project that involves travel and/or short assignments in other regions of the world. Think through the information you will need to gather and set some time lines to get this done.

Take time to reflect...

If you feel networking is a lot of effort for little reward...

...then you need to think about it in a different way. Networking is not all about getting an immediate return. It's about expanding your effectiveness by knowing people and being known.

If you tend to be unfocused in your approach...

...then define your purpose. Think quality not quantity. Being clear on what you hope to gain from building your network will help ensure you get what you need.

If you find yourself interacting with the same people again and again...

...then discover pleasant surprises by branching out. Be bold. Step into new territory. Building networks in areas that are far removed from your work—whether different industries or geographies—can be refreshing, enlightening, and rewarding.

" *You can make more friends in two months by becoming interested in other people than you can in two years by trying to get other people interested in you.* **"**

Dale Carnegie – American author and speaker

Learn more about *Builds* networks

Anklam, P. (2007). *Net work: A practical guide to creating and sustaining networks at work and in the world.* Burlington, MA: Butterworth-Heinemann.

Baber, A., & Waymon, L. (2007). *Make your contacts count: Networking know-how for business and career success* (2nd ed.). New York, NY: AMACOM.

Beasley, J. S., & Nilkaew, P. (2012). *Networking essentials* (3rd ed.). Upper Saddle River, NJ: Pearson Education, Inc.

Bjorseth, L. D. (2009). *Breakthrough networking: Building relationships that last* (3rd ed.). Lisle, IL: Duoforce Enterprises, Inc.

Zack, D. (2010). *Networking for people who hate networking: A field guide for introverts, the overwhelmed, and the underconnected.* San Francisco, CA: Berrett-Koehler Publishers, Inc.

 Deep dive learning resource links

Clark, D. (2014, January 9). How networking can become your competitive advantage. *Forbes.* Retrieved from http://www.forbes.com/sites/dorieclark/2014/01/09/how-networking-can-become-your-competitive-advantage/

Debaise, C. (2012, May 3). 7 Tips for networking. *Entrepreneur.* Retrieved from http://www.entrepreneur.com/blog/223468

Dishman, L. (2013, November 22). How the most productive people grow their network while still getting it all done. *Fast Company.* Retrieved from http://www.fastcompany.com/3022043/secrets-of-the-most-productive-people/how-the-most-productive-people-grow-their-network-with

Fitzgerald, J. (2014, January 12). Fine-tune your networking skills. *The Boston Globe.* Retrieved from http://www.bostonglobe.com/business/2014/01/12/not-about-networking-about-doing-right/pfqZqjJMBIJSRSEL3Qfp4I/story.html

Hauer, C. (2012, June 14). Networking tips: Win friends, influence others [Video file]. *Bloomberg Businessweek.* Retrieved from http://www.businessweek.com/videos/2013-06-14/networking-tips-win-friends-influence-others

HBR IdeaCast. (2011, July 21). Getting networking right [Podcast]. *Harvard Business Review Blog Network.* Retrieved from http://blogs.hbr.org/2011/07/getting-networking-right/

21

Misner, I. (2012, September 6). 5 Ways to use your network to grow your business. *Entrepreneur.* Retrieved from http://www.entrepreneur.com/article/224344

Ryan, L. (2010, April 7). Ten things that are not networking: Consulting edition. *The Huffington Post*. Retrieved from http://www.huffingtonpost.com/liz-ryan/ten-things-that-are-not-n_b_528019.html

Sharma, G. (2013, February 28). How to start networking – and succeed. *Forbes*. Retrieved from http://www.forbes.com/sites/gaurisharma/2013/02/28/a-force-to-be-networked-with/

Recommended search terms

If you'd like to explore *Builds* networks further, try searching online using the following terms:

- Getting your employees to network.
- How to start networking.
- Leveraging networks.
- Networking.
- What not to do while networking.

21

(i) More help...

Go to www.kornferry.com/fyi-resources and link directly to the deep dive resources in this chapter. Visit the site often to see the additional resources that are uploaded on a regular basis.

22. Nimble learning

Actively learning through experimentation when tackling new problems, using both successes and failures as learning fodder.

Most of us are good at applying what we have seen and done in the past and utilizing solutions that have worked for us before. A rarer skill is doing things for the first time. Solving problems we've never come across. Trying solutions we have never tried before. Analyzing problems in new contexts and in new ways. With the increasing pace of change, being quick to learn and apply first-time solutions is becoming a crucial skill. It involves taking risks, being less than perfect, discarding the past, going against the grain, and cutting new paths. It requires patience, persistence, and a positive attitude. Organizations need people who can quickly adapt their thinking to the current situation. People who can draw on their past experience and apply the learning to a new and different setting. To become a nimble learner is to be engaged in the present while drawing on past learnings and thinking about future needs. Ask good questions. Learn from experience. Be willing to try new things. And be flexible in the face of new or changing information.

"Negative results are just what I want. They're as valuable to me as positive results. I can never find the thing that does the job best until I find the ones that don't."

Thomas Edison – American inventor and businessman

Nimble learning is in the **Self** factor (IV) in the Korn Ferry Leadership Architect™. It is part of Cluster L, **Being flexible and adaptable,** along with *Manages* ambiguity (3), *Being* resilient (26), and Situational adaptability (31). You may find it helpful to also take a look at some of the tips included in those chapters to supplement your learning.

Skilled

Learns quickly when facing new situations.

Experiments to find new solutions.

Takes on the challenge of unfamiliar tasks.

Extracts lessons learned from failures and mistakes.

Less skilled

- Struggles to learn in new situations.
- Becomes frustrated or confused by unfamiliar tasks.
- Gives up on new ideas too soon.
- Resists taking a chance on untested solutions.

Talented

- Tries multiple times using multiple methods to find the right solution.
- Views mistakes as opportunities to learn.
- Enjoys the challenge of unfamiliar tasks.
- Seeks new approaches to solve problems.

Overused skill

- Takes on new challenges for the sake of it rather than in the interest of making a positive impact.
- Focuses on unvetted ideas simply because they are new.
- May take unnecessary risks in the name of learning.

Some possible causes of lower skill

Causes help explain *why* a person may have trouble with Nimble learning. When seeking to increase skill, it's helpful to consider how these might play out in certain situations. And remember that all of these can be addressed if you are motivated to do so.

- Isn't willing to ask questions.
- Fails to look outside of the box.
- Doesn't analyze successes and failures for clues.
- Solves problems based only on what has worked in the past.
- Isn't a risk taker.
- Isn't self-confident.
- Perfectionist.
- Stuck in the past.
- Can't do more than one thing at a time.
- Doesn't have learning role models.
- Poor observer of others.

Brain booster

Believe you can't teach an old dog new tricks? Early scientific research supported the mindset that there are specific periods in a person's life when they learn certain capabilities. Language. Vision. Social attachment. And once that period has passed, the learning stops. The capabilities become hardwired and hard to change. For instance, the first 8–10 months is critical for a child in learning to detect phonetic distinctions in speech. By 12 months, this ability diminishes. The "fixed" mindset supports this view. However, the growing evidence for neuroplasticity in the past two decades has challenged this. Neuroplasticity refers to the brain's ability to adapt and change as a result of effort and experiences. And not just through childhood. The physical structure of the brain continues to change, which means that our learning is not limited in the way early research suggested. This is good news for nimble learning. The brain is sensitive to experience, meaning even old dogs can and do learn new tricks if they're willing to try new things, take risks, and dive into the unfamiliar.[32]

Tips to develop Nimble learning

1. **Facing a new or unknown situation? Embrace ambiguity.** Not many people are motivated by uncertainty and chaos. But sometimes they can bring rewards. Envision the payoff of the unknown and you'll become more comfortable being a pioneer. Solving problems no one has solved before. Cutting paths where no one has been before. Instead of getting overwhelmed by the problem, seek to find a solution. Ask yourself questions. What do you know about the situation? How can you use your experience/expertise and relate it to the setting? Where do you need insight from others? Look for opportunities to gain exposure to new situations, new perspectives, and new insights. Become comfortable with the unknown. Be curious.

2. **Too focused on a solution? Take time to ask questions and define the problem.** Too often we think first and only of solutions. It's easy and tempting. In studies of problem-solving sessions, solutions outweigh questions eight to one. Most meetings on a problem start with people offering solutions. Early solutions are not likely to be the best. If you move to decisions too quickly, analyze the factors that cause you to avoid taking the time to consider complexity. Set aside the first 50% of the time for questions and problem definition and the last 50% of the time for solutions. Asking more questions early helps you rethink the problem and come to more and different solutions. Ask how many elements this problem has. What is related to it? What is not related to it? What are the root causes? Sometimes by understanding the cause, the best solution comes to light. Try to solve the problem as close to the root cause as possible.

22

3. **Where to start? Locate the essence of the problem.** What are the key factors or elements in this problem? Experts usually solve problems by figuring out what the deep, underlying principles are and working forward from there. The less adept focus on desired outcomes/solutions and work backward or concentrate on the surface facts. What are the deep principles of what you're working on? Once you've done this, search the past for parallels—your past, the business past, the historical past. One common mistake here is to search in parallel organizations because "only they would know." Backing up and asking a broader question will aid in the search for solutions. When Motorola wanted to find out how to process orders more quickly, they went not to other electronics firms, but to Domino's Pizza and Federal Express.

Want to learn more? Take a deep dive...

Anthony, S. (2010, July 6). Grooming leaders to handle ambiguity. *Harvard Business Review Blog Network.*

Llopis, G. (2013, November 4). The 4 most effective ways leaders solve problems. *Forbes.*

Zwilling, M. (2011, July 19). *Nine steps to effective business problem solving.* Business Insider.

4. **Trouble making sense of the issues? Dig for root causes.** Keep asking why. See how many causes you can come up with and how many organizing buckets you can put them in. This increases the chance of a better solution because you can see more connections. Chess masters recognize thousands of possible patterns of chess pieces. Look for patterns in data. Don't just collect information. Put it in categories that make sense to you. Use other people to help you best analyze issues. Ask for their understanding of the core problem. Where do they see themes? Draw upon the expertise of others to help you analyze more deeply.

5. **How to generalize? Look for patterns.** Look for personal patterns, organizational patterns, or world patterns when analyzing general successes and failures. What was common to each success or what was present in each failure but never present in a success? Focus on both the successes and failures. Failures are easier to analyze but don't in themselves tell you what would work. But they give you great incentive to learn, which leads to results. Comparing successes, while less exciting, yields more information about underlying principles. Be careful, though. If you only focus on what went well, you could assume improvement isn't necessary. You might get lazy. By focusing on where you can make improvements, even in successful situations, you can ensure stronger results next time. When analyzing either a success or a failure, it is best to be as specific as possible. Specificity gets to the subtle issues that can make or break a decision in the future. The bottom line is to reduce your insights to principles or rules of thumb you think might be repeatable. When faced with the next new problem, those general underlying principles will apply again.

6. **Need help? Use others.** Teams of people with the widest diversity of backgrounds produce the most innovative solutions to problems. Get others with different backgrounds to analyze and make sense of

the issue with you. When working together, come up with as many questions about it as you can. Set up a competition with another group or individual. Ask them to work on exactly what you are working on. Have a postmortem to try to deduce some of the practices and procedures that work best. Find a team or individual that faces problems quite similar to what you face and set up dialogues on a number of specific topics. Ask them what they think about when they make decisions. Have them tell you how they thought through a new problem in this area. The major skills they look for in sizing up people's proficiency in this area. Key questions they ask about a problem. How they would suggest you go about learning quickly in this area.

Want to learn more? Take a deep dive...

Cherry, K. (n.d.). *What is problem-solving?* About.com Psychology.

Dreifus, C. (2008, January 8). In professor's model, diversity = productivity. *The New York Times*.

Mind Tools. (n.d.). *Root cause analysis: Tracing a problem to its origins*. Mind Tools.

7. **Want to speed up the learning cycle? Try different solutions and learn from the results.** Don't expect to get it right the first time. Being safe and doing what has worked in the past leads to stale solutions. Instead, be willing to experiment. Many studies show that the second or third try is when we really understand the underlying dynamics of problems. If you have trouble going back the second or third time to get something done, then switch approaches. Sometimes people get stuck in a repeating groove that's not working. Do something different next time. To increase learning, build feedback loops into your experimentation. Aim for immediate and timely feedback from others. If it's not forthcoming, ask for it. The more frequent the cycles, the more opportunities to learn. Try something new on a regular basis. Instead of looking at learning as a formal process that has to be scheduled, try to learn one new thing every day. This increases your learning opportunities and increases the chance of finding the right answer.

8. **Want to innovate but don't know how? Do quick experiments.** Studies show that 80% of innovations occur in unexpected places and by unexpected people. Dye makers developed detergent. Post-it® Notes came from an error in a glue formula. These people

were not looking for this solution. They stumbled upon it. They experimented. Build time into your schedule to try new things. Think outside of the box. Pursue a new idea. Try lots of quick, inexpensive experiments to increase the chances of success. Be curious. Draw on ideas from other people. Other industries. Other functional areas. Even if you come up with an idea that you can't use yourself, think about where else it can be applied. Sometimes the best ideas won't work in your area. Will it help in other areas? Can you pass it along?

9. **Afraid of failure? Take more risks.** Not all new ideas are successful. Prepare yourself for this. About 30%–50% of technical innovations fail in tests within the company. Even among those that make it to the marketplace, 70%–90% fail. The bottom line on change is a 95% failure rate, and the most successful innovators try lots of quick, inexpensive experiments to increase the chances of success. Research indicates that more successful people have made more mistakes than the less successful. Try new things often. Go for small wins. You can recover quickly if you miss, and more importantly, learn from the results. Start with the easiest challenge, then work up to the tougher ones. Recognize that you won't always be successful. But keep trying. Never give up when you believe there is a way to make something better. Many problem-solving studies show that the second or third try is when we really understand the underlying dynamics of problems. Think of exploring as a series of try-learn-try again-learn some more.

Want to learn more? Take a deep dive...

Baldoni, J. (2010, January 29). How to encourage small innovations. *Harvard Business Review Blog Network*.

Cain, M. (2013, April 23). 5 Ways to conquer your fear of failure. *Forbes*.

Laufenberg, D. (2010, December). Diana Laufenberg: How to learn? From mistakes [Video file]. TED.

10. **Want to use current learning in the future? Reflect.** Once you have completed a task or a project, build in time for reflection. The best way to become a nimble learner is to take the time to consider what you have learned from an experience and then apply that learning to future situations. Pause. Reflect. On your own? Take a walk. Journal. Sit in silence. With others? Do a post-project review. Set up an off-site session. Ask questions. What went well? What didn't? How

could you have done things differently? If you face a similar challenge in the future, what can you take from this experience to be even more successful? Don't just think about this reflection as a review of the past. Think forward. What can you take with you to be more successful in future challenges? As you grow, think about your learning journey. What have you learned and developed along the way? How are you thinking about problems from a different perspective now compared to 10 years ago? Five years ago? Three months ago? Last week?

11. **Don't see much change or growth? Make learning a priority and a goal.** Research indicates that when a person not only seeks to make a good decision but also proactively seeks to learn from an experience, they are more successful in the future. They not only solve the problem but also become a better thinker. This helps the person solve future problems more effectively. When reflecting on the experience, don't just think about the impact of the solution. Consider what you have learned about yourself. What is your best learning style? In what situations would you benefit from using a new or different learning style? What approach is typical for you? What has been most difficult for you in this challenge? Be aware of what is restricting your thinking and perspective. When approaching any new situation, shift your thinking to be learning oriented.

12. **Fall back to how you've always done it? Override your default comfort zone.** If you find yourself defaulting to the established way of doing things, you're not alone. It turns out our brains are conditioned to be more comfortable with the status quo. We have a natural tendency to stick to what is already known. What we've already decided. What's comfortable. Change of any kind makes our brains work harder than staying the same. The good news is that we can override our brain's natural tendency toward inertia. How? By constantly trying something new—new ways of doing things, new experiences, new people. There will be challenges for you at first. You're bound to feel a decreased sense of mastery and will likely fail sometimes too. Focus on the payoff—being able to adapt more easily, being out in front of change. This will silence the worry voice inside your head that keeps you tethered to what's comfortable and familiar.

Want to learn more? Take a deep dive...

Haque, U. (2010, November 24). Making room for reflection is a strategic imperative. *Harvard Business Review Blog Network*.

Latham, G. P., & Seijts, G. (2006, May/June). Learning goals or performance goals: Is it the journey or the destination? *Ivey Business Journal*.

Warrell, M. (2013, April 22). Why getting comfortable with discomfort is crucial to success. *Forbes*.

Job assignments

- Join professional organizations that will build your knowledge and allow you to meet your counterparts from other organizations. Ask them about their approaches, systems, or solutions and assess the relevance to your business.

- Look for opportunities to gain experience working in a cross-cultural setting where you are required to work with people who come from different backgrounds and have different experiences.

- Work on a cross-functional task force where you interact with people from different backgrounds and areas of the organization.

- Volunteer to lead a project or take on a role that is related to your area of expertise where you have less experience.

- Find a mentor. Look for a person who you admire and who demonstrates very strong skills in analyzing issues and solving problems creatively.

22

Take time to reflect...

If you rely on your past experience when faced with new situations...

...then recognize that what worked before might not always work going forward. A situation may look exactly the same, but there could be differences you're not seeing. Adapt. Try new things.

If you lean toward doing rather than taking time to learn...

...then understand that these aren't mutually exclusive. You're learning every day, even if you don't always stop to think about it. Set aside time to reflect and draw vital lessons from your experiences.

If you prefer to reflect on successes and bury the failures...

...then keep in mind that some of the most powerful learning comes from unsuccessful projects. Studying your mistakes may be painful, but it can turn an experience to forget into a lesson to remember.

"*You don't learn to walk by following rules.
You learn by doing, and by falling over.* **"**

Sir Richard Branson – English business magnate and investor

Learn more about Nimble learning

Bruno, H. E., Gonzalez-Mena, J., Hernandez, L. A., & Sullivan, D. R. (2013). *Learning from the bumps in the road: Insights from early childhood leaders*. St. Paul, MN: Redleaf Press.

Tugend, A. (2011). *Better by mistake: The unexpected benefits of being wrong*. New York, NY: Penguin Group.

Watanabe, K. (2009). *Problem solving 101: A simple book for smart people*. New York, NY: Portfolio Hardcover.

Weinzimmer, L. G., & McConoughey, J. (2013). *The wisdom of failure: How to learn the tough leadership lessons without paying the price*. San Francisco, CA: Jossey-Bass.

Wilkinson, D. J. (2006). *The ambiguity advantage: What great leaders are great at*. Hampshire, England: Palgrave MacMillan.

Deep dive learning resource links

Anthony, S. (2010, July 6). Grooming leaders to handle ambiguity. *Harvard Business Review Blog Network*. Retrieved from http://blogs.hbr.org/2010/07/grooming-leaders-to-handle-ambiguity/

Baldoni, J. (2010, January 29). How to encourage small innovations. *Harvard Business Review Blog Network*. Retrieved from http://blogs.hbr.org/2010/01/how-to-encourage-small-i-innov/

Cain, M. (2013, April 23). 5 Ways to conquer your fear of failure. *Forbes*. Retrieved from http://www.forbes.com/sites/glassheel/2013/04/23/5-ways-to-conquer-your-fear-of-failure/

Cherry, K. (n.d.). *What is problem-solving?* About.com Psychology. Retrieved from http://psychology.about.com/od/problemsolving/f/problem-solving-steps.htm

Dreifus, C. (2008, January 8). In professor's model, diversity = productivity. *The New York Times*. Retrieved from http://www.nytimes.com/2008/01/08/science/08conv.html?_r=0

Haque, U. (2010, November 24). Making room for reflection is a strategic imperative. *Harvard Business Review Blog Network*. Retrieved from http://blogs.hbr.org/2010/11/reflection-items-not-action-it/

Latham, G. P., & Seijts, G. (2006, May/June). Learning goals or performance goals: Is it the journey or the destination? *Ivey Business Journal*. Retrieved from http://iveybusinessjournal.com/topics/leadership/learning-goals-or-performance-goals-is-it-the-journey-or-the-destination#.UuwaqdTnZdg

| 269

Laufenberg, D. (2010, December). Diana Laufenberg: How to learn? From mistakes [Video file]. TED. Retrieved from http://www.ted.com/talks/diana_laufenberg_3_ways_to_teach.html

Llopis, G. (2013, November 4). The 4 most effective ways leaders solve problems. *Forbes*. Retrieved from http://www.forbes.com/sites/glennllopis/2013/11/04/the-4-most-effective-ways-leaders-solve-problems/

Mind Tools. (n.d.). *Root cause analysis: Tracing a problem to its origins*. Mind Tools. Retrieved from http://www.mindtools.com/pages/article/newTMC_80.htm

Warrell, M. (2013, April 22). Why getting comfortable with discomfort is crucial to success. *Forbes*. Retrieved from http://www.forbes.com/sites/margiewarrell/2013/04/22/is-comfort-holding-you-back/

Zwilling, M. (2011, July 19). *Nine steps to effective business problem solving*. Business Insider. Retrieved from http://www.businessinsider.com/nine-steps-to-effective-business-problem-solving-2011-7

Recommended search terms

If you'd like to explore Nimble learning further, try searching online using the following terms:

- Defining the problem.
- Embracing ambiguity.
- Finding and generalizing patterns.
- Learning from past mistakes.
- Overcoming a fear of failure.
- Personal reflection.

(i) More help...

Go to www.kornferry.com/fyi-resources and link directly to the deep dive resources in this chapter. Visit the site often to see the additional resources that are uploaded on a regular basis.

---

23. Organizational savvy

Maneuvering comfortably through complex policy, process, and people-related organizational dynamics.

Organizations are made up of formal structure, policies, buildings, inventory, intellectual property, and so forth. They may be logically planned and brilliantly orchestrated, but while human beings are still at the core, things can get messy. It's the human element that interjects politics, emotion, uncertainty, intrigue, and conflict. Often, we end up dealing with a confusing blend of the rational and irrational, the controlled and the random, the spoken and the unsaid. It's easy to get lost in the fog. Organizational savvy is the compass that guides you swiftly and without mishap to your destination. People who do this well understand the difference between what the organization intends to be versus the reality. They read the unwritten signs to navigate the organizational maze. They know who has power and influence. They appreciate who has respect. And they are aware of who only has a title. They know which messages work and which ones don't. They use their understanding to move things forward for the greater good. In short, they're masters at getting work done in an organizational setting. So accept the complexity of your organization. Don't fight it. Learn how to work with it to your advantage.

> **"** One of the penalties for refusing to participate in politics is that you end up being governed by your inferiors. **"**

Plato – Greek philosopher

Organizational savvy is in the **People** factor (III) in the Korn Ferry Leadership Architect™. It is part of Cluster I, **Influencing people,** along with Communicates effectively (7), *Drives* engagement (16), Persuades (24), and *Drives* vision and purpose (37). You may find it helpful to also take a look at some of the tips included in those chapters to supplement your learning.

Skilled

Is sensitive to how people and organizations function.

Anticipates land mines and plans approach accordingly.

Deals comfortably with organizational politics.

Knows who has power, respect, and influence.

Steers through the organizational maze to get things done.

Less skilled

- Overlooks or disregards the political complexities of the organization.

- Pursues own area's goals without considering the impact on other groups.

- Says and does things that strain organizational relationships.

- Tends to be impatient with organizational processes and makes political errors.

Talented

- Navigates the political complexities of the organization easily.

- Has a clear understanding of other groups' business priorities.

- Avoids provoking tension between groups.

- Uses knowledge of organizational culture to achieve objectives.

Overused skill

- May prioritize organizational positioning, even when straightforward action is called for.

- May be seen as excessively political.

- May tell others what they want to hear instead of what he/she knows to be true.

Some possible causes of lower skill

Causes help explain *why* a person may have trouble with Organizational savvy. When seeking to increase skill, it's helpful to consider how these might play out in certain situations. And remember that all of these can be addressed if you are motivated to do so.

- Ignores or denies the reality of the system.
- Inexperienced.
- Resists the reality of complexity.
- Weak negotiator.
- Rejects the need to "play politics."
- Doesn't read others or their interests well.
- Excessively direct and straightforward.
- Lacks influence.
- Low ambiguity tolerance.
- Cynical.

Culture card

Organizational savvy in the United States may be organizational taboo in Japan. Individual versus collective orientation drives a variety of these differences. In the US, there is strong emphasis on contribution of the individual. In Japan, while individual achievements matter, the greater focus is on the whole group succeeding. Without this collective success, individual contribution is meaningless. Self-promotion and celebration of individual accomplishments are accepted and expected in a US business environment. Assertiveness, too, while often applauded in the US, can be perceived as aggression in Japan. Expressing views contrary to the rest of the team isn't common practice in a Japanese business environment. Deciding the most appropriate way to maneuver through the organization requires cultural savvy, especially in the global community.[33, 34, 35, 36, 37]

23

Tips to develop Organizational savvy

1. **Frustrated? Consider the nature of the organization.** Do you always want to think things are simpler than they are? Sometimes the problem is underestimating the complexity of organizations. While it's possible that some organizations are simple, most are not. Understanding how organizations function takes some discipline. Accept this. Look beyond the obvious to see what's really in the background. Take time to identify both the formal and informal structures that exist in the organization. Notice how they work. The intricacies of both. Use what you learn to facilitate more efficient ways of getting things done.

2. **Lost in the fog? Sharpen your focus.** Proactively navigate your social environment at work. Be an astute observer of others. Look below the surface. See beyond the behavior being displayed and learn to notice the motivation driving the behavior. Observe people. In meetings. During formal and informal conversations. Notice patterns of power and deference. Where do alliances and power coalitions exist? Who do people go to for advice? Who seems to know what's going on? Who shares new insights, information, and news? Noticing these small but significant things will help you build a picture of the informal networks that exist. When you know where these networks are, you can join them.

3. **Outmaneuvered? Learn to read the political landscape.** The political landscape is often viewed as the "dark side" of the organization. Navigating it isn't easy, but it is necessary if you are going to operate effectively. Start by viewing organizational politics as something neutral. As a necessary part of how the organization functions. As the system through which power and influence is applied and distributed. Be bold in the way you maneuver through it. Take time to diagnose the paths, turns, dead-ends, and zigzags that might exist. Be prepared to take a wrong turn now and then. Reflect on what you learn from your successes and failures along the way. People who are politically savvy know the organization. They know how to get things done.

4. **Don't know the movers and shakers? Identify the key players and their roles.** How do they get things done? Who do they rely on for expediting things through the maze? How do you compare to them? Who are the major gatekeepers who control the flow of resources, information, and decisions? Who are the guides and the helpers? Get to know them better. Build or join coalitions. Who are the major

resisters and stoppers? Try to avoid them. Go around them if you have to.

Want to learn more? Take a deep dive...

Bergstrand, J. (2013, March 27). Great CIOs are politically savvy. *CIO*.

Bryan, L. L., Matson, E., & Weiss, L. M. (2007, November). Harnessing the power of informal employee networks. *McKinsey Quarterly*.

Goldsmith, M., & Katzenbach, J. (2007, February 14). Navigating the "informal" organization. *Bloomberg Businessweek*.

---

5. **Right audience, wrong message? Understand what makes individuals and groups distinct.** Become people sensitive. Learn to read people. Predict how they are going to react to you and to what you are trying to get done. Some studies argue that your ability to identify with others is a critical success factor in getting things done. The magic and the complexity of life is that people are different. Each requires special consideration and treatment. Take time to observe others. How do they react to people and situations? If you are able to predict what individuals or groups will do, you will be able to select from among your various tactics, skills, tones, and styles to get done what you need.

6. **Getting a poor response from others? Make a positive impression.** Personal style can get in the way. People differ in the impression they leave. Study the individual or group you need to influence. What do they value? What would impress them? What steps can you take to achieve this? Research shows that if you are to influence successfully, others need to be positively impressed by your integrity, authenticity, and sincerity. They must see that you are genuine, honest, and forthright. Do this well and you will inspire trust and confidence. As a result, you will achieve more than those who leave a negative impression.

23

7. **Taking more than you're giving? Think equity.** Relationships that work are built on equity and considering the impact on others. Don't just ask for things; find some common ground where you can provide help, not just ask for it. What does the unit you're contacting need in the way of problem solving or information? Do you know how they see the issue? Is it even important to them? How does what you're working on affect them? If it affects them negatively, can you trade something, appeal to the common good, figure out

some way to minimize the work or other impact (volunteering staff help, for example)?

8. **Too agreeable? Balance being agreeable with being political.** Do you value harmony and getting along with others over getting things done? Are you quick to compromise your interests? Do you tend to be compassionate, cooperative, and considerate toward others? Your accommodating nature alone will not always be enough to drive results. Some circumstances will require you to behave politically. To be more assertive. More competitive. Studies have shown that individuals who combine a highly agreeable approach with high political skill demonstrate higher levels of job performance than those who display low levels of either or both.

9. **Others not coming through for you? Consider your sources of help.** Sometimes the problem is in assessing people. Who really wants to help? Who is going to get in the way? What do they really want? What price will they ask for helping? People are more likely to come through when ideas and suggestions match their needs and fit into their view of the world. Are in line with their values, principles, beliefs, and opinions. Notice what's important to those around you. Check with others who know them well. Use what you learn to target the right sources of help and to position your request in the most influential way for them and their needs.

Want to learn more? Take a deep dive...

Deutschman, A. (September 18, 2009). How authentic leaders 'walk the walk.' *Bloomberg Businessweek*.

Fried, J. (2010, November). Jason Fried: Why work doesn't happen at work [Video file]. TED.

Warrell, M. (2013, August 20). Are you too agreeable? 7 Strategies to push back without coming off pushy. *Forbes*.

10. **Lost in the maze? Go with the flow.** Some people know the steps necessary to get things done but are too impatient to allow events to run their course. Maneuvering through the maze includes stopping once in a while to let things happen. It may mean waiting until a major gatekeeper has the time to pay attention to your needs. Be patient.

11. **Thrown off track? Expect the unexpected.** Always have a plan of attack but also have a contingency plan. Be ready for instant change. What's the worst that could happen and what will you do? People who are organizationally savvy are personally flexible. They anticipate that things can and will go wrong, but balance this with a can-do attitude and a Plan B up their sleeve. So, faced with a surprise, take a step back. Consider your options. Call on your resources. Accept that things have changed and adjust your course to stay on the right route.

12. **Playing the blame game? Keep political conflicts small and concrete.** The more abstract it gets, the more unmanageable it becomes. Separate the people from the problem. Attack problems by looking at the nature of the problem, not the person presenting the problem. Avoid direct blaming remarks; describe the problem and its impact. Focus on finding the shared meaning and conclusion to be drawn from the situation. Find a collaborative solution. If you can't agree on a solution, agree on procedure, or agree on a few things, and list all the issues remaining. This creates some motion and breaks political stalemates.

13. **Struggling to find the right approach? Find a mentor.** Seek out someone who has a long tenure of success in your organization. Someone whose behavior and style you'd like to emulate. Pay special attention to how they accomplish their work. Let the mentor know that you're especially interested in the process of work— how things "best get done around here." Experiment with new approaches based on what you see and hear from them. Keep a log of what worked and what didn't.

14. **Not sure why you're having difficulty? Get some feedback.** Often, we're unaware of the obstacles we create for ourselves. For instance, being too assertive or too submissive in different contexts. It is difficult to pull back and monitor, especially in emotionally charged situations. Those who work closest with you are best equipped to tell you how you're doing. Do they perceive you as organizationally savvy, politically aware and agile? Ask at least one person from each group you work with for feedback. Give yourself some honest feedback too. What do you think is blocking you from getting things done smoothly and effectively in the organization?

23

Want to learn more? Take a deep dive...

Brim, B. (2006, February 9). The best way to influence others. *Gallup Business Journal*.

Marcus, B. (2012, September 5). Hate politics? You still need to be political to advance your career. *Forbes*.

Musselwhite, C. (2007, October 1). Self-awareness and the effective leader. *Inc.*

Job assignments

- Relaunch an existing product or service that's not doing well. Investigate why it's not successful. Identify what is needed for it to be successful.

- Work on a team looking at a reorganization plan. Work on fully understanding where the organization is headed. Do your homework on the organization, including any strategic planning or vision statements to help inform the organizational structure.

- Conduct a postmortem on a failed project and present the findings to the people involved. Involve them in discussions about how things will need to be approached differently next time.

- Write a proposal for a new policy, process, mission, charter, product, service, or system and sell it to management. Anticipate the challenges and questions they will have and be prepared to handle these.

- Volunteer to find a way of bringing together and/or aligning processes, systems, or procedures from across a range of business units.

Take time to reflect...

If you think formal channels are the only route to get things done...

> ...then ask whether the path less traveled can bring you to a more rewarding destination. Looking behind the scenes can introduce you to information and ideas you didn't even know existed.

If you're baffled by the maze of organizational politics...

> ...then take a step back to see connections. To understand how things work and why they sometimes don't. Listen. Observe. Analyze. Learn.

278 |

If you don't take time to understand what's going on around you...

...then recognize that you could be making your job a lot harder for yourself. Knowing who's who and what's what can help you make a far more valuable contribution to the organization.

"*The closer I watch politics, the more it looks like professional wrestling in business suits.* **"**

Bosley Gravel – American author

23

Learn more about Organizational savvy

Barnes, B. K. (2007). *Exercising influence: A guide for making things happen at work, at home, and in your community*. San Francisco, CA: Pfeiffer.

Brandon, R., & Seldman, M. (2004). *Survival of the savvy: High-integrity political tactics for career and company success*. New York, NY: Free Press.

George, B., & Sims, P. (2007). *True north: Discover your authentic leadership*. San Francisco, CA: Jossey-Bass.

Katzenbach, J. R., & Khan, Z. (2010). *Leading outside the lines: How to mobilize the (in)formal organization, energize your team, and get better results*. San Francisco, CA: Jossey-Bass.

Showkeir, J., & Showkeir, M. (2008). *Authentic conversations: Moving from manipulation to truth and commitment*. San Francisco, CA: Berrett-Koehler Publishers.

▢ **Deep dive learning resource links**

Bergstrand, J. (2013, March 27). Great CIOs are politically savvy. *CIO*. Retrieved from http://www.cio.com/article/730538/Great_CIOs_Are_Politically_Savvy

Brim, B. (2006, February 9). The best way to influence others. *Gallup Business Journal*. Retrieved from http://businessjournal.gallup.com/content/21325/best-way-influence-others.aspx

Bryan, L. L., Matson, E., & Weiss, L. M. (2007, November). Harnessing the power of informal employee networks. *McKinsey Quarterly*. Retrieved from http://www.mckinsey.com/insights/organization/harnessing_the_power_of_informal_employee_networks

Deutschman, A. (September 18, 2009). How authentic leaders 'walk the walk.' *Bloomberg Businessweek*. Retrieved from http://www.businessweek.com/managing/content/sep2009/ca20090918_716655.htm

Fried, J. (2010, November). Jason Fried: Why work doesn't happen at work [Video file]. TED. Retrieved from http://www.ted.com/talks/jason_fried_why_work_doesn_t_happen_at_work.html

Goldsmith, M., & Katzenbach, J. (2007, February 14). Navigating the "informal" organization. *Bloomberg Businessweek*. Retrieved from http://www.businessweek.com/stories/2007-02-14/navigating-the-informal-organizationbusinessweek-business-news-stock-market-and-financial-advice

Marcus, B. (2012, September 5). Hate politics? You still need to be political to advance your career. *Forbes*. Retrieved from http://www.forbes.com/sites/bonniemarcus/2012/09/05/hate-politics-you-still-need-to-be-political-to-advance-your-career/

Musselwhite, C. (2007, October 1). Self-awareness and the effective leader. *Inc*. Retrieved from http://www.inc.com/resources/leadership/articles/20071001/musselwhite.html

Warrell, M. (2013, August 20). Are you too agreeable? 7 Strategies to push back without coming off pushy. *Forbes*. Retrieved from http://www.forbes.com/sites/margiewarrell/2013/08/20/are-you-too-agreeable-7-strategies-to-push-back-without-coming-off-pushy/

Recommended search terms

If you'd like to explore Organizational savvy further, try searching online using the following terms:

- Authentic leadership.
- Becoming politically savvy.
- Influencing others at work.
- Navigating informal organizations.
- Seeking feedback at work.
- Separating the people from the problem.

 More help...

Go to www.kornferry.com/fyi-resources and link directly to the deep dive resources in this chapter. Visit the site often to see the additional resources that are uploaded on a regular basis.

23

24. Persuades

Using compelling arguments to gain the support and commitment of others.

Work gets done through relationships. Sometimes it can be hard to make things happen unless people are persuaded to adapt their point of view and take action. Effective persuasion requires skillful delivery of a message and adjusting to the audience. An emotional connection with others needs to be formed while offering compelling, logical arguments, including data to support viewpoints. Persuasion requires adhering firmly to ideas with strength of resolve, but also knowing when to yield to another's point of view. Sometimes tough-minded individuals need to be persuaded. Groups of people may need to be influenced to think in a different way. One-to-one or one-to-many, persuading can be challenging. But handled effectively, it may change a small part of a project or completely alter the strategic direction of an organization. Whether you simply want to be more effective in your daily relationships through winning hearts and minds, or you need to influence senior stakeholders' decisions, there's a great deal at stake. Learn to be inspiring, motivating, and compelling.

"Let him who would be moved to convince others, be first moved to convince himself."

Thomas Carlyle – Scottish philosopher, writer, teacher, and historian

Persuades is in the **People** factor (III) in the Korn Ferry Leadership Architect™. It is part of Cluster I, **Influencing people,** along with Communicates effectively (7), *Drives* engagement (16), Organizational savvy (23), and *Drives* vision and purpose (37). You may find it helpful to also take a look at some of the tips included in those chapters to supplement your learning.

Skilled

Positions views and arguments appropriately to win support.

Convinces others to take action.

Negotiates skillfully in tough situations.

Wins concessions without damaging relationships.

Responds effectively to the reactions and positions of others.

Less skilled

- Pushes own point of view too strongly.

- Fails to win support or buy-in from others.

- Is unable to negotiate solutions that are agreeable to all.

- Responds negatively to the reactions and positions of others.

- Has difficulty articulating a logical argument that supports own position.

Talented

- Shares own ideas in a compelling manner that gains commitment from others.

- Negotiates skillfully and creates minimal noise when working toward an agreed-upon solution.

- Finds common ground and acceptable alternatives that satisfy the needs of multiple stakeholders.

Overused skill

- Attempts to negotiate when the situation calls for tough and decisive action.

- Spends so much time persuading that timely results are missed.

- May come across as manipulative.

Some possible causes of lower skill

Causes help explain *why* a person may have trouble with Persuades. When seeking to increase skill, it's helpful to consider how these might play out in certain situations. And remember that all of these can be addressed if you are motivated to do so.

- Low personal confidence.
- Lacks allies or supporters.
- No credibility.
- Not confident in ideas.
- Comes on too strong.
- Does not listen or respond to objections.
- No plan for action or follow-up.
- Does not have a clear purpose and vision.
- Poor presentation skills.
- Too easily discouraged.

Brain booster

It seems common sense that the most successful persuaders are those who have a genuine passion for their ideas. But it's not just logic that suggests this to be the case; this is also supported by neuroscience. When someone successfully influences another person, neural regions related to the brain's reward system are highly activated. This tells us the influencer feels positive about the idea. Genuinely believes in it. We also know that successful persuasion involves the influencer going a step further than this by putting themselves in the shoes of the person they're trying to persuade. They imagine the value of the idea to the other person. How does brain function substantiate this? The other area of the brain activated during effective persuasion includes the neural network that relates to perspective-taking or imagining the views of others. So, before you try to persuade, get your own house in order first. If you don't have passion, find it. If you don't see the benefits to others, figure them out. And don't try to fake it. We also know that brain activities of message recipients mirror those of the communicator. If you don't believe, then most likely, neither will they.[38, 39]

24

| 285

Tips to develop Persuades

1. **Need to be heard? Speak up.** Ever proposed a great idea only to see it die? Then someone else stole your thunder with the same idea? Did it feel like a conspiracy? The fault may lie with you. Perhaps you hung back at a critical moment. Maybe you were too polite to get out in front. Too modest and quiet. If you hesitate to put a stake in the ground, someone with fewer inhibitions will beat you to it. Learn to step into the spotlight. Lean into the conversation. Celebrate the cause. Push yourself to speak up in meetings. Call meetings of your own and build enthusiasm. Look for opportunities to establish yourself as an expert on certain topics. Put together a session and invite colleagues to tap into your knowledge. Share links that support your point of view. Write an article or blog on the topic. If you're uncomfortable claiming the spotlight, remember this is not about you but about the value of your ideas.

2. **No allies? Build relationships first.** Persuaders have a good reputation that precedes them. They find like-minded allies. They perform at a high level, turn in results, keep their promises, and reach out to help others. They build rapport and trust. Their ideas get implemented because they know people, and people know them. If you doubt this, try asking someone you don't know to join you for lunch. Notice how hard it is to convince them to spend time with you. Even before you have a need, build relationships. Reach out across the organization. Be curious. Tear yourself away from your e-mail, get up from your desk, walk down the hall. Visit other offices. Arrive early to meetings, introduce yourself, and find common ground. Follow up on a teleconference with a personal call to someone you'd like to know better. Learn about other functions. Find out who people are, what interests them, what concerns them, and how they are motivated. Get behind their ideas and you can better persuade them to get behind yours.

3. **Need more help? Start with your boss.** If you're very independent or reluctant to ask your boss for help, this is a good time to practice new behaviors. Sometimes you are empowered to lead the charge. But sometimes you need the support of your boss or someone else in the upper echelon. Set up the meeting. Then be sure you are prepared with the full picture, including what you want to do and what kind of support you need. Recognize that your boss has a network of relationships and responsibilities and that your request for support may align with other initiatives already underway. Or it may clash. There may be competition for scarce resources. Ask for your boss's perspective and advice on how you can and should

proceed. If you get the go-ahead and/or an offer of support, plan the next steps.

4. **Lack confidence? Address root causes.** Not sure how your ideas will be received? Intimidated when you have to persuade your boss of something? Worried about working in a part of the world you've never experienced before? Everyone can lose confidence under certain circumstances. A little anxiety is normal. But successful people don't let it hold them back. When you're losing confidence, start by noticing exactly what makes you anxious. Then do something to address the problem. If you're not sure of your basic ideas, run a pilot. Get input, ask questions, search for examples of what has been tried and proven. If asking for your boss's support makes you tongue-tied, try thinking of them as a customer who needs what you have to offer. Going to a new country? Get information. Go online, get a guidebook, talk to someone who has been there. Build your confidence and you will build your skill in persuading. And when you really need courage, contemplate Eleanor Roosevelt's assertion: "You must do the thing you think you cannot do."

Want to learn more? Take a deep dive...

Blalock, B. (2013, October 15). 10 Steps to executive-level confidence. *The Wall Street Journal*.

Michaels, S. (2011, August 22). 3 Powerful skills you must have to succeed in sales. *Forbes*.

5. **Ahead of the crowd? Explain your thinking.** You may be a trend-spotter. An intuitive decision maker. A conceptual thinker, comfortable with ambiguity. You can leap to conclusions or set direction without much data. If so, congratulations! Your agile thinking is needed. But to be credible, you need to let others in on the secrets. Tell them what information underlies your idea. They need to relate to it. See the rationale. Understand what inspired you. Can you show others how your vision will help the business perform better? Describe how it will keep your organization ahead of the competition. Search for like-minded people who support your thinking. Use data from emerging demographics, leading-edge product ideas, or industry best practices to bolster your credibility. Explain how your credentials and experience qualify you as an expert. Share stories of past success. Build a prototype to show how this could work. Speak in the language of your audience. Fill in the dots. Use data if others need it, even if you don't.

24

6. **Poor presenter? Get some training—and relax.** Giving a presentation is the greatest human fear, after dying. To reduce your fear of presenting, eliminate the need to be perfect and instead aim for being practiced, confident, and engaging. Great presenters are human. They are comfortable because they know they are imperfect. Unfazed by glitches. Familiar with their material. Connected with the audience. Prepared but not robotic. Be eager to share your thoughts. Dress well but comfortably. Breathe and smile. Acquaint yourself with the technology and don't get flustered when it acts up—as it often does. Your audience is not a panel of judges scoring your performance, but interested learners who are on your side. Observe presenters whose style you admire. How do they keep themselves comfortable and the audience engaged? Browse YouTube to see what works and what doesn't. Watch the movie *The King's Speech* to learn how George VI worked toward overcoming his fear. Hire a presentation or media coach to help you get comfortable on a stage, behind a podium, and on the screen.

7. **Can't get others to see what you see? Draw the complete picture.** "Trust me" is not enough to win over busy people. When things are about to change, people want the full picture. They need to see the vision and the process for getting there. To know not only *what* the end game is, but *how* it will happen. *Why* is it happening. And what is needed from them. Be honest about what you want them to do. Be clear on how they will benefit. Share initial process plans. Be prepared to literally draw pictures. Show them a path toward completion, then work with them to build the roadway.

Want to learn more? Take a deep dive...

DeGideo, A. (2009, July 7). *Communication keys: 7 Steps to more compelling arguments*. Business Brief.

Gallo, A. (2010, November 15). How to get your idea approved. *Harvard Business Review Blog Network*.

8. **Can't engage the team? Give them a challenge.** Persuaders don't have all the answers. But they do ask great questions. In the book *Hot Spots*, author Lynda Gratton writes that one way to motivate teams is to ask a challenging question that inspires purposeful action. When the CEO of BP asked "How can a large oil company become a creator of value in the world?" the teams at BP created significant investments in alternative energy. Ask: What if...? How can we...? What else...? Igniting questions catalyze change. Get the

best from yourself and others. In every endeavor, ask, "How can we do this better?"

9. **Getting resistance? Establish common ground.** Seeing a lot of folded arms in meetings? Getting the silent treatment when it's time for questions in the town hall? Negotiations at a standstill? Some people need lots of information to be convinced—especially when the stakes are high. When you are at an impasse, stop the meeting and go back to basic causes. Tell them why this agreement is important to you and ask what is important to them. Identify what you each need and ask how you can get it. Skeptics are more likely to get on board if they understand that you care about what they care about. Like customers. Or financial clarity. Or plant safety. Or the company's reputation for great products. Disclose your own intentions and stay open to others' deepest values. Have an honest conversation about why you are there. You will build a sense of trust and shared purpose that brings people together.

10. **Hearing emotional objections? Use empathy with sound thinking.** People getting emotional about a proposed change? You might want to try to leave emotion out of it and move immediately to action. But that's like trying to rearrange the furniture while the room is on fire. Emotion is powerful. Until it is dealt with, it can derail any initiative. To win over groups or individuals, you must first empathize with them. See it from their point of view. Understand and acknowledge emotional objections. Allow time for emotional venting and conversation. Only then—when emotions have calmed—can you move to the logical side of the equation. Douse the fire first—by listening. Then use good thinking to show the objective soundness of your ideas. Come to an understanding that will work for all parties.

Want to learn more? Take a deep dive...

Moss Kanter, R. (2012, September 25). Ten reasons people resist change. *Harvard Business Review Blog Network*.

Quast, L. (2012, November 26). Overcome the 5 main reasons people resist change. *Forbes*.

11. **Seen as stubborn or rigid? Get input early and often.** You have great ideas. So do your colleagues, managers, customers, vendors, and team members. Persuasive people are clear on overall objectives and impact. And they are curious about others' reactions and open to new thinking. If you're too rigid in your beliefs or exert too much

24

control over the process, creative and potentially interested people will drop by the wayside. Hold brainstorming sessions or work with a few colleagues to get good ideas on the table. Seek people's input at the creation phase. What are their views? What concerns do they have? What can they add? Allow course corrections and creative refinements in the execution phase. People are more likely to come round to your way of thinking if they feel they've had the chance to contribute to its shaping.

12. **Getting worked up? Pause to regroup.** Passionate? Frustrated? Convinced that you have the answer? Want to do it now? It's easy to come on too strong. Especially if you're getting attacked, being rejected, or not feeling heard. But raised voices and frustration only drive people away. If you're heated in meetings or tempted to fire off an e-mail you'll regret, take a break. Sit down and figure out what has you so upset. Process all of your hurt feelings and personal emotions. Did something like this happen to you when you were younger and you still feel the pain? Let it go. List all of the reasons why something seems like a great idea. Then list all of the reasons why others might not be so enthusiastic. Face facts until you see things clearly. Remember, this is not about you but about the value of the idea. When you are emotionally calm and thinking clearly, make a strategic decision about whether to proceed and, if you do, how to go about it. Resolve to try a new and more inclusive approach. Engage a friend or coach to help you understand how others see you and how you can behave differently.

13. **Have positional power? Use it wisely.** As the saying goes, "Power corrupts." But we expect our leaders to be decisive, optimistic, in charge, and making things happen. Good leaders are comfortable using positional and functional power for the right reasons. When you want to change others' behavior, reassess the tools and resources at your disposal. Sales executive? Sales contests create healthy competition that drives action. CEO or HR leader? Compensation structures reward performance. Virtual team leader? Face-to-face meetings build morale. Sometimes a title alone can persuade others to follow your lead, at least in the short-term. Inhabit your role as executive, expert, team manager, member of the leadership team. Step lightly but firmly. Proceed with respect and integrity. You are here for a reason.

14. **Situation stalled? Don't quit yet.** Persuasion is rarely a one-time event. Life changes. Situations are fluid. Needs shift over time. Persuasive people are both flexible and determined. They know what's negotiable and where the line is drawn. What they can

concede and what they need to hold on to. When to walk away and when to return. They process situations and find a way to bounce back. If you encounter "no" or indifference, don't quit. "No" might mean "not now" or "I need to think about this some more." Ask what is needed to get to "yes." Will time, more information, or the support of your peers get the negotiation back on track? Do you need to give in order to get? Be firm but be resilient. Use respectful persistence. Plan some follow-up tactics. Get perspective and be patient. You may be in this for the long haul. Don't give up until you have decided that a different idea is the way forward.

Want to learn more? Take a deep dive...

Goulston, M., & Ullmen, J. (2013, March 19). For real influence, listen past your blind spots. *Harvard Business Review Blog Network*.

Hall, J. (2013, June 19). Don't let your ego grow bigger than your influence. *Forbes*.

Job assignments

- Lead or participate in a change initiative, such as a business integration, that requires people from different organizations to create a new structure.
- Volunteer to represent your organization as the keynote speaker or expert panelist at an upcoming industry conference.
- Invite the most skeptical member of your peer group to partner with you on a change initiative. Get to the root of their resistance and help them understand the importance of the change.
- Create and lead a webinar discussion on the value of self-awareness in persuasive leaders. Create a compelling session that will engage your audience.
- Handle a tough negotiation with an internal or external client or customer. Beforehand, find out as much as you can about them and try to understand the situation from their viewpoint.

24

Take time to reflect...

If you have good ideas that no one seems to want to hear about...

>...then realize that a strong idea requires a strong case behind it. Delivering compelling evidence and capturing people's imaginations can help ensure a win.

If you're frustrated by the endless debates that simple changes require...

>...then reconcile yourself with the need to be persistent. Your strength of resolve will pay dividends in the long run and get you the results you're looking for.

If you find relating to others tough and a chore...

>...then recognize the importance of people feeling connected in order to accept a point of view. It's easier for them to buy into your idea if they buy into you.

❝*The key to successful leadership today is influence, not authority.* **❞**

Ken Blanchard – American author and management expert

24

Learn more about Persuades

Bacon, T. R. (2011). *Elements of influence: The art of getting others to follow your lead*. New York, NY: AMACOM.

George, B., & Sims, P. (2007). *True north: Discover your authentic leadership*. San Francisco, CA: Jossey-Bass.

Goulston, M., & Ullmen, J. (2013). *Real influence: Persuade without pushing and gain without giving in*. New York, NY: AMACOM.

Mortensen, K. W. (2013). *Maximum influence: The 12 universal laws of power persuasion* (2nd ed.). New York, NY: AMACOM.

Scharlatt, H., & Smith, R. (2011). *Influence: Gaining commitment, getting results* (2nd ed.). Greensboro, NC: Center for Creative Leadership.

 ## Deep dive learning resource links

Blalock, B. (2013, October 15). 10 Steps to executive-level confidence. *The Wall Street Journal*. Retrieved from http://blogs.wsj.com/speakeasy/2013/10/15/10-steps-to-executive-level-confidence/

DeGideo, A. (2009, July 7). *Communication keys: 7 Steps to more compelling arguments*. Business Brief. Retrieved from http://www.businessbrief.com/communication-keys-7-steps-to-more-compelling-arguments/

Gallo, A. (2010, November 15). How to get your idea approved. *Harvard Business Review Blog Network*. Retrieved from http://blogs.hbr.org/2010/11/how-to-get-their-approval/

Goulston, M., & Ullmen, J. (2013, March 19). For real influence, listen past your blind spots. *Harvard Business Review Blog Network*. Retrieved from http://blogs.hbr.org/2013/03/for-real-influence-use-level-f/

Hall, J. (2013, June 19). Don't let your ego grow bigger than your influence. *Forbes*. Retrieved from http://www.forbes.com/sites/johnhall/2013/06/19/dont-let-your-ego-grow-bigger-than-your-influence/

Michaels, S. (2011, August 22). 3 Powerful skills you must have to succeed in sales. *Forbes*. Retrieved from http://www.forbes.com/sites/womensmedia/2011/08/22/3-powerful-skills-you-must-have-to-succeed-in-sales/

Moss Kanter, R. (2012, September 25). Ten reasons people resist change. *Harvard Business Review Blog Network*. Retrieved from http://blogs.hbr.org/2012/09/ten-reasons-people-resist-chang/

24

293

Quast, L. (2012, November 26). Overcome the 5 main reasons people resist change. *Forbes*. Retrieved from http://www.forbes.com/sites/lisaquast/2012/11/26/overcome-the-5-main-reasons-people-resist-change/

Recommended search terms

If you'd like to explore Persuades further, try searching online using the following terms:

- Building confidence.
- Building real influence.
- Dealing with resistance to change.
- Making a compelling argument in business.
- Persuading others in business.

 More help...

Go to www.kornferry.com/fyi-resources and link directly to the deep dive resources in this chapter. Visit the site often to see the additional resources that are uploaded on a regular basis.

24

294 |

25. Plans and aligns

Planning and prioritizing work to meet commitments aligned with organizational goals.

Nothing helps move things along better than a good plan. And a clear marker of a good plan is one that is aligned with strategic priorities. Plans lay a foundation. Aligned plans enable you, your team, and the entire organization to move in the right direction. Plans help people get organized and remain focused. They lead to better use of resources. Reduce scrambling. Help people anticipate problems. And prompt them to proceed with more confidence. This is particularly important given the rapid change and uncertainty prevalent in organizational life. Bob Johansen of the Institute for the Future describes the importance of providing clarity as a smart way to address chaos and confusion. Plans do just that. Instead of jumping into action, use the planning process to deliberate on what you're trying to accomplish. Line up your plans and projects so they are in sync with strategic organizational priorities. Collaborate with others to develop robust, flexible plans that guide you where you want to go.

" *The end we aim at must be known before the way can be made.* **"**

Jean Paul – German writer

Plans and aligns is in the **Results** factor (II) in the Korn Ferry Leadership Architect™. It is part of Cluster E, **Managing execution,** along with Directs work (15) and *Optimizes* work processes (38). You may find it helpful to also take a look at some of the tips included in those chapters to supplement your learning.

Skilled

Sets objectives to align with broader organizational goals.

Breaks down objectives into appropriate initiatives and actions.

Stages activities with relevant milestones and schedules.

Anticipates and adjusts effective contingency plans.

Less skilled

- Gets caught up in immediate needs without attending to larger priorities.

- Spends time and resources without a clear purpose.

- Gets caught off guard by problems due to the lack of contingency plans.

- Haphazardly tracks progress or performance.

Talented

- Focuses on highest priorities and sets aside less critical tasks.

- Lays out a thorough schedule and steps for achieving objectives.

- Makes implementation plans that allocate resources precisely.

- Looks for obstacles and develops excellent contingency plans.

- Uses milestones to diligently track and manage the progress of the work.

Overused skill

- Is so focused on completing only mission-critical tasks that he/she lets the trivial many accumulate into a critical problem.

- Persistently follows plans, allowing little room for change.

- May leave out the human element of the work.

- Spends an inordinate amount of time planning for unlikely obstacles or roadblocks.

Some possible causes of lower skill

Causes help explain *why* a person may have trouble with Plans and aligns. When seeking to increase skill, it's helpful to consider how these might play out in certain situations. And remember that all of these can be addressed if you are motivated to do so.

- Doesn't think ahead.
- Short-term focus.
- Lacks structure; disorganized.
- Avoids communication.
- Impatient.
- Oversimplifies.
- Poor time management.
- Not detail oriented.

25

. . . .

 Did you know?

In a 2011 survey of 1,500 executives conducted globally, McKinsey & Company found that only 9% of those surveyed were "very satisfied" with how they allocated time. One-third of the respondents were "actively dissatisfied." The survey also explored the degree to which these executives were strategically aligned in terms of the use of their time. Only 52% said the way they spent their time largely matched the strategic priorities of their organization. With nearly half admitting they were not focusing sufficiently on guiding the strategic direction of the business, this shows that the time challenges experienced by executives not only affect them as individuals, but is also likely to impact the well-being of the company.[40]

. . . .

Tips to develop Plans and aligns

1. **Planning without clarity? Define overall goals and objectives.** Before developing a plan, take time to understand its purpose. What exactly needs to be accomplished and why? Is there a problem that needs to be solved? An initiative that needs to be organized? An effort that needs to be managed? Who has identified the need? What's the context? What's at stake? Who will benefit from a successful outcome? What will success look like according to key customers and stakeholders? What criteria will be used to measure success? Defining clear goals and objectives from the beginning is critical to plan effectively and deliver the desired results. The more specific you are, the less disagreement there will be about whether you have achieved your objectives.

2. **Don't know what to include? Lay out the work and tasks.** Most successful projects begin with a good plan. Once you've identified the objectives, outline the scope, desired outcomes, and key measures. What skills are needed to accomplish the goals? Who should be on the team? What additional resources are required? Then create a schedule using the appropriate level of detail for the project team, sponsors, and stakeholders. A high-level overview typically includes phases, milestones, and key deliverables set to a time line. A detailed plan adds all the steps from A to Z. Take special care outlining these steps—many people are perceived as lacking planning skills because they leave important things out. Consider starting at the end or from a deadline, working backward from Z to A when mapping out the steps. Laying out tasks in reverse order can help you develop a realistic schedule. Ask others for feedback on the plans and incorporate their input.

3. **Want more structure? Use planning tools and software.** Become an expert on frameworks and tools to create flowcharts, visualize plans, and monitor progress. A Work Breakdown Structure (WBS) prompts you to subdivide activities into the smallest possible task. For each task, ask, "What has to be done in order to accomplish this?" until nothing else can be subdivided. Estimate the duration and resources needed for each task. A Critical Path diagram shows all essential activities needed to complete the project, plus the total time it will take. The activities should be in the right order. Some must be sequential—they depend on others being completed first. Other activities can happen concurrently or in parallel. There are two other widely used flowcharting tools that show time lines, sequences, and

dependencies. Gantt charts are a bar-type visual for smaller projects. A PERT diagram is used for more complex projects, often as a monitoring tool. Share the output of the various tools with others so everyone stays up-to-date and can see when a plan is off track. Select software that meets your needs but isn't too difficult to learn. Find someone to train you and to share frequently used templates so you don't have to reinvent the wheel.

4. **Limited resources? Obtain and manage resources wisely.** Nothing stalls the execution of a plan like lack of resources. Think through what you'll need for each phase and activity of your plan. People, funding, tools, technology, space, materials. Which resources can you obtain easily and control on your own? Which do you need to locate, negotiate for, or get help securing? Present a clear rationale to decision makers. Outline the difference these resources will make toward effectively meeting your objectives. How will they impact results? Completion time? Budget? What short- and long-term implications exist? How will other areas of the enterprise be impacted? Explain how you'll allocate the resources efficiently and avoid waste. Describe the risks of not obtaining needed resources. Get creative and be willing to bargain for needed resources. What can you trade with other groups? What can you share? Discuss viable options along with their associated costs/benefits.

> ## Want to learn more? Take a deep dive...
>
> For Dummies. (n.d.). *How to create a work breakdown structure.* For Dummies: A Wiley Brand.
>
> Larson, E., & Larson, R. (2004, September 10). How to create a clear project plan. *CIO Magazine.*
>
> Mind Tools. (n.d.). *Locke's goal setting theory: Understanding SMART goal setting.* Mind Tools.
>
> Stolovitsky, N. (2012, October 19). *Top 10 tips for effective resource management whether jumping from space or not.* Genius Project.

5. **Unsure how things fit with the big picture? Align your objectives.** It's common sense to align objectives with broader organizational goals. Unfortunately, it's not always common practice. Connecting the strategic dots helps create a common mindset. Reduces confusion. Increases efficiency of effort. Each individual's goals

should align with and support the team's objectives. Each team should have goals that align with and support the department's objectives. And so forth on up. Once alignment is clear, you'll have a better sense of what to prioritize in your daily work. With goals as the guide, separate potential actions into four areas: mission critical, important to get done, nice to do if time is left over, and unrelated to the organization's main goals. When choosing what to do, apply the scale and always choose the highest level. Plan and execute what matters most.

6. **Operate in a silo? Engage in collaborative planning.** Research has found that one of the best ways to gain commitment is to ask people for their ideas—especially when the work is first taking shape. Consult with others from the beginning to build support for the project. Meet with those who will be implementing the plan. Share the overall intent so they understand the context. Work together to map things out and then ask them to review your drafts. Is the sequencing correct? Are the right people involved? Can they commit to this schedule? What gaps exist? Gather their input about the many moving parts. How will outputs from one group relate to the work of other units? Where can you consolidate or streamline tasks to save time and accomplish more? What risks should be addressed? Make sure all team members understand and agree to the plan. Also seek advice from those who have planned or worked on similar projects. What did they learn that could be applied to the current project? Always remember that what you do is part of a broader strategy and interconnected system.

7. **Keeping others in the dark? Communicate plans with stakeholders.** The cooperation and engagement of stakeholders will be crucial to achieving your plan's objectives. Identify your key stakeholders. What are their interests and needs? How much information do they want? What vehicles of communication do they prefer? At what frequency? Develop and follow a communication plan to stay in touch with them. Communicate the overall aims, approach, and time line of your project. Include meaningful milestones, such as when you need their input on decisions or for approvals. Let stakeholders know what's progressing according to plan and what is not. If you anticipate problems or delays, inform those who will be affected as soon as possible and determine workable solutions.

Want to learn more? Take a deep dive...

Harding, C. (2010, January 14). *Project status reporting process*. Project Management Online.

Lavoie, A. (n.d.). *Ignoring this issue could ruin your company*. CEO.

Mekšs, D. (2012). *30 Greatest online project management and collaboration tools for easy communication!* 1st Web Designer.

Merrett, R. (2012, July 31). Want project success? Engage stakeholders. *CIO Magazine*.

8. **Not tracking details closely enough? Monitor progress against the plan.** If a leader or stakeholder asks an important question related to the status of your project, could you respond quickly and accurately? Could you estimate time to completion? Provide a budget update? At the outset of the project, develop a system for tracking time lines and measures that are meaningful to team members and stakeholders—cost and quality control, scheduling variances, scope changes, resource usage. When in doubt, return to your objectives. What are you trying to do? Review success criteria regularly—have a dashboard of these metrics within easy reach. Periodically distribute executive summaries to all parties. Supplement the summaries with additional information relevant for specific groups. Give everyone involved in implementing the plan progress reports. When you reach milestones, share updates related to achievements, decisions, potential risks, and next steps.

9. **Not anticipating potential roadblocks? Envision the plan in process.** Take time to picture what could go wrong from the start of the plan to its completion. Discuss potential scenarios with colleagues who have diverse vantage points. How might things play out? What's the worst-case scenario? What other setbacks or glitches might occur? Rank the potential problems from highest likelihood to lowest likelihood. What will you do if the highest likelihood things happen? Create contingency plans for each. Take steps to prevent problems and monitor warning signs. Pay close attention to the weakest links. These are usually groups or elements you have the least interface with or control over (perhaps someone in a remote location, a consultant or supplier). Stay doubly in touch with the potential weak links. Things can change quickly, so at various milestones, go back through your mental checklist. Anticipate and have Plan B ready.

10. **Overly optimistic when developing plans? Plan for the unplanned.** Many use "best-case scenario" formulas when making initial plans. They're eager to please the customer. To deliver top-quality results quickly and affordably. Stretch goals are admirable. But overpromising isn't practical or smart—it can lead to execution problems and fallout from unmet expectations. It can also make the planner seem naive. Strive to make your plans realistic. Get input from others experienced with similar projects. Take into account challenges that are likely to crop up. When dealing with unknowns, give yourself time to become familiar with the territory. There are human and unforeseen aspects related to every plan. Anticipate challenges without letting them overwhelm you. Adapt the plan in light of new insights.

11. **Prefer plans to stay the same? Be ready to adapt and act.** Are you naturally wired to want to finalize plans and move on? Think revisiting plans is a waste of time? Given how frequently plans are launched in dynamic and unpredictable environments, changes should be expected. Even welcomed. Change can mean that people are paying close attention to evolving information. It can signal that they're discovering new opportunities for innovation. If you or your organization values innovation and entrepreneurial zeal, you may want to reassess how you approach planning. An overemphasis on plans can slow things down. Research conducted by Saras Sarasvathy at the Darden School of Business indicates that many entrepreneurs begin with action rather than planning. They take "smart steps," evaluate what is learned, then build on it to pursue their goals. Traditional organizations often fear that a lack of planning will increase risk. The entrepreneurs studied believe that risk is actually reduced, given the real-world data they obtain during a series of quick, inexpensive steps.

12. **Changes getting out of hand? Beware of scope creep.** An important aspect of planning is managing scope. Scope creep occurs when stakeholders' expectations have expanded, but the changes have not been vetted and time lines and resources have not been adjusted to accommodate. It could stem from customer requests, unforeseen complications, cost overruns, resource constraints, scheduling adjustments. Whatever the case, scope creep results in additional work. If not identified and managed properly, the plan could get behind schedule, run over budget, or not meet agreed-upon objectives. Guard against pressure to deliver more than was originally planned without going through a proper revision process. Establish standard change procedures and make sure people are aware of them. Typically, this includes a change request form that states the

reasons, costs, and sign-offs needed by project leads and sponsors. Change is inevitable—be ready to manage it.

Want to learn more? Take a deep dive...

Knight, J., Thomas, R., & Angus, B. (2013, June 4). Battle scope creep in your projects. *Harvard Business Review Blog Network*.

Mochari, I. (2014, January 15). 3 Risks of not tracking your progress. *Inc.*

Pitagorsky, G. (2011, January 26). Project managers are change managers. *Project Times*.

Stolovitsky, N. (2010, August 4). *Planning for the unplanned. Including risk in your project management strategy*. Genius Project.

Job assignments

- Plan an off-site meeting, conference, convention, or trade show where you'll need to closely monitor the time line leading up to the event.

- Lead a strategic alignment initiative to ensure your team/department/unit goals and plans are integrated with those from other areas, and that all are aligned with broader organizational priorities.

- Take on a project or assignment that requires collaborative planning with colleagues from various disciplines, divisions, or geographies.

- Plan the renovation of an office, floor, building, service center, lab, warehouse, etc., that requires you to carefully manage scope and resources.

- Plan the installation and integration of a new process or system (e.g., IT, HR, finance, procurement), making sure stakeholders remain engaged and updated throughout the process.

Take time to reflect...

If you'd rather improvise than take the time to come up with a plan...

> ...then consider that there are many destinations you'll never reach without a map. A strong plan allows you to take well-considered steps in new territory. Avoid hazards. Arrive sooner.

If you're spontaneous by nature...

> ...then recognize the potential pitfalls of doing things without the benefit of forethought. Aligning resources, ideas, and goals requires anticipation and planning. It doesn't happen by accident.

If you're easily unsettled when things go off track...

> ...then acknowledge that sometimes plans go awry. Obstacles are inevitable, so staying open to a shift in route is pragmatic and realistic. Detours can turn out to be the best part of any trip.

"*It is a bad plan that cannot be changed.* **"**

Publilius Syrus – Assyrian aphorist

Learn more about Plans and aligns

Chermack, T. J. (2011). *Scenario planning in organizations: How to create, use and assess scenarios*. San Francisco, CA: Berrett-Koehler Publishers.

Kerzner, H. (2005). *Project management: A systems approach to planning, scheduling, and controlling* (9th ed.). Hoboken, NJ: John Wiley & Sons.

Manas, J. (2006). *Napoleon on project management: Timeless lessons in planning, execution, and leadership*. Nashville, TN: Thomas Nelson.

Ogilvy, J. A. (2002). *Creating better futures: Scenario planning as a tool for a better tomorrow*. New York, NY: Oxford University Press, Inc.

Tomczyk, C. A. (2005). *Project manager's spotlight on planning*. Alameda, CA: SYBEX, Inc.

Deep dive learning resource links

For Dummies. (n.d.). *How to create a work breakdown structure*. For Dummies: A Wiley Brand. Retrieved from http://www.dummies.com/how-to/content/how-to-create-a-work-breakdown-structure.html

Harding, C. (2010, January 14). *Project status reporting process*. Project Management Online. Retrieved from http://projectmanagementonline.wordpress.com/2010/01/14/project-status-reporting-process/

Knight, J., Thomas, R., & Angus, B. (2013, June 4). Battle scope creep in your projects. *Harvard Business Review Blog Network*. Retrieved from http://blogs.hbr.org/2013/06/battling-scope-creep-in-your-p/

Larson, E., & Larson, R. (2004, September 10). How to create a clear project plan. *CIO Magazine*. Retrieved from http://www.cio.com.au/article/166486/how_create_clear_project_plan/

Lavoie, A. (n.d.). *Ignoring this issue could ruin your company*. CEO. Retrieved from http://www.ceo.com/leadership_and_management/ignoring-this-issue-could-ruin-your-company/

Mekšs, D. (2012). *30 Greatest online project management and collaboration tools for easy communication!* 1st Web Designer. Retrieved from http://www.1stwebdesigner.com/design/project-management-collaboration-tools/

Merrett, R. (2012, July 31). Want project success? Engage stakeholders. *CIO Magazine*. Retrieved from http://www.cio.com.au/article/432205/want_project_success_engage_stakeholders/

Mind Tools. (n.d.). *Locke's goal setting theory: Understanding SMART goal setting*. Mind Tools. Retrieved from http://www.mindtools.com/pages/article/newHTE_87.htm

Mochari, I. (2014, January 15). 3 Risks of not tracking your progress. *Inc.* Retrieved from http://www.inc.com/ilan-mochari/3-risks-not-tracking.html

Pitagorsky, G. (2011, January 26). Project managers are change managers. *Project Times*. Retrieved from http://www.projecttimes.com/george-pitagorsky/project-managers-are-change-managers.html

Stolovitsky, N. (2010, August 4). *Planning for the unplanned: Including risk in your project management strategy*. Genius Project. Retrieved from http://www.geniusproject.com/blog/pm-best-practices/planning-for-the-unplanned-including-risk-in-your-project-management-strategy/

Stolovitsky, N. (2012, October 19). *Top 10 tips for effective resource management whether jumping from space or not*. Genius Project. Retrieved from http://www.geniusproject.com/blog/famous-projects/top-10-tips-for-effective-resource-management-when-jumping-from-space/

Recommended search terms

If you'd like to explore Plans and aligns further, try searching online using the following terms:

- Dealing with and preventing scope creep.
- Effectively managing resources.
- Project planning.
- Regular status reporting in project management.
- Setting clear goals.
- Tracking project progress and change.

 More help...

Go to www.kornferry.com/fyi-resources and link directly to the deep dive resources in this chapter. Visit the site often to see the additional resources that are uploaded on a regular basis.

26. *Being* resilient

Rebounding from setbacks and adversity when facing difficult situations.

Setbacks are often unavoidable. Potential pitfalls are everywhere, especially in today's demanding, adverse, and often volatile working environment. Even the most resilient people experience setbacks. The difference is they anticipate them. Meet them head-on. Have the ability to withstand them. They use their resilience to stay in control. To keep positive and believe there is a way forward, even when it can't be seen. They recover quickly, learn, and move forward. But resilience doesn't come easy. It requires courage and commitment. But without it, stress can rise to unmanageable levels. Performance can fall away. You can burn out. The more resilient you become, the more you'll stay calm under pressure and positively adapt to difficult situations. You'll keep going when you feel like giving up. You'll bounce back to baseline levels of performance, confidence, and satisfaction sooner. Not only that, you'll be better equipped to confront the next challenge that arises. You'll be stronger.

> " Do not judge me by my successes, judge me by how many times I fell down and got back up again. "

Nelson Mandela – South African anti-apartheid revolutionary, politician, and former president of South Africa

Being resilient is in the **Self** factor (IV) in the Korn Ferry Leadership Architect™. It is part of Cluster L, **Being flexible and adaptable,** along with *Manages* ambiguity (3), Nimble learning (22), and Situational adaptability (31). You may find it helpful to also take a look at some of the tips included in those chapters to supplement your learning.

Skilled

Is confident under pressure.

Handles and manages crises effectively.

Maintains a positive attitude despite adversity.

Bounces back from setbacks.

Grows from hardships and negative experiences.

Less skilled

- Gets easily rattled in high-pressure situations.

- Exhibits low energy and motivation during times of stress and worry.

- Acts defensively when faced with criticism or roadblocks.

- Takes too long to recover from setbacks.

Talented

- Stays focused and composed in stressful situations.

- Maintains a positive attitude and forward-thinking approach despite troubling circumstances or setbacks.

- Takes constructive action to navigate difficulties or obstacles.

- Is viewed as a source of confidence in high-stress situations.

Overused skill

- Is unreasonably confident and optimistic; could miss the early signs of trouble.

- Fails to show emotion in appropriate circumstances; comes across as cold and uncaring.

- May allow stress to pile up, risking burnout.

- Minimizes the implications or severity of the situation.

Some possible causes of lower skill

Causes help explain *why* a person may have trouble with *Being* resilient. When seeking to increase skill, it's helpful to consider how these might play out in certain situations. And remember that all of these can be addressed if you are motivated to do so.

- Doesn't push hard enough.
- Withdraws when faced with resistance.
- Gives up too soon.
- Lacks composure.
- Takes things personally.
- Won't take charge.
- Lacks belief and passion.
- Freezes when situations change quickly.
- Uncomfortable with rejection.
- Lacks physical/mental fitness.

Brain booster

Losing composure is often an instantaneous reaction that we have not "filtered" through our rational brain. In fact, it's the brain's limbic system that drives the increased heartbeat, flushed face, sweaty palms, and the flash of emotion that accompany a loss of composure. The limbic system is one of the most primitive areas of the brain and it's designed to detect threats of all kinds. A perceived lack of fairness, lack of certainty, or lack of respect are all modern-day threats that our limbic system is attuned to. Once your brain detects a threat and your amygdala (emotional response center) is activated, the prefrontal cortex (PFC), which is responsible for rational thinking, is impaired. In this frame of mind, you are more likely to miss details, draw incorrect conclusions, and make rash moves in an effort to regain control and obliterate the threat. That could be detrimental to your relationships and reputation. The next time you start to "lose it," pause. Take some slow, deep breaths. This reduces the stress reactions. Notice what is upsetting you. Ask yourself why you feel threatened. Put it in context so it doesn't seem overwhelming. Tell yourself that it's time to be constructive. Talk your limbic system off the ledge so you can get back to using your PFC.

Tips to develop *Being* resilient

1. **Meeting resistance? Push through it.** Hesitate in the face of resistance? Do you backpedal? Give in too soon? Remember, resistance is normal, not abnormal. Some of the time it's legitimate; most of the time it's just human nature. An unconscious defense mechanism. People resist until they understand. They are just protecting territory. Don't take it personally. Remind yourself what you are there to do. Return to the facts and your agenda. Keep making the business case. Invite the resisters in. Find out what's causing them to behave that way. Maybe your audience isn't ready to do what you need; it's not on their agenda. Help them understand what's in it for them. Invite their ideas, input, and critique. Listen. Adjust if you need to. Push ahead again.

2. **Lose confidence when challenged? Prepare to present a strong case.** Question your ability at the first sign of a challenge? Tell yourself that others are better, smarter than you? That this is never going to work? That your performance won't be good enough and that you are bound to fail? Confidence comes from having absolute belief in what you stand for. Being secure in yourself that you're on the right track. Being determined that this thing must get done. Feeling good about it. Do you feel good about yourself? Can you confidently defend to a critical and impartial audience the wisdom of what you're doing? Work on presenting your case. Practice mental interrogation until you can clearly state in a few sentences what you stand for. Use definite, direct language. People don't line up behind laundry lists or ambiguous objectives. Don't make what you're doing sound like a trial balloon. Don't be vague or tentative. Use the business case to support what you are asking for and to explain how everybody can gain. Do your homework. Anticipate tough questions, attacks, and countering views. Expect pushback. Rehearse how you will respond. Practice your style, tone, pace, and volume. Plan as if you're only going to have one shot.

3. **Giving up after one or two tries? Try something different.** If you find yourself stuck in a repeating groove that's not working, it's time to switch approaches. To do something different. After all, if you always do what you've always done, you'll always get what you've always got. Don't give up. Identify what's getting in the way. If you think you might be missing something, take a step back. Look at the situation from a range of perspectives: yours, theirs, and that of an objective observer. Think about multiple ways to get the same outcome. Use the insights you gain to give yourself some advice about what to do differently. For example, to push a decision through, you could meet

with stakeholders first, go to a single key stakeholder, study and present the problem to a group, call a problem-solving session, or call in an outside expert. Be prepared to do them all when obstacles arise. Persevere. Go back a second, third, or fourth time if you have to.

4. **Path blocked at every turn? Learn to navigate the maze.** Organizations can be complex mazes. Full of obstacles, with many turns and dead ends. Even worse, organizations are staffed with people, which makes it more complex. Egos. Gatekeepers. Resisters. The best path to get something done may not be direct. The formal organization works only some of the time. Most of the time, the informal organization runs the show. To overcome obstacles and drive things through, you have to know how to work the maze. Be prepared to tread new paths. Learn the informal organization. Identify the key players, especially the gatekeepers and the traffic controllers. Maybe the best way to approach someone is through someone else. Maybe you have to work on your timing. Be patient with process. Things sometimes take time. People need to be ready to move. When is the best time to approach someone for a decision or an action? Ask others the best way to get things done in this organization. Watch others. What path do they follow?

Want to learn more? Take a deep dive...

Hannon, K. (2012, December 26). 6 Key steps for career resilience. *Forbes*.

Ireland, K. (2013, August 16). *How to show self-confidence tips & tricks*. Livestrong.

Wakeman, C. (2009, June 8). A guide to dealing with resistant employees. *Fast Company*.

---

5. **React defensively when criticized? Respond constructively instead.** There will always be people who are quick to criticize. To point out what you've done wrong. Tell you how something should be done differently. Sometimes it's well intended; sometimes it isn't. But, as Aristotle once said, the only way to avoid criticism is "...by saying nothing, doing nothing, and being nothing." Resist your natural impulse to react defensively. This is rarely a wise or productive move. It's emotionally driven and likely to make your critic feel attacked. It could escalate into conflict. Learn to respond instead by staying calm and pausing. Listen to and think about what you're hearing. Treat it as information, even if you don't agree with it or feel hurt.

Accept you have flaws and that sometimes it's helpful to have these pointed out to you. Be open to the fact that others may be right. Pay attention to any quality feedback that is being given. Focus on what you can learn. Apply constructive thinking. If the criticism feels unjust, ask your critic to repeat their viewpoint. Listen carefully. You may spot that it's based on a misunderstanding or different perspective. Work with them to straighten things out. When you choose your response, you are taking control of the situation and of your emotions. You'll make better choices about what you do with the information.

6. **Trying to do too much? Regain your balance.** Being pulled in multiple directions? Managing conflicting demands? Lost your sense of priority? Trying to make everyone happy? Stop. You can't please all of the people all of the time. You can't fight every battle and hope to be effective. You only have a finite amount of energy and quality thinking time each day, so you need to balance it across the things that matter. Focus your effort on driving through the priorities. Not sure what they are? Establish them. Find out. Agree on them with your boss/stakeholders where you need to. Write them down. Use them to stay focused. Priorities act like a guiding compass when you're faced with managing conflicting demands. They help you maintain perspective in terms of what must be done. Be sure your priorities are right.

7. **No energy? Get fit and healthy.** You need energy to be resilient. Physical and mental energy feed off of each other. Work on your physical fitness. Join a health club, walk, exercise, and eat well. Look after your mental well-being. Regularly engage in activities that you find mentally restorative. Develop a habit for a physical activity you enjoy and that makes you feel good. Practice yoga, mindfulness, or meditation techniques. Scientific studies show doing things that "center" you can give your mind greater clarity. Renewed thinking. If you're physically and mentally fit and healthy, you'll have more energy. It'll feel easier to attack and finish projects. Easier to stay focused and positive. To persevere when you feel like giving up. You'll perform better, feel stronger.

8. **Blow up under pressure? Regulate your internal pressure gauge.** Demanding role? Challenging projects? Tough environment? Pressure building? Resilience being tested? Find ways to stay in control. Pressure can be productive if regulated effectively—just like a pressure cooker. Not enough pressure, the meal won't cook. Too much and the lid will blow. Contents all over—a chaotic mess. Try to

understand what causes you to blow up. Maybe your fuse is too long. You wait and wait. You keep concerns to yourself. Let the pressure build to the point where you're unable to control its release, so you blow up. Maybe it's too short and you don't see the signs in time. Either way, uncontrolled pressure release is likely to have negative implications, for you and those around you. Regulate your internal pressure gauge. Learn how much pressure you need to be productive. Recognize the signals that the pressure's getting too high. That you need to let off some steam. Maybe you're faltering? Losing your confidence? Your composure? Agitating others? Find constructive ways to release the pent-up energy and emotion. Work on releasing your work frustration off-work. Get a physical hobby. Physical activity helps relieve pent up energy. Detaches you from daily pressures. It also bumps up the production of endorphins, your brain's feel-good neurotransmitters. These help combat the negative effects of stress. Try writing down what you're concerned about. Talk about it with confidantes and trusted coworkers. Take action as soon as you feel your pressure gauge rising. The sooner you can dissipate the unhelpful energy, the sooner you will bounce back to your baseline levels of composure and performance.

26

9.   **Burning out? Learn to manage stress.** Physically and emotionally exhausted? Dread going to work? Trouble sleeping? Exhausted all the time? No interest in your work? Feeling overwhelmed? Getting short-tempered? These could be warning signs that your stress levels are too high and that you could be heading towards burnout. Stress can be caused by anything. Your daily commute. Heavy workload. Difficult customers. Delivering results quarter after quarter. It's different for everyone. Unchecked, it can affect your productivity and, worse still, your health. Find out what situations cause you to become stressed. Keep a stress diary. Make an entry after any stressful event. Note down when it happened. How you felt about it. How high your stress level became on a scale of 0–10. How you responded. How your response helped or hindered the situation. Any physical or emotional reaction (sweaty palms, tears, etc.). Review your diary entries regularly and establish what situations cause you the most stress. How do they affect your productivity? Your health? What can you do to change these situations for the better? What strategies will help you deal with them? Some stress at work will be unavoidable and resilience means recognizing and responding to your signals early. Finding better ways to manage stress and pressure. Talk to your boss or mentor about getting some relief if you're about to crumble. If you feel you're already burned out, maybe think about moving to a less stressful job.

Want to learn more? Take a deep dive...

Collingwood, J. (2010). *Dealing with anger constructively*. Psych Central.

Goudreau, J. (2013, March 20). 12 Ways to eliminate stress at work. *Forbes*.

Mayo Clinic Staff. (2013). *Coping with stress: Workplace tips*. Mayo Clinic.

10. **Lost your passion? Rediscover what matters.** Heart's not in it anymore? Hard to stay positive? Not 100% committed? Maybe you don't bounce back or drive to overcome difficulties because deep down you don't care anymore—you're sick of doing this job or working for this organization or pushing against a particular person or group. Ask what it is that you want. Find your passion again. To make the best of your current job, make a list of what you like and don't like to do. Concentrate on doing more liked activities each day. Work to delegate or task trade the things that are no longer motivating to you. Do your least preferred activities first to get them out of the way; focus not on the activity, but on your sense of accomplishment. Change your work activity to mirror your interests as much as you can. Volunteer for task forces and projects that would be motivating for you.

11. **Caught off guard by crises? Prepare for them.** Resilience is a key skill for crisis management. When a crisis strikes, you need to keep a firm, confident hand on the tiller. During a crisis, time is the enemy. Pressure is high and quick action is needed. So be prepared for them. Learn to anticipate them. Come up with signal detectors— such as an increase in costs or threats—for all potential crises. Collect all the data you can. Think through all of the worst-case consequences and assign a person or a team to prepare for them. When a crisis strikes, use the data you have and ask others for suggestions and thoughts. Decide and execute decisions with an instant feedback loop. Make adjustments to your course as you go. Stay focused and in control. And communicate, communicate, communicate.

12. **Suffered a setback? Take positive action.** Setbacks can happen at any time and are caused by many things. Environmental factors. Or individual mistakes. Whatever the cause, it can be easy to be thrown off track and harder to bounce back. Maybe you're embarrassed? Perhaps you feel you've failed, lost the battle. Recognize what has

happened and accept your own role in the situation. Bring yourself to a physical and emotional state where you can focus on moving forward. Confront the issue. Plan your recovery. Ask yourself: What do I want to have happen? What is within my control? What do I have influence over? How can I make the most immediate, positive difference in this situation? What's the best and worst outcome from here? What do I want success to look like on the other side of this setback? How can I get there quickly? What will I do first? Don't retreat into isolation. Surround yourself with wise counsel—people who will help you stay balanced. Challenge your perspective. Guide you through making the tough decisions. Encourage you to keep going; to recover quickly. Resilience is about taking action. A positive step forward, a small win, a new goal that takes attention off of the past and creates excitement about the future. A belief that you will succeed eventually.

26

Want to learn more? Take a deep dive...

Kleiman, J. (2013, January 28). 7 Ways to bounce back from career mistakes, missteps, and misunderstandings. *Forbes*.

Levin, H. (2012, May 3). *How to stay motivated at work*. Fox Business.

Ryan, J. R. (2010, June 11). Four ideas for a positive workforce. *Bloomberg Businessweek*.

Job assignments

- Take on a task or assignment that you dislike doing. Manage your own resistance to driving it through.

- Prepare and present, with confidence, a significant proposal to your management team. Anticipate the resistance you may get and prepare to counter it.

- Offer to take the lead on getting a derailed project back on track. Dig beneath the surface to find out what went wrong so you can work out how things need to be approached differently.

- Solicit constructive criticism from a customer or stakeholder that you've had trouble with or find it hard to get along with. Look for what you can learn from the information you receive.

- Develop and implement your own personal stress- and pressure-management plan. Seek input from experts who can help guide you.

Take time to reflect...

If you feel like giving up when people push back...

> ...then ask yourself if you tend to give up too soon. Don't be discouraged by resistance. If your goal is worthwhile, you owe it to yourself to persist.

If you find it hard to stay focused when the pressure is on...

> ...then find your release valve to reduce your stress levels. Keep things in perspective. Talk to trusted friends. Find ways to laugh.

If you're feeling drained from things not working out...

> ...then take a break from the battle. Do whatever re-energizes you most. Recharge your batteries. Return to the situation with renewed vigor and focus.

26

"It's hard to beat a person who never gives up."

Babe Ruth – American baseball player and member of the Baseball Hall of Fame

Learn more about *Being* resilient

Beer, M. (2009). *High commitment high performance: How to build a resilient organization for sustained advantage*. San Francisco, CA: Jossey-Bass.

Cashman, K. (2008). *Leadership from the inside out: Becoming a leader for life*. San Francisco, CA: Berrett-Kohler Publishers.

Paulson, T. L. (2010). *The optimism advantage: 50 simple truths to transform your attitudes and actions into results*. Hoboken, NJ: Wiley & Sons.

Trestman, M. (2010). *Perseverance: Life lessons on leadership and teamwork*. Edina, MN: Bernstein Books.

Zolli, A., & Healy, A. M. (2013). *Resilience: Why things bounce back*. New York, NY: Simon & Schuster.

 # Deep dive learning resource links

26

Collingwood, J. (2010). *Dealing with anger constructively*. Psych Central. Retrieved from http://psychcentral.com/lib/dealing-with-anger-constructively/0003155

Goudreau, J. (2013, March 20). 12 Ways to eliminate stress at work. *Forbes*. Retrieved from http://www.forbes.com/sites/jennagoudreau/2013/03/20/12-ways-to-eliminate-stress-at-work/

Hannon, K. (2012, December 26). 6 Key steps for career resilience. *Forbes*. Retrieved from http://www.forbes.com/sites/kerryhannon/2012/12/26/6-key-steps-for-career-resilience/

Ireland, K. (2013, August 16). *How to show self-confidence tips & tricks*. Livestrong. Retrieved from http://www.livestrong.com/article/191199-how-to-show-self-confidence-tips-tricks/

Kleiman, J. (2013, January 28). 7 Ways to bounce back from career mistakes, missteps, and misunderstandings. *Forbes*. Retrieved from http://www.forbes.com/sites/work-in-progress/2013/01/28/7-ways-to-bounce-back-from-career-mistakes-missteps-and-misunderstandings/

Levin, H. (2012, May 3). *How to stay motivated at work*. Fox Business. Retrieved from http://www.foxbusiness.com/personal-finance/2012/05/03/how-to-stay-motivated-at-work/

Mayo Clinic Staff. (2013). *Coping with stress: Workplace tips*. Mayo Clinic. Retrieved from http://www.mayoclinic.org/coping-with-stress/art-20048369

Ryan, J. R. (2010, June 11). Four ideas for a positive workforce. *Bloomberg Businessweek*. Retrieved from http://www.businessweek.com/managing/content/jun2010/ca2010068_804146.htm

Wakeman, C. (2009, June 8). A guide to dealing with resistant employees. *Fast Company*. Retrieved from http://www.fastcompany.com/1293211/guide-dealing-resistant-employees

Recommended search terms

If you'd like to explore *Being* resilient further, try searching online using the following terms:

- Becoming resilient.
- Being persistent at work.
- Building perseverance.
- Showing confidence at work.
- Working through resistance.

ⓘ More help...

Go to www.kornferry.com/fyi-resources and link directly to the deep dive resources in this chapter. Visit the site often to see the additional resources that are uploaded on a regular basis.

318 |

27. Resourcefulness

Securing and deploying resources effectively and efficiently.

So much to do; so little time to do it. Finite resources; infinite needs. Everyone having more to do than they can get to. Sound familiar? That's life in organizations today. There are often more opportunities than there are people, time, and money available. Most anyone can produce results, given unlimited resources. The real trick is to produce results by making the best use of the limited resources available. Resourcefulness means finding a way to get things done, even when the odds are against you. Not getting stalled at the first roadblock but, instead, looking beyond the obvious for other viable approaches to accomplishing the goal. Knowing how to find and secure scant resources. Orchestrating efforts so that assignments are executed efficiently and effectively. Challenging yourself to do more with less. And redefining what's possible.

❝It's not the lack of resources, it's your lack of resourcefulness that stops you. ❞

Tony Robbins – American entrepreneur and motivational speaker

Resourcefulness is in the **Results** factor (II) in the Korn Ferry Leadership Architect™. It is part of Cluster D, **Taking initiative,** along with Action oriented (2). You may find it helpful to also take a look at some of the tips included in that chapter to supplement your learning.

Skilled

Marshals resources (people, funding, material, support) to get things done.

Orchestrates multiple activities simultaneously to accomplish a goal.

Gets the most out of limited resources.

Applies knowledge of internal structures, processes, and culture to resourcing efforts.

Less skilled

- Has difficulty figuring out where to get resources.
- Relies on the same resources over and over.
- Gets frustrated and becomes inefficient when things don't go as planned.
- Tries to impose one way of doing things; doesn't adjust swiftly enough.

Talented

- Gets the most out of available resources and secures rare resources others can't get.
- Adapts quickly to changing resource requirements.
- Enjoys multi-tasking; applies knowledge of the organization to advance multiple objectives.

Overused skill

- Stretches available resources beyond capacity.
- Hoards resources from others.
- Sometimes gathers resources too far ahead of time or obtains excess resources.
- Diverts too quickly from planned approach when something unexpected happens.

320 |

Some possible causes of lower skill

Causes help explain *why* a person may have trouble with Resourcefulness. When seeking to increase skill, it's helpful to consider how these might play out in certain situations. And remember that all of these can be addressed if you are motivated to do so.

- Poor planner.
- Disorganized.
- Doesn't delegate.
- Not flexible.
- Inexperienced.
- Slow decision maker.
- Poor time management.
- Uncomfortable with ambiguity.

Did you know?

Resourcefulness is such an integral part of life in bustling India, it has given rise to a particularly Indian form of innovation known as *jugaad*. Tracing its popular roots to Indian farmers' construction of jitney-like vehicles from scrap wood and irrigation pump motors, jugaad has found its way into the management lexicon as companies increasingly turn to "frugal innovation" practices to fuel their R&D operations. Recent innovations in everything from cars to medical devices to mobile banking all owe some inspiration to the principles of jugaad.[41, 42]

27

Tips to develop Resourcefulness

1.   **Need a plan? Lay out the work.** Resourcefulness starts out with a plan. A good plan helps everyone who has to work under it. It leads to better use of resources and facilitates getting things done efficiently. Lay out the work from A to Z. What are your goals? What's mission critical and what's trivial? What's the time line? What resources will you need? Who controls the resources (time, people, funding, tools, materials, support)? What's your currency? How can you pay for or repay the resources you need? Break complex and multi-tracked projects down into a series of tasks. Ask others to comment on your ordering and note what's missing. When you're ready, set the plan. Use flowcharting or project planning software that does PERT and Gantt charts. Set aside 20 minutes at the start of each week to review your plan, prioritize, and manage your resources.

2.   **Wasting time? Invest it wisely.** Your time and that of others is a precious resource not to be wasted. At some point, everyone has wished for more hours in the day. Be time sensitive. Accurately plan your time and the time you need from others and manage against it. Set deadlines for yourself. Use your best time of day for the toughest and most critical projects—your "A" tasks. If you're best in the morning, don't waste it on "B" and "C" level tasks. Don't secure and deploy resources too early or too late in a project; both can lead to time being wasted. Attach a monetary value to time. Figure out what you and your other people resources are worth per hour based on gross salary plus overhead and benefits. Then ask: Is this task worth that amount of time and money? What would be a more valuable investment? Remember that the higher up you go, the higher the monetary value on time will be.

3.   **Difficulty securing all you need? Work with what you have.** You can't always delay taking action while you wait to get every last bit of resources that you need. It might never happen and doing nothing is likely not an option. Have the courage to make a start. Be clear about what resources you have, where they are, and what they can do. Focus on what can be achieved. Visualize how you can achieve what you need to. If you were making the most of the resources you have, what would you be doing? What's the best possible result you could deliver? Invite others who are involved to offer suggestions on how to best use the available resources. Be pragmatic. Manage stakeholder expectations where you need to and start small where you have to. But start anyway.

Want to learn more? Take a deep dive...

Kimbrell, G. (2014, January 31). Four project management lessons you can learn from software engineers. *Forbes*.

Larson, E., & Larson, R. (2004, September 10). How to create a clear project plan. *CIO Magazine*.

Saunders, E. G. (2013, January 7). How to allocate your time, and your effort. *Harvard Business Review Blog Network*.

Trammell, J. (2013, June 18). The resource allocation dilemma faced by CEOs every single day. *Forbes*.

4. **Operating on a shoestring? Bargain for resources.** Sometimes you'll need to be creative to get what you need. That means learning to bargain, negotiate, trade, cajole, and influence. What can you borrow? What do you have that you can trade? What do you need to trade for? Who do you know that could help? What could you provide in return? How can you make it a win for everyone? Use relationships to help where you can; find people in your network to borrow from. Working internationally? Adjust your resource-bargaining approach to match the local culture. Worried you may be pushing the ethics envelope? Study up on the legal practices of the country in which you are operating and how they may influence or limit what you can do. If you are operating in a questionable area, get help from legal or others who have worked in similar situations.

5. **Money tight? Watch the budget.** Be clear on exactly what funding you have and plan spending carefully. Write down all your funding sources along with when each element of funding will be available. Make a list of the costs you're anticipating and when they are likely to occur. Which are fixed and which might vary? Align the funding coming in to the expenditures going out. If you can, have a reserve in case the unexpected comes up. Projected spending higher than the funding available? Look at the variable costs to find areas to cut back. Or work backwards—take the funding you have available and consider how to best spend it in line with what needs to be delivered. Set up a funding time line to track ongoing expenditures. Review your spending regularly to keep on track.

6. **Not getting the most out of people resources? Delegate.** On long, complex, multi-track projects, you can't do everything yourself. Your people resources each come with a unique set of skills, knowledge, experience, and ideas. All available for you to tap into. Get

comfortable giving up control. Give away as much as possible along with the authority that goes with it. Be clear on the outcome required but open on how it's achieved. Give people leeway, encourage experimentation. One clear finding in research is that people are more motivated when they have control over their work, can determine how to do it, and have the authority to make decisions. It's also developmental. Telling them how to do it may help you in the short-term, but if people just carry out your instructions, they won't grow. Agree on boundaries and authority levels. Give context to the bigger strategic picture—take three extra minutes to talk about its importance to the goals and objectives of the unit.

7. **Limited pool of resources to draw upon? Observe master resource builders in action.** Do you tend to rely on the same resources over and over? Amazed by others who get resources from far and wide? Who find and secure the rare resources others can't? Don't just wonder at them, actively observe their behavior. How do they get things done? How do they use internal culture, structures, and processes to get what they need? How do they influence and negotiate? What tactics do they use to expedite things through the organizational maze? How do they use their networks? Who do they rely on for help and to get things done? What relationship do they have with the gatekeepers who control the flow of resources? Compare your approach to theirs. What do they do that you don't? Who do they know that you don't? Get to know them better; use them as a mentor. Learn their strategies then borrow them for yourself.

27

Want to learn more? Take a deep dive...

Green, H. (2012, June 12). Four strategies for getting it done in your organization. *Forbes*.

Lawrence, L., Hernandez Requejo, W., & Graham, J. L. (2011, June 28). Negotiating over a limited resource: What would you do? *Harvard Business Review Blog Network*.

Mind Tools. (n.d.). *Successful delegation: Using the power of other people's help*. Mind Tools.

Westland, J. (2011, June 23). Project management: 4 Ways to manage your budget. *CIO Magazine*.

8. **Overwhelmed? Manage your state of mind.** Think it can't be done? That it'll never work? This is negative self-talk. It reinforces beliefs that limit what is possible. Learn to eliminate negative self-talk and

replace it with something more helpful. Look at complex problems and hold the belief that they can be solved, even when others are telling you otherwise. Turn negatives like "I can't do this" or "This is impossible" into positive questions: "How can I do this?" "How is this possible?" It shifts your thinking from the problem to the solution. From what you can't do to what you can do. What you think shapes your reality. And in the words of Henry Ford, "Whether you think you can, or you think you can't—you're right."

9. **Frustrated when things don't go according to plan? Expect the unexpected.** Are you a perfectionist? Create plans and expect to follow them without deviation? Get frustrated when circumstances change? Even the best laid plans go astray when the unexpected happens. Resourcefulness is about knowing this and preparing for it. Build contingency into your resources where you can. Have a Plan B as well as a Plan A. Anticipate changes in circumstances and prepare how you might respond. What will you do if you lose some of your resources? If the time lines are tightened? Funding cut? Stay calm when the unexpected does happen. Take an objective look at what's changed and avoid the urge to act impulsively. Don't waste time and energy on things you can't change. Focus on what you *can* do. Ask questions that provoke resourceful thinking. What result am I working toward? Where am I now? What's my best option? What do I have influence and/or control over? How much do I need to adapt my plan? What help do I need? What adjustments do I need to make to my resources—time, people, funding, etc.? Adapt swiftly. Remember, resourcefulness is measured by the ability to achieve the outcome, not follow the plan.

10. **Stuck with one way of doing things? Be creative.** Resourcefulness is, in part, about finding creative new ways of doing things. Experimenting when an initial approach doesn't work. If you find yourself relying on the same methods time after time, reflect on what's preventing you from being more creative. Fear of failure? Creative people see failure as an opportunity to learn. Worried what people may think? Being creative means putting up the new and unique for review and critique. Get out of your comfort zone. Beware of "I have always..." or "Usually, I..." Focus on "What haven't I tried" or "What would happen if..." Learn from others who've achieved the outcome you're seeking. Find out what made them effective. Take a risk. Don't carelessly disregard the rules, but do find unconventional ways to do things if it helps. Be prepared to explain yourself and apologize if you overstep. Think and act differently; try new things; break free of your restraints.

11. **Think there's only one way to get things done? Try different solutions and learn from the results.** Don't expect to get it right the first time. A low-risk, perfectionist mindset leads to safe and stale solutions. Many studies show that the second or third try is when we really understand the underlying dynamics of problems. To increase learning, shorten your action time and get feedback loops—aiming to make them as immediate as possible. The more frequent the cycles, the more opportunities to learn. If we do something in each of three days instead of one thing every three days, we triple our learning opportunities and increase our chances of finding the right answer.

Want to learn more? Take a deep dive...

Clark, N. F. (2013, July 15). A surprising way to get things done on time. *Forbes*.

Conlon, C. (2011, October 12). *7 Wise ways to find focus and get things done*. Life Hack.

Mayo Clinic Staff. (2011, May 28). *Positive thinking: Reduce stress by eliminating negative self-talk*. Mayo Clinic.

Pitagorsky, G. (2011, January 26). Project managers are change managers. *Project Times*.

Job assignments

- Offer to lead an underresourced project that requires you to bargain and trade with others to get what you need to succeed.

- Begin something from scratch that requires your bringing a team together and initiating simultaneous actions under a tight time frame.

- Take on a task where you've failed in the past. Push yourself outside your comfort zone and experiment with new ways of achieving success.

- Consider tasks that are no longer developmental for you but would be for others, and delegate them.

- Volunteer to plan an off-site meeting, conference, convention, trade show, or other event where you're almost certain to encounter changing requirements and obstacles that will test your resourcefulness.

Take time to reflect...

If the task seems impossible with the resources you have...

> ...then renegotiate and refocus. Figure out what's possible with limited resources. The resources that have brought you this far can probably take you even further. Use old tools in new ways. Improvise and adapt. Find a way.

If your "go to" resources have got up and gone...

> ...then recognize the risks of relying on the same sources again and again. Seek out new options. Use your knowledge of your environment. Tap into connections. Always be on the lookout.

If you don't have what you need to get the job done...

> ...then consider that the solution doesn't always stare you in the face. Look beyond the obvious. Get creative. Think possibilities and "what ifs." Sometimes the most unlikely options turn out to be the best fit.

❝ *I will either find a way or make one.* **❞**

27

Hannibal – Punic Carthaginian military commander

Learn more about Resourcefulness

Achor, S. (2010). *The happiness advantage: The seven principles of positive psychology that fuel success and performance at work.* New York, NY: Crown Business.

Chandler, S. (2011). *Time warrior: How to defeat procrastination, people-pleasing, self-doubt, over-commitment, broken promises and chaos.* Anna Maria, FL: Maurice Bassett.

Gordon, J. (2008). *The no complaining rule: Positive ways to deal with negativity at work.* Hoboken, NJ: John Wiley & Sons, Inc.

Hall, D. (2013). *Time management: How to take charge of your schedule, reduce stress, be productive, and effective!* [Kindle edition]. Amazon Digital Services.

Kerzner, H. R. (2009). *Project management: A systems approach to planning, scheduling, and controlling.* Hoboken, NJ: John Wiley & Sons, Inc.

Deep dive learning resource links

Clark, N. F. (2013, July 15). A surprising way to get things done on time. *Forbes.* Retrieved from http://www.forbes.com/sites/womensmedia/2013/07/15/a-surprising-way-to-get-things-done-on-time/

Conlon, C. (2011, October 12). *7 Wise ways to find focus and get things done.* Life Hack. Retrieved from http://www.lifehack.org/articles/productivity/7-wise-ways-to-find-focus-and-get-things-done.html

Green, H. (2012, June 12). Four strategies for getting it done in your organization. *Forbes.* Retrieved from http://www.forbes.com/sites/work-in-progress/2012/06/12/four-strategies-for-getting-it-done-in-your-organization/

Kimbrell, G. (2014, January 31). Four project management lessons you can learn from software engineers. *Forbes.* Retrieved from http://www.forbes.com/sites/theyec/2014/01/31/four-project-management-lessons-you-can-learn-from-software-engineers/

Larson, E., & Larson, R. (2004, September 10). How to create a clear project plan. *CIO Magazine.* Retrieved from http://www.cio.com.au/article/166486/how_create_clear_project_plan/

Lawrence, L., Hernandez Requejo, W., & Graham, J. L. (2011, June 28). Negotiating over a limited resource: What would you do? *Harvard Business Review Blog Network.* Retrieved from http://blogs.hbr.org/2011/06/negotiating-over-a-limited-res/

328 |

Mayo Clinic Staff. (2011, May 28). *Positive thinking: Reduce stress by eliminating negative self-talk*. Mayo Clinic. Retrieved from http://www.mayoclinic.org/positive-thinking/art-20043950

Mind Tools. (n.d.). *Successful delegation: Using the power of other people's help*. Mind Tools. Retrieved from http://www.mindtools.com/pages/article/newLDR_98.htm

Pitagorsky, G. (2011, January 26). Project managers are change managers. *Project Times*. Retrieved from http://www.projecttimes.com/george-pitagorsky/project-managers-are-change-managers.html

Saunders, E. G. (2013, January 7). How to allocate your time, and your effort. *Harvard Business Review Blog Network*. Retrieved from http://blogs.hbr.org/2013/01/how-to-allocate-your-time-and/

Trammell, J. (2013, June 18). The resource allocation dilemma faced by CEOs every single day. *Forbes*. Retrieved from http://www.forbes.com/sites/joeltrammell/2013/06/18/the-resource-allocation-dilemma-faced-by-ceos-every-single-day/

Westland, J. (2011, June 23). Project management: 4 Ways to manage your budget. *CIO Magazine*. Retrieved from http://www.cio.com/article/684978/Project_Management_4_Ways_to_Manage_Your_Budget

Recommended search terms

If you'd like to explore Resourcefulness further, try searching online using the following terms:

- Bargaining for limited resources.
- How to work with limited resources.
- Planning your time effectively.
- Reducing negative self-talk.
- Using different strategies to get things done.

 More help...

Go to www.kornferry.com/fyi-resources and link directly to the deep dive resources in this chapter. Visit the site often to see the additional resources that are uploaded on a regular basis.

28. *Drives* results

Consistently achieving results, even under tough circumstances.

Driving results Is an overall achievement mindset, a bias for action, an eagerness to take the initiative. People who drive for results infuse their teams and organizations with a sense of urgency. They help create a culture where organizational performance is always top of mind. Results might be quantifiable—measured in terms of P&L, sales growth, customer satisfaction ratings, new products launched. Or results may be qualitative—an enhanced reputation among customers, a more vibrant brand that attracts customers and employee talent. In successful organizations, the efforts of individuals, teams, functions, departments, and business units are aligned around these objectives. Driving results means communicating a vision, setting priorities, developing and executing plans that achieve the desired outcome—for the organization and the world. As a leader, you *must* be willing to act and follow through to drive results.

" If my mind can conceive it, and my heart can believe it, I know I can achieve it! "

Jesse Jackson – American civil rights activist

***Drives* results** is in the **Results** factor (II) in the Korn Ferry Leadership Architect™. It is part of Cluster F, **Focusing on performance,** along with *Ensures* accountability (1). You may find it helpful to also take a look at some of the tips included in that chapter to supplement your learning.

Skilled

Has a strong bottom-line orientation.

Persists in accomplishing objectives despite obstacles and setbacks.

Has a track record of exceeding goals successfully.

Pushes self and helps others achieve results.

Less skilled

- Is reluctant to push for results.
- Does the least to get by.
- Is an inconsistent performer.
- Gives up easily; doesn't go back with different strategies for the third and fourth try.
- Often misses deadlines.
- Procrastinates around whatever gets in the way.

Talented

- Sets aggressive goals and has high standards.
- Is consistently one of the top performers.
- Pursues everything with energy, drive, and the need to finish.
- Persists in the face of challenges and setbacks.
- Always keeps the end in sight; puts in extra effort to meet deadlines.

Overused skill

- Goes for results at all costs without appropriate concern for people, teams, due process, or possibly norms and ethics.
- May be so deadline oriented that he/she pushes to get something done rather than taking the time to do it right.
- Even in the face of near insurmountable obstacles, sticks with the effort beyond reason.
- Puts too much pressure on self and others to achieve the impossible.
- May not celebrate and share successes.

332 |

Some possible causes of lower skill

Causes help explain *why* a person may have trouble with *Drives* results. When seeking to increase skill, it's helpful to consider how these might play out in certain situations. And remember that all of these can be addressed if you are motivated to do so.

- Loses focus.
- Disorganized.
- Not strategic.
- Procrastinates.
- Sets unrealistic expectations.
- Poor planner.
- Burned out.
- Afraid of mistakes.
- Lacks commitment and accountability.

 Brain booster

So driven that you can't relax? For the highest achievers, it can be hard to stop and take a break, but it turns out that rest and relaxation is exactly what helps us maintain high levels of achievement. This may feel like a paradox, but conduct your own experiment to see for yourself. Research has shown that short naps improve the vigilance and judgment of air traffic controllers. Getting a full night's sleep improves memory. Staying unplugged on vacation decreases the likelihood that you'll leave your company. Stepping away, switching off, relaxing, and protecting your workout time all contribute to higher productivity and better job performance. While wishing for more hours in your day is futile, wishing for more energy during your day is achievable.[43]

28

Tips to develop *Drives* results

1. **Have a big idea? Convert it to action.** Ever get on board with a big initiative, only to run out of steam? Create inspiring plans in an off-site and then forget about them? Or set an audacious goal in January and lose track of it by February? Big ideas produce big results over the long haul. In fact, they can be downright transformative. But to see results, you need to translate ideas into action. If you are part of something big, keep it front of mind by making it visible. Post a photo or other reminder on your screensaver so you see it every time you open your laptop. Create a visual model or time line and share it with others. If it involves the whole organization, get HR, marketing, communications, or other relevant groups involved. Create a communications plan. Put time on the calendar to get things moving. A vision is just a good idea until you take action.

2. **Not bold enough? Take reasonable risks.** Won't take a risk? Micromanaging to avoid mistakes? Running another analysis of last month's figures? Rethinking decisions? If this is you, practice pushing yourself forward. Sometimes producing results involves taking chances and trying bold new initiatives. Doing those things leads to more misfires and mistakes but sometimes better results. Treat any mistakes or failures as chances to learn. Nothing ventured, nothing gained. Up your risk comfort. To get results, you need to keep things moving. Making decisions. Approving plans. Start small so you can recover more quickly. See how creative and innovative you can be. Let go of perfection and aim for excellence. Satisfy yourself; people will always say it should have been done differently. Listen to them, but be skeptical. Ask yourself what's at stake. And what's the worst that can happen. Then turn the question around: What good things will *not* happen if you fail to act? Allow reasonable time to consider options, then make the best decision possible. Conduct a postmortem immediately after finishing. This will indicate to all that you're open to continuous improvement whether the result was stellar or not.

3. **Procrastinator? Start now.** Are you a lifelong procrastinator? Do you perform best in crises and under impossible deadlines? Do you wait until the last possible moment? If you do, you may miss deadlines and performance targets. You might not produce consistent results. Some of your work will be marginal because you didn't have the time to do it right. You settled for a B when you could have gotten an A if you had one more day to work on it. And you might be causing yourself and your teammates unnecessary stress. Save "crisis mode" for your own time. When others are depending on you, get going. Start earlier. Try doing 10% of each task immediately after

it is assigned so you can better gauge what it is going to take to finish the rest. Divide tasks and assignments into thirds and schedule time to do them spaced over the delivery period. Let others know how you are progressing. Always leave more time than you think it's going to take.

4. **Overwhelmed? Focus on priorities.** You're already working at top speed on a full schedule. Then your boss asks you to take on something new—right now. You feel like you need to go in eight different directions and don't know where to start. Before you panic, do some planning. What's mission-critical? What are the three to five things that most need to get done to achieve your goals? Effective performers typically spend about half their time on a few mission-critical priorities. Don't get diverted by trivia and things you like doing but aren't tied to the bottom line. When you've laid out your top priorities, identify a few critical action steps that will move you forward on each one. Notice what is demanding immediate attention—and what is actually already on track. Put some space on your calendar to take care of what is important but not urgent now. Then take care of the urgent. This planning will take just a few minutes and will get you back on track. If you're still uptight, ask for help. And remember to manage your expectations of yourself: as good as you may be, you can't be in two places at once.

Want to learn more? Take a deep dive...

Driscoll, M. (2013, July 18). Research: Why companies keep getting blind-sided by risk. *Harvard Business Review Blog Network*.

Giang, V. (2012, March 18). *15 Ways to stop procrastinating right now*. Business Insider.

Llopis, G. (2013, April 1). The 12 things that successfully convert a great idea into a reality. *Forbes*.

Mind Tools. (n.d.). *Taking initiative: Making things happen in the workplace*. Mind Tools.

28

5. **Problem getting work done through others? Focus on the fundamentals.** Many people can produce results themselves but struggle to make the transition to getting results from the team. Having trouble getting your team to work with you to get the results you need? Have the resources and the people but things just don't run well? Maybe you do too much of the work yourself. You don't

delegate or empower. You don't communicate well. Struggle to motivate. Plan poorly. Find prioritizing difficult. You may need to learn the basics of delegation and good management. To let go of doing it all yourself. To learn to show others what you want done— and let them do it. To paint a clear picture of what is important and why. Delegation is a complex skill. It takes effort to show others what you want. But it pays off over time. The team will become stronger. Results will be better. Read *Becoming a Manager* by Linda A. Hill. Learn from others around you who delegate well.

6. **Trouble getting buy-in? Listen before you act.** Focused on action? Eager to get started? Anxious to get results? These are great qualities for getting to the bottom line. But if you're driving results through others, you need to slow down and include them in your thinking. People can't follow you if they don't know where you are going, and why. Give them the big picture of what needs to happen. Invite them to flesh out ideas and plans. Work with them to define plans and expectations. Help them prioritize their own efforts. Start with a brainstorming session. "Here's what we need to do. How can we do this?" Collaborate on creating a plan. Or hand it off to them. Check in. Stay involved to see how things are going. Let them know how their efforts align with the organizational goals.

7. **People not committed? Set stretch goals and stay involved.** High expectations are great. But if goals are perceived as unachievable, people become skeptical and discouraged. They give up and performance lags. Or, if goals are too low, boredom sets in and performance lags. People lose interest and end up underperforming. Setting stretching but achievable goals shows confidence. It creates optimism and an expectation for success. But don't just set goals. Ask what is needed to get there. Get the resources and support you need—and set checkpoints along the way to measure progress. Give yourself and others as much feedback as you can. Get buy-in. Recognize improvement. Celebrate success. Then agree on next steps to even higher performance.

8. **Group not performing? Address team dynamics.** Leading a stalled project? In danger of missing the goal? Delivering subpar performance? Every group and team is made up of individuals. Some who may be giving more than others. Some who may be willing but struggling. Some may have "checked out" for reasons of their own. If this is happening, assess the team as a whole. Does it have an agreed-upon goal? The right mix of skills? The resources it needs? Adequate support from the organization? Make the changes

you need to make to ensure results are achieved. Look at individuals. Do you need to switch out some team members or bring in new skills? Encourage different working relationships? Stimulate new collaborations? Address conflict? Figure out what's not working and make it right. Ask HR for help or bring in a team consultant if you are really stumped.

9. **Getting resistance? Deal with objections.** It's your job to drive a major change initiative. You've got your resources, your time line, your plans. Everything looks good. Until a key group or person raises objections. Why are we doing this? What will this cost? Why are we changing what we've done for 20 years? The best change leaders don't get derailed by pushback. They anticipate resistance. They are equipped to handle the heat of controversy. They allow time to hear objections. Individual meetings. Town halls. Phone conferences. They answer objections and make course corrections. But they don't lose sight of the endgame. The vision. The results. Encourage more objections. If you sense people are holding back, get concerns out on the table. Ask for specifics. Dig deep. Get to the root of the resistance. Understand what's behind the dissent. See it from their point of view. If you were in their shoes, what would you need to hear to be converted?

Want to learn more? Take a deep dive...

Gleeson, B. (2012, December 28). Setting stretch goals: All in, all the time. *Inc*.

Hill, L., & Lineback, K. (2012, April 3). Good managers lead through a team. *Harvard Business Review Blog Network*.

Russell, N. S. (2013, February 8). Six ways to get things done when you're not the boss. *Forbes*.

Sevier, R. A. (2006, September). Moving a team forward. *University Business*.

28

10. **Derailed by the unexpected? Define and address the problem.** You're working hard, focused on getting things done. Then something unexpected happens. A system glitch destroys last night's work. An important meeting gets cancelled. Maybe you get stuck in traffic and arrive at the office two hours late. When you are thrown off track by the unexpected, you have two choices. You can either tense up, throw up your hands, snap at a few coworkers, and generally make the situation worse, or you can take a breath, stay calm, and

find a way around or through the situation. Pick up the phone, get on e-mail, reach out to others, and work the problem. Use your brain, use your resources. Envision a good outcome. Shift your attitude from "Why is this happening to me?" to "Interesting development. Let's see what we can do with it."

11. **Disorganized? Use systems to stay on track.** Running late? Missed a phone call? Lost a critical e-mail? When you're going in more than one direction, the occasional slip-up is inevitable. But you can't consistently deliver results if you can't stay on top of the details. Use systems to have a fighting chance of completing things on time and within budget. Log contact info into your phone or e-mail system. Deal with e-mail two to three times a day. Answer, forward, or act on anything you can. File the rest in project folders and put time on your calendar for follow-up. Have a to-do list or system for immediate tasks. Look at it at the beginning or end of the day. Add new items; delete those you've completed. Learn some basic Excel skills to create simple project sheets. Use just one calendar. Color code your files and tasks. Use mobile technology to access your e-mail and calendar on the go. Learn to live without paper. Back up your laptop. Remember that when it comes to being organized, less is more.

12. **Tempted to quit before the end? Refocus and stick with it.** It may be tempting to reduce your efforts when the end is in sight. After all, your customers have been delighted with the new products. The economy has run strong all year. Things are going well, so results are in the bag—right? Not necessarily. Surprises happen. Contracts get cancelled. Opportunities and sure things fizzle out. Markets crash. If you find your attention flagging, refocus. Winning teams play with the same intensity the whole game, no matter the score. Driving for results means not quitting before the end. Getting results means sticking with the project until it is completed successfully. Keep up a review of what has been done, what remains to be done, and where results will come from. Be persistent. Follow through on every task. Sometimes you'll head off a disaster. Sometimes you'll find an unexpected late win. Check the details. It's not over until it's over.

13. **Lost in the detail? Focus on the essentials.** Good with the detail? Pride yourself on your expertise? Remember names, dates, and places? Can relate the history of any product your company ever produced? Have the answer to any question? Being this detail oriented doesn't mean you're the quickest to get results. While you're stuck in what you know, the people around you want to move on. To create the next generation of products. To adopt some new

ideas. To get up to speed, you don't need to abandon valuable detail. But you do need to streamline your thinking—and your communication. Focus on the endpoint and ask yourself, "How much detail is needed to paint the picture and move us forward?" Use what is needed now. Archive or jettison the rest.

14. **Driving too hard? Learn to manage stress.** Pride yourself on exceeding goals? Push yourself every day to produce? Always ready for a challenge? Individual responses to stress vary. But for most people, driving for results day after day, quarter after quarter, year after year is stressful. If you're close to burnout or if people can't keep up with you, you're overdoing it. Sustainable performance requires rest and recovery. Athletes train hard, then enjoy the off-season. Performance will improve if you disconnect once in a while. Use your commute to work to get perspective. Enjoy friends and family. Make personal connections at work. Stop to celebrate wins. Learn to take pride in your great results, but balance action with recovery. Take a time out.

Want to learn more? Take a deep dive...

Grant Halvorson, H. (2011, June 22). How to become a great finisher. *Harvard Business Review Blog Network*

Mayo Clinic Staff. (2011, May 28). *Positive thinking: Reduce stress by eliminating negative self-talk*. Mayo Clinic.

Stolovitsky, N. (2010, August 4). *Planning for the unplanned: Including risk in your project management strategy*. Genius Project.

Wilkinson, M. (2010, June 18). *Why perseverance is an essential quality to possess in the workplace*. Career Path 360.

28

Job assignments

• Lead a team in launching a new product or service with a large potential impact on the business. Involve them in thinking through how to maximize benefit to the business.

• Manage the successful installation of a new process or system under a tight deadline. Secure the right support and build a strong sense of commitment to making it a success.

| 339

- Lead a stalled project to successful completion within the next few weeks. Identify the issues and generate solutions to move it forward.

- Develop an actionable time line to improve performance in a group that has lost momentum. Dig deep for the reasons and take action to get them back on track.

- Create, champion, and track a fundraising campaign with a clear financial goal. Get creative about how it can be exceeded.

Take time to reflect...

If the goal ahead seems unattainable...

> ...then make it your mission to get others on board. Securing the commitment of the team is critical. Clarify the goal. Sell the vision. Share the plan. Define roles. Turn them loose.

If you've been pushing hard and don't see an end in sight...

> ...then remember the goal you are striving toward. Celebrate what you've achieved so far. Regroup. Plunge back in with renewed vigor.

If you can't face those last few steps of the task...

> ...then ask yourself what's holding you back. Inspiration and aspiration are just the start. Action is what will take you across the finish line. Craft a plan. Carve out the time. Focus on the goal in sight.

28

"One never notices what has been done;
one can only see what remains to be done."

Marie Curie – Polish and naturalized-French physicist and chemist

Learn more about *Drives* results

Baldoni, J. (2006). *How great leaders get great results*. New York, NY: McGraw-Hill.

Hiam, A. (2003). *Motivational management: Inspiring your people for maximum performance*. New York, NY: AMACOM.

Meier, J. D. (2010). *Getting results the agile way: A personal results system for work and life*. Bellevue, WA: Innovation Playhouse, LLC.

Myers, B. (2012). *Take the lead: Motivate, inspire, and bring out the best in yourself and everyone around you*. New York, NY: Atria Paperback.

Thomas, K. W. (2009). *Intrinsic motivation at work: What really drives employee engagement* (2nd ed.). San Francisco, CA: Berrett-Koehler Publishers.

 # Deep dive learning resource links

Driscoll, M. (2013, July 18). Research: Why companies keep getting blind-sided by risk. *Harvard Business Review Blog Network*. Retrieved from http://blogs.hbr.org/2013/07/research-why-companies-get-blindsided/

Giang, V. (2012, March 18). *15 Ways to stop procrastinating right now*. Business Insider. Retrieved from http://www.businessinsider.com/15-ways-to-stop-procrastinating-right-now-2012-3?op=1

Gleeson, B. (2012, December 28). Setting stretch goals: All in, all the time. *Inc*. Retrieved from http://www.inc.com/brent-gleeson/setting-stretch-goals.html

Grant Halvorson, H. (2011, June 22). How to become a great finisher. *Harvard Business Review Blog Network*. Retrieved from http://blogs.hbr.org/2011/06/how-to-become-a-great-finisher/

Hill, L., & Lineback, K. (2012, April 3). Good managers lead through a team. *Harvard Business Review Blog Network*. Retrieved from http://blogs.hbr.org/2012/04/good-managers-lead-through-a-t/

Llopis, G. (2013, April 1). The 12 things that successfully convert a great idea into a reality. *Forbes*. Retrieved from http://www.forbes.com/sites/glennllopis/2013/04/01/12-things-successfully-convert-a-great-idea-into-a-reality/

Mayo Clinic Staff. (2011, May 28). *Positive thinking: Reduce stress by eliminating negative self-talk*. Mayo Clinic. Retrieved from http://www.mayoclinic.org/positive-thinking/art-20043950

28

Mind Tools. (n.d.). *Taking initiative: Making things happen in the workplace*. Mind Tools. Retrieved from http://www.mindtools.com/pages/article/initiative.htm

Russell, N. S. (2013, February 8). Six ways to get things done when you're not the boss. *Forbes*. Retrieved from http://www.forbes.com/sites/deborahljacobs/2013/02/08/six-ways-to-get-things-done-when-youre-not-the-boss/

Sevier, R. A. (2006, September). Moving a team forward. *University Business*. Retrieved from http://www.universitybusiness.com/article/moving-team-forward

Stolovitsky, N. (2010, August 4). *Planning for the unplanned: Including risk in your project management strategy*. Genius Project. Retrieved from http://www.geniusproject.com/blog/pm-best-practices/planning-for-the-unplanned-including-risk-in-your-project-management-strategy/

Wilkinson, M. (2010, June 18). *Why perseverance is an essential quality to possess in the workplace*. Career Path 360. Retrieved from http://www.careerpath360.com/index.php/why-perseverance-is-an-essential-quality-to-possess-in-the-workplace-4-9318/

Recommended search terms

If you'd like to explore *Drives* results further, try searching online using the following terms:

- Effectively reducing stress at work.
- Getting work done through others.
- Planning for unexpected problems at work.
- Risk management.
- Setting stretch goals for employees.
- Turning an idea into reality.

28

(i) More help...

Go to www.kornferry.com/fyi-resources and link directly to the deep dive resources in this chapter. Visit the site often to see the additional resources that are uploaded on a regular basis.

342 |

29. *Demonstrates self-awareness*

Using a combination of feedback and reflection to gain productive insight into personal strengths and weaknesses.

Self-awareness, the ability to clearly assess your own capabilities, gives a foundation upon which to grow, develop, and take on new challenges. Deploying yourself against life and work is greatly helped by really knowing what you're good at, average at, and bad at, what you're untested in, and what you overdo or overuse. It is not a new concept—it was Socrates who said "Know thyself." The fact that over 2,000 years later we're still figuring out how to be more self-aware is an indication of how challenging it is for us to see ourselves as we are. Self-aware people are able to connect the external perspective—how they are perceived by others—with the internal—how they see themselves. And that can be uncomfortable. But with great risk comes the potential for great reward—both for yourself personally and for your organization. That is, if you take action. Just increasing your self-awareness is not enough. You must do something with that knowledge, if it is to have an impact. Accepting that you have changes to make is your choice—it's up to no one but you. That means aligning your strengths and development areas with what's important for your career growth and deciding how to apply your increased self-awareness. Knowing how it can make you more effective and doing something about it.

> " *The more you know yourself,*
> *the more patience you have for what you see in others.* "

Joan Erikson – Canadian psychologist

***Demonstrates* self-awareness** is in the **Self** factor (IV) in the Korn Ferry Leadership Architect™. It is part of Cluster K, **Being open,** along with Self-development (30). You may find it helpful to also take a look at some of the tips included in that chapter to supplement your learning.

Skilled

Reflects on activities and impact on others.

Proactively seeks feedback without being defensive.

Is open to criticism and talking about shortcomings.

Admits mistakes and gains insight from experiences.

Knows strengths, weaknesses, opportunities, and limits.

Less skilled

- Doesn't reflect on past mistakes.

- Acts defensively when given feedback.

- Is unaware of own skills and interpersonal impact.

- Makes excuses and blames others.

Talented

- Seeks and acts on feedback from a wide variety of people.

- Willingly admits and takes responsibility for mistakes and shortcomings.

- Views criticism as helpful.

- Can articulate the causes behind own feelings and moods.

Overused skill

- Overthinks or overanalyzes feedback from others.

- May be self-critical to the point of risking credibility and appearing insecure.

- Spends too much time on building self-insight and not enough time on making meaningful changes to behavior or skills.

29

Some possible causes of lower skill

Causes help explain *why* a person may have trouble with *Demonstrates* self-awareness. When seeking to increase skill, it's helpful to consider how these might play out in certain situations. And remember that all of these can be addressed if you are motivated to do so.

- Arrogant.
- Defensive.
- Doesn't get any feedback.
- Doesn't know how to get feedback.
- Too much success.
- Blames others.
- Shuts down in the face of criticism.
- Spends too much time on reflection before acting.
- Sways too much based on feedback.
- Unable to learn from mistakes.
- Doesn't take the time to reflect on experience.
- Too modest.
- Too self-critical.

 Brain booster

Your brain has an observer that sits above all the activity and notices, monitors, and directs your thinking. Sometimes the observer is in narrative mode and is processing memories, making plans, and interpreting information. Sometimes the observer is in sensation mode and is focusing on all of the information coming in to your senses in real time—including feelings, thoughts, and internal states. Being mindful and self-aware involves activating this observer, knowing whether you are in narrative or sensation mode, and consciously being able to shift between the two. Practice focusing your attention on one of your five senses. Observe the thoughts and interpretations that cross your mind. Practice noticing without judging. All of these exercises can help restructure your brain to make it easier to be aware of what you are feeling, experiencing, and thinking. And, once you are aware, you have more control to decide what you will do, how you will interpret something, and how you will respond.[44, 45]

29

Tips to develop *Demonstrates* self-awareness

1. **Not sure how others see you? Get feedback.** People can be reluctant to give feedback, especially negative or corrective information. Generally, to get it, you must ask for it. Seeking negative feedback increases both the accuracy of our understanding and people's evaluation of our overall effectiveness. A person who wants to know the bad must be pretty good. People will increase their estimation of you as you seek out and accept more feedback. If people are reluctant to give criticism, help by making self-appraisal statements rather than asking questions. Saying, "I think I focus too much on operations and miss some of the larger strategic connections; what do you think?" is easier for most people to reply to than a question which asks them to volunteer this point.

2. **Want to get the real story? Keep it confidential and balanced.** Confidential feedback, a private discussion, or a private 360 feedback tool tends to be more accurate than public feedback. Don't assume everything is OK just because you aren't getting feedback. For most of us, when people give us feedback in public, it's an excessively positive view. Don't get too comfortable with what people tell you in public settings. Use private feedback as a means to understand how others see you and to get the most accurate information. Try not to stack the deck, asking for feedback only from people you get along with or like most. The best way to get good feedback data is to choose wisely. Choose people who are in the best position to observe your skills and capabilities, friendship or warm feelings aside.

3. **Want a broader view of yourself? Seek feedback from more than one source.** Different people know about your performance in different areas. When asking for feedback, make sure you are involving people who see you from a variety of angles. It doesn't have to be a big production. Seek out feedback on a daily basis by asking others how they think things are going. Ask others what they'd like to see you continue. Do differently. Where you can improve. Bosses tend to know about your strategic grasp, selling-up skills, comfort around higher management, presentation of problems and solutions, clarity of thinking, team building, confronting and sizing up people skills. Customers will have a view on responsiveness, listening, quality orientation, problem-solving skills, understanding of their business needs, persuasiveness. Peers observe persuasion, selling, negotiation, listening to find common cause, keeping the interests of the organization in mind, follow-through on promises, and attention to give-and-take in 50/50 relationships. Direct reports

29

know about your day-to-day behavior of leadership, management, team building, delegation, confronting, approachability, time use. When you get feedback, ask yourself if the person is in a position to know that about you. You may be the only one who doesn't know the truth about yourself. Other sources agree much more with one another about you than you will likely agree with any one of the sources. Even though your own view is important, don't accept it as fact until verified by more than one other person who should know.

Want to learn more? Take a deep dive...

Ask a Manager. (2011, March 9). *How can I get critical feedback?* Askamanager.org.

Donnelly, T. (2010, August 10). How to get feedback from employees. *Inc.*

Gallo, A. (2012, May 15). How to get feedback when you're the boss. *Harvard Business Review Blog Network.*

4. **Getting ruffled? Manage your response.** Sometimes feedback doesn't seem to fit and it's easy to become defensive or upset. Defensiveness is a major blockage to self-knowledge. When you respond in a defensive manner, people suspect you really can't take it, that you are defending against something, probably by blaming it on others or the job context. Defensive people get less feedback. To break this cycle, you will need to follow the rules of good listening. Work on keeping yourself in a calm state when getting negative feedback. Change your thinking. When getting the feedback, your only task is to accurately understand what people are trying to tell you. It is not your task at that point to accept or reject. That comes later. Mentally rehearse how you will calmly react to tough feedback situations before they happen. Develop automatic tactics to shut down or delay your usual emotional response. Some useful tactics are to slow down, take notes, ask clarifying questions, ask them for concrete examples, and thank them for telling you since you know it's not easy for them. While this may sound unfair, you should initially accept all feedback as accurate, even when you know it isn't. On those matters that really count, you can go back and fix it later.

29

5. **Can't make sense of it? Analyze the feedback.** Too much information coming at you at once? You need to prioritize. Once you have understood the feedback, carry out the following exercise:

(1) Write down all of the viewpoints on Post-it® Notes.

(2) Create two categories: 1) The criticisms that are probably true of you. 2) The criticisms that are probably not true of you. Ask someone you trust who knows you well to help you so you don't delude yourself.

(3) For those that are true, signal to the people who gave you the feedback that you have understood, think it was accurate, and will try to do something about it.

(4) For those that are not true, re-sort the comments into criticisms that are important to you and those that are small and trivial or unimportant. Throw the unimportant ones away.

(5) With those that are probably not true but important, re-sort them into:

(6) Career threatening—if people above me really thought this was true about me, my career would be damaged.

(7) Not career stopping. Throw the not-career-stopping pile away.

(8) With the remaining comments, review them with your boss and/or mentor to see what the general opinion is about you.

(9) This leaves you with two categories: those that people do believe—even though they are not true—and those they don't. Throw the don't-believe pile away.

(10) With the remaining pile, plot a strategy to convince people around you by deeds, not words, that those criticisms are untrue of you.

6. **Feeling overwhelmed? Think before you act.** Feel like you're constantly trying to change based on comments from others? Head spinning? Not sure which way to go? Developing your self-awareness means being open to feedback, but it can be exhausting, especially when it comes from various directions. It's a valuable source of information, so don't waste it, but think carefully how you use it. First, consider the source. Do you trust this person? Do you look up to them and value their opinion? Do you need to work with them on a regular basis? Second, get to the behavior. If feedback is too general, it is not helpful. Distill the comments down to the core behavior or message. What is it this person is trying to tell you? Third, reflect. Is this consistent with what you've heard in the past? Does it fit with what you know of yourself? Is it important? Even if it doesn't seem to be true, is there something here that needs attention? Fourth, decide. Do you want to do anything about it? You do have a choice, but think it through. The feedback was given for a reason. Understand it before you dismiss it. Decide to change? Make a plan. Decide to do nothing? Move on.

Want to learn more? Take a deep dive...

Robles, P. (2009, October 2). *How do you handle feedback?* Ecoconsultancy.com.

Smith, J. (2013, January 29). How negative feedback can help your career. *Forbes*.

Wright, K. (2011, March 15). How to take feedback. *Psychology Today*.

7. **Come across as arrogant? Adopt some humility.** Arrogance is a major blockage to self-knowledge. Many people who have a towering strength or lots of success get little feedback and roll along until their careers get in trouble. They're so sure of themselves that often they're caught off guard. If you are viewed as arrogant, you may have to repeatedly ask for feedback, and when you get it, there may be some anger with it. Almost by definition, arrogant people overrate themselves in the eyes of others. Others who think you are arrogant might rate you lower than neutral observers. If you devalue others, they will return the insult. When others give you feedback, look at it as an opportunity to grow and develop. Feedback is a gift. If you don't appear to be genuinely interested in what others have to say to you, you risk cutting off the source. If their feedback falls on stony ground, why should they bother providing any more? By demonstrating openness to others' feedback, you're more likely to get more valuable feedback in the future.

8. **Got blind spots? Turn them into known weaknesses.** Blind spots are things you think you're good at, but others don't see it that way. They're an overestimation of your competence. The thing that gets us into the most career trouble is a blind spot that matters. Better to have a known and admitted weakness. We know we are not good at it so we try harder, ask for help, delegate it, get a consultant, get a tutor, read a book, or loop around it. Ignorance is not bliss when it comes to blind spots. How do you identify your blind spots? Think about what really drives you crazy about other people. Perhaps you have similar challenges. Often what frustrates us most about other people is something we need to work on ourselves. Consciously observe others' reactions and subtle cues. Ask for feedback from people you trust. Listen. Consider. Reflect. Bring blind spots out into the light. Turn all of your blind spots into known weaknesses and then the known weaknesses into skills. Make it a quest to find out what everybody really thinks about you.

29

9. **Not sure of what you are good at? Find your hidden strengths.** You may have hidden strengths. Others see strengths that you don't know you have or don't think are stand-out skills. If you don't see them, you won't draw upon them. How do you find these strengths? First, through self-reflection. What comes easily to you? What do you enjoy? When does time fly by? In what settings or capacities do you get results? Think through situations, challenges, or interactions where you were at your best. What positive feedback have you received in the past? Like, "I always feel like you listen to what I am saying." Or, "Projects seem so easy when you are in the lead." When you hear something new, perk up your ears. Ask for clarification—seek to understand what the other person saw but you were unaware of. This can help you uncover some hidden strengths. Use feedback not only to learn what you're doing wrong, but what you're doing right. Last, use self-reflection tools such as journaling to uncover hidden thoughts and ideas. After recording your experiences for a period of time, scan your journal. What themes do you see? What strengths are coming through?

Want to learn more? Take a deep dive...

Baldoni, J. (2009, November 5). Use humility to improve performance. *Harvard Business Review Blog Network*.

Canaday, S. (2012, October 8). How to detect your blind spots that make your colleagues disrespect you. *Forbes*.

Smith, L. (2012, March). Larry Smith: Why you will fail to have a great career [Video file]. TED.

10. **Stuck in a personal awareness rut? Move to action.** Read a lot of self-help or personal development books? Like the content but have a hard time putting it into practice? Pore over your 360 results but aren't sure what to do with them? Caught off guard when given unanticipated feedback? Have trouble integrating it into your development strategy? It's easy to get stuck in a rut and fail to act. Reflection and information are valuable. But you can overdo self-reflection and get stuck in the process rather than taking action. Take stock of your strengths and development areas. Pick one or two and create a development plan. Focusing on fewer themes increases the likelihood that you can actually make a difference. Work with your boss, an HR representative, your coach to review your plan. Ask them to hold you accountable by checking in with you for progress.

350 |

11. **Don't have time to reflect? Build in a pause.** Life is busy. Urgent tasks get priority. Self-aware people build in time for what Kevin Cashman calls *The Pause Principle.* "The conscious, intentional process of stepping back, within ourselves and outside of ourselves, to lead forward with greater authenticity, purpose, and contribution." It looks different for different people. Meditation works for some. Others recognize they need daily physical activity. This becomes valuable reflection time for them. Daily walks. Journaling. The key is to take the time to reflect, however it makes sense to you. Consider. Appreciate. Debrief before moving forward or taking action. When you've completed a task or a project, hit the pause button. Rewind. Press play and review. What went well? What didn't? What will you do differently next time? Ask others for their feedback. Reflect as a team. Allow the comments—yours and theirs—to settle before moving on. Self-aware people learn from experience and build it into their next activity.

12. **Avoid admitting mistakes? Take ownership.** Self-awareness is knowing when you are wrong and owning it. Admitting it not just to yourself, but to others. Made a mistake? Own up to it. Would have done something differently? Talk about it with others. Showing ownership to others helps them feel more comfortable giving you feedback and offering suggestions. Take the lead. Identify what you think went wrong. Talk first about what you would have done differently. Then ask others what they'd like to see you do differently in the future. Learn from experience. Reflect. Taking ownership shows openness to reflection and willingness to change.

Want to learn more? Take a deep dive...

Bregman, P. (2011, January 3). The best way to use the last five minutes of your day. *Harvard Business Review Blog Network.*

Jensen, K. (2012, July 3). Success is overrated: How do you handle your mistakes? *Forbes.*

Zwilling, M. (2012, May 26). *Don't be too busy to do some reflective thinking.* Business Insider.

29

Job assignments

• Volunteer for an assignment in a different culture. Use this to become more aware of how you may respond in new or unfamiliar settings.

- Start something new. Begin something from scratch or build a new area of the organization. Build a new team.

- Take on an assignment that stretches your skills or pushes you to embrace a new challenge. Move to a new location, take on a position in a different area of the organization.

- Complete a 360. Consider who may be able to give you the best feedback, not just those who will tell you what you want to hear.

- Take on a new project outside your area of expertise. Make a point of asking those working with you for specific, honest, and regular feedback.

Take time to reflect...

If reflection doesn't come naturally to you...

> ...then recognize that taking the time to look back and learn is an important part of moving forward. Think about what worked and what didn't. Understand why. Modify your behavior to keep on the right track.

If you've ever been surprised by feedback you've received...

> ...then be aware that behaviors that feel natural to you may rub others the wrong way. Examine the disconnect between your intentions and others' perceptions. Work to close the gap.

If you're happy with how you are and don't want to change...

> ...then reflect before you reject. You might not recognize the feedback you receive or you may not like it, but don't discount it too early. Bite your tongue, take a deep breath, digest what you hear—then decide.

29

"*Know yourself to improve yourself.* **"**

Auguste Comte – French philosopher

Learn more about *Demonstrates* self-awareness

Beh, E. (2012). *Powerful guidelines on effectively writing a personal development plan*. Self-Improvement Mentor. Retrieved from http://www.self-improvement-mentor.com/writing-a-personal-development-plan.html

Cashman, K. (2012). *The pause principle: Step back to lead forward*. San Francisco, CA: Berrett-Koehler Publishers, Inc.

Kabat-Zinn, J. (2011). *Mindfulness for beginners: Reclaiming the present moment – and your life*. Boulder, CO: Sounds True, Inc.

London, M. (2003). *Job feedback: Giving, seeking, and using feedback for performance improvement*. Mahwah, NJ: Lawrence Erlbaum Associates, Inc.

Rock, D. (2009). *Your brain at work: Strategies for overcoming distraction, regaining focus, and working smarter all day long*. New York, NY: HarperCollins Publishers.

Siegel, D. J. (2007). *The mindful brain: Reflection and attunement in the cultivation of well-being*. New York, NY: W. W. Norton & Company.

Van Hecke, M. L. (2007). *Blind spots: Why smart people do dumb things*. Amherst, NY: Prometheus Books.

Deep dive learning resource links

Ask a Manager. (2011, March 9). *How can I get critical feedback?* Askamanager.org. Retrieved from http://www.askamanager.org/2011/03/how-can-i-get-critical-feedback.html

Baldoni, J. (2009, November 5). Use humility to improve performance. *Harvard Business Review Blog Network*. Retrieved from http://blogs.hbr.org/2009/11/use-humility-to-improve-perfor/

Bregman, P. (2011, January 3). The best way to use the last five minutes of your day. *Harvard Business Review Blog Network*. Retrieved from http://blogs.hbr.org/2011/01/the-best-way-to-use-the-last-f/

Canaday, S. (2012, October 8). How to detect your blind spots that make your colleagues disrespect you. *Forbes*. Retrieved from http://www.forbes.com/sites/forbesleadershipforum/2012/10/08/how-to-detect-your-blind-spots-that-make-your-colleagues-disrespect-you/

Donnelly, T. (2010, August 10). How to get feedback from employees. *Inc.* Retrieved from http://www.inc.com/guides/2010/08/how-to-get-feedback-from-employees.html

Gallo, A. (2012, May 15). How to get feedback when you're the boss. *Harvard Business Review Blog Network*. Retrieved from http://blogs.hbr.org/2012/05/how-to-get-feedback-when-youre/

29

Jensen, K. (2012, July 3). Success is overrated: How do you handle your mistakes? *Forbes*. Retrieved from http://www.forbes.com/sites/keldjensen/2012/07/03/success-is-overrated-how-do-you-handle-your-mistakes/

Robles, P. (2009, October 2). *How do you handle feedback?* Ecoconsultancy.com. Retrieved from http://econsultancy.com/blog/4705-how-do-you-handle-feedback

Smith, J. (2013, January 29). How negative feedback can help your career. *Forbes*. Retrieved from http://www.forbes.com/sites/jacquelynsmith/2013/01/29/how-negative-feedback-can-help-your-career/

Smith, L. (2012, March). Larry Smith: Why you will fail to have a great career [Video file]. TED. Retrieved from http://www.ted.com/talks/larry_smith_why_you_will_fail_to_have_a_great_career.html

Wright, K. (2011, March 15). How to take feedback. *Psychology Today*. Retrieved from http://www.psychologytoday.com/articles/201103/how-take-feedback

Zwilling, M. (2012, May 26). *Don't be too busy to do some reflective thinking*. Business Insider. Retrieved from http://www.businessinsider.com/dont-be-too-busy-to-do-some-reflective-thinking-2012-6

Recommended search terms

If you'd like to explore *Demonstrates* self-awareness further, try searching online using the following terms:

- Dealing with feedback.
- Finding your blind spots.
- How to gather feedback from colleagues.
- How to learn from feedback.
- Learning your hidden strengths.
- Personal development tips.

(i) More help...

Go to www.kornferry.com/fyi-resources and link directly to the deep dive resources in this chapter. Visit the site often to see the additional resources that are uploaded on a regular basis.

354 |

30. Self-development

Actively seeking new ways to grow and be challenged using both formal and informal development channels.

The bottom line is, those who learn, grow, and change continuously across their careers are the most successful. The skills someone has now are unlikely to be enough in the future. Acquiring new skills is the best way to navigate an uncertain future. Some won't face their limitations. They make excuses. Blame it on the boss or the job or the organization. Others are defensive and fight any corrective feedback. Some are reluctant to do anything about their problems. Some want a quick fix—they don't have time for development. Other times, people simply don't know what to do. There is great value in learning to learn from experience. Becoming a lifelong learner isn't just a catchphrase. Being committed to self-development means you look for ways to build skills that you will need in the future. You look to grow from experience. Seek out feedback and are open to what you hear. Challenge yourself in unfamiliar settings. Try out new skills. Learn from others. Outcome? Work is more interesting. You are less likely to get stuck in a rut—or in your current position. You can stretch yourself to develop and grow in ways that perhaps you didn't think you could. Development is a personal commitment. You make the choice.

> **"** *Celebrate what you've accomplished, but raise the bar a little higher each time you succeed.* **"**

Mia Hamm – American soccer player

Self-development is in the **Self** factor (IV) in the Korn Ferry Leadership Architect™. It is part of Cluster K, **Being open,** along with *Demonstrates* self-awareness (29). You may find it helpful to also take a look at some of the tips included in that chapter to supplement your learning.

Skilled

Shows personal commitment and takes action to continuously improve.

Accepts assignments that broaden capabilities.

Learns from new experiences, from others, and from structured learning.

Makes the most of available development resources.

Less skilled

- Doesn't put in the effort to grow and change.
- Is comfortable with current skills.
- Is fearful of making mistakes that accompany development.
- Lacks awareness or interest in using available developmental resources.

Talented

- Takes consistent action to develop new skills.
- Finds ways to apply strengths to new issues.
- Is aware of the skills needed to be successful in different situations and levels.
- Seeks assignments that stretch him/her beyond comfort zone.

Overused skill

- Develops just for the sake of development, without focus or objective.
- Focuses on own development at the expense of meeting other obligations.
- May be susceptible to the latest self-help fads.

30

356 |

Some possible causes of lower skill

Causes help explain *why* a person may have trouble with Self-development. When seeking to increase skill, it's helpful to consider how these might play out in certain situations. And remember that all of these can be addressed if you are motivated to do so.

- Arrogant; doesn't have any weaknesses.
- Defensive.
- Doesn't know what to develop.
- Doesn't know what to do.
- Doesn't think people really can change.
- Fears failure or admitting shortcomings.
- Too busy getting work done.
- Afraid of new experiences.
- Unsure of what is needed at the next level.
- Relies on the organization for development.
- Satisfied with current skills.

Brain booster

Everything we do demands some level of energy and attention. The newer the task, the more challenging the task, the more brain fuel is required. When your brain is busy putting forth tremendous effort on one activity, there is less capacity for other things. And you become depleted and need to recharge. Improving your skill diminishes the energy required to do a particular task. Make an up-front investment to hone a skill, then once you've mastered something, take the most economical approach to it. This frees up your brain to pay attention to more things at once. Take on more complex problems. Learn new skills.[46]

30

Tips to develop Self-development

1. **See yourself as not being able to develop? Change your mindset.** Some people are natural learners. They always look to learn something new from every situation. Some people are not natural learners. They are more performance oriented—get the job done and move on. Performance-oriented people tend to avoid new situations in which they may fail. Why? Because failing at a task translates to judgment, in their mind. Natural learners are more willing to take the risk because they are less worried about how they may be perceived by others. To them, the learning is the outcome. It is less about confidence in their ability and more about growing. Did you know you can shift your mindset? You can train yourself to be a learner. But you must be willing to expand your horizon. Be curious. Continuously look for opportunities to stretch yourself. See each situation as a learning opportunity.

2. **Not sure where to start? Do a skills audit.** First, get a good multi-source assessment, a 360 questionnaire, or poll 10 people who know you well to give you detailed feedback. What are you doing well? Not so well? What should you keep doing? Stop doing? You don't want to waste time on developing things that turn out not to be needs. At the same time, rate yourself. What do you see as your strengths? What areas do you need to develop? Where do you suspect you have strengths but you haven't had the opportunity to try? Group your skills into categories. Clear strengths—me at my best. Overdone strengths—I do too much of a good thing. So much so that it is limiting my success. Hidden strengths—others rate me higher than I rate myself. These are untapped resources. Blind spots—I rate myself higher than others rate me. These are behaviors that get in the way of your success without your awareness. Weaknesses—I don't do it well. Obvious areas that you know you need to improve upon. Untested areas—I've never been involved in that area. Don't knows—I need more feedback. Once you have your skills grouped into categories, create a plan of attack. What is most important for you to work on now? Where can you have the biggest impact now and for the future? Figure out a plan for how to grow in this area.

3. **Wondering what to focus on? Identify your values and organizational priorities.** Feedback is helpful, but you need to place it in context to determine priorities. First, ask yourself a few questions. What matters to you? What motivates you? What is most interesting to you? What do you want to accomplish in your career? What is important for success in your current role? What would help you be more successful here? Leveraging strengths? Overcoming certain weaknesses? Also consider your future. Where do you want to go?

What are the skills that are needed in your next position? When you compare your current capabilities with where you want to go, you can identify areas for development that are most essential. Second, identify what matters to others. What do other people—such as your boss, senior management, and others—expect from you and desire from you? What is important to the organization? Identify the sweet spot between what is important to you, important to the organization, and where there are gaps between these values and your skill set. These are your developmental priorities.

4. **Want to be ready for your next role? Do your research and be prepared.** Think about what you want to accomplish next in your career. A lateral move? International assignment? More leadership responsibility? Moving to a new functional area? Think through what skills are necessary to be successful in this role. Do your research. Work with HR or ask someone who's currently in the job. What skills do people have who are successful in this role? Then, compare. How do your strengths align with this new role? Where do you need further development? Where are the gaps? Start working toward closing those gaps. When the opportunity arises, you want to be ready to move.

5. **Know what you need to develop? Prioritize.** Once you have compared your skill set to what is important for success now and in your next role, identify your development priorities. But not too many! People are most successful when they work on one or two things at a time. Set your development goals. Make a plan. Share your plan with someone else. You are more likely to achieve success if you have built in accountability measures. Ask for their help. Make sure that your goals are SMART (Specific, Measurable, Achievable, Relevant, Time-bound) goals. Start small and work up as you experience success.

Want to learn more? Take a deep dive...

Goodman, N. (2012, September 18). 4 Ways to discover your strengths. *Entrepreneur*.

Guey, L. (2013, May 24). *Instant MBA: Most people don't know themselves as well as they think*. Business Insider.

Olson, L. (2011, January 27). How to set yourself up for promotion. *U.S. News & World Report*.

Scivicque, C. (2011, June 21). Creating your professional development plan: 3 Surprising truths. *Forbes*.

30

6. **Not applying your talents? Leverage your strengths.** A Gallup study found that individuals who are coached to utilize their strengths are more engaged employees in terms of productivity and tenure. Part of self-development is knowing when to draw upon the strengths you already possess. Where do you have skills that aren't being utilized? What have you mastered? What do you learn quickly? What gives you the most satisfaction at work? What are three things you can start doing today? Where can you use your strengths to help others? Can't use your strengths in your current job? How about a project, special assignment, or a task trade? Maintain the clear strengths you will need in the future by testing them in new task assignments. Coach others on your strengths. In turn, ask others to coach you on theirs.

7. **Never tried it? Focus on untested areas.** Minimize weaknesses, but also go after untested areas—skills that you have not developed but are likely to be important in the future. Often, people are promoted based on their performance in their current job. But the skills needed in their next position may be very different. In our research, we find that managers are rated as "highly skilled" on behaviors that are more tied to performance at the individual contributor level. Not enough development is happening over time. Few managers are good at developing talent at first. Few executives are good at driving vision and purpose. But did they ever have a real chance to develop in these areas? The key is to find out the core demands of performance in a role, then develop the skills before they are necessary. Get involved in small versions of your untested areas. Write a strategic plan for your unit, then show it to people. Negotiate the purchase of office furniture. Onboard someone new. Write down what you did well and what you didn't do well. Then try a second, bigger task. Again, assess the experience. At this point, you may want to read a book or attend a course in this area. Keep upping the size and stakes until you have the skill at the level you need it to be.

8. **Signing up for class after class? Learn on the job.** Learning does not only happen in a classroom or through a book. The best learning happens when you are on the job. Use real-life challenges as learning experiences. Volunteer for a special project. Help a person learn something within your expertise. Take on a project. Volunteer to sit on a task force. Task forces are an effective way to learn from your peers and expand your business knowledge. They require learning other functions and businesses. Work with different cultures or nationalities. Work with others in a collaborative manner to rapidly address an issue. Diversity of experience is the single best way to develop new skills. Try something new every day to force yourself

outside of your comfort zone. These opportunities stretch your skills in a real-life way. They push you to work with different people. They broaden your horizon. Venture beyond your normal experience and look at things from a different light.

9. **Not leveraging development resources available to you? Find a coach or a mentor.** Pick a person in the organization who is known for their strength in the area that you'd like to develop. Observe what they do and how they do it. If possible, ask for a meeting/lunch to discuss their success and the things they have learned. See if the person has any interest in teaching you something and being a temporary coach. Get to know other potential advocates on- and off-work. Go for maximum variety in the towering strengths they possess. Working with a mentor is a great way to develop. But, vary your mentors and coaches. Try not to get stuck in a rut relying on the same people for much of your career. You don't want to become a "mini me" of your mentor. Utilize a variety of people to help you develop the skills you are looking to grow.

Want to learn more? Take a deep dive...

Burns, K. (2010, January 13). 13 Tips on finding a mentor. *U.S. News & World Report*.

Garnett, L. (2013, August 16). How to leverage your true talent. *Inc.*

Herbert, W. (2012, July 2). *Learning on the job: Myth vs science*. Association for Psychological Science.

Zenger, J. (2013, July 16). Throw your old plan away: 6 New ways to build leadership development into your job. *Forbes*.

10. **Don't learn from experience? Become reflective.** People who are good at self-development build time into their schedule to develop from experiences. They seek to achieve results but also look to learn and grow from a situation. After each experience—whether a project, task force, new challenge—reflect. What went well? What didn't? What could you have done differently to achieve a better outcome? What skills were you lacking? Where do you need additional expertise or experience? Take your learning and put it into practice the next time. Add the learning to your development plan. How can you continue to build on it? Use your experience to help drive your future growth. Watch out for the "haven't the time" trap. There's always something that seems more important than reflection. But check yourself. Don't rush to the next task. Plan to reflect.

30

11. **Need support? Show others you take your development seriously.** State your development needs and ask for their help. Research shows that people are much more likely to help and give the benefit of the doubt to those who admit their shortcomings and try to do something about them. They know it takes courage. Don't stop at asking for feedback. Ask people for their help in your development. Can they act as a coach? Can they teach you a new skill? Can they be a springboard for new ideas? Utilize the people around you to help in your development.

12. **Frustrated by lack of progress? Understand that development takes time.** Development doesn't happen overnight. It takes time to make changes that are noticeable, sustainable, and position you well for future success. Just like there is no "easy" button to prepare for a marathon, plan a significant event, or write a book, there are no shortcuts for your own growth. Research suggests that deliberate and sustained practice is necessary to really hone a skill to make it a strength. Malcolm Gladwell, in *Outliers: The Story of Success,* reports that people need to practice something for 10,000 hours before they master the skill. It can be a long haul. Set your goals. Work your plan. Celebrate small wins along the way.

Want to learn more? Take a deep dive...

Capture Your Flag. (2013, June 14). Learning to reflect more and get to know yourself better [YouTube].

Petriglieri, G. (2013, February 6). Getting stuck can help you grow. *Harvard Business Review Blog Network.*

Tjan, A. K. (2012, July 19). How leaders become self-aware. *Harvard Business Review Blog Network.*

Zenger, J. (2013, August 29). Personal development isn't personal: 3 Tips for getting your manager involved. *Forbes.*

Job assignments

- Take on a task that you have never tried, dislike or hate to do, and is outside of your domain. Stick to it and focus on the learning you're deriving from it.

- Teach/coach someone how to do something you're an expert in. Invite them to tap into your knowledge and the lessons you took from your experiences.

- Attend a course or event which will push you personally beyond your usual limits or outside your comfort zone.

- Find and spend time with an expert to learn something in an area new to you, in either a work or non-work setting.

- Take on an assignment outside of your current organizational area or region to practice working within a different organizational or global culture.

Take time to reflect...

If you think development is always a formal affair...

> ...then consider that you've probably been learning through new challenges you take on. Accelerate the process by being conscious of it. Consider how you want to grow. Make a plan. Take action every day.

If you know you have skill gaps and are uncomfortable with that...

> ...then accept that fallibility is not failure. There's no disgrace in being less than perfect. Most flaws can be fixed. Design your development plan to fill the most important gaps.

If you can't seem to find time to learn anything new...

> ...then recognize that developing yourself doesn't have to be a separate event. Take just a few minutes a day to try something you've never tried before or do something in a different way. Practice a new skill each week.

" *The only difference between a rut and a grave are the dimensions.* **"**

Ellen Glasgow – American author

30

Learn more about Self-development

Beh, E. (2012). *Powerful guidelines on effectively writing a personal development plan*. Self-Improvement Mentor. Retrieved from http://www.self-improvement-mentor.com/writing-a-personal-development-plan.html

Hunt, J. M., & Weintraub, J. R. (2011). *The coaching manager: Developing top talent in business* (2nd ed.). Thousand Oaks, CA: Sage Publications.

Kahneman, D. (1973). *Attention and effort*. Upper Saddle River, NJ: Prentice-Hall.

Pavlina, S. (2008). *Personal development for smart people: The conscious pursuit of personal growth*. Carlsbad, CA: Hay House.

Smilansky, J. (2007). *Developing executive talent: Best practices from global leaders*. Chichester, West Sussex, England: John Wiley & Sons.

Throop, R. K., & Castellucci, M. B. (2011). *Reaching your potential: Personal and professional development*. Boston, MA: Cengage Learning.

 Deep dive learning resource links

Burns, K. (2010, January 13). 13 Tips on finding a mentor. *U.S. News & World Report*. Retrieved from http://money.usnews.com/money/blogs/outside-voices-careers/2010/01/13/13-tips-on-finding-a-mentor

Capture Your Flag. (2013, June 14). Learning to reflect more and get to know yourself better [YouTube]. Retrieved from http://www.youtube.com/watch?v=iGFXAfUMmS8

Garnett, L. (2013, August 16). How to leverage your true talent. *Inc.* Retrieved from http://www.inc.com/laura-garnett/how-to-leverage-your-true-talent.html%25E2%2580%258E

Goodman, N. (2012, September 18). 4 Ways to discover your strengths. *Entrepreneur*. Retrieved from http://www.entrepreneur.com/blog/224433

Guey, L. (2013, May 24). *Instant MBA: Most people don't know themselves as well as they think*. Business Insider. Retrieved from http://www.businessinsider.com/know-your-strengths-and-weaknesses-hiroshi-mikitani-2013-5

30

Herbert, W. (2012, July 2). *Learning on the job: Myth vs science.* Association for Psychological Science. Retrieved from http://www.psychologicalscience.org/index.php/news/were-only-human/learning-on-the-job-myth-vs-science.html

Olson, L. (2011, January 27). How to set yourself up for promotion. *U.S. News & World Report.* Retrieved from http://money.usnews.com/money/blogs/outside-voices-careers/2011/01/27/how-to-set-yourself-up-for-promotion

Petrieglieri, G. (2013, February 6). Getting stuck can help you grow. *Harvard Business Review Blog Network.* Retrieved from http://blogs.hbr.org/2013/02/getting-stuck-can-help-you/

Scivicque, C. (2011, June 21). Creating your professional development plan: 3 Surprising truths. *Forbes.* Retrieved from http://www.forbes.com/sites/work-in-progress/2011/06/21/creating-your-professional-development-plan-3-surprising-truths/

Tjan, A. K. (2012, July 19). How leaders become self-aware. *Harvard Business Review Blog Network.* Retrieved from http://blogs.hbr.org/2012/07/how-leaders-become-self-aware/

Zenger, J. (2013, August 29). Personal development isn't personal: 3 Tips for getting your manager involved. *Forbes.* Retrieved from http://www.forbes.com/sites/jackzenger/2013/08/29/personal-development-isnt-personal-3-tips-for-getting-your-manager-involved/

Zenger, J. (2013, July 16). Throw your old plan away: 6 New ways to build leadership development into your job. *Forbes.* Retrieved from http://www.forbes.com/sites/jackzenger/2013/07/16/throw-your-old-plan-away-6-new-ways-to-build-leadership-development-into-your-job/

Recommended search terms

If you'd like to explore Self-development further, try searching online using the following terms:

• Creating a personal development plan.

• Developing in your role.

• How to leverage your own talent.

• Looking for a mentor.

• Patience with personal development.

• Personal SWOT analysis.

30

More help...

Go to www.kornferry.com/fyi-resources and link directly to the deep dive resources in this chapter. Visit the site often to see the additional resources that are uploaded on a regular basis.

31. Situational adaptability

Adapting approach and demeanor in real time to match the shifting demands of different situations.

Those skilled at situational adaptability recognize the need to be flexible and act differently because no two situations are exactly alike. They know that using the same approach, tone, and style in different settings may be consistent but not necessarily effective. You wouldn't behave the same way in a team brainstorming discussion as you would when managing a customer complaint or navigating a politically charged strategy session. Quickly adjusting and fine-tuning your behavior in real time allows you to be versatile in different situations and interactions with others. Situational adaptability means paying attention to circumstances and adjusting accordingly. Bringing empathy in times of stress and change, firm direction in times of uncertainty, or diplomacy in times of conflict. Continuously gauge the impact you're having and stay alert to make adjustments to your demeanor and approach. Be flexible to meet the needs of the moment. The outcome will be ease of transaction and effectiveness of interaction.

"*A wise man adapts himself to circumstances, as water shapes itself to the vessel that contains it.***"**

– Chinese proverb

Situational adaptability is in the **Self** factor (IV) in the Korn Ferry Leadership Architect™. It is part of Cluster L, **Being flexible and adaptable,** along with *Manages* ambiguity (3), Nimble learning (22), and *Being* resilient (26). You may find it helpful to also take a look at some of the tips included in those chapters to supplement your learning.

Skilled

Picks up on situational cues and adjusts in the moment.

Readily adapts personal, interpersonal, and leadership behavior.

Understands that different situations may call for different approaches.

Can act differently depending on the circumstances.

Less skilled

- Uses same style and approach regardless of the situation.

- Fails to notice changing situational demands.

- Expects others to adjust to his/her preferred style and approach.

- Thinks being true to self is all that matters.

- Doesn't take time to understand interpersonal dynamics.

Talented

- Picks up on the need to change personal, interpersonal, and leadership behavior quickly.

- Observes situational and group dynamics and selects best-fit approach.

- Seamlessly adapts style to fit the specific needs of others.

Overused skill

- May be seen as a social chameleon, leaving others unsure of when he/she is being genuine.

- Is hypervigilant in monitoring situational dynamics to the point that the desired outcome isn't met; may come across as indecisive or wavering.

Some possible causes of lower skill

Causes help explain *why* a person may have trouble with Situational adaptability. When seeking to increase skill, it's helpful to consider how these might play out in certain situations. And remember that all of these can be addressed if you are motivated to do so.

- Sticks to a single preferred style.
- Oblivious to interpersonal dynamics.
- Focused only on own agenda.
- Subscribes to "I am what I am."
- Defensive in the face of criticism.
- Doesn't read others well.
- Poor communication skills.
- Rigid in values and beliefs.

Does it best

Rock star, business partner, philanthropist, and political activist. U2's Irish-born Bono wears many hats. Whether he's on tour or at a charity event, he is arresting and dynamic. As a business partner, he is shrewd and solution oriented. As a philanthropist, he is empathetic and creative—seeking ways to raise money to fight poverty and disease. As a political activist, Bono is respectful and focused on dialogue when he meets with world leaders to discuss debt relief and other humanitarian efforts. And, while he didn't begin his career with the ability to play all of these roles, he has gradually grown comfortable in a variety of situations: guest editing an issue of *Vanity Fair,* launching (PRODUCT)RED™ with iconic global brands, collaborating with a diverse list of artists and writers, and graciously receiving countless awards for his music as well as his humanitarian work.[47, 48]

Tips to develop Situational adaptability

1. **Find it hard to read others? Tune in.** Everyone is different. Some differences are easy to see. Height. Weight. Speed. Others are a little harder to gauge. Motivated; not so motivated. Engaged; disengaged. Confident; anxious. To really understand what's going on with people in a given situation, you need to tune in to what's going on beneath the surface. Pay close attention to what people say or do first. What do they emphasize in their behavior or speech? People focus on different things—taking action, details, concepts, feelings, other people. What's their interaction style? Pushy, tough, soft, matter-of-fact, and so on. Listen for values, for the things that ignite passion and emotion. Don't fight their style; accept their preferred mode of doing things. Take control of the situation by adapting your style and behavior and by responding in a way that eases the transaction and promotes a productive outcome.

2. **Not sure what approach to take? Think about the consequences.** Use mental rehearsal to think about different ways you could engage. Picture the response. Try to see yourself acting in opposing ways to get to the same outcome—being tough, letting others decide, deflecting the issue. What cues would you look for to select an approach that matches what you want to accomplish? Imagine trying to get the same thing done with two different groups with two different approaches. How do they play out in your mind? Now focus on the situation at hand and the players involved—which approach will likely yield the best outcome?

3. **Struggle to control your instant reaction? Press pause.** You may have been told that you need to practice self-control. That you respond to situations as if they were threats instead of the way life is. That you're too quick to react. When your emotions and fears are triggered, it can cause an initial anxious response. It usually lasts around 40–60 seconds. You need to buy some time before you say or do something inappropriate. Practice holding back your first response long enough to think of a second and third. Research shows that, generally, somewhere between the second and third thing you think to say or do is the best option. Rather than reacting, adapt and thoughtfully respond to the situation instead. Stay in control. Focus on the impression you want to make, given the situation. Manage your shifts, don't be a prisoner of them.

4. **Make snap judgments about what's going on? Listen more.** Listening helps you get a read on what's going on with others. When you listen, you're suspending judgment. You're taking in information that

will allow you to select the best response to the situation. You're pausing to see what you might be missing. Don't interrupt and don't instantly judge. Speak briefly and summarize often. Give reasons for everything you're saying. When you disagree, do so in a way that invites others to respond. For example, "I don't think so, but what do you think?" Restate what others have said to signal understanding. Nod. Jot down notes. Elicit and listen to as much information as you can about what's going on. Use that information to adapt your behavior as needed.

5. **In a hurry to get down to business? Manage the first three minutes.** Managing the first three minutes of any situation is essential. The tone is set. First impressions are formed. Work on being open and approachable. On taking in information during the beginning of a transaction. This means putting others at ease so that they feel OK about disclosing. It means initiating rapport, listening, sharing, understanding, and comforting. Approachable people get more information, know things earlier, and can get others to do more things. The more you can get others to speak up early in the transaction, the more you'll know about where they're coming from and the better you can tailor your approach.

Want to learn more? Take a deep dive...

Bhasin, K., & Nisen, M. (2013, March 27). *26 Tips on how to read people*. Business Insider.

Biro, M. M. (2013, August 4). 5 Leadership lessons: Listen, learn, lead. *Forbes*.

Goudreau, J. (2013, January 9). From crying to temper tantrums: How to manage emotions at work. *Forbes*.

Mind Tools. (n.d.). *The Hersey-Blanchard Situational Leadership® Theory*. Mind Tools.

---

6. **Need exposure to different ways of behaving? Go for more variety.** Repeatedly taking on the same assignments, dealing with the same situations, or continually playing the same role prevents you from expanding your repertoire. Get out of your comfort zone. Put yourself into very different situations than those you typically encounter. Volunteer for assignments that represent a new challenge. Push yourself forward to play different situational roles. From facilitator to director. From harmonizer to orchestrator of productive conflict. From leader to follower. Operating in a variety of situations

and roles will help you become more flexible and adaptable. Research shows that people with a broad behavioral repertoire and the ability to perform roles that include contradictions will be the most effective.

7. **Trouble shifting gears? Practice the transitions.** As one song says, "I've gotta be me." Not many of us have that luxury all the time. Each situation we deal with is a little bit, somewhat, or a lot different. To be effective, you need to read the situation and the people, then behave appropriately. Be in control at 9 a.m., a follower at 10 a.m., quiet at 11 a.m., and dominating at noon. Respectful with the boss, critiquing with peers, caring for direct reports, and responding to customers. Go from confronting people to being approachable. From firing someone to a business-as-usual staff meeting. It's all in a day's work. Monitor your gear-shifting behavior for a week at work and at home. Between activities, if only for a few seconds, think about the transition you're making and the frame of mind needed to make it work well. Which do you find easy? Why? Which do you find toughest? List the five transitions you find most difficult. Write down how each one makes you feel and what stops you from being effective. Create a plan that focuses on developing the skills and behaviors required to skillfully execute what needs to be done.

8. **Ready to learn from others? Study transition experts.** Interview people who are good at shifting gears, such as fix-it managers (tear down and build back up), shutdown managers (fire people yet support them and help them find other employment, and motivate those who stay), or excellent parents. Talk to an actor or actress to see how they can play opposing roles back-to-back. Talk to people who have recently joined your organization from places quite different than yours. Talk to a therapist who hears a different problem or trauma every hour. See if you can figure out some rules for making comfortable transitions.

9. **Unsure of your impact in certain situations? Get feedback.** People can be reluctant to give you feedback, especially negative or corrective information. Generally, to get it, you must ask for it. The best time to ask for it is while the situation is happening or immediately after. If people are reluctant to give criticism, help by making self-appraisal statements—"I think I talked too long on that topic in the meeting, what do you think?" Do some self-refection too. How did you think, feel, and behave in the situation? Did you achieve the right outcome? How did others react to you? Use the feedback you get from others, and yourself, to determine what you'd

do differently next time. Research shows that people who reflect on their performance are more likely to be flexible in adapting to changes in their environment. And therefore better able to identify alternative ways of behaving to be more effective in given situations.

10. **Afraid to make a mistake? Laugh at yourself.** Having a sense of humor about yourself only serves to humanize you. Funny stories about situations where you were embarrassed, did the wrong thing, fumbled a well-rehearsed line, or committed a faux pas are opportunities to learn while entertaining yourself and others. When you fail, reflect on what went wrong, adjust course, and don't repeat the same mistake next time. Learning and improving your adaptability along the way is the goal, not perfection.

31

Want to learn more? Take a deep dive...

Allworth, J. (2012, March 22). How to get into your zone. *Harvard Business Review Blog Network*.

Dehne, S. (2009, March 27). *5 Tips for facing change at work*. Career Builder.

Huffington Post. (2013, November 14). Why it's incredibly important to learn to laugh at yourself. *The Huffington Post*.

Warrell, M. (2013, April 22). Why getting comfortable with discomfort is crucial to success. *Forbes*.

11. **Too much of a good thing? Pull back on overused skills.** Tend to overdo things, especially things you're good at? Lots of people overuse their strengths. Push for results too hard. Analyze data too long. Try to be too nice. For those overdone behaviors, it's hard to do the opposite. Get feedback to find out what you overdo. Either through a 360 feedback instrument or by polling your closest associates. Find out how adaptable people think you are under pressure and how well you handle the fragmentation of a typical day. Work on balancing your behavior. If you get brusque under pressure, take three deep breaths and consciously slow down or use some humor. If you're too tough, ask yourself how you'd like to be treated in this situation. If you run over others, tell them what you're thinking about doing and ask them what they think should be done. If you habitually go into an action frenzy or grind to a halt, ask yourself what would be more effective right now. Strengths become overused skills when you use them, regardless of the situation. Be more precise and adjust to the specific need.

|

12. **Trouble finding balance? Combine seemingly opposite behaviors.** Many situations call for mixed responses and behaviors. Kaiser and Overfield (2010) labeled this type of approach the "mastery of opposites"—combining opposing but complementary behaviors. Delivering a tough message on layoffs but doing it in a compassionate way. Taking strong stands but listening and leaving room for others to maneuver. Having a strong personal belief about an issue but loyally implementing an organization plan which opposes your view. Being playful but firm. Being loose with parts of the budget but unyielding in others. Doing two opposing things at once isn't comfortable for everyone. Many pride themselves on being just one person, believing and following one set of beliefs. Situational adaptability doesn't really violate that. It just means within your normal range of behaviors and style, you use two of your extremes— being as quiet as you can be in the first half of the meeting and as loud as you ever are in the second half.

13. **Selling someone else's vision? Get comfortable walking someone else's talk.** Having to support someone else's program or idea when you don't really think that way or agree is a common paradox. You have to be a member of the loyal opposition. Most of the time, you may be delivering someone else's view of the future. Top management and a consultant created the mission, vision, and strategy off somewhere in the woods. You may or may not have been asked for any input. You may even have some doubts about it yourself. Don't offer conditional statements to your audience. Don't let it be known to others that you are not fully on board. Your role is to manage this vision and mission, not your personal one. If you have strong contrary views, be sure to demand a voice next time around.

14. **Adjusting too much or too little? Redress the balance.** Focus too much on pleasing and accommodating others and not enough on being you? You could be at risk of adjusting too much, too often. People may perceive that you're inconsistent and waffling or, even worse, manipulative and inauthentic. If you're making wild swings in personality between different interactions and situations, stop. Take steps to redress the balance. Pay as much attention to your own needs and values as you do those of others. Focus on being authentic while being sensitive to the needs of the situation. Maybe you're the opposite? Maybe you don't adjust your approach for fear of not presenting your "true self" or projecting a "false image." If you neglect to adjust, you risk being seen as someone who tramples over others, is overly rigid, or dogmatic. Remember, adjusting your approach isn't about being disingenuous or inauthentic. It's about introducing the right approach and behavior at the right time to get

the right result. Don't stick rigidly to one way of operating. Pay attention to what the situation requires of you and adjust accordingly.

Want to learn more? Take a deep dive...

Lie, E. (2010, November 18). *Instant MBA: Striking the right balance between rigid and flexible management will motivate employees.* Business Insider.

Martinuzzi, B. (n.d.). *The agile leader: Adaptability.* Mind Tools.

Vlachoutsicos, C. (2012, December 7). What being an "authentic leader" really means. *Harvard Business Review Blog Network.*

Warrell, M. (2013, May 20). Why leaders must "get real"— 5 ways to unlock authentic leadership. *Forbes.*

Job assignments

- Set tasks that force you to shift gears, such as being a spokesperson in a tough issue, making peace with an enemy, or managing a team of novices. Try new behaviors and seek feedback on your approach.

- Support the implementation of a controversial new project or process that wasn't your idea and that you don't fully agree with. Mentally rehearse how you will respond to challenges from your audience.

- Take on a tough project where there are no clear answers or paths to completion. Wear different hats as you figure out how to deal with the variety of situations.

- Help people infuse humor into their presentations. Adept use of humor requires a good understanding of the situation, the audience, what will play, what would go over their heads and what would fall flat.

- Volunteer to teach others something you don't know how to do the next time a new procedure, policy, or technology appears. This will force you to shift from experienced expert to novice.

Take time to reflect...

If you rely on one or two ways of handling most situations...

>...then think of behaviors as tools. You don't need a sledge hammer to crack a walnut. A spoon won't help when you need a shovel. Use what's best to get the job done.

If you feel self-conscious when trying out different ways...

>...then recognize that adaptability is like a muscle. It gets stronger with exercise. Relax. Have fun with it. Today's awkward straining can be tomorrow's natural flexing.

If you feel changing too much means you're not being yourself...

>...then understand that if situations shift, staying the same isn't always an option. When the old route is blocked, you need a new map to guide you to the new route.

"*When you are frustrated and do not know a way out,*
only flexibility and moderation toward difficulties will save you. **"**

Husayn ibn Ali – Early Muslim Imam

Learn more about Situational adaptability

George, B., & Sims, P. (2007). *True north: Discover your authentic leadership*. San Francisco, CA: Jossey-Bass.

Gurvis, J., & Calarco, A. (2007). *Adaptability: Responding effectively to change*. Greensboro, NC: Center for Creative Leadership.

Hamel, G. (2012). *What matters now: How to win in a world of relentless change, ferocious competition, and unstoppable innovation*. San Francisco, CA: Jossey-Bass.

Heath, C., & Heath, D. (2010). *Switch: How to change things when change is hard*. New York, NY: Broadway Books.

Kaiser, R. B., & Overfield, D. V. (2010). Assessing flexible leadership as a mastery of opposites. *Consulting Psychology Journal: Practice and Research, 62*(2), 105-118.

31

 Deep dive learning resource links

Allworth, J. (2012, March 22). How to get into your zone. *Harvard Business Review Blog Network*. Retrieved from http://blogs.hbr.org/2012/03/how-to-get-into-your-zone/

Bhasin, K., & Nisen, M. (2013, March 27). *26 Tips on how to read people*. Business Insider. Retrieved from http://www.businessinsider.com/how-to-read-other-people-2013-3

Biro, M. M. (2013, August 4). 5 Leadership lessons: Listen, learn, lead. *Forbes*. Retrieved from http://www.forbes.com/sites/meghanbiro/2013/08/04/5-leadership-lessons-listen-learn-lead/

Dehne, S. (2009, March 27). *5 Tips for facing change at work*. Career Builder. Retrieved from http://www.careerbuilder.com/Article/CB-1192-The-Workplace-5-Tips-for-Facing-Change-at-Work/

Goudreau, J. (2013, January 9). From crying to temper tantrums: How to manage emotions at work. *Forbes*. Retrieved from http://www.forbes.com/sites/jennagoudreau/2013/01/09/from-crying-to-temper-tantrums-how-to-manage-emotions-at-work/

Huffington Post. (2013, November 14). Why it's incredibly important to learn to laugh at yourself. *The Huffington Post*. Retrieved from http://www.huffingtonpost.com/2013/11/14/10-successful-people-who-_n_4262766.html

Lie, E. (2010, November 18). *Instant MBA: Striking the right balance between rigid and flexible management will motivate employees*. Business Insider. Retrieved from http://www.businessinsider.com/instant-mba-hit-the-right-balance-between-rigid-and-flexible-2010-11

Martinuzzi, B. (n.d.). *The agile leader: Adaptability*. Mind Tools. Retrieved from http://www.mindtools.com/pages/article/newLDR_49.htm

Mind Tools. (n.d.). *The Hersey-Blanchard Situational Leadership® Theory*. Mind Tools. Retrieved from http://www.mindtools.com/pages/article/newLDR_44.htm

Vlachoutsicos, C. (2012, December 7). What being an "authentic leader" really means. *Harvard Business Review Blog Network*. Retrieved from http://blogs.hbr.org/2012/12/what-being-an-authentic-leader-really-means/

Warrell, M. (2013, April 22). Why getting comfortable with discomfort is crucial to success. *Forbes*. Retrieved from http://www.forbes.com/sites/margiewarrell/2013/04/22/is-comfort-holding-you-back/

Warrell, M. (2013, May 20). Why leaders must "get real" – 5 ways to unlock authentic leadership. *Forbes*. Retrieved from http://www.forbes.com/sites/margiewarrell/2013/05/20/why-leaders-must-get-real/

Recommended search terms

If you'd like to explore Situational adaptability further, try searching online using the following terms:

- Embracing change in the workplace.
- Flexible leadership.
- Knowing when to change your approach.
- Learning to read others.
- Managing your emotions in the workplace.
- Situational leadership.

 More help...

Go to www.kornferry.com/fyi-resources and link directly to the deep dive resources in this chapter. Visit the site often to see the additional resources that are uploaded on a regular basis.

32. *Balances* stakeholders

*Anticipating and balancing the needs
of multiple stakeholders.*

A stakeholder has a legitimate claim, or a "stake." Stakeholders affect or are affected by the actions of an individual or the organization. They may be internal to the organization or external. Decision makers or decision approvers. Information providers or information seekers. They may be actively involved or on the sidelines. They may have different priorities—sometimes complementary, sometimes conflicting. That's what makes balancing stakeholder needs so important. Getting anything of value done today isn't a go-it-alone proposition. Stakeholders are critical to the success of any strategy, initiative, or project. They may be the team in charge of executing your vision. Or the person who pulls the approval strings. They could be the customer. Investors. The board. Stakeholders can be advocates for you or just as easily be blockers. Creating the right balance in working with stakeholders can mean the difference between a project flying or crashing. And it's a juggling act. Knowing who to engage with and when. Who to inform and to what degree. Who has something you need to be successful and what they expect in return. And recognizing that balancing often means you won't please every stakeholder every time.

> " *Find the appropriate balance
> of competing claims by various groups of stakeholders.
> All claims deserve consideration
> but some claims are more important than others.* "

Warren G. Bennis – American scholar, organizational consultant, and author

***Balances* stakeholders** is in the **Thought** factor (I) in the Korn Ferry Leadership Architect™. It is part of Cluster B, **Making complex decisions,** along with *Manages* complexity (8) and Decision quality (12). You may find it helpful to also take a look at some of the tips included in those chapters to supplement your learning.

Skilled

Understands internal and external stakeholder requirements, expectations, and needs.

Balances the interests of multiple stakeholders.

Considers cultural and ethical factors in the decision-making process.

Acts fairly despite conflicting demands of stakeholders.

32

Less skilled

- Focuses on meeting current expectations and needs of a limited number of stakeholders.

- Considers some stakeholders' interests more strongly than others'.

- Allows conflicting stakeholder demands to unfairly influence actions.

Talented

- Maintains frequent interactions with a broad stakeholder network.

- Takes a proactive approach to shape and influence stakeholder expectations.

- Serves as a liaison between different stakeholder groups.

- Effectively aligns the interests of multiple, diverse stakeholders.

Overused skill

- Spends too much time interacting with stakeholders, slowing down decision making.

- Is too focused on clarifying stakeholder needs and building consensus among stakeholders when others are looking for clear direction on day-to-day business matters.

380 |

Some possible causes of lower skill

Causes help explain *why* a person may have trouble with *Balances* stakeholders. When seeking to increase skill, it's helpful to consider how these might play out in certain situations. And remember that all of these can be addressed if you are motivated to do so.

- Poor communication skills.
- Wants to please everyone.
- Poor influencer.
- Ineffective networker.
- Not attuned to others' needs.
- Weak at building relationships.
- Not strategic.
- Avoids conflict.
- Narrow perspective.
- Uncomfortable with complexity.

Does it best

With around 44,000 service stations and 10 million customers to satisfy every day, balancing stakeholders is a tall order for Shell's leaders. They recognize five areas of stakeholder responsibility: shareholders, customers, employees, suppliers, and society. All have different priorities and all are essential to Shell's success. Shareholders want their investment protected. Employees need to be safe, healthy, and motivated. Suppliers need good business relationships with Shell. Customers want value for their money as well as cleaner, more efficient fuels. Communities need to be reassured of a safe environment. To ensure the needs of all its stakeholder groups are met, Shell applies three criteria in its decision making: the economic impact, the social impact, and the long-term effect. Shell leaders make it their business to understand what's important to people and go the extra mile to act upon it. For example, Shell LiveWire is an online community for young entrepreneurs. Shell provides resources and information to help them turn their ideas into reality. With annual revenue in excess of US$480 billion, Shell was number one in Fortune's Global 500 in 2013. Shell's efforts to balance stakeholder relationships have led to significant competitive advantage.[49, 50]

Tips to develop *Balances* stakeholders

1. **Don't know where to start? Identify your stakeholders.** Balancing stakeholders effectively starts with knowing who they are. And often your stakeholder group will extend further than you think. Start by considering everyone who could be impacted by what you're working on. Better to start big and narrow it down than overlook people. Who is impacted by the change your strategy or project will bring? Who will support it? Who will fight it? Who has influence and power over what you're doing? Who has an interest in whether the project succeeds or fails? Who has something to contribute—information, time, resources? Get others to help you identify stakeholders. Involve your sponsor, a trusted advisor, or someone in the know. Who do they see as your stakeholders? Scan internally and consider the less obvious functions. Look outside the organization to groups who may also have a stake. Customers. Suppliers. Community groups. Governmental agencies. Analysts. Make your list, then critique it. Who have you missed? Who's on it that shouldn't be? Leave it. Go back to it. Update it. Keep at it until you're satisfied.

2. **Not sure who you're dealing with? Get to know your stakeholders.** It's one thing to determine who your stakeholders are, but how much do you actually know about them? To manage them and balance their needs, you have to know what makes them tick. Analyze your stakeholder group. Get to know them. Understand them. Complete a stakeholder analysis to structure your thinking and ensure you cover everything. Here's a start:

   - What's their connection to the project?
   - What financial interests do they have?
   - What motivates them?
   - What's their current view of the situation?
   - How are they likely to feel about the intended outcome of what you're working on?
   - Who else might influence their opinions?
   - What information do you want from them?
   - What's strategically important to them?
   - What's their vision for their part of the organization?
   - Where is their thinking in terms of changes taking place in the organization?
   - What history do they have that could be significant to the future?

Test yourself. If you can't answer the questions, then do some research. Ask people who know them. Ask the stakeholders themselves. Look into their background and experience. Think about how your work links to their role. Build a clear picture that will form the foundation of your interaction with them.

3. **Stuck at the starting gate? Engage key stakeholders early.** Getting an idea off the ground can be a tricky business. Sometimes you need all the help you can get to start things moving. So make use of some of your most powerful stakeholders. Those who know the organization well. Those who can influence decisions. Get them on board right from the beginning by asking them to help you define and shape the thinking. Call on their experience to ensure you plan things in the right way. Tap into their knowledge. Ask for their guidance on potential pitfalls. Use their positional power to get heard. Involving them from the kick-off can mean you're more likely to have their support going forward. People generally have a higher level of interest in both progress and outcomes when they've been involved from the start.

4. **Only consider the upsides? Think worst-case scenario.** In planning to get the balance right, think what could go wrong. Anticipate the obstacles before they appear. Part of preparing for things to go right with stakeholders is to think through what could go wrong. What's the worst possible scenario when it comes to balancing your stakeholders? Sponsors who don't buy into the benefits of your strategy? Team members who have no idea what's expected of them to execute on the plan? Peers caught off guard by how much time they must invest in your pet project? Customers blindsided by a large-scale change that impacts their own business? Power players who feel excluded from the decision-making process? Think about all that could go wrong, and then plan to get it right.

Want to learn more? Take a deep dive...

Giang, V. (2013, September 8). *How to win loyalty from others.* Business Insider.

Hack, N. B. (2011, May 3). How deeply engaging stakeholders changes everything. *Forbes.*

Kokemuller, N. (n.d.). How to deal with multiple stakeholders in organizations. *Chron.*

Springman, J. (2011, July 28). Implementing a stakeholder strategy. *Harvard Business Review Blog Network.*

5. **Struggling with juggling? Prioritize.** Stakeholder groups can become very large, which will have an impact on your success in getting the balance right. You can't hope to give everyone the same level of attention, nor should you. You need to determine where to channel your energy and define the type of interaction you should have with each individual or group. Create an Influence/Interest grid—a 2X2 with "High to Low" axes describing the level of influence, or power, each stakeholder has, including their degree of interest. Classify each of your stakeholders. Use their position on the grid to determine how to interact with each of them. High Power/High Interest are the stakeholders you must manage most closely. Fully engage them and make the greatest effort to meet their needs. If you can't, explain why. High Power/Low Interest—keep them engaged, but don't bore them with too much detail. Low Power/High Interest—keep them adequately informed, but don't expend too much energy on them. Low Power/Low Interest—monitor them, but dedicate minimum effort. Keep in mind that influence and interest can change due to a number of factors: role change, resource reallocation, other projects in the works, change in strategic direction. Keep alert to these changes and assess the effect they may have on your stakeholders. Keep your picture current.

6. **Unsure how to involve stakeholders? Differentiate involvement.** Involving everyone fully can become difficult to manage and slow down decision making. How actively involved should each of your stakeholders be? How do you decide how to balance involvement with just keeping them informed? Will they be on the periphery—on the outside looking in? Or will they be pivotal—at the hub of the action? It depends on a number of factors: The stakeholder's role and level of authority. The degree to which the project depends on their input. Their attitude toward the project. Supportive? They can be a great influence on others. Negative? On the one hand, they can derail, but on the other, you may want them where you can keep an eye on them—"Keep your friends close and your enemies closer." Consider these factors in your stakeholder analysis and categorize each individual or group's involvement: Essential—their input could make the difference between success and failure. Not involving them could cause issues with engagement and support. Optional— you can get there without their active contribution, but their involvement will make things quicker, easier, and more effective. Non-essential—others could contribute on their behalf. Make your assessment. Monitor progress. Adjust as needed.

7. **Dealing with differing support? Manage collaborations.** Your stakeholder group is a great resource. Leverage the power by

creating good connections and encouraging productive interactions. Make use of the differing viewpoints within the group. Assess people's attitudes and understand their points of view. Who will gain? Winners are likely to be positive. Who will lose? Those who are disadvantaged are more likely to be a challenge. Consider who has something that could be helpful to other stakeholders. Who has information? Facts and figures? Background details not readily available? Historical data? Establishing where people fall will help you decide who should communicate with whom. Who to group together in meetings concerning the project. Try to avoid your negative people having too much contact with each other. Mix your positive people with your negative people. Connect your dissenters with those who can help them see the benefits of the project. If someone has had a bad past experience that's tainting their view of the way forward, encourage their interaction with people who are open-minded and have a fresh outlook. Connect them with people who see the benefits and are not constrained by the past. If someone can't see the advantages of change, have them spend time with people who thrive on the new and different. Managing collaborations will help foster project success.

8. **Out of sight, out of mind? Engage stakeholders near and far.** It's easier to focus on stakeholders you come into contact with more frequently. Those you bump into at the water cooler. The people who attend the same meetings as you. But it's likely you have stakeholders at different locations. Those internal to the organization's home office or located in different regions. Externals like customers, the board, outside agencies. These may be the stakeholders who need more engagement but could end up getting far less because of proximity. Beware the distance trap. Draw up a communications plan and stick to it. Make sure to include external stakeholders when you provide updates. Alert them to news that's relevant to the project and impacts them. Give them as much opportunity as possible to have direct contact with other stakeholders. Go see them at their own location.

Want to learn more? Take a deep dive...

Duff, V. (n.d.). How can stakeholders negatively influence a project? *Chron*.

Ernst, C. (2009, October 28). Leadership beyond bounds. *Forbes*.

Thompson, R. (n.d.). *Stakeholder analysis: Winning support for your projects*. Mind Tools.

9. **Unhappy stakeholders? Listen to what matters to them.** Don't confuse being a stakeholder with being a supporter. Supporters emerge when they can see clear benefits from the project's success. Economic gain. Status improvement. An easier way to operate. Stakeholders can be non-supporters or resisters too. The strategy, once executed, will mean more work. Loss of relationships. Less security. Departure from something they know and are comfortable with. Understanding resisters' points of view is essential if you are to balance their concerns with the reality of what needs to happen. Chances are you won't be able to give them everything they want, but you can show that you empathize and recognize what's important to them. Make a point of understanding their concerns. Find out why they feel as they do. Understand the history that's driving their view of the future. Have they been here before? Have they had a bad experience with something similar? Are they threatened by potential outcomes? What are they missing that could help them see the benefits of your direction? If they're going to lose out, how can you cushion that blow? They may never be your greatest advocate, but you can help them accept.

10. **Conflicting viewpoints? Focus on strategy.** Stakeholders often have conflicting priorities and your challenge is to manage those. One person's loss can be another person's gain. A reduction in resources may mean cost savings for one stakeholder but a major execution challenge for another. A new process may mean more work for one team while effort is reduced in another. A change or variation in a product may be disappointing for one customer but exactly what the other customer is looking for. Start with empathy. Understand each point of view and recognize why their views are important to them. A rule of thumb in dealing with conflicting viewpoints is to try to find some common ground. In the case of your stakeholders, this may be difficult. Each likely has a solid rationale to back up their view. You need to be seen as objective and not playing favorites. So be impartial. Make it about the purpose, not about them. Show how the objectives of the project align with the strategic intent of the organization. Help them see the benefits more broadly than strictly how it impacts them. You may never get to a meeting of minds, but you can help them understand why you're doing what you're doing.

11. **Once-and-done stakeholder planning? Monitor changes.** People change. Views alter. Priorities shift. Don't assume that where your stakeholders were when you first engaged with them is where they are now. You need to be on the ball and keep up-to-date about stakeholder changes so you can modify your approach. Their role could have changed. Their position as a stakeholder may not be as

influential. Perhaps they now have *more* power. Their interest level may not be what it was. Keep track. Stay in touch. Check the status quo when it comes to your stakeholders to ensure you understand their position. Don't make assumptions. Check in with them regularly. Take a temperature check on how they're feeling about things. What do they need more of? Less of? What's going on in their world that may affect their stakeholder position? Monitor continuously to keep balance in check.

Want to learn more? Take a deep dive...

Blanch, A. (2013, August 5). *How to manage difficult stakeholders*. Business Think Tank.

Hack, N. B. (2012, May 30). Improving stakeholder engagement increases productivity, profit and sustainability. *The Huffington Post*.

Merrett, R. (2012, July 31). Want project success? Engage stakeholders. *CIO*.

ProjectManager.com. (2013, November 11). *Project stakeholder communication tips*. Project Manager.

32

Job assignments

- Take on a project with a wide variety of internal and external stakeholders. Rise to the challenge of juggling priorities, preferences, and needs.

- Design a communications plan to inform stakeholders about a change that is not likely to be well-received.

- Get a group of stakeholders together who were involved in a recent project. Gather information from them regarding what worked well for them and what didn't.

- Present the strategic imperatives of the organization to your team, explaining where their efforts fit into the larger goals.

- Volunteer to rescue a project with unhappy stakeholders. Find out what's gone wrong. Engage them in moving forward in the right direction.

32   **Factor I:** Thought
Cluster B: Making complex decisions
Competency 32: *Balances* stakeholders

Take time to reflect...

If you focus purely on results and forget about people...

> ...then understand that stakeholders can help you get there faster, but they can also hold you back. Get them on board. Understand them. Engage them.

If you think that having a multitude of stakeholders will slow progress...

> ...then remember investing time up front can save you time later on. It's less about the number of stakeholders and much more about taking the right approach. The more stakeholders in your corner, the more your ideas will gain traction.

If you think you can predict what each stakeholder group needs...

> ...then tread carefully. Making assumptions can be dangerous and lead you down the wrong path entirely.

32

"*When one has so many different people
with different opinions to deal with in a new affair,
one is obliged sometimes to give up some smaller points
in order to obtain greater.* **"**

Benjamin Franklin – American inventor, politician,
and one of the founding fathers of the United States

Learn more about *Balances* stakeholders

Kuenkel, P., Gerlach, S., & Frieg, V. (2011). *Working with stakeholder dialogues*. Norderstedt, Germany: Books on Demand GmbH.

Lewis, J. P. (2010). *Project planning, scheduling and control* (5th ed.). New York, NY: McGraw-Hill.

Roeder, T. (2013). *Managing project stakeholders: Building a foundation to achieve project goals*. Hoboken, NJ: John Wiley & Sons, Inc.

Shireman, B., Wohlgemuth, E., & Pfahl, D. (2013). *Engaging outraged stakeholders: How-to guide for uniting the left, right, capitalists, and activists*. New York, NY: Affinity Press.

Walker, S. F., & Marr, J. W. (2001). *Stakeholder power: A winning plan for building stakeholder commitment and driving corporate growth*. Cambridge, MA: Perseus Publishing.

32

 Deep dive learning resource links

Blanch, A. (2013, August 5). *How to manage difficult stakeholders*. Business Think Tank. Retrieved from http://www.businessthinktank.com.au/how-to-guides/how-to-manage-difficult-stakeholders

Duff, V. (n.d.). How can stakeholders negatively influence a project? *Chron*. Retrieved from http://smallbusiness.chron.com/can-stakeholders-negatively-influence-project-36026.html

Ernst, C. (2009, October 28). Leadership beyond bounds. *Forbes*. Retrieved from http://www.forbes.com/2009/10/28/boundaries-collaboration-teams-leadership-managing-ccl.html

Giang, V. (2013, September 8). *How to win loyalty from others*. Business Insider. Retrieved from http://www.businessinsider.com/how-to-win-loyalty-from-others-2013-9

Hack, N. B. (2011, May 3). How deeply engaging stakeholders changes everything. *Forbes*. Retrieved from http://www.forbes.com/sites/85broads/2011/05/03/how-deeply-engaging-stakeholders-changes-everything/

Hack, N. B. (2012, May 30). Improving stakeholder engagement increases productivity, profit and sustainability. *The Huffington Post*. Retrieved from http://www.huffingtonpost.com/nadine-b-hack/stakeholder-engagement_b_1556070.html

Kokemuller, N. (n.d.). How to deal with multiple stakeholders in organizations. *Chron*. Retrieved from http://smallbusiness.chron.com/deal-multiple-stakeholders-organizations-62017.html

Merrett, R. (2012, July 31). Want project success? Engage stakeholders. *CIO*. Retrieved from http://www.cio.com.au/article/432205/want_project_success_engage_stakeholders/

ProjectManager.com. (2013, November 11). *Project stakeholder communication tips.* Project Manager. Retrieved from http://www.projectmanager.com/project-stakeholder-communication-tips.php

Springman, J. (2011, July 28). Implementing a stakeholder strategy. *Harvard Business Review Blog Network*. Retrieved from http://blogs.hbr.org/2011/07/implementing-a-stakeholder-str/

Thompson, R. (n.d.). *Stakeholder analysis: Winning support for your projects.* Mind Tools. Retrieved from http://www.mindtools.com/pages/article/newPPM_07.htm

Recommended search terms

If you'd like to explore *Balances* stakeholders further, try searching online using the following terms:

- Collaborating with stakeholders.
- Dealing with stakeholder conflict.
- How to identify your stakeholders.
- Managing difficult/challenging stakeholders.
- Project stakeholder communication.
- Stakeholder engagement.

(i) More help...

Go to www.kornferry.com/fyi-resources and link directly to the deep dive resources in this chapter. Visit the site often to see the additional resources that are uploaded on a regular basis.

33. Strategic mindset

Seeing ahead to future possibilities and translating them into breakthrough strategies.

Being strategic involves looking, planning, and moving into the future with clear intentions and purposeful actions. Some think being strategic is an either-or proposition —that a person is either tactical or strategic. Focused on the short-term or long-term. Interested in details or the big picture. While many people gravitate toward one side, a strategic mindset requires readiness for both. It's about doing things today with an eye toward tomorrow. Making decisions now that will lead the organization toward its future objectives. Like deciding where to invest to capitalize on emerging trends in your market. Like building internal capabilities that will help bring a new strategy to life. To develop a strategic mindset, you need to thoroughly understand the territory in which you operate. You need to understand what unique capabilities your unit or organization has to offer. You need to consistently ask where you are going and how you will get there.

" In strategy, it is important to see distant things as if they were close and to take a distanced view of close things. "

Miyamato Musashi – Japanese swordsman and samurai

Strategic mindset is in the **Thought** factor (I) in the Korn Ferry Leadership Architect™. It is part of Cluster C, **Creating the new and different,** along with Global perspective (18) and *Cultivates* innovation (19). You may find it helpful to also take a look at some of the tips included in those chapters to supplement your learning.

Skilled

Anticipates future trends and implications accurately.

Readily poses future scenarios.

Articulates credible pictures and visions of possibilities that will create sustainable value.

Creates competitive and breakthrough strategies that show a clear connection between vision and action.

Less skilled

- Is more comfortable in the tactical here and now.
- Spends little time or effort thinking about or working on strategic issues.
- Contributes little to strategic discussions.
- Lacks the disciplined thought processes to pull together varying elements into a coherent view.

Talented

- Sees the big picture, constantly imagines future scenarios, and creates strategies to sustain competitive advantage.
- Is a visionary and able to articulately paint credible pictures and visions of possibilities and likelihoods.
- Formulates a clear strategy and maps the aggressive steps that will clearly accelerate the organization toward its strategic goals.

Overused skill

- May be seen as too theoretical.
- May be so far ahead that others have trouble seeing how the organization will get from here to there.
- May be impatient with day-to-day tactical issues.
- May overcomplicate plans.

392 |

Some possible causes of lower skill

Causes help explain *why* a person may have trouble with Strategic mindset. When seeking to increase skill, it's helpful to consider how these might play out in certain situations. And remember that all of these can be addressed if you are motivated to do so.

- Doesn't like complexity.
- Prefers what is familiar.
- Short-term focus.
- Lacks competitive drive.
- Overly tactical.
- Low curiosity.
- Too busy with today's tasks.
- Likes things to be predictable.
- Narrow perspective.
- Low-variety background.

Did you know?

33

A strategic approach to leadership is, on average, 10 times more significant to your perceived effectiveness than other behaviors. At least that's what a global survey of 60,000 managers conducted by the Management Research Group in 2013 found. Strategic-minded leaders tend to look much more broadly when they solve problems and make decisions. They think in multiple time frames, balancing achieving things now with planning for potential future outcomes. They think systemically, making connections and understanding the impact their decisions have on other parts of the organization. The study also revealed that those with the highest ratings on these skills associated with strategic mindset were four times more likely than their lower-scoring counterparts to be viewed as high potential within their organization.[51, 52]

Tips to develop Strategic mindset

1. **Can't anticipate what's to come? Become a trend-watcher.** Too busy getting today's work done to think about tomorrow? To cultivate a strategic mindset, keep one eye toward the horizon. Study emerging trends inside and outside your field. Get in the habit of questioning what things will mean for the future. How is technology driving greater efficiency and breakthrough innovation? How is social media altering the way people make purchasing decisions? Tap into future-focused resources such as the World Future Society, Institute for the Future, or Faith Popcorn's TrendBank. Join the Future Trends group in LinkedIn. Listen to thought-provoking speakers live or online. Meet with colleagues to discuss how events and trends may impact your organization's strategy. Brainstorm ways you can capitalize on emerging opportunities. When examining trends, Rosabeth Moss Kanter advises zooming in and zooming out. Zoom in for sharp focus on important details. Zoom out to see how details form patterns and fit into the bigger picture.

2. **Out of touch with customers? Make customer intimacy a priority.** A winning strategy is designed around the customer. Understand your customers historically, today, and most importantly, tomorrow. What products and services do they want more or less of? How can you improve the user experience? What do your competitors offer that you don't? What trends do you need to monitor and plan for? Analyze market and customer data. Gather fresh insights. Watch customers as they interact with your products or services. Meet with your internal or external customers on a regular basis to understand their needs and desires. Determine which customers you want to keep and which you want to attract in the future. Plan how you'll accomplish these goals. Allocate your greatest resources to your primary customers.

3. **Unclear about the competitive landscape? Get market smart.** Know the industry inside and out, from the smallest to the largest player. Study the competition's annual reports, websites, press releases, social media sites. What are their strengths and weaknesses? What is their strategy related to speed, growth, customers, products/services, innovation, talent, and global reach? How does their strategy compare to yours? Leverage knowledge about your similarities and differences to make better strategic decisions. Apply Michael Porter's Five Forces model to assess the intensity of the competition's power and the profitability of your industry. (*For more information, visit* http://www.mindtools.com/pages/article/newTMC_08.htm.) Spark conversations about how to anticipate the different moving parts in

the marketplace. How might you best differentiate and keep your organization out in front?

4. **Not standing out in the marketplace? Identify your distinctive advantage.** A strategy is about what you do and what you want to become. It's also about what you don't do and do not aspire to be. No organization can be all things to all people. You have to make choices. Differentiation can take many forms. You can be a low-cost leader. Deliver quality products, services, or experiences. Or have superior customer relationships. A distinctive advantage is something that is hard for competitors to copy or develop. Spend time understanding your unique capabilities and offerings. Take a stand on what you'll continue to strengthen and promote in the future. Embed this strategy into the culture—employees of low-cost providers hunt for cost-savings; quality-first employees demonstrate an eye for detail; customer-service leaders treat everyone as special. Identify concrete ways to leverage what makes you distinct.

5. **Developing a strategy in a vacuum? Scan the environment first.** Before crafting a strategic plan, you need to get a handle on the context in which you operate. Pull together people with diverse knowledge and create a detailed picture. There are a number of scanning frameworks you can use. The SWOT analysis (Strengths, Weaknesses, Opportunities, Threats) is widely used to identify internal and external factors that define and shape a competitive position in the marketplace. A PEST analysis helps to capture the big picture in terms of Political, Economic, Social, Technological topics. (Some add Legal and Environmental.) Bennis and Nanus suggest using the Quick Environmental Scanning Technique (QUEST). In this framework, trends are observed, potential market conditions are forecasted, and options are discussed to address evolving conditions.

6. **Can't predict the future? Consider multiple scenarios.** It's not easy to develop strategic plans when faced with so many unknowns. Scenario planning can assist by generating useful dialogue and insights. It's not about predicting the future. It's about considering various possibilities. Discuss your assumptions about what might happen. Develop a small number of plausible scenarios (stories) about how the future might unfold. Think through how the organization could/should respond if faced with shifts in socioeconomic, political, technological, environmental, or social areas. Then do what expert Peter Schwartz calls "rehearsing the implications." How might things impact your industry, organization,

stakeholders? What decisions would you need to make? What else might be triggered? What contingencies should be in place? Scenario planning makes you better prepared to recognize signals that warrant a response. And better able to anticipate, plan, and adapt when changes arise.

Want to learn more? Take a deep dive...

Edin, P., Lingqvist, O., & Tamsons, A. (2012, July 26). The best sales leaders are trend hunters. *Harvard Business Review Blog Network*.

Howes, L. (2012, December 11). 7 Steps to become an authority in your industry. *Entrepreneur*.

Straub, M. (2013, April 9). Does your business stand out in the marketplace? *The Business Times*.

---

7. **Think strategy is a waste of time? Recognize the value of strategy.** Some reject strategic work. They avoid it. They say they'd rather be doing something useful, like solving today's problems. That they've never seen a plan actually happen as projected anyway. While it's true that most strategic plans don't materialize as planned, that doesn't mean it was a wasted effort. A good strategy leads to practical decisions about what to do, who to hire, how to allocate funds and deploy resources. If you have doubts about whether to go ahead with a project, ask: Is this in line with our strategy? If you're wondering which option to choose, ask: Which best aligns with our key priorities? If your team is losing steam, ask: How will what we're doing now position us well for the future? A good strategy energizes people to move in the same direction. It makes choices clear and leads to less wasted effort.

8. **Looking for certainty? Embrace the unknown.** Strategic planning is one of the most uncertain things leaders do. It's speculating on the near-unknown. It requires projections into foggy landscapes. It requires making assumptions about unfamiliar terrain. Many are uncomfortable making statements they can't back up with facts. Uncomfortable committing resources when there's no money-back guarantee. All adventures come with potential risks and rewards. Most strategies can be challenged and questioned. If you are questioned, think of it as a good thing. Questions from others are really opportunities to further vet your strategic direction. Questions raise issues you may not have thought of and likely yield a sounder approach as a result.

9. **Consumed with daily demands? Make room for strategic priorities.** Burning issues require attention. It wouldn't be wise to ignore important demands of the day. Neither would it be wise to avoid what will matter most in the long run. You need to strike the right balance. Talk with colleagues to be sure you agree on what projects are mission critical vs. important vs. nice to have. If your team is engaged in activities that don't drive the strategy forward, make the case for discontinuing them. Create a culture of questioning. If people can't justify why something is important, they should question why it's on their plate. Reserve "thinking time" on your calendar to weed out distractions and make strategic adjustments.

Want to learn more? Take a deep dive...

Birshan, M., & Kar, J. (2012, July). Becoming more strategic: Three tips for any executive. *McKinsey Quarterly*.

Clark, D. (2013, October 8). What's keeping you from being strategic? *Forbes*.

Lester, A. (2012, December 7). More companies include retreat time to innovate. *The Boston Globe*.

33

10. **Looking for some quick strategic wins? Play to your strengths.** Executing on your strategy may require that you and your team develop new skills. But that doesn't mean you should discount the strengths you already possess. Strategically smart organizations leverage their core capabilities. How can you build upon what is already great to drive your strategy forward? How can your talents' skills be applied more broadly? How can existing infrastructure be advanced? What products or services can be repurposed, redefined, or relaunched? Consider how you can take what's solid and extend it into new ventures. Disney's core is family-friendly entertainment. Over time, they extended their core beyond cartoons into theme parks, media, products, and retail, unlocking progressively more value. Consider how to capitalize on less obvious assets too—your intellectual property, materials, distribution networks, alliances.

11. **Outdated strategic plan? Keep it fresh, fluid, and flexible.** It used to be that strategic plans were created once a year or every few years. They sat in binders on a shelf. Not today. To stay competitive and nimble, the neat and tidy plans of the past have been transformed into a continuous strategic planning process. Make sure to revisit your strategy frequently. Debate key topics when they arise and focus on making sound decisions quickly. What are the mission-critical

priorities? What key metrics will inform and guide you? Whose interests come first—customers, shareholders, employees? When difficult trade-offs surface, look to your core values to determine which way to go. Develop simple rules of thumb to guide people to make on-the-spot decisions, ensuring they stay aligned with the bigger picture.

12. **Not sure how your role fits in? Identify a clear strategic line of sight.** Understanding strategy is important for people in every role. Learn about your organization's strategy. What primary objectives is it aiming toward? How does it plan to reach them? What critical capabilities and resources does the organization need to succeed? Talk about how your department supports or drives the organization's strategy directly or indirectly. How do you create value? Serve customers? Contribute to growth or the bottom line? Strengthen the brand? Support the community in which you operate? How do other functions build on the work your group produces? Spend time connecting the dots, and you'll have a better sense of what to emphasize in your daily work. If you can't demonstrate how a job aligns with the strategy, why do you have it?

13. **Get tongue-tied when talking strategy? Learn to speak the language of strategy.** You may have a knack for thinking strategically but not know how to express it very well. Strategy is an emerging and ever-changing field. At any time, there are gurus who create new words and concepts to describe it. If you don't use these words, others may not perceive you as being strategic. Learn from the latest experts. Watch their videos. Read their blogs and articles in the *Harvard Business Review* and similar publications. Read case studies about strategy and find parallels between other organizations and yours. Also pay attention to what your senior leaders are reading and talking about. Offer ideas on topics that match their strategic interests. Use the same terms and metaphors they use in their messages. Practice thinking and speaking more broadly than your own function and level. Go for form *and* substance.

14. **Plans interrupted by unwanted change? Approach the future with optimism.** It's important to face undesirable realities—competitors disrupting the industry, regulators halting progress, unforeseen events crushing otherwise perfect plans. But doom and gloom forecasts do little to rouse energy and commitment. Make it a point to view needed changes in strategy with an optimistic lens. Reinforce your confidence in the resourcefulness, drive, and competence that you and your colleagues possess. It's hard to imagine new possibilities

if you allow crises large and small to dampen your belief in a positive future. When change forces your strategy to change, regroup. Together, paint a new portrait of what's possible.

Want to learn more? Take a deep dive...

Green, H. (2012, September 11). Strategy ain't what it used to be. *Forbes*.

Hatch, J., & Zweig, J. (2001, March/April). Strategic flexibility – The key to growth. *Ivey Business Journal*.

Sirkin, H. L. (2013, September 23). The key to corporate fitness: Agility and flexibility. *Bloomberg Businessweek*.

Job assignments

- Take on a project or assignment that requires significant strategic thinking and planning with colleagues from various disciplines, divisions, or geographies.

- Prepare and present a strategic proposal to senior leaders that involves charting new ground. Identify the trade-offs inherent in any strategic decision.

- Do a thorough trend analysis and environmental scan of your function, unit, or organization as part of the strategic planning process.

- Manage an aspect of a rapidly expanding or growing operation that is instrumental to the organization's strategy.

- Conduct a competitive analysis of your organization's products/ services and position in the marketplace.

33

Take time to reflect...

If you focus on the here and now...

> ...then understand that strategy is foresight. What got you here today will not get your there tomorrow. Keep one eye on the present, and focus the other on looking to the future.

If seeing ahead brings more fog than clarity...

> ...then recognize that a strategic mindset isn't about absolutes. Being curious and well-informed will help shed light on an uncertain future and make you more prepared for that future when it arrives.

If you see strategy as abstract and not concrete enough...

> ...then make your strategies solid. As you forecast what the organization can become, figure out what needs to happen along the way. Turn abstract goals into a tangible path to action.

"*When you find a good move, look for a better one.***"**

Emanuel Lasker – German chess player and philosopher

Learn more about Strategic mindset

Dranove, D., & Marciano, S. (2005). *Kellogg on strategy: Concepts, tools, and frameworks for practitioners*. Hoboken, NJ: John Wiley & Sons.

Hoffman, A. J., & Woody, J. G. (2008). *Climate change: What's your business strategy? (Memo to the CEO)*. Boston, MA: Harvard Business School Publishing.

Kim, W. C., & Mauborgne, R. (2005). *Blue ocean strategy: How to create uncontested market space and make competition irrelevant*. Boston, MA: Harvard Business School Publishing.

Magretta, J. (2011). *Understanding Michael Porter: The essential guide to competition and strategy*. Boston, MA: Harvard Business School Publishing.

Morgan, M., Levitt, R. E., & Malek, W. A. (2008). *Executing your strategy: How to break it down and get it done*. Boston, MA: Harvard Business School Publishing.

Porter, M. (1979). How competitive forces shape strategy. *Harvard Business Review, 57*(2), 86-93.

 Deep dive learning resource links

33

Birshan, M., & Kar, J. (2012, July). Becoming more strategic: Three tips for any executive. *McKinsey Quarterly*. Retrieved from http://www.mckinsey.com/insights/strategy/becoming_more_strategic_three_tips_for_any_executive

Clark, D. (2013, October 8). What's keeping you from being strategic? *Forbes*. Retrieved from http://www.forbes.com/sites/dorieclark/2013/10/08/whats-keeping-you-from-being-strategic/

Edin, P., Lingqvist, O., & Tamsons, A. (2012, July 26). The best sales leaders are trend hunters. *Harvard Business Review Blog Network*. Retrieved from http://blogs.hbr.org/2012/07/sales-is-all-about-hitting/

Green, H. (2012, September 11). Strategy ain't what it used to be. *Forbes*. Retrieved from http://www.forbes.com/sites/work-in-progress/2012/09/11/strategy-aint-what-it-used-to-be/

Hatch, J., & Zweig, J. (2001, March/April). Strategic flexibility – The key to growth. *Ivey Business Journal*. Retrieved from http://iveybusinessjournal.com/topics/strategy/strategic-flexibility-the-key-to-growth

| 401

Howes, L. (2012, December 11). 7 Steps to become an authority in your industry. *Entrepreneur*. Retrieved from http://www.entrepreneur.com/blog/225225

Lester, A. (2012, December 7). More companies include retreat time to innovate. *The Boston Globe*. Retrieved from http://www.bostonglobe.com/business/2012/12/07/companies-set-aside-time-for-employees-innovate/Y4cWITyVjmpvKhOfV0GQiM/story.html

Sirkin, H. L. (2013, September 23). The key to corporate fitness: Agility and flexibility. *Bloomberg Businessweek*. Retrieved from http://www.businessweek.com/articles/2013-09-23/the-key-to-corporate-fitness-agility-and-flexibility

Straub, M. (2013, April 9). Does your business stand out in the marketplace? *The Business Times*. Retrieved from http://thebusinesstimes.com/does-your-business-stand-out-in-the-marketplace/

Recommended search terms

If you'd like to explore Strategic mindset further, try searching online using the following terms:

33

- Creating strategic flexibility.
- Implementing strategy.
- Learn more about your industry.
- Learn to be more strategic at work.
- Strategic adaptability.

(i) **More help...**

Go to www.kornferry.com/fyi-resources and link directly to the deep dive resources in this chapter. Visit the site often to see the additional resources that are uploaded on a regular basis.

402 |

34. *Builds effective* teams

Building strong-identity teams that apply their diverse skills and perspectives to achieve common goals.

Teams are the primary way to accomplish coordinated, integrated tasks. Team members need each other and work interdependently to achieve common goals. For some, this is good news—a chance to collaborate with a variety of people. For others, it's a burden—a productivity drain. Many have had a peak experience working with a dream team that clicked from the start and went on to achieve great things. They wonder why all teams can't be like that. Here's the reality— great teams rarely just happen. They require attention to purpose, tasks, relationships, and processes. The rewards can be significant for you and your organization when you set teams up for success. Whether you're a team leader or team member, whether your team works under the same roof or across several time zones, it pays to be smart about how to structure things and contribute so your team performs at its best.

"*Talent wins games, but teamwork and intelligence win championships.* **"**

Michael Jordan – American basketball player and member of the NBA Hall of Fame

34 Factor III: People
    Cluster H: Optimizing diverse talent
    Competency 34: *Builds effective* teams

Builds effective teams is in the **People** factor (III) in the Korn Ferry Leadership Architect™. It is part of Cluster H, **Optimizing diverse talent,** along with Attracts top talent (4), Develops talent (13), and *Values* differences (14). You may find it helpful to also take a look at some of the tips included in those chapters to supplement your learning.

Skilled

Forms teams with appropriate and diverse mix of styles, perspectives, and experience.

Establishes common objectives and a shared mindset.

Creates a feeling of belonging and strong team morale.

Shares wins and rewards team efforts.

Fosters open dialogue and collaboration among the team.

Less skilled

- Doesn't create a common mindset or challenge.

- Fails to recognize that morale, recognition, and belongingness are integral ingredients of effective teams.

- Prioritizes and rewards individual efforts rather than team achievements.

- Doesn't shape and distribute assignments in a way that encourages teamwork.

Talented

- Defines success in terms of the whole team.

- Recognizes that leveraging each team member's unique background and perspective is critical to achieving team goals.

- Rallies others behind common team goals.

- Places team goals ahead of own goals.

Overused skill

- May focus so much on teaming behavior that results may suffer.

- May build such a strong sense of team identity that it is hard for new members to break in and get up to speed.

- May not develop individual leaders.

Factor III: People
Cluster H: Optimizing diverse talent
Competency 34: *Builds effective* teams

34

Some possible causes of lower skill

Causes help explain *why* a person may have trouble with *Builds effective* teams. When seeking to increase skill, it's helpful to consider how these might play out in certain situations. And remember that all of these can be addressed if you are motivated to do so.

- Prefers working alone.
- Not clear about team purpose and goals.
- Doesn't engage others.
- Needs to be in control.
- Avoids sharing information.
- Excessively action oriented.
- Conflict averse.
- Poor process management skills.
- Avoids holding people accountable.
- Incentives are based upon individual achievement.
- Has difficulty motivating others.

Does it best

In the early days of what would become the Walt Disney Company, there was a core team of animators known colloquially as "Disney's Nine Old Men" (a name derived from President Franklin D. Roosevelt's nickname for the nine US Supreme Court Justices). Disney's team has become an icon in the field of animation, credited with establishing the modern art of animation and revolutionizing children's films. They created some of the most beloved characters in cartoon history. The team was comprised of very different men, each of whom brought something unique to the table during the creative process. Walt was known as the "Agitator," stirring debate and playing devil's advocate. Ub Iwerks was the "Expert." With a background in animation, Ub created the iconic Mickey Mouse. Walt's older brother, Roy, was the "Glue," securing the financial backing needed to build an organization to compete with the larger studios in New York. The Nine Old Men were the "Workhorses," originating the animated characters that have helped Disney become one of the most widely recognized brands in the world.[53, 54]

34

34

Factor III: People
Cluster H: Optimizing diverse talent
Competency 34: *Builds effective* teams

Tips to develop *Builds effective* teams

1. **Not sure why you're here? Identify clear goals and a uniting purpose.** A common thrust energizes high-performing teams—goal clarity adds focus, power, and efficiency. Set team goals together, prioritize them, and establish ways to measure outcomes and chart progress. What will success look like? How will you know if you meet expectations? Get each team member involved in setting a meaningful purpose—something they believe in that will rouse commitment. Reinvigorate people with the mission when times get tough. Why does the work matter? What will happen as a result of your accomplishments? If it's a long-standing team or if focus scatters over time, regroup. Ask each person to individually write and rank the team's current top three priorities. Compare notes. Discuss what needs to be emphasized now and how to better align and execute.

2. **Need solid team players? Select and leverage the right mix.** Analyze the key purpose, tasks, and deliverables of the team, then ask: Who is best suited to do the work? What knowledge, expertise, and skills are critical? Don't stop with the obvious technical/functional requirements. Consider the optimal mix of diverse experiences, backgrounds, and styles. Aim for complementary skills, not more of the same. Who collaborates well? Knows how to make decisions? Keeps people on track? Challenges the status quo? Generates enthusiasm? Isn't afraid to tackle problems head-on? Can build trust inside, build bridges outside? Share each other's strengths so you can capitalize upon them and learn from each other. Talk about your weaknesses and vulnerabilities, too, so that you can work around them for the good of the whole. The team should know who they are and what they stand for, individually and collectively.

3. **Questioning team size? Bigger is not usually better.** There's a tendency for leaders to err on the side of making teams too large, often because they want to be (or seem) inclusive. Watch out, because coordination problems can mount when more people are added. Other downsides: difficulty keeping people on the same page, less active participation from all, people more concerned about projecting an image vs. doing substantive work, greater conformity to the majority view. Most experts agree that it's best to have the smallest number of team members as possible who can still successfully do the work (generally fewer than 10). Break teams up into sub-teams with sub-leaders if needed.

Factor III: People
Cluster H: Optimizing diverse talent
Competency 34: *Builds effective* teams

34

Want to learn more? Take a deep dive...

Wharton School. (2006, June 14). *Is your team too big? Too small? What's the right number?* Wharton School of the University of Pennsylvania.

Young Entrepreneurial Council. (2013, June 7). Five ways to build an effective team. *Forbes*.

4. **Too much guesswork? A little structure goes a long way.** Who does what? How is information shared? Resources obtained? Feedback given? Crises handled? Everyone wants to know. Patterns are often unconsciously set, then unquestionably maintained. Collaboratively design what team expert Richard Hackman calls "an enabling structure." That means establishing norms that will support rather than impede the team's work. Be explicit about what's expected around roles, decision making, running meetings, communication, accountability, processes—anything that will set you up for success. Revisit and adjust things along the way to best support your collective efforts.

5. **Need a clear course of action? Create a game plan.** Once the mission and outcomes and goals are established, a plan is necessary to avoid duplicate work and things falling through the cracks. Use visuals and project management tools that clearly show interdependencies and deliverables. Surface potential risks and discuss how you'll handle them. Given how dynamic things are, expect plans to change. It's usually better to be responsive than to stick to a plan that no longer serves the team's purpose.

6. **Too much individualism? Shift the focus from "me" to "we."** Resistance to the idea of a team is best overcome by focusing on common goals, priorities, and challenges. Stress the benefits of teamwork: different perspectives on old issues, creativity, an expanded network, a better outcome. Treat each meeting as a chance to celebrate team successes. Cite examples of how people on your team have worked together to solve problems, improve performance, or achieve results. Encourage naturally competitive people to channel it toward the external competition instead of inside the team. Remind people that you're all on the same side. Promote a sense of belonging by saying: "*Our* objectives," "*Our* challenges," "*Our* solutions," "*We* did it."

34

Factor III: People
Cluster H: Optimizing diverse talent
Competency 34: *Builds effective* teams

Want to learn more? Take a deep dive...

Hall, H., & Thompson, B. (2012, March 30). The secret sauce of teamwork. *Harvard Business Review Blog Network*.

Hall, J. (2013, January 29). 12 Simple things a leader can do to build a phenomenal team. *Forbes*.

7. **Want higher performance? Go for higher-impact communication.** Research scientists at MIT collected loads of data on teams outfitted with electronic sensors. They found that the most important predictors of a team's success were patterns of communication (more than intelligence, skill, and personality combined). It was the manner in which teams communicated—not the content—that made the biggest difference, such as more face-to-face exchanges; exuding energy when communicating; balancing listening and speaking; using brevity; engaging directly with many others on the team, not just with the team leader or a select few; talking between meetings; making frequent connections outside the team and incorporating fresh input that's been picked up. Bottom line? Orchestrate ways for people to interact more often, making sure everyone is involved and dialogue keeps circulating.

8. **All work and no play? Build team spirit.** Even though some—including you—may resist it, social events like parties, group charity work, activities, and outings build group cohesion. Cohesion is about what makes you bond or stick together during good times and bad. There's good chemistry. The team feels it and those outside the team sense it. Chemistry can be instant, but it usually comes from mixing together, through challenge and fun, on and off the job. Research tells us cohesive teams are more productive too—another reason to take fun seriously. Make it easy for team members to get to know each other as whole people. When you laugh together, it releases stress, builds trust, and opens up ways to solve problems more creatively.

9. **Losing momentum? Monitor and publicize short-term wins.** Long-term goals/visions are an important part of inspiring others, but if these are the only carrots, progress toward your vision will lose traction. You need momentum, and you can create momentum by recognizing short-term progress and making it visible. Lessons learned through hardship are also wins if you make "failing forward" part of the team's DNA. This means talking openly about mistakes, turning them into stepping stones toward achievement so everybody can learn.

Factor III: People
Cluster H: Optimizing diverse talent
Competency 34: *Builds effective teams*

34

10. **Have virtual team challenges? Keep them connected and motivated.**
Virtual teams are everywhere now. A sense of isolation and maintaining morale are common challenges, so dial up on tactics to stay well connected. Frontload face-to-face time when possible. Schedule frequent conference calls. Leverage multiple technologies (videoconferencing, groupware, etc.). If dispersed members dial in to large meetings, be sure to interact with them. Schedule off-line one-on-one contact for deeper conversations, mindful that e-mail and texting are the least effective forms of communication for virtual teams. Be extra sensitive to cultural differences or language barriers—things may be misconstrued when there isn't a way to decipher non-verbals and check for understanding. Create an expertise directory or webpage to showcase the diverse capabilities of the team. Include non-work aspects, such as the person's hobbies or interests, to strengthen bonds.

Want to learn more? Take a deep dive...

Llopis, G. (2013, September 23). 6 Ways to make your leadership and workplace fun again. *Forbes*.

Moran, G. (2013, March 13). 3 Ingredients for building effective teams. *Entrepreneur*.

---

11. **Tension brewing? Strengthen trust through mutual accountability.**
Trust is the foundation of effective teams. You need to know you can rely on each other to follow through. When that doesn't happen and trust begins to erode, the antidote is candid conversation. Team members—not just the leader—need to let each other know when they've been let down. Describe the consequences when someone doesn't deliver. Call each other on actions that seem counterproductive. Clarify expectations and agree on productive next steps. You'll know that trust is strengthened when people admit shortcomings and ask for help before their teammates mention it.

12. **Not benefiting from diverse views? Practice perspective-taking.**
Could be that even after you've selected team members for their diverse value, you still get too much sameness. Could be that those with minority views are just quiet. Could be they're snuffed out. Be assertive and gather input from everyone, not just the dominant players. Ask for different ways to frame a problem. If an idea initially seems ridiculous, get curious instead of judgmental. "Tell us more." Play out various "what ifs" and "how abouts." Encourage people to

34

Factor III: People
Cluster H: Optimizing diverse talent
Competency 34: *Builds effective* teams

question assumptions and poke holes in solutions. Make perspective-taking a habit to sharpen the team's mind and arrive at better outcomes. You'll also boost morale, because everyone wants to be heard and understood.

13. **Arguments heating up? Referee unproductive infighting.** Passionate debates are good for a team and generally get out information and ideas that might remain hidden. These should not be stifled. But do monitor the degree of heat and jump in early if people are headed toward personal attacks that are counterproductive. Steer the focus to the task or process issues that are causing conflict. If personal attacks occur or feelings are hurt, let things chill a bit. Then get both sides together to speak their minds. Remind them not to take things personally (e.g., "both sides presented good arguments and the team would not have made an informed decision if we hadn't viewed the issue from all sides"). Redirect the energy toward common goals and productive next steps.

Want to learn more? Take a deep dive...

The HR Specialist. (2012, February 29). Team dysfunction: Why it happens and how to fix it. *Business Management Daily*.

Zwilling, M. (2010, July 26). *How the best bosses foster team accountability*. Business Insider.

34

14. **The team losing its spark? Prioritize continuous learning and development.** Development is motivating and productive. Provide team members with challenging assignments that are in sync with their career aspirations and also accelerate the team's progress. Who can mentor whom to grow knowledge and expertise? Provide training or coaching to help the team collaborate better, like learning problem-solving or idea-generating techniques. Gain insights together with trips to see customers. Conduct periodic team assessments—even if things are going pretty well, the best like to keep getting better. Try making a list of 10 key factors of team effectiveness. Have each person indicate whether they think it's a strength, OK, or area for improvement. Tally up the scores, talk it through, and decide how to leverage strengths and address weaknesses.

15. **Strong headwinds? Ensure organizational support for teams.** No team is—nor should be—an island. Develop strong relationships with leaders, sponsors, stakeholders, and other groups for

Factor III: People
Cluster H: Optimizing diverse talent
Competency 34: *Builds effective* teams

34

necessary information, technology, resources, collaboration, and troubleshooting. Influence people to get *team* efforts rewarded more than individual achievements—through recognition and other incentives. On a broader scale, when attracting and promoting talent, go for those with a track record and motivation to excel in team settings.

Want to learn more? Take a deep dive...

Ashkenas, R. (2010, May 11). How to build an A-team from day one. *Harvard Business Review Blog Network*.

Wolski, C. (2013). Factors that promote effective teamwork. *Chron*.

Job assignments

- Be an active member of a virtual team, ensuring all members stay connected, motivated, and productive.

- Work on a team handling a high-stakes business issue, where you will need to share information and make sense of it quickly.

- Assemble a team of diverse people to accomplish a difficult task that requires collaboration and creative thinking. Agree on purpose, goals, roles, and a structure that best supports the team's work.

- Coach a team that is demonstrating lack of trust, split focus, or suboptimal performance.

- Lead a community project team outside the workplace, practicing teaming skills you want to improve. Gather feedback from members of the project team, then apply the feedback on the job.

34

34

Factor III: People
Cluster H: Optimizing diverse talent
Competency 34: *Builds effective* teams

Take time to reflect...

If you like to go it alone...

...then understand the benefits to be gained from pulling people together. Encourage mutual support. Build a sense of commitment and cooperation. Instill this in the team and become more comfortable with it yourself.

If your long-standing team works just fine the way it is...

...then ask yourself is it effective, or does it just feel good? Is it actually performing or just a comfortable place to be? A positive team atmosphere is only great when team results are also great.

If you think every group is automatically a team...

...then recognize that teams have to be formed and nurtured. It takes effort, commitment, alignment, and a great deal besides. Teamwork doesn't happen by accident; it happens by design.

" *When was ever honey made with one bee in a hive?* **"**

Thomas Hood – British humorist and poet

34

Factor III: People
Cluster H: Optimizing diverse talent
Competency 34: *Builds effective* teams

34

Learn more about *Builds effective* teams

Duke Corporate Education. (2005). *Building effective teams (leading from the center)*.Chicago, IL: Dearborn Trade Publishing.

Grimshaw, J., & Baron, G. (2010). *Leadership without excuses: How to create accountability and high performance (instead of just talking about it)*. New York, NY: McGraw-Hill.

Lencioni, P. (2005). *Overcoming the five dysfunctions of a team: A field guide for leaders, managers, and facilitators*. San Francisco, CA: Jossey-Bass.

Miller, B. C. (2004). *Quick team-building activities for busy managers: 50 Exercises that get results in just 15 minutes*. New York, NY: American Management Association.

Veeck, M., & Williams, P. (2005). *Fun is good: How to create joy and passion in your workplace and career*. Emmaus, PA: Rodale, Inc.

Deep dive learning resource links

Ashkenas, R. (2010, May 11). How to build an A-team from day one. *Harvard Business Review Blog Network*. Retrieved from http://blogs.hbr.org/2010/05/how-to-build-an-a-team-from-da/

Hall, H., & Thompson, B. (2012, March 30). The secret sauce of teamwork. *Harvard Business Review Blog Network*. Retrieved from http://blogs.hbr.org/2012/03/the-secret-sauce-of-teamwork/

Hall, J. (2013, January 29). 12 Simple things a leader can do to build a phenomenal team. *Forbes*. Retrieved from http://www.forbes.com/sites/johnhall/2013/01/29/team-building-leader/

The HR Specialist. (2012, February 29). Team dysfunction: Why it happens and how to fix it. *Business Management Daily*. Retrieved from http://www.businessmanagementdaily.com/29865/team-dysfunction-why-it-happens-and-how-to-fix-it#_

Llopis, G. (2013, September 23). 6 Ways to make your leadership and workplace fun again. *Forbes*. Retrieved from http://www.forbes.com/sites/glennllopis/2013/09/23/6-ways-to-make-your-leadership-and-workplace-fun-again/

Moran, G. (2013, March 13). 3 Ingredients for building effective teams. *Entrepreneur*. Retrieved from http://www.entrepreneur.com/article/226063

34

34

Factor III: People
Cluster H: Optimizing diverse talent
Competency 34: *Builds effective* teams

Wharton School. (2006, June 14). *Is your team too big? Too small? What's the right number?* Wharton School of the University of Pennsylvania. Retrieved from http://knowledge.wharton.upenn.edu/article/is-your-team-too-big-too-small-whats-the-right-number-2/

Wolski, C. (2013). Factors that promote effective teamwork. *Chron*. Retrieved from http://smallbusiness.chron.com/factors-promote-effective-teamwork-1932.html

Young Entrepreneurial Council. (2013, June 7). Five ways to build an effective team. *Forbes*. Retrieved from http://www.forbes.com/sites/theyec/2013/06/07/five-ways-to-build-an-effective-team/

Zwilling, M. (2010, July 26). *How the best bosses foster team accountability*. Business Insider. Retrieved from http://www.businessinsider.com/how-the-best-bosses-foster-team-accountability-2010-7

Recommended search terms

If you'd like to explore *Builds effective* teams further, try searching online using the following terms:

- Building effective teams.
- Building team capabilities.
- Overcoming team dysfunction.
- Team accountability.
- Team building.

34

 More help...

Go to www.kornferry.com/fyi-resources and link directly to the deep dive resources in this chapter. Visit the site often to see the additional resources that are uploaded on a regular basis.

35. Tech savvy

Anticipating and adopting innovations in business-building digital and technology applications.

What once seemed impossible is now commonplace, thanks to technology. Digital media can put entire libraries into the palm of a hand. Computers as eyewear and wrist watches are no longer part of science fiction but are a reality. 3-D printing is set to revolutionize manufacturing, medical, and other industries. New inventions and engineering marvels are emerging every day, in every part of the world. Whether people are thrilled or intimidated by the tech world, the simple truth remains: it's inescapable. Disruptive technologies are entering the market at breakneck speed. You and your organization can't be cutting edge without being out front on at least some technology and digital fronts. Being tech savvy is not just nice to have for success today. It's very much a must-have. It can enable people to do their jobs better and quicker. It can ensure that organizations stay ahead of the pack. Embrace what's new and confusing. Learn what's coming in the future. Marshal the power and promise of technology.

" *Technology is a useful servant but a dangerous master.* **"**

Christian Lous Lange – Norwegian historian and Nobel Peace Prize recipient

Tech savvy is in the **Thought** factor (I) in the Korn Ferry Leadership Architect™. It is part of Cluster A, **Understanding the business,** along with Business insight (5), Customer focus (11), and Financial acumen (17). You may find it helpful to also take a look at some of the tips included in those chapters to supplement your learning.

Skilled

Anticipates the impact of emerging technologies and makes adjustments.

Scans the environment for new technical skills, knowledge, or capabilities that can benefit business or personal performance.

Rejects low-impact or fad technologies.

Readily learns and adopts new technologies.

Less skilled

- Is inexperienced with key technology tools or too comfortable with existing applications to willingly adopt new technologies.

- Fails to seek out new or innovative technologies that could add business value.

Talented

- Continually scans the environment for technology breakthroughs.

- Experiments with a wide range of existing technologies while applying new and emerging options that can enhance organizational outcomes.

- Encourages others to learn and adopt new technologies.

35 Overused skill

- Focuses too much on learning new technology or exploring technology applications rather than applying it effectively to meet business goals.

- Overlooks when others may not have the same level of tech savvy.

Some possible causes of lower skill

Causes help explain *why* a person may have trouble with Tech savvy. When seeking to increase skill, it's helpful to consider how these might play out in certain situations. And remember that all of these can be addressed if you are motivated to do so.

- Inexperienced with technology.
- Anxious about learning something new.
- Lacks interest in technology.
- Time management; haven't gotten around to it.
- Stuck in the past with older technology.
- Skeptical about what technology can do.
- Prefers traditional approaches over new tools.

 Does it best

Three CEOs – Robert McDonald at Procter & Gamble, Massimo Bongiovanni with Coop Centrale in Italy, and Toshifumi Suzuki of 7-Eleven Japan. What do they all have in common? What differentiates them from the majority of their peers? They're all known for being tech savvy business leaders. They keep IT at the center of business strategy. They are fully involved in strategic IT decisions, something they expect their senior management team to follow suit on. They ensure that the partnership between business and IT is on an equal footing. And the result of their efforts? Superior rates of return. Research shows that organizations that spend more on IT and have higher levels of tech savvy can achieve 20% greater margins than the competition. Those spending the least on IT and with poor standards of tech savvy earn 32% lower margins than their competitors.[55]

35

Tips to develop Tech savvy

1. **Not sure where to start? Prioritize what will make the most difference.** There are millions of technologies out there, with more being created every day. Chances are that you will only be called upon to understand and use a small fraction of them. Tech savvy involves determining the right innovations for the benefit of the organization. It doesn't mean throwing out what already works well in favor of something unproven and novel. The innovations used at work tend to be both more useful than what existed before (think of e-mail versus fax machines) and easier to use (think of small, elegant tablet devices versus huge desktop computers). If you are overwhelmed by the sheer number of options technology provides, ask which ones will make your work easier, better, and more efficient. There's no victory in being the first adopter of a new technology that isn't compatible with what customers or suppliers use. Similarly, it's not a wise investment to plunge precious dollars into a technology that will likely be supplanted by something far better and cheaper in just six months.

2. **Technophobic? Shift your attitude about technology.** Many people find technology more daunting than exciting. It can be frustrating to be faced with a tool that you have no idea how to use. You may find yourself making basic mistakes or getting confused by some of the simpler features. Perhaps it feels like everyone gets it, but you. Don't let this deter you. View technology as a tool to help you be more successful, not as something that gets in the way, is irritating, or makes you feel inadequate. Remember, everyone starts off as a novice when learning new technologies. Focus on the benefits the technology provides, not the trouble it might initially cause you. Get comfortable being an amateur with new technology. Have confidence that one day you will master it.

3. **Learn best through others? Seek out formal and informal experts.** Desktop Support? IT Helpdesk? Executive Services? Tech support comes from many different directions in different organizations. But experts do not always have job titles that lead you to them. They're everywhere, in all sorts of roles. The people who love to discover by playing with technology. Those who just naturally gravitate to the digital solution for everything. Scope out your colleagues and others in the organization who always seem to have the latest tech gadget first. Learn what technology does for them. How does it save time? What doors does it open? What does it replace? What does it add to their day that's missing from yours? Most people good at something don't mind having a few apprentices around.

|

4. **Need a good reference? Get support online.** Most technologies—software or hardware—have online support. People who create technology want you to use it, so there are often many online tutorials, documents, and discussion boards to facilitate learning. Independent sites where users can read experts' thoughts on new technologies and hear about others' experiences in applying them. Online communities offer the flexibility to research on your own with a safety net of anonymity. Crowdsourcing is a user-driven way to show how digital innovations play out in practice.

5. **Prefer to learn in a formal setting? Take a class.** Your local college or trade school likely offers nighttime or weekend courses on various digital and technology topics. Look into community groups or professional organizations as well. Many of these provide courses in technologies that are essential to particular roles. Check into your organization's training resources. Ask around. What have people found useful? Where did they go to get help? For current technologies, choose courses that emphasize application and do-it-now tips. That provide hands-on experience and lots of practice with the technologies you need to excel in your role. Don't just focus on current state. Take classes or attend seminars on new digital innovations that are on the horizon. Don't just aim to learn about what's top of mind now. Find out what's coming and learn about it before you need to.

6. **Too busy? Find time to play.** Building tech savvy doesn't need to be an ordeal. It doesn't need to be a source of anxiety and stress. Instead, it's a skill that can grow naturally if you have fun with it. Consider another area that people frequently find very challenging: public speaking. It's not uncommon for people to build this capability, not through making formal speeches, but by joining improv comedy groups or amateur dramatics companies. Performing on stage can take away the fear and make them more accomplished public speakers. They lose their self-consciousness and gain confidence in front of audiences. Tech savvy can grow much the same way. Find things you enjoy about technology—video games, entertaining websites, cool new gadgets, music-making software. Spend time unwinding with them. When you have fun with technology, you train your brain to accept and adopt new tools.

35

Want to learn more? Take a deep dive...

Haggerty, N. (2012, July/August). On becoming an IT savvy CEO. *Ivey Business Journal*.

Nisen, M. (2012, November 14). *There's a big misconception about how companies become tech savvy*. Business Insider.

Smoot, N. (2013, March 28). 3 Free apps to make you a tech-savvy business professional. *The Huffington Post*.

7. **Want to stay ahead of the curve? Become an early adopter.** Tech savvy people don't simply adjust to change. They actively seek out the new, the improved, the cutting edge. Be an early tester of new and emerging technology. Don't wait until you have to hurry and catch up. Whenever a new technology surfaces, volunteer to learn and try it first. That gives you a head start and allows you to stumble a bit because you are the first. You may discover glitches. You might struggle with some aspects of it. Dealing with the risk that it might not work and facing the uncertainty that comes with being an amateur are all part of the process.

8. **Hoarding your knowledge? Advocate and educate.** Think about how you can use your growing tech savvy to support the aims of your organization. If you encounter a new application or innovation that could add value, encourage others to adopt it. Make the case for the benefits it can bring. Demonstrate the value it can add. Present the business case for purchasing it and deploying it widely. Teach others how to use it, and serve as the organization's go-to expert for the new technology.

9. **Facing skepticism about new technologies? Empathize with concerns about innovation.** People resist technology for a wide variety of reasons. Some don't want to learn new things. Others have had bad experiences in the past. A few may be wary of how much of modern life is influenced by the digital age. If you understand the source of both your own and other people's concerns, you will find it easier to address them. If you are implementing or advocating new technology, ensure that everyone has ample time to get comfortable with it. Acceptance of technology across a group seldom comes all at once. It's likely to happen gradually. Allow people to learn at their own pace. Recognize some may struggle with the change. Encourage fast learners to help teach those who take a little longer.

Want to learn more? Take a deep dive...

Davidson, E. (n.d.). The advantages of new technology for businesses. *Chron*.

HBS Working Knowledge. (2014, January 6). Technology re-emergence: Creating new value for old innovations. *Forbes*.

Sylva, J. (2012, August 17). Leverage technology for business transformation [Video file]. *Harvard Business Review Blog Network*.

10. **Out of touch? Stay on top of new communications technologies.** Technology has created a world that is far more interconnected than ever before. Social media has transformed the way people interact with their personal and career networks. Blogs have given people new forums to express their views and share their wisdom. New teleconferencing, instant messaging, and desktop video tools can enable real-time, face-to-face chats with team members across the globe. In our virtual world, distance is no excuse for falling out of touch. Stay current on collaboration technologies. Gartner Research (www.gartner.com) is a great resource to check out the latest technologies and how they apply to your business. Consider how you can use new technologies to build and strengthen relationships. Think about how you can keep dialogue flowing through new media. Scan the Internet to learn what others are saying about your field, organization, or industry. Make new connections via the Internet. Get to know people you'd never otherwise have a chance to meet. Build a presence on social/virtual platforms. If you rely only on a limited range of well-established communication tools, you may miss out on the discoveries, discussions, and insights that are happening online.

11. **Uncertain what the future holds? Stay in touch with experts and innovators.** Being tech savvy doesn't require you to be a computer genius or a brilliant inventor. However, it does mean being knowledgeable of what these innovators are doing today, and what impact emerging technologies might have on your business. Get familiar with the technology press. Read publications like *Fast Company* and *Wired*. Find out who the technology gurus and big thinkers are in your field. Follow them on social media. Learn what's coming and consider how you can capitalize on tomorrow's technologies. What's most relevant to your role? What is going to make a difference to the organization going forward?

35

12. **Confident about your technological edge? Stay attuned to disruptive innovations.** Technology brings change. These changes bring opportunity, but they can also cause upheaval. The internal combustion engine spelled doom for horse-drawn buggies. Digital cameras, now commonplace, created brand-new markets and competition. One CEO of a popular school picture company put it this way: "Suddenly every mom with a camera was the competition instead of the customer." The Internet has created markets, killed off markets, and transformed many others. Retail, publishing, music, and countless other industries face new challenges and opportunities. No organization can afford to ignore technology, since it has the power to make almost anything obsolete. Keep abreast of what new technologies are emerging, not just in your industry, but also in ones that are adjacent and distant. Talk with others about what implications these developments might have for your organization. Ensure your confidence doesn't become complacency.

Want to learn more? Take a deep dive...

Fitzgerald, M., Kruschwitz, N., Bonnet, D., & Welch, M. (2013). Embracing digital technology. *MIT Sloan Management Review*.

Krippendorff, K. (2011, May 26). The flow of technology adoption reverses. *Fast Company*.

McAfee, A. (2010, August 10). Can technology optimists and pessimists get in the same room? *Harvard Business Review Blog Network*.

Job assignments

- Offer to manage the process of identifying, selecting, purchasing a new technology for the organization.

- Serve on the group responsible for launching a new technology; become a resource to support others as they transition to new tools.

- Help the organization enhance or update its presence on digital channels (external/internal websites, social media, etc.).

- Initiate or join a group to study future innovations that may benefit the organization over the long-term.

- Perform an analysis of a tech launch that has gone poorly; investigate the underlying issues and make recommendations for how to make future launches more successful.

Take time to reflect...

If you're most comfortable with the technologies you already know...

> ...then embrace the discomfort of what you don't know. Welcome the disruption that a new technology can bring. Go through the pain for the gain.

If you adopt ideas late and tend to hang back...

> ...then aim to become a pioneer. Blaze the trail with a new technology and recruit others along the way. Build a reputation for being first to go live with new technology.

If you can't imagine how technology is going to evolve...

> ...then realize that if you think to the future, you'll be prepared when it arrives. Today's science fiction is tomorrow's competitive advantage. Study the horizon. Learn what's coming.

" *Television won't last. It's a flash in the pan.* **"**

Mary Somerville – Pioneer of radio broadcasting

35

Learn more about Tech savvy

Beekman, G., & Beekman, B. (2011). *Tomorrow's technology and you* (10th ed.). Upper Saddle River, NJ: Prentice Hall.

Burgelman, R. A., Christensen, C. M., & Wheelwright, S. C. (2008). *Strategic management of technology and innovation*. New York, NY: McGraw-Hill.

Christensen, C. M. (1997). *The innovator's dilemma: When new technologies cause great firms to fail (Management of innovation and change)*. Boston, MA: Harvard Business Review Press.

Mueller-Eberstein, M. (2010). *Agility: Competing and winning in a tech-savvy marketplace*. Hoboken, NJ: John Wiley & Sons, Inc.

Pfleging, B., & Zetlin, M. (2006). *The geek gap: Why business and technology professionals don't understand each other and why they need each other to survive*. Amherst, NY: Prometheus Books.

 ## Deep dive learning resource links

Davidson, E. (n.d.). The advantages of new technology for businesses. *Chron*. Retrieved from http://smallbusiness.chron.com/advantages-new-technology-businesses-4047.html

Fitzgerald, M., Kruschwitz, N., Bonnet, D., & Welch, M. (2013). Embracing digital technology. *MIT Sloan Management Review*. Retrieved from http://sloanreview.mit.edu/projects/embracing-digital-technology/

Haggerty, N. (2012, July/August). On becoming an IT savvy CEO. *Ivey Business Journal*. Retrieved from http://iveybusinessjournal.com/topics/leadership/on-becoming-an-it-savvy-ceo

HBS Working Knowledge. (2014, January 6). Technology re-emergence: Creating new value for old innovations. *Forbes*. Retrieved from http://www.forbes.com/sites/hbsworkingknowledge/2014/01/06/technology-re-emergence-creating-new-value-for-old-innovations/

Krippendorff, K. (2011, May 26). The flow of technology adoption reverses. *Fast Company*. Retrieved from http://www.fastcompany.com/1755281/flow-technology-adoption-reverses

McAfee, A. (2010, August 10). Can technology optimists and pessimists get in the same room? *Harvard Business Review Blog Network*. Retrieved from http://blogs.hbr.org/2010/08/ive-been-hankering-to-hang/

424 |

Nisen, M. (2012, November 14). *There's a big misconception about how companies become tech savvy*. Business Insider. Retrieved from http://www.businessinsider.com/theres-a-big-misconception-about-how-companies-become-tech-savvy-2012-11

Smoot, N. (2013, March 28). 3 Free apps to make you a tech-savvy business professional. *The Huffington Post*. Retrieved from http://www.huffingtonpost.com/nick-smoot/3-free-apps-to-make-you_b_2973243.html

Sylva, J. (2012, August 17). Leverage technology for business transformation [Video file]. *Harvard Business Review Blog Network*. Retrieved from http://blogs.hbr.org/2012/08/leverage-technology-for-busine/

Recommended search terms

If you'd like to explore Tech savvy further, try searching online using the following terms:

- Adopting new technology in business.
- Building technical savvy.
- Learning to use new technology in business.
- Overcoming fear/resistance of new technology.
- Tech savvy business.

 More help...

Go to www.kornferry.com/fyi-resources and link directly to the deep dive resources in this chapter. Visit the site often to see the additional resources that are uploaded on a regular basis.

35

36. *Instills* trust

Gaining the confidence and trust of others through honesty, integrity, and authenticity.

Trust lies at the heart of effective relationships. Whether in or out of the workplace, trust generates feelings of goodwill. It enables successful collaboration and more productive outcomes. When there's trust, things go more smoothly. People pull together, relying on each other to do their part. They're better able to work through conflicts and tough times. Without trust, there are unnecessary speed bumps, heightened doubt, dips in performance. Being trustworthy is about being honest and authentic. It's about acting with integrity. Showing consistency. Being credible. If you're trusted, it means others can count on you to deliver and to look after their highest interests. Trust is based on reciprocity—you need to give it to get it.

" *No legacy is so rich as honesty.* "

William Shakespeare – English playwright and poet

***Instills* trust** is in the **Self** factor (IV) in the Korn Ferry Leadership Architect™. It is part of Cluster J, **Being authentic,** along with Courage (10). You may find it helpful to also take a look at some of the tips included in that chapter to supplement your learning.

Skilled

Follows through on commitments.

Is seen as direct and truthful.

Keeps confidences.

Practices what he/she preaches.

Shows consistency between words and actions.

Less skilled

- Lacks consistent follow-through on commitments.
- Betrays confidences and covers up mistakes.
- Misrepresents facts for personal gain.
- Has trouble keeping confidences.
- Makes promises but doesn't always keep them.

Talented

- Gains the confidence and trust of others easily.
- Honors commitments and keeps confidences.
- Expresses self in a credible and transparent manner.
- Models high standards of honesty and integrity.

Overused skill

- May push openness and honesty to the point of being disruptive.
- May come across as overly judgmental of those not quite as overtly authentic.

36

Some possible causes of lower skill

Causes help explain *why* a person may have trouble with *Instills* trust. When seeking to increase skill, it's helpful to consider how these might play out in certain situations. And remember that all of these can be addressed if you are motivated to do so.

- Lacks follow-through.
- Guarded; holds back.
- Won't admit mistakes.
- Breaks confidentiality.
- Overpromises.
- Doesn't "walk the talk."
- Puts self-interests first.
- Avoids sharing information.
- Bends the rules.
- Unclear about own values.

· ·

Brain booster

Neurochemistry can shed some light on how to build trust and foster a sense of team, which can lead to greater productivity. There are some basic sources of stress that decrease trust, undermine relationships, and reduce productivity:

- Being evaluated by others in a work setting.
- Being evaluated by others in a social setting.
- Rejection.
- Unfairness.
- Dealing with ambiguity and uncertainty.
- Delivering results under pressure.

Obviously, many of these are an inherent part of living and working in the 21st century. While providing feedback to help people grow can build trust, constantly scrutinizing people's work can erode it. Find the right balance. If you can reduce these stress triggers among your team members, you will be able to reduce cortisol levels, have happier, healthier, more relaxed and more productive team members. Encourage team members with positive comments. Build a sense of community and cohesion

36

so that no one feels like an outsider. Be fair. Help people find answers to questions that are preventing them from getting their work done. And, when you don't have the answers, help team members define what they do have control over, what choices they can make. Finally, in a time of doing more with less, be compassionate about how much you are expecting and ask yourself how you can do a better job of balancing how realistic and ambitious your expectations are.[56, 57]

Tips to develop *Instills* trust

1. **Failing to deliver? Be more reliable.** People rely on each other to follow through on their commitments. To meet deadlines. To contribute their fair share. The research of Mishra and Mishra shows that reliability is one of the quickest ways you can demonstrate trust. You can show it during your first meeting with someone by being on time. By returning calls. By passing on information you promised to send. By giving people a "heads up" if circumstances have changed or trouble is brewing. Failing to do these things damages relationships and decreases productivity. If following through isn't your strength, identify the main reasons and address them. If you tend to forget, write things down or set up alerts on your smartphone. If you're often running behind, work on better time management. At the beginning and end of each day, review the commitments you've made and decide when you'll follow through.

2. **Trouble with consistency? Align your words and actions.** Probably nothing chills trust more than a person saying one thing and doing something else. People want consistency. You can deliver an inspiring message with convincing calls-to-action. But, if the next day you do something quite contrary, people may no longer buy it. Worse yet, they may question your credibility. Having integrity means representing yourself accurately. Knowing who you are. What you believe. And practicing what you preach regardless of the setting. If you're not sure if there's a gap between your words and deeds, ask someone you trust to give you feedback. Then you can begin to close any gaps.

3. **Withholding too much? Share more openly.** Do you often keep things to yourself? Tend to hold back information or opinions? Err on the side of non-disclosure? It may not be your intention, but people around you may begin to wonder. Wonder what you're up to, what your agenda is, whether you're hoping to gain an advantage over them. Why aren't you sharing more openly? It may be that you have a reserved nature or prefer privacy. Or that you don't want to

lose control or appear less authoritative. Regardless of the reasons, it may be time to make some adjustments. Organizations function on the flow of information. Greater transparency is expected at all levels, in and outside the firm. So find out what people want and need to know and begin to comply. Sending information on relevant topics is a start. Better still, talk or meet with people for open, two-way exchanges. Practice showing and telling it like it is.

4. **Trying too hard to impress? Don't exaggerate or overpromise.** Does your enthusiasm to make the sale or win approval cause you to commit to too many things? Do you stretch the truth? Say "yes" to a stakeholder or customer request by default? The customer you gain by overpromising is the customer you may lose forever when they find out you can't deliver. Word spreads quickly. When doubts are raised, customers go on guard—not sure they'll believe the next thing you say, ready to shift their loyalty somewhere else. Reflect a bit on when and where you tend to exaggerate. Is it under most circumstances or when the pressure is particularly intense? Were you rewarded for it in another setting? Is it serving you well now? Observe your patterns and begin adjusting your approach. Be authentic—we're in an era when truth carries greater weight than fiction. Don't promise something unless you can deliver. If you don't know for sure, say, "I'll look into it and get back with you when I do."

5. **Unable to meet expectations? Grow your capability.** If someone isn't trusted, it's not necessarily about a lack of honesty or integrity. It might be that people lack confidence in your ability to perform your job well. To meet or exceed requirements. To execute at the top of your game. As a result, they probably feel on edge, especially if their success depends on your contribution. If more than one colleague is checking up on you, questioning your judgment or skill, it may be a wake-up call. Conduct an inventory of your strengths and weaknesses. Gather feedback from a variety of people and work to gain skill where you're not measuring up.

Want to learn more? Take a deep dive...

Graybill, M. (2013, August 8). *Leadership fundamentals: Transparency and trust*. About Leaders.

Llopis, G. (2012, September 10). 5 Powerful things happen when a leader is transparent. *Forbes*.

Scott, S. (2011, June 30). TEDxOverlake – Susan Scott – The case for radical transparency [YouTube]. TED

36

6. **Difficulty admitting mistakes? Take responsibility.** Everyone makes mistakes. It's how you deal with them that determines whether or not people view you as trustworthy. History is full of examples where the cover-up of a mistake does more damage than the original misstep. Resist any temptation to hide it, deny it, play dumb, or blame someone else. Apologize with sincerity. Admit when you were wrong as soon as you can, informing everyone who may be affected. Offer to help with workarounds or potential repercussions. Share what you learned and what steps you'll take to prevent it from happening again. When someone's feelings have been hurt, trust is particularly fragile, so take time to talk things through. It's never too late to repair a damaged relationship. Come to terms with your part in the situation. Take steps to rectify things. Finally, move on. Dwelling on past mistakes distracts you from doing your best now.

7. **Tempted to spread someone else's news? Maintain confidentiality.** Some people are viewed as untrustworthy because they've shared information intended to be kept confidential. Revisit what keeping a confidence means. Some guidelines: Ask up front, "Is this to be kept confidential?" "Is this mine to share?" Don't let social media norms sway you—always keep personal information someone shares to yourself. Read and follow your organization's guiding principles. If someone shares legal or ethical breaches, let them know you can't promise confidentiality on those topics. If you learn information that might compromise people's safety, there is also no guarantee of confidentiality. In most cases, apply the golden rule—would you want someone to pass it on if you had shared it? If you're not sure, ask. It doesn't take many slip-ups before people say you can't be trusted with confidential information. Err on the side of discretion.

8. **Lacking an ethical compass? Take corrective action.** People rarely start their careers planning to be unethical. More often it comes about slowly. Occasionally taking home office supplies, fudging numbers on an expense report. It might spread—condoning unfair treatment of employees, using lower quality parts that could jeopardize product safety, keeping silent about corruption or fraud. There are countless ways to rationalize unethical choices: *Everyone else is doing it. Nobody will find out. My boss told me to. It's not exactly illegal. The end justifies the means. We didn't have time to check. It won't hurt anybody.* Review and comply with the ethical codes provided by your organization and profession. But don't stop there—identify your own code of conduct. What values will you choose to uphold? What lines will you refuse to cross? Work with leaders to incorporate practices to detect and report missteps. Talk about how to handle "gray zones," where there are no easy answers.

How to do what is right, even if it's unpopular. How to surface conflicts of interest. What may seem minor at the time can ripple out, harming the reputations of both individuals and organizations.

Want to learn more? Take a deep dive...

Bailey, S. (2013, May 15). Business leaders beware: Ethical drift makes standards slip. *Forbes*.

Guest, G. (2013, May 1). *Workplace ethics rub off on employees.* Futurity.org.

Pastin, M. (2013, November 11). The different ways people handle ethical issues in the workplace. *Bloomberg Businessweek*.

---

9. **Perceived to be self-centered? Put the team or organization first.** Do others sense you care more about your own agenda than the larger group's? If so, they may doubt whether you'll operate in their best interests. Shuffle and prioritize the team. Talk about what "we" have accomplished—not "I" or "me." Recognize others' contributions and spread credit where it's due. Research shows you can also build trust through self-sacrifice. This means doing things that postpone your own interests, privileges, or rewards for the benefit of the group. Like working overtime with the team to finish a task. Giving up your weekend or holiday to meet a deadline. If you're a leader with status, it could mean relinquishing your large office when space is tight. Or taking a pay cut during challenging times. Research shows that trust built through self-sacrifice can have a long-term positive impact.

10. **Lack of trust between groups? Build cross-boundary bridges.** Sometimes trust is high for people *within* a team or department, but not *between* groups or functions. Maybe there's a long history of "us vs. them." Maybe something recent has caused friction. Maybe you stereotype each other. Or just don't know each other. To better coordinate efforts and leverage synergies, foster cross-boundary trust. Find out what's causing any past or current problems. If your team hasn't delivered the goods, decide how you'll fix things to build credibility. If the others have fallen short, clarify what's needed going forward. In all cases, look for ways to connect. Identify common objectives and values. Share resources, expertise, information. Collaborate to solve problems and drive new initiatives. Incorporate getting-to-know-you time in neutral settings. Make use of what the authors of *Boundary Spanning Leadership* call "attractor spaces"— informal community spots like libraries or cafés that encourage

36

relationships to form spontaneously. Become a self-appointed bridge-builder, forging intergroup trust.

11. **Sense trust may be eroding? Pay attention to warning signs.** Keep alert to signs that trust may be breaking down in your department or team. Are people talking about one another behind their backs? Are they withholding information or resources? Are they undermining each other to make themselves look good? Stifling authentic feelings about issues? Do some members cast blame or criticism unfairly? Do people feel compelled to cover their tracks? Do decisions get made during sidebar conversations or in cliques? Trust takes a long time to build and can deteriorate rather quickly. Don't just wait and see what happens. Directly confront warning signs with the group. If things are especially tense, ask a facilitator or coach to help the group get back on track through a series of candid conversations.

12. **Reluctant to bring your heart to work? Show genuine concern for people's needs.** Many think the workplace should be all about business. That compassion doesn't belong. In reality, a culture of caring is good for business—it strengthens trust and collaboration. Showing you care goes beyond remembering someone's birthday. For a trust-based relationship to flourish, there needs to be mutual concern for what matters to the other person. Listen closely to discover what that is. Even five minutes of focused, quality time can go a long way. Involve people in decisions that are important to them. Ask what you can do to help them. Follow up. When times are tough, be even more accessible, providing empathy and support.

Want to learn more? Take a deep dive...

Bryant, A. (2011, July 30). The trust that makes a team click. *The New York Times*.

Clark, D. (2012, March 28). Five ways to become a better team player. *Forbes*.

Voortman, P. (2013, May 23). Trust in organisations: Pauline Voortman at TEDxRadboudU 2013 [YouTube]. TED.

36

Job assignments

• Make peace with a colleague or customer you've disappointed in the past, apologizing for any mistakes and taking steps to renew trust.

- Mediate a conflict between two people or groups, where you'll need to gain the trust of both parties and facilitate an honest discussion leading toward resolution.

- Be a liaison or spokesperson for your organization in the local community, requiring you to instill trust while addressing the concerns they have related to your company's practices.

- Lead a team or group that is experiencing resistance due to a change that was imposed upon them (e.g., new structure, downsizing); practice restoring trust between the group and management.

- Teach a leadership or orientation course/webinar on your organization's code of ethics, including discussion on how to show integrity and handle challenging dilemmas.

Take time to reflect...

If you're concerned that others don't have full trust in you...

...then find out why and take clear action to turn things around. Do the right thing—always. Be patient. Trust cannot be claimed; it needs to be earned.

If you talk a good story but don't follow through...

...then be aware that people will soon lose confidence if they hear the words but don't see the action. Demonstrate your commitment right through to the end result.

If you sense that gossip is running rampant...

...then understand that allowing negative "hearsay" can lead to a culture of distrust. Address rumors with speed and honesty. Focus on the underlying reasons.

" *Always do right.*
This will gratify some people
and astonish the rest. **"**

Mark Twain – American writer, humorist, and lecturer

36

Learn more about *Instills* trust

Boyatzis, R. E., Smith, M., & Blaize, N. (2006). Developing sustainable leaders through coaching and compassion. *Academy of Management Learning & Education, 5*(1), 8-24.

Covey, S. M. R., & Merrill, R. R. (2006). *The speed of trust: The one thing that changes everything.* New York, NY: Free Press.

Dobrin, A. (2002). *Ethics for everyone: How to increase your moral intelligence.* New York, NY: John Wiley & Sons.

Galford, R. M., & Siebold Drapeau, A. (2002). *The trusted leader: Bringing out the best in your people and your company.* New York, NY: Free Press.

Reina, D. S., & Reina, M. L. (2010). *Rebuilding trust in the workplace: Seven steps to renew confidence, commitment, and energy.* San Francisco, CA: Berrett-Koehler.

Rock, D. (2009). *Your brain at work: Strategies for overcoming distraction, regaining focus, and working smarter all day long.* New York, NY: HarperCollins Publishers.

Solomon, R. C., & Flores, F. (2001). *Building trust: In business, politics, relationships, and life.* New York, NY: Oxford University Press.

Tracy, D., & Morin, W. J. (2001). *Truth, trust, and the bottom line.* Chicago, IL: Dearborn Trade.

Deep dive learning resource links

Bailey, S. (2013, May 15). Business leaders beware: Ethical drift makes standards slip. *Forbes.* Retrieved from http://www.forbes.com/sites/sebastianbailey/2013/05/15/business-leaders-beware-ethical-drift-makes-standards-slip/

Bryant, A. (2011, July 30). The trust that makes a team click. *The New York Times.* Retrieved from http://www.nytimes.com/2011/07/31/business/siemens-ceo-on-building-trust-and-teamwork.html?pagewanted=all&_r=0

Clark, D. (2012, March 28). Five ways to become a better team player. *Forbes.* Retrieved from http://www.forbes.com/sites/dorieclark/2012/03/28/five-ways-to-become-a-better-team-player/

Graybill, M. (2013, August 8). *Leadership fundamentals: Transparency and trust.* About Leaders. Retrieved from http://www.aboutleaders.com/leadership-fundamentals-transparency-and-trust/

Guest, G. (2013, May 1). *Workplace ethics rub off on employees.* Futurity.org. Retrieved from http://www.futurity.org/workplace-ethics-rub-off-on-employees/

Llopis, G. (2012, September 10). 5 Powerful things happen when a leader is transparent. *Forbes.* Retrieved from http://www.forbes.com/sites/glennllopis/2012/09/10/5-powerful-things-happen-when-a-leader-is-transparent/

Pastin, M. (2013, November 11). The different ways people handle ethical issues in the workplace. *Bloomberg Businessweek.* Retrieved from http://www.businessweek.com/articles/2013-11-11/the-different-ways-people-handle-ethical-issues-in-the-workplace

Scott, S. (2011, June 30). TEDxOverlake – Susan Scott – The case for radical transparency [YouTube]. TED. Retrieved from https://www.youtube.com/watch?v=oVKaXUB4LTg

Voortman, P. (2013, May 23). Trust in organisations: Pauline Voortman at TEDxRadboudU 2013 [YouTube]. TED. Retrieved from https://www.youtube.com/watch?v=Z-HY2mdm_JI

Recommended search terms

If you'd like to explore *Instills* trust further, try searching online using the following terms:

- Building trust in the workplace.
- Business ethics.
- Effective business communication.
- Personal integrity in business.
- Reliable employee performance.
- Transparent leadership.

 More help...

Go to www.kornferry.com/fyi-resources and link directly to the deep dive resources in this chapter. Visit the site often to see the additional resources that are uploaded on a regular basis.

36

37. *Drives* vision and purpose

Painting a compelling picture of the vision and strategy that motivates others to action.

When faced with ongoing uncertainty and change, people look for something they can hold on to. Believe in. Aspire toward. They want to know that what they do matters. That they're contributing to something worthwhile. Larger than themselves. A sound purpose and inspiring vision—whether for an organization, team, project, or initiative—fuel commitment and unify efforts. People are more engaged when they understand how what they do connects to the big picture. They make better decisions when they know where they're headed. They're more resilient when setbacks occur, knowing they're on the right path. To influence others to pursue a meaningful direction, create a vision of the future you want to achieve together. A future that captivates the group's imagination. If that vision isn't inspiring to you on a personal level, it won't light any fires in others either. If you are passionate about the purpose, about closing the gap between current reality and the future you desire, you still need to find a way to ignite that passion in others. Shape and deliver a message that appeals to the core interests and values of your audience. But words alone aren't enough. You need to demonstrate your commitment to the purpose and vision you espouse. This will inspire others to show their commitment as well.

> **"** If one does not know to which port one is sailing, no wind is favorable. **"**
>
> Seneca – Roman philosopher and statesman

Drives **vision and purpose** is in the **People** factor (III) in the Korn Ferry Leadership Architect™. It is part of Cluster I, **Influencing people,** along with Communicates effectively (7), *Drives* engagement (16), Organizational savvy (23), and Persuades (24). You may find it helpful to also take a look at some of the tips included in those chapters to supplement your learning.

Skilled

Talks about future possibilities in a positive way.

Creates milestones and symbols to rally support behind the vision.

Articulates the vision in a way everyone can relate to.

Creates organization-wide energy and optimism for the future.

Shows personal commitment to the vision.

Less skilled

- Fails to personally connect with the organization's vision.
- Has difficulty describing the vision in a compelling way.
- Can't simplify enough to help people understand complex strategy.
- Struggles to energize and build excitement in others.

Talented

- Articulates a compelling, inspired, and relatable vision.
- Communicates the vision with a sense of purpose about the future.
- Makes the vision sharable by everyone.
- Instills and sustains organization-wide energy for what is possible.

Overused skill

- May lack follow-through to execute the vision.
- Communicates at a high level too often.
- May lack patience when others don't share the same vision and sense of purpose.

Some possible causes of lower skill

Causes help explain *why* a person may have trouble with *Drives* vision and purpose. When seeking to increase skill, it's helpful to consider how these might play out in certain situations. And remember that all of these can be addressed if you are motivated to do so.

- Not possibility oriented.
- Resists change.
- Doesn't relate well with others.
- Lacks ambition.
- Ineffective communicator.
- Stuck in the past.
- Doesn't show emotion or passion.
- Lacks authenticity.
- Not focused or committed.

 Does it best

Half a century ago, Lee Kuan Yew, former Singaporean prime minister, often referred to as the father of modern Singapore, had a vision for what was possible in his country. Lee's "big idea" was that, in order for Singapore to realize its potential, the citizens would first need a prosperous livelihood and have a sense of nationalism. One thing Lee did immediately was to compel citizens to adopt English as their working language. This helped forge a unified society and laid the foundation to unite the island's many different ethnic groups. Lee wanted to instill in his fellow Singaporeans a sense that they all shared a future, in his words, that "if Singapore goes down everyone goes down."

Through Lee's vision, Singapore has been transformed from a fishing village with a port to an intellectual and technical center of the region. Due in large part to his leadership, per capita income has grown from about US$400 a year to close to US$40,000. What was a medium-sized city has become a significant international and economic player.[58, 59]

Tips to develop *Drives* vision and purpose

1. **Individuals unclear about how they fit in? Connect work to the big picture.** Understanding the vision is important for people in every role. Draw the link between your goals, projects, and deliverables and the organization's destination. Initiate conversations with peers and leaders. Get clear about how what you do moves the organization toward its vision. Get clear about how your efforts activate the strategy directly or indirectly. Get clear about how the vision fits into the larger context of your industry and society. Articulate why this matters to you personally and professionally—purpose and passion fuel individual and group performance. Discuss upcoming initiatives that don't fully align with the vision. What adjustments need to be made? Outline the specific actions you'll take to remove obstacles and drive the vision forward.

2. **Missing a sense of purpose? Inquire about peak experiences.** An effective way to uncover or revive a sense of purpose in a group or organization is through a process originally developed by David Cooperrider called "Appreciative Inquiry." It involves asking about the best of what already exists and finding ways to build upon that. Through surveys or dialogue, ask people to (1) Reflect on times that stand out as being a high point in their work with the organization or team—when they felt the most alive, effective, or really proud of their involvement. (2) Identify three things they appreciate about the organization/team that they'd like to maintain going forward. (3) Describe what they want the organization/team to look like in the future. Then gather the varied responses and cluster them around key themes. Identify the core values and shared sense of purpose. Talk about how to leverage, communicate, and reinforce these throughout the organization/team.

3. **Confusion about what's critical? Craft a clear mission statement.** A mission statement is a short description of the purpose of an organization, team, or individual. It answers the fundamental questions: Why do we exist? How do we add value? Effective purpose statements are clear and concise. They signal what's mission critical. They help people decide how to allocate time, energy, and resources. They often follow a simple framework, e.g., "Our mission is to _____ for _____ so that _____." For example, "Our mission is to provide nutritious, delicious snacks for active families so that health and taste aren't compromised when people are on the go." Or "Our team's purpose is to deliver zero-defect parts so that customers receive the highest standards in safety and reliability." The tone of your mission should reflect your unique identity, culture, or style.

Above all, the statement should be meaningful for those who adopt it. Write a draft, then ask others for suggestions on how to improve it.

4. **Vision too long or complex? Keep it simple.** A vision is what you or the organization aim to become in the future. Your destination. The best visions are concise, clear, and compelling. Try to articulate your vision in no more than two to three minutes. Even shorter sound bites work well for quick conversations. The vision should make sense rationally and draw people in emotionally. It should be clear enough that people know when it's reached. It should be compelling enough that people mobilize to make it happen. Vision is about where you are going—not about how you will get there. Whet people's appetite with your vision so they understand it. Then ask them to help you realize it.

Want to learn more? Take a deep dive...

Baskin, E. (2014, January 6). *To align employees, keep the vision simple – and unique to your culture*. Good Company.

Frost, S. (n.d.). How to align employees with company goals. *Chron*.

Mind Tools. (n.d.). *Appreciative inquiry: Solving problems by looking at what's going right*. Mind Tools.

Tabaka, M. (2010, August 24). 3 Steps to make your vision work for you. *Inc*.

5. **Not connecting well with people? Tailor the message to match the audience.** You may have a clear picture of the future in your own mind, but it won't do you any good unless you can paint that picture for others. A one-size-fits-all delivery usually isn't the answer. While keeping the essence of the message intact, adjust your language and style to suit particular groups. What's their background? How much do they know about the topic? What would motivate them to embrace the vision? Object to it? How might someone from finance relate to it differently than someone from IT or marketing? A new hire vs. a board member? Your own team vs. an external party? Is the setting formal or informal? When in doubt, skip the jargon and use language people easily understand. Your approach should be determined by the other person or group, not by your own preferences.

37

6. **Your words falling flat? Communicate with charisma.** You may have been told that you aren't inspiring enough. That your words don't captivate. That you should show more charisma. Some think you need to be born with charisma—that it cannot be developed. Researchers at the University of Lausanne have found that it can. They've identified twelve key tactics that when practiced and adopted, help listeners remember and relate to a message. They also cause speakers to be viewed as more credible and trustworthy leaders. Nine of the twelve are verbal and three are non-verbal. They are: (1) Metaphors and analogies. (2) Stories and anecdotes. (3) Contrasts (e.g., "it's not about what you'll get, but about what you can give"). (4) Rhetorical questions. (5) Three-part lists. (6) Expressions of conviction and integrity. (7) Showing empathy. (8) High goals. (9) Conveying confidence that goals can be attained. (10) Animated voice. (11) Facial expressions. (12) Gestures. The tactics help create emotional connections whether used with a group or in one-to-one conversations. (*See* Antonakis, Fenley, and Liechti, 2012.)

7. **Not appearing consistent? Align your words and actions.** Probably nothing chills trust more than a person saying one thing and doing something else. You can deliver an inspiring vision. Speak eloquently of future possibilities. But if the next day you do something that undermines your words, people may no longer buy it. They may question your vision and your credibility. Show integrity by representing yourself accurately. Be authentic about who you are. What you believe. And practice what you preach, regardless of the setting. If you're not sure if there's a gap between your words and deeds, ask someone you trust to give you feedback. Then you can begin to close any gaps.

8. **Meeting resistance? Be prepared for skeptics.** There will always be those who don't buy your vision. They may be private about it or come at you in public. Be prepared to answer the 10 most likely questions/critiques that may surface. "Is this realistic? Our customers won't go for it. Where will we get the resources?" Write out your answers and rehearse how you'll respond. Listen patiently to people's concerns—there may have been a time when you weren't convinced this was the way to go either. They may simply want to protect the organization's best interests. Approach resistance as a positive thing. If you handle questions openly, others will feel free to voice their concerns. It's better to have the issues on the table than to have them fester below the surface. Empathize with people. If more dialogue is needed to get on the same page, welcome it. Contrary opinions may ultimately strengthen the vision. If resistance becomes

entrenched and people won't collaborate, reinforce why the vision has merit and the timing is now. Occasionally, you may have to pull someone aside and say, "I understand your concerns, but we're moving on. Are you with us or not?"

Want to learn more? Take a deep dive...

Chappelow, C. (2012, September 5). 5 Rules for making your vision stick. *Fast Company*.

Genard, G. (2012, March 25). *4 Easy ways to become a more charismatic speaker*. Public Speaking International.

Harrison, C. (2007, December). *Who's your audience? Ways to win your audience through inclusion*. Toastmasters International.

Kaipa, P. (2012, July 2). Recover your credibility. *Harvard Business Review Blog Network*.

---

9. **Team losing its forward momentum? Envision team success.** To help team members embrace new possibilities, engage them in a visioning exercise. Ask the team to picture completing its work and successfully reaching its goals. What does the future state look like? How do customers/stakeholders feel? What actions did they take? What did the team do to be successful? What did it avoid doing that could have been a barrier? What were the tangible and intangible rewards of working together to realize the vision? Then discuss and log what the team specifically wants to start, stop, and continue doing to be more effective. Identify some quick wins you can achieve to build momentum. Come up with an image, symbol, or slogan that inspires the team and can serve as a reminder. Monitor your progress and hold each other accountable for achieving your shared vision.

10. **Want to rally people around an opportunity? Add urgency.** Change expert John Kotter advocates showing a high degree of "strategic fitness" when it's vital to jump on opportunities quickly. Strategic fitness means being able to act faster, more nimbly, more creatively to what's new. A well-crafted vision can accelerate your efforts. It can create a sense of urgency around a high-stakes opportunity. Get people excited about what's possible. In the vision, vividly portray what success looks like. Include a time frame that's ambitious yet attainable. Then encourage people to step up and participate. Recognize those who galvanize others to get involved. Notice how people embrace the vision and make it their own. Socialize

catchphrases that go viral. Keep the urgency going. Remove barriers. Communicate and celebrate wins from the start.

11. **Experiencing roadblocks? Show optimism and persevere.** Your vision may not materialize at the pace you want. It may be sidetracked by problems or unforeseen events. The destination may no longer seem feasible. But doom and gloom forecasts do little to rouse energy needed to achieve a vision. So make a conscious effort to address difficulties without letting them drag you down. Talk about what you've learned from setbacks. Use delays as opportunities to regroup and reinvigorate. Then get back to work. According to the research of Angela Duckworth, showing "grit"—sustained interest and effort toward long-term goals—is a primary predictor of success. Grit surpassed intelligence and talent as key for achievement in a wide variety of contexts—business, the military, education. Work hard to make your *vision* a reality.

12. **Vision fading? Keep it in focus.** Given all the things that compete for attention, even a compelling vision may fade into the background. Make sure it stays at the forefront. Reinforce it repeatedly. Refer to it in meetings, updates, videos, conversations. Create a memorable symbol, slogan, or image of the vision that makes the cause come alive. Something that captures the imagination. Conjures up exciting possibilities. Set up a friendly competition or get others involved in creating it so more people are invested. Use visual scorecards—such as dashboards or thermometers—to show progress toward realizing the vision. Regularly share stories that illustrate progress. Reward those who move the needle in the desired direction.

Want to learn more? Take a deep dive...

Barón, M. (2013, August 28). *Top tips for creating a clear vision for your business*. Small Business UK.

Kotter, J. (2011, April 27). The biggest mistake I see: Strategy first, urgency second. *Forbes*.

Moss Kanter, R. (2012, October 23). 12 Guidelines for deciding when to persist, when to quit. *Harvard Business Review Blog Network*.

Spiro, J. (2010, August 30). How to get employees excited about your business vision. *Inc.*

Job assignments

- Be a change agent for a new process, product, or service. Create a symbol for the change and champion it through to implementation.

- Assist a floundering team in developing a clear sense of purpose and a compelling vision for the future.

- Take a strategic assignment that involves charting new ground and communicating the vision to a critical audience.

- Prepare and present a strategic proposal to senior leaders that involves a change in direction and a request for sponsorship and resources.

- Lead or be a team member on a start-up that requires creating a team charter to unify, focus, and inspire the team.

Take time to reflect...

If you see that people are not tracking with your message or with the strategy overall...

> ...then emphasize the importance of being as one. Bring into focus the purpose that everyone has in common. The goals you all share. The customers you all serve. The future you are trying to create.

If you sense that excitement about the strategy is losing steam...

> ...then relight the fire. Bring the mission to life. Create milestones for people to rally around. Celebrate successes along the way. Build enthusiasm for goals that everyone buys into.

If you feel people don't see the importance of what they do...

> ....then keep the vision front and center. Make it real. Show them the difference their contribution makes. Let them see how significant their role is in the grand scheme of the organization.

"Good business leaders create a vision,
articulate the vision, passionately own the vision, and relentlessly
drive it to completion. **"**

Jack Welch – American business executive, author, and chemical engineer

Learn more about *Drives* vision and purpose

Antonakis, J., Fenley, M., & Liechti, S. (2012). Learning charisma: Transform yourself into someone people want to follow. *Harvard Business Review*, June, 127-130.

Belsky, S. (2010). *Making ideas happen: Overcoming the obstacles between vision and reality*. New York, NY: Portfolio.

Center for Creative Leadership, Cartwright, T., & Baldwin, D. (2007). *Communicating your vision*. Hoboken, NJ: Pfeiffer.

Kouzes, J. M., & Posner, B. Z. (2012). *The leadership challenge: How to make extraordinary things happen in organizations*. (5th ed.). San Francisco, CA: Jossey-Bass.

Kurtzman, J. (2010). *Common purpose: How great leaders get organizations to achieve the extraordinary*. San Francisco, CA: Jossey-Bass.

Reiman, J. (2012). *The story of purpose: The path to creating a brighter brand, a greater company, and a lasting legacy*. Hoboken, NJ: John Wiley & Sons.

 ## Deep dive learning resource links

Barón, M. (2013, August 28). *Top tips for creating a clear vision for your business*. Small Business UK. Retrieved from http://www.smallbusiness.co.uk/starting-a-business/ideas-and-business-planning/2392048/top-tips-for-creating-a-clear-vision-for-your-business.thtml

Baskin, E. (2014, January 6). *To align employees, keep the vision simple – and unique to your culture*. Good Company. Retrieved from http://blog.tribeinc.com/2014/01/06/to-align-employees-keep-the-vision-simple-and-unique-to-your-culture/

Chappelow, C. (2012, September 5). 5 Rules for making your vision stick. *Fast Company*. Retrieved from http://www.fastcompany.com/3000998/5-rules-making-your-vision-stick

Frost, S. (n.d.). How to align employees with company goals. *Chron*. Retrieved from http://smallbusiness.chron.com/align-employees-company-goals-11667.html

Genard, G. (2012, March 25). *4 Easy ways to become a more charismatic speaker*. Public Speaking International. Retrieved from http://www.publicspeakinginternational.com/blog/bid/131382/4-Easy-Ways-to-Become-a-More-Charismatic-Speaker

448 |

Harrison, C. (2007, December). *Who's your audience? Ways to win your audience through inclusion*. Toastmasters International. Retrieved from http://www.toastmasters.org/ ToastmastersMagazine/ToastmasterArchive/2007/December/ WhosYourAudience.aspx

Kaipa, P. (2012, July 2). Recover your credibility. *Harvard Business Review Blog Network*. Retrieved from http://blogs.hbr.org/2012/07/ recover-your-credibility/

Kotter, J. (2011, April 27). The biggest mistake I see: Strategy first, urgency second. *Forbes*. Retrieved from http://www.forbes.com/ sites/johnkotter/2011/04/27/the-biggest-mistake-i-see-strategy- first-urgency-second/

Mind Tools. (n.d.). *Appreciative inquiry: Solving problems by looking at what's going right*. Mind Tools. Retrieved from http:// www.mindtools.com/pages/article/newTMC_85.htm

Moss Kanter, R. (2012, October 23). 12 Guidelines for deciding when to persist, when to quit. *Harvard Business Review Blog Network*. Retrieved from http://blogs.hbr.org/2012/10/12-guidelines-for- deciding-whe/

Spiro, J. (2010, August 30). How to get employees excited about your business vision. *Inc*. Retrieved from http://www.inc.com/ guides/2010/08/how-to-get-employees-excited-about-your- business-vision.html

Tabaka, M. (2010, August 24). 3 Steps to make your vision work for you. *Inc*. Retrieved from http://www.inc.com/marla-tabaka/3-steps- to-make-your-vision-work-for-you.html

Recommended search terms

If you'd like to explore *Drives* vision and purpose further, try searching online using the following terms:

- Aligning employees with company goals.
- Aligning your words and actions.
- Appealing to different audiences.
- Getting employees excited about your vision.
- Persevering through roadblocks at work.
- Strategic fitness and urgency.

More help...

Go to www.kornferry.com/fyi-resources and link directly to the deep dive resources in this chapter. Visit the site often to see the additional resources that are uploaded on a regular basis.

450 |

38. *Optimizes* work processes

Knowing the most effective and efficient processes to get things done, with a focus on continuous improvement.

Great processes simplify work. They align jobs and systems to better serve customers. Streamline communication. Cut costs and increase efficiency. Process touches everything from simple job task planning to complex supply chain management. From workstation layout to supercomputer data management. Streamlined processes drive improvements in quality, customer satisfaction, sales and profitability. With a well-designed process, performance is measured in results— not activity. The best processes are dynamic. Nimble. Able to flex with changing conditions. These processes are designed so that problems can be quickly and easily spotted and corrected. They're optimized for efficiency. Understanding and designing processes like these means knowing that there is no real finish line. It means continuously asking, "How can we make this better?" It's building in measurement and control methods and feedback loops. Knowing how all the pieces interrelate. How a change in one part of the process will affect upstream and downstream elements. With every incremental process improvement, you impact one or more important aspects of the work. Quality. Productivity. Timeliness. Cost. Safety. Keep a laser focus on continuously upgrading and optimizing your work processes. Chances are they are an untapped source of competitive advantage for your organization.

" *It is not a question of how well each process works, the question is how well they all work together.* **"**

Lloyd Dobyns – American broadcaster and quality expert

***Optimizes* work processes** is in the **Results** factor (II) in the Korn Ferry Leadership Architect™. It is part of Cluster E, **Managing execution,** along with Directs work (15) and Plans and aligns (25). You may find it helpful to also take a look at some of the tips included in those chapters to supplement your learning.

Skilled

Identifies and creates the processes necessary to get work done.

Separates and combines activities into efficient workflow.

Designs processes and procedures that allow managing from a distance.

Seeks ways to improve processes, from small tweaks to complete reengineering.

38

Less skilled

- Works in a disorganized fashion.

- Has difficulty figuring out effective and efficient processes to get things done.

- Accepts processes as they are; pays little attention to process improvement.

- Doesn't take advantage of opportunities for synergy and efficiency.

Talented

- Figures out the processes necessary to get things done.

- Separates and combines tasks into efficient and simple workflow.

- Thinks about the whole system.

- Focuses efforts on continuous improvement; has a knack for identifying and seizing opportunities for synergy and integration.

Overused skill

- May have trouble explaining to others how processes work.

- May attempt to put too much together at once.

- Oversimplifies processes.

- Tinkers with processes that are working sufficiently well already.

- Is so focused on efficiency that the human element of the work is left out.

452 |

Some possible causes of lower skill

Causes help explain *why* a person may have trouble with *Optimizes* work processes. When seeking to increase skill, it's helpful to consider how these might play out in certain situations. And remember that all of these can be addressed if you are motivated to do so.

- Not focused on improvement.
- Doesn't view things in terms of systems.
- Disorganized.
- Stuck in old ways; rejects emerging science and technology.
- Too autonomous or independent.
- Lacks knowledge of process tools.
- Resists learning and change.
- Dislikes structure and routine.

Does it best

When it comes to work process optimization, no company is quite like Toyota. The car manufacturer's Lean production process, known as "The Toyota Way," shifted the focus from the utilization of individual machines to the flow of the product through the total process. The process is underpinned by 14 principles, including the elimination of wasted time and resources, finding low-cost but reliable alternatives to expensive technology, and holding little or no inventory. But the approach is not just about the efficiency of the machine setup and the throughput. Toyota has recognized the critical human element by holding every employee accountable for inspecting quality and for continuous improvement. Since its full implementation in the 1950s, Lean manufacturing has helped Toyota become the 14th largest company in the world by revenue.[60, 61, 62]

Tips to develop *Optimizes* **work processes**

1. **Just starting out? Understand how to connect.** New in your role? Or maybe you've just joined the organization. There is a lot of evidence that early wins get noticed and it's the first 90 days that count. New contributors can be eager to change the way things are done. But before you suggest new processes, survey what already exists. What are the key responsibilities of your new role? What other groups and functions does it touch on and how are they connected? What information do you collect, analyze, and/or provide to others? Where does it come from? Where is it stored or processed? How is it acted upon? These are the working details of your position. Take time to understand how they interact with others. Create a process map centered on your role to help you identify opportunities for process improvement.

2. **Not sure where to focus? Start with your customers.** Organizations exist to provide products and services to customers. Even internal functions ultimately impact the customer experience. So it makes sense to improve process starting with the customer perspective. Many of your processes will link into those directly relating to customers. You can start internally. Name the functions and people you support and find out what you can do better. A simple survey is a good start. Or you can go bigger. Collect data to analyze the customer experience. Where are the most complaints coming from? What do they like best? What needs to change to serve them better? Dig into the data to identify root causes and design solutions. There is always something you can do better. If customers are happy, don't stop there. What further improvements can be made to increase their satisfaction? Set things up to provide service and support they didn't even know they needed.

3. **Not a linear thinker? Use process mapping.** When it comes to creating and using process, human beings are wired differently. Some are organized, scheduled, and methodical. They see clearly what needs to happen to reach a goal—on time and under budget. They plot a step-by-step path and rarely deviate until they reach the end. Others jump in at the middle and just keep going until they're done. If you struggle with laying out a process, mapping can help. A process map provides a visual depiction of workflow. It can show who is involved, what happens, what needs to happen, and in what order. It creates clarity and context from seemingly disjointed information. And it can show how processes need to flex to fit different situations. It literally draws a picture. You can find process-mapping tools online, including several you can try for free. Work by

yourself or with others to bring clarity to process, using these tools. To go deeper, find a short course at a local tech school or university. For major projects, hire a consultant to facilitate the conversation, and learn along with others.

4. **Hate routine? Use process to focus on what's important.** Great processes enable creative thinking. They provide a way to take care of the mundane and free you up for the fun stuff. Like strategizing a new acquisition. Hiring new talent. Planning your next market move. If you're action oriented, don't ignore or resist process. Find out how it can make your life—and your customers' lives—better. Learn about some of the tools of business analysis. Meet with some engineers for a brainstorming session. Ask how your competitors are using process tools. Turn on your competitive juices to figure out how you can do it even better.

38

Want to learn more? Take a deep dive...

Heye, S. (2007, November 5). Quick overview of process mapping [YouTube].

Pavey, S. (n.d.). *Creativity techniques – start here!* Mind Tools.

Sugars, B. (2012, July 2). Need a vacation? 4 Steps to a business that thrives without you. *Entrepreneur*.

YEC Women. (2011, November 15). How to create systems that enable business growth. *Forbes*.

5. **Planning a project? Lay out the process.** Well-run projects start out with a plan and a process. What do you need to accomplish? What's the time line? What resources will you need? Who controls the resources—people, funding, tools, materials, and support that you need? Go online to find project flowcharting software such as PERT and Gantt charts. Some are available for free. Or, if it's a less complex project, use Excel or even a Word-based table to lay out necessary steps, resources, deadlines, and action steps. Follow the process but don't be too rigid about keeping things moving. Following a process to get things done includes stopping once in a while to let things play out. Share the goals of your process with the people you need to support you. Work with them to get the tools and resources you need. If you're working with a team, match their skills to tasks. Estimate time to completion. Set goals for the whole project and the subtasks. Set measures so you and others can track progress against the goals. Running a project like this is a great way to begin thinking about process improvement.

6. **Creating team process? Align it with objectives.** Team processes need to support the end objective of the group—anything else just slows down results. In strong, self-managed groups, the team makes decisions on process as they work together. For other teams, the leader designs the process—ideally with input from team members. Start with objectives. What are they going to deliver and when? Do they need to meet tight deadlines? Meet regulatory requirements or stay within a budget? What else might affect their ability to deliver? Then get ideas on process. When and how often do they want to meet? What tools do they need? How will they store and share documents? How will they track progress? Hold meetings to resolve early difficulties. Ask frequently how things are going and what needs to change. Keep an eye on the goal: change any element of the system or process that hinders communication and goal achievement.

7. **Running process change? Use proven methodologies.** Systems engineering and business process improvement have been in use for decades. Great thinkers like Deming and Juran led the way. Companies like Toyota and GE use methodologies to make comprehensive changes in the way they do business. You don't have to invent a new process to improve processes—the methods and models are already available. A quick Internet search brings up the Lean Enterprise Institute, where you can learn about the customer-focused Lean methodology that transformed Toyota. Or go to GE.com/sixsigma, where you can learn the process that is embedded in the GE culture. Or you can search sites to find out about KISS ("Keep It Simple, Stupid"), a change model focused on simplicity—and other ways of thinking about change. Even a little knowledge of these methods will help you think about process in a new way. Ask an analyst or process leader which models apply to your situation—and how you can use them. Go deeper by taking a longer course or pursuing certification.

8. **Using data? Get the big picture.** Most organizations are rich with data. Financial results. Customer satisfaction surveys. Quality ratings. Sales information. Billions of bits of information created every minute through online shopping, web searches, and other Internet interactions. All of this information can help you improve process—if you know where to look. Want to grow sales, create new services, or streamline time to market? Start by asking questions that the data could help you answer. Find out what is available in your organization. Engage an analyst or data mining consultant to help you interpret what you find. Go deep to look for root causes, identify patterns, and develop a clear picture of what is happening. Pull together a

brainstorming session to explore the information and generate ideas for business improvement. What opportunities do you see? Work backwards from the data to design a process for improvement.

9. **Think process is its own end? Don't let process improvement turn into process bureaucracy.** It's tempting to become so focused on the merits of process optimization that you lose sight of the true end in mind—getting better results. Beware of creeping bureaucracy, overzealous process auditing, or any activity created in the name of process improvement. The irony being that these very systems could end up impeding the efficiency you were seeking in the first place. Management expert Oren Harari describes driving for zero defects as being just one small piece of the package. He also recommends treating your suppliers as partners to improve quality.

Want to learn more? Take a deep dive...

38

Evison, A. (n.d.). *The planning cycle: A planning process for medium-sized projects*. Mind Tools.

Power, B. (2012, September 27). Understanding fear of process improvement. *Harvard Business Review Blog Network*.

Satell, G. (2013, December 3). Yes, big data can solve real world problems. *Forbes*.

Tobak, S. (2010, September 22). *Entrepreneurs: Learn to improve processes without adding bureaucracy*. CBS News.

10. **Overcomplicating matters? Learn to streamline.** Enjoy designing processes? Like describing how to get from point A to point B through XYZ and back? Your skills are useful. But your processes may be complex and cumbersome. Unnecessarily redundant. Overengineering hurts efficiency. Look at the drawings of Rube Goldberg—a cartoonist who drew complex devices that performed simple tasks in convoluted ways. His drawings are humorous—but there's nothing funny about slowing down productivity or creating systems that people won't use. Look for ways to streamline. Find the place where five steps could become two. Cut pieces of old processes that no longer serve a purpose. Eliminate redundancies unless they are needed for security and risk reduction. Check for things like reporting requirements that can be simplified. Ask others how processes can be changed for greater ease and productivity.

11. **Avoiding new technologies? Ask for help.** Technology continuously evolves. DVDs are replaced by video streaming. New websites revolutionize communications. System upgrades appear overnight. Last year's hot smartphone is this year's recycling. Work process optimizers have a talent for evaluating new technologies. They understand intuitively how the technologies work and how they streamline communication, move information, and save time. But for some, the pace of technological change is dizzying. How many new tools and processes do you need to master, and when will it stop? Your challenge is to adapt, not resist. Start by being open. Be curious about the latest. Engage an internal geek who can show you shortcuts and features. Browse the Internet for clues as to what's coming. Ask your colleagues what they're using. If you resist—you risk being labeled a dinosaur. Have fun exploring. Learn to use helpful or necessary new technologies.

12. **Like things the way they are? Open yourself to change.** You like your job. The work gets done and customers seem satisfied. And then something happens to change all of that. There's a new emphasis on data. Measurements. Reporting requirements. Methodologies. It's hard to accept the new reality. But change is essential to growth. Ask questions. Be curious not only about what is happening, but why. Look for ways to influence—not block—changes. Learn all you can. Step up as a learner and leader. Volunteer to join the change team. Form or lead a process group for your area. Help develop and teach user training. Accept that change is unsettling. But it's the new constant—at least for a while.

13. **Afraid of breaking a process you're trying to improve? Create an environment for experimentation and learning.** One principle of these techniques is to drive for continuous improvement. Never be satisfied. Always drive to improve all work. Don't expect to get it right the first time. This leads to safe and stale solutions. If you have trouble going back the second or third time to get something done, then switch approaches. Sometimes people get stuck in a repeating groove that's not working. Do something different next time. Think about multiple ways to get the same outcome. To increase learning, shorten the action phases of process improvement efforts and insert feedback loops—aiming to make them as immediate as possible after any action. The more frequent the cycles, the more opportunities to learn.

Want to learn more? Take a deep dive...

Dumbill, E. (2014, February 5). The experimental enterprise. *Forbes*.

Morgan, J. (2013, August 27). The 5 must-have qualities of the modern employee. *Forbes*.

Pavey, S. (n.d.). *Improving business processes: Streamlining tasks to improve efficiency*. Mind Tools.

Pozen, R. C. (2013, January 3). Embrace change, but still stand for something. *Harvard Business Review Blog Network*.

Job assignments

- Develop a process to improve the efficiency of services delivered to internal or external customers of your group or function. Monitor it. Learn from it. Further improve it.

- Create and present a process time line for a change initiative incorporating goals, deadlines, resources, and measurement metrics.

- Learn as much as you can about Lean methodology and outline how it could be used to improve your organization's product delivery processes. Apply it to an area you are working on.

- Shadow the person in your organization responsible for quality. Deliver a presentation on quality processes used in your organization.

- Monitor and follow a new product or service through the entire idea, design, test market, and launch cycle.

Take time to reflect...

If you'd rather tolerate a bad process than spend time getting it fixed...

...then reflect on the problems it's caused you over the last six months. The holdups. The wasted effort. The rework. The frustration. The missed opportunities. Invest time now; be glad you did later.

If keeping everything running smoothly is a challenge for you...

...then recognize that you may have to prioritize what you focus on. Channel your energy where the benefit of the improvement is worth the cost of the effort.

If you see process as the critical aspect of any project...

...then watch that the process doesn't dominate the outcome. Remember, processes are the means to an end. Strive to improve, but keep your focus on the final result.

"*Great things are done by a series of small things brought together.* **"**

Vincent Van Gogh – Dutch painter

Learn more about *Optimizes* work processes

Damelio, R. (2011). *The basics of process mapping* (2nd ed.). Boca Raton, FL: CRC Press.

Evans, J. R., & Lindsay, W. M. (2010). *Managing for quality and performance excellence* (8th ed.). Mason, OH: Cengage Learning.

Jacka, J. M., & Keller, P. J. (2009). *Business process mapping: Improving customer satisfaction*. Hoboken, NJ: John Wiley & Sons, Inc.

Page, S. (2010). *The power of business process improvement: 10 Simple steps to increase effectiveness, efficiency, and adaptability*. New York, NY: AMACOM.

Soares, S. (2012). *Big data governance: An emerging imperative*. Boise, ID: MC Press.

 ## Deep dive learning resource links

38

Dumbill, E. (2014, February 5). The experimental enterprise. *Forbes*. Retrieved from http://www.forbes.com/sites/edddumbill/2014/02/05/the-experimental-enterprise/

Evison, A. (n.d.). *The planning cycle: A planning process for medium-sized projects*. Mind Tools. Retrieved from http://www.mindtools.com/pages/article/newPPM_05.htm

Heye, S. (2007, November 5). Quick overview of process mapping [YouTube]. Retrieved from http://www.youtube.com/watch?v=UDXngerDmWQ

Morgan, J. (2013, August 27). The 5 must-have qualities of the modern employee. *Forbes*. Retrieved from http://www.forbes.com/sites/jacobmorgan/2013/08/27/5-must-have-qualities-modern-employee/

Pavey, S. (n.d.). *Creativity techniques – start here!* Mind Tools. Retrieved from http://www.mindtools.com/pages/article/newCT_00.htm

Pavey, S. (n.d.). *Improving business processes: Streamlining tasks to improve efficiency*. Mind Tools. Retrieved from http://www.mindtools.com/pages/article/improving-business-processes.htm

Power, B. (2012, September 27). Understanding fear of process improvement. *Harvard Business Review Blog Network*. Retrieved from http://blogs.hbr.org/2012/09/understanding-fear-of-process-improvement/

Pozen, R. C. (2013, January 3). Embrace change, but still stand for something. *Harvard Business Review Blog Network*. Retrieved from http://blogs.hbr.org/2013/01/embrace-change-but-still-stand/

Satell, G. (2013, December 3). Yes, big data can solve real world problems. *Forbes*. Retrieved from http://www.forbes.com/sites/gregsatell/2013/12/03/yes-big-data-can-solve-real-world-problems/

Sugars, B. (2012, July 2). Need a vacation? 4 Steps to a business that thrives without you. *Entrepreneur*. Retrieved from http://www.entrepreneur.com/article/223919#

Tobak, S. (2010, September 22). *Entrepreneurs: Learn to improve processes without adding bureaucracy*. CBS News. Retrieved from http://www.cbsnews.com/news/entrepreneurs-learn-to-improve-processes-without-adding-bureaucracy/

YEC Women. (2011, November 15). How to create systems that enable business growth. *Forbes*. Retrieved from http://www.forbes.com/sites/yec/2011/11/15/how-to-create-systems-that-enable-business-growth/

Recommended search terms

If you'd like to explore *Optimizes* work processes further, try searching online using the following terms:

- Creating an environment of experimentation and change.
- Effective business process mapping.
- Integrating big data.
- Process management and improvement.
- Streamlining business processes.
- Systemizing your work processes.

 More help...

Go to www.kornferry.com/fyi-resources and link directly to the deep dive resources in this chapter. Visit the site often to see the additional resources that are uploaded on a regular basis.

Career stallers
and stoppers

101.   *Poor* administrator

People differ widely on personal organization, ranging from the perfectionist with everything having to be just so, to the disorganized absent-minded professor never knowing where things are and never being on time with anything. There are really two issues. The first is personal disorganization. The fallout is having too much to do, being late on commitments, having to work longer hours to keep up, losing key documents, forgetting appointments, not doing things completely that have to be redone later, etc. It leads to personal inefficiency and ineffective use of personal time and resources. The second issue is many times worse than the first. It's the disruption your personal disorganization has on the processes managed by others. When your reports are late, others get delayed. When you're late, others have to wait. When the form isn't completed properly, someone else has to take the time to get it corrected. Many people go through life happily disorganized and disheveled. The key is its impact on the people around you.

" *I must govern the clock,*
not be governed by it. **"**

Golda Meir – Israeli teacher, politician, and former Prime Minister of Israel

101

Factor: N/A
Cluster N: Doesn't inspire or build talent
Career staller and stopper 101: *Poor* administrator

A problem

- Has low detail-orientation.
- Lets things fall through the cracks.
- Overcommits and underdelivers.
- Misses key details.
- Forgets undocumented commitments.
- Has to scramble to pull things together at the last minute.
- Moves on without completing the task.

Not a problem

- Well organized and detail skilled.
- Reliable—keeps tabs on work in process; remembers commitments.
- Good administrator; keeps things on track.
- Sets tight priorities.
- Uses time well.
- Says no if they can't get to it.
- Completes most things on time and in time.

Some possible causes

- Can't say no to people; gets overloaded.
- Impatient.
- Poor grasp of due process as seen by others.
- Poor mental organization.
- Poor sense of time.
- Procrastinates.
- Too busy to get organized.

Other causes

Being less skilled at, or overusing, some competencies may also be the cause of an issue with *Poor* administrator.

Being less skilled at:

12. Decision quality
25. Plans and aligns

466 |

Factor: N/A
Cluster N: Doesn't inspire or build talent
Career staller and stopper 101: *Poor* administrator

101

27. Resourcefulness
38. *Optimizes* work processes

Overusing:

3. *Manages* ambiguity
18. Global perspective
19. *Cultivates* innovation
20. Interpersonal savvy

Tips to overcome being a *Poor* administrator

1. **Unsure where to start? Make a list of things to fix.** Do an upstream and downstream check on the people you work for, work around, and those who work for you, to create a list of the administrative slip-ups you make that give them the most trouble. Be sure to ask them for help creating the list. That way, you have a focused list of the things you need to fix first. If you fix the top 10, maybe that will do and the rest of your habits can stay the same.

2. **Overbooked? Practice good time management.** Personal time management is a known technology. There are countless books on the topic as well as a number of good personal time management courses you could attend. Search online for "tips for good time management." Try out some different approaches. Some will work for you; some won't and may actually get in the way. Adopt practices you like. Don't waste time on things you don't.

3. **Disorganized? Get organized.** Put the things you have to do in two piles—things I have to do that are for me, and things I have to do that are for others or that will affect others. Do the second pile first. Further divide the second pile into the mission critical, important, and things that can wait. Do them in that order.

4. **Need more help? Hire people with organization skills.** If you have the luxury of an administrative assistant, select on the ability to organize themselves and you. Pick someone who is candid, who will stand up to you and help you be successful.

5. **Messy work environment? Contain the clutter.** Make your personal disorganization less obvious to others. If you are a pile manager, get shelving that has addressable cubbyholes so you can get your piles

101

Factor: N/A
Cluster N: Doesn't inspire or build talent
Career staller and stopper 101: *Poor* administrator

out of the way. Get an L-shaped desk, one for your piles and one that you keep clean for only the project you are working on at the moment. Put the pile table in back of you toward the wall. Have an area of your office—a couple of chairs and a table that you never put anything on—that you can use for visitors. Frame this quotation and put it on your wall so others know you are not very organized: "If a cluttered desk is the sign of a cluttered mind, what is an empty desk the sign of?"

6. **Personal preferences getting in the way? Focus on priorities.** Don't work based upon your feelings. Don't organize your work around what you like to do and put off what you don't like to do. That's one reason people get into organization problems. Use priorities of what needs to be done instead.

7. **Failing to keep your commitments? Let others help you prioritize.** Ask your internal and external customers for the order in which they need things. If there is going to be a delay beyond the commitment you've made, send an e-mail or call and tell them when to expect what you've promised. You can only do this once.

8. **Trouble meeting deadlines? Set your own deadline.** Set false deadlines for yourself that are ahead of the real deadlines. Delegate any of the things you have trouble getting done.

9. **Don't care? Check your attitude toward administrative tasks.** Some people ignore this need as not that important; administration has a trivial sound to it. The problem is, what else does it say about you? Most likely it tells people what you overdo. You're an action junkie and leave a trail of problems around you, you're creative and have your fingers in too many pies, or you're a strategist or a visionary and show disdain for details, which suggests to others that what they do isn't very important. People rightly see this as a sort of arrogance. Demonstrate that you appreciate the importance of administrative tasks. Show respect for the people who execute them.

10. **Not dependable? Build trust.** The bottom line for this need is that people don't trust people who are disorganized, particularly if you indicate you don't much care. They feel they can't count on you, that your actions may wreak havoc for them. Behaving as a consistently responsible administrator will eliminate this problem.

Factor: N/A
Cluster N: Doesn't inspire or build talent
Career staller and stopper 101: *Poor* administrator

101

Job assignments

- Manage the renovation of an office, floor, building, meeting room, warehouse, etc.

- Work on a process-simplification team to take steps and costs out of a process.

- Plan an off-site meeting, conference, convention, trade show, event, etc.

- Manage the purchase of a major product, equipment, materials, program, or system.

- Manage a dissatisfied internal or external customer; troubleshoot a performance or quality problem with a product or service.

" *Our greatest weariness comes from work not done.* **"**

Eric Hoffer – American writer on social and political philosophy

101

Factor: N/A
Cluster N: Doesn't inspire or build talent
Career staller and stopper 101: *Poor* administrator

101

Learning resources

Allen, D. (2003). *Getting things done: The art of stress-free productivity*. New York, NY: Penguin Books.

Bossidy, L., & Charan, R. (with Burck, C.). (2002). *Execution: The discipline of getting things done*. New York, NY: Crown Business.

Byfield, M. (2003). *It's hard to make a difference when you can't find your keys: The seven-step path to becoming truly organized*. New York, NY: Viking Press.

Charan, R. (2007). Know-how: *The 8 skills that separate people who perform from those who don't*. New York, NY: Crown Business.

Cramer, K. D. (2002). *When faster harder smarter is not enough: Six steps for achieving what you want in a rapid-fire world*. New York, NY: McGraw-Hill.

Crouch, C. (2005). *Getting organized: Improving focus, organization, and productivity*. Memphis, TN: Dawson Publishing.

Cunningham, M. J. (2006). *Finish what you start: 10 Surefire ways to deliver your projects on time and on budget*. Chicago, IL: Kaplan Business.

Dittmer, R. E., & McFarland, S. (2008). *151 Quick ideas for delegating and decision making*. Franklin Lakes, NJ: Career Press.

Dodd, P., & Sundheim, D. (2005). *The 25 best time management tools and techniques: How to get more done without driving yourself crazy*. Windham, NH: Peak Performance Press.

Dotlich, D. L., Cairo, P. C., & Rhinesmith, S. H. (2006). *Head, heart, and guts: How the world's best companies develop complete leaders*. San Francisco, CA: Jossey-Bass.

Drucker, P. F. (2006). *The effective executive* (Rev. ed.). New York, NY: HarperBusiness.

Hoover, J. (2007). *Time management: Set priorities to get the right things done*. New York, NY: HarperCollins Business.

Kaplan, R. S., & Norton, D. P. (2008). *Execution premium: Linking strategy to operations for competitive advantage*. Boston, MA: Harvard Business School Press.

Limoncelli, T. A. (2005). *Time management for system administrators*. Sebastopol, CA: O'Reilly Media.

Whipp, R., Adam, B., & Sabelis, I. (Eds.). (2002). *Making time: Time and management in modern organizations*. Oxford, UK: Oxford University Press.

102. Blocked personal learner

People say you're stuck in the past. For some reason, you resist learning new personal and managerial behaviors. You're the last to get on board a new initiative. You're from Missouri (the "Show Me" state)—we have to prove it to you before you'll move. Surveys done with a major outplacement firm show that those most likely to be let go during a downsizing have good technical and individual skills but poor learning to do anything new or different skills. You can't survive today without keeping you and your skills fresh. There's not much room anymore for someone stuck in the past.

" I do not think much of a man who is not wiser today than he was yesterday. "

Abraham Lincoln – 16th President of the United States

102

Factor: N/A
Cluster M: Trouble with people
Career staller and stopper 102: Blocked personal learner

A problem

- Is closed to learning new personal, interpersonal, managerial, and leadership skills, approaches, and tactics.
- Prefers staying the same, even when faced with new and different challenges.
- Is narrow in interests and scope.
- Uses few learning tactics.
- Doesn't seek input.
- Lacks curiosity.
- Is not insightful about self.

Not a problem

- Eager to learn; interested in what's new or better.
- Has broad interests and perspective.
- Seeks and listens to feedback.
- Takes criticism to heart.
- Always looking to improve self.
- Carefully observes others for their reactions and adjusts accordingly.
- Reads people and groups well.
- Picks up on subtle corrective cues from others.
- Is sensitive to different challenges and changes accordingly.

Some possible causes

- Hangs on, hoping to make it without changing.
- Low risk taker.
- May block change for others.
- Narrow in scope and interests.
- Not open to new approaches.
- Perfectionist.
- Prefers the tried and true.
- Self-learning/development interest is low.
- Too busy to learn anything new.
- Too comfortable.

Factor: N/A
Cluster M: Trouble with people
Career staller and stopper 102: Blocked personal learner

102

Other causes

Being less skilled at, or overusing, some competencies may also be the cause of an issue with Blocked personal learner.

Being less skilled at:

6. Collaborates
29. *Demonstrates* self-awareness
30. Self-development
31. Situational adaptability

Overusing:

2. Action oriented
5. Business insight
10. Courage
25. Plans and aligns

Tips to overcome being a Blocked personal learner

1. **Need a defined approach? Work from the outside in.** People who are good at this work from the outside in (the customer, the audience, the person, the situation), not from the inside out ("What do I want to do in this situation? What would make me happy and feel good?"). Practice not thinking inside out when you are around others. What are the demand characteristics of this situation? How does this person or audience best learn? Which of my approaches or styles or skills or knowledge would work best? How can I best accomplish my goals? How can I alter my approach and tactics to be the most effective? The one-trick pony can only perform once per show. If the audience doesn't like that particular trick, no oats for the pony, no encore.

2. **Caught in your comfort zone? Find new solutions.** You're probably caught in your comfort zone. You rely on historical, tried-and-true solutions. You use what you know and have seen or done before. So when faced with a new issue, challenge, or problem, first figure out what causes it. Don't go to the solution or conclusion first. Keep asking "Why?" See how many causes you can come up with and how many organizing buckets you can put them in. This increases the chance of a better solution because you can see more connections. Look for patterns in data, don't just collect information or assume that you know what to do. People are telling you that you often don't.

102

Factor: N/A
Cluster M: Trouble with people
Career staller and stopper 102: Blocked personal learner

3. **Failing to connect with others? Adjust to your audience.** You must constantly observe others' reactions to you to be good at adjusting to others. You must watch the reactions of people to what you are saying and doing while you are doing it in order to gauge their response. Are they bored? Change the pace. Are they confused? State it in a different way. Are they angry? Stop and ask what the problem is. Are they too quiet? Stop and get them involved in what you are doing. Are they fidgeting, scribbling on their pads, or staring out the window? They may not be interested in what you are doing. Move to the end of your presentation or task, end it, and exit. Check in with your audience frequently and select a different tactic if necessary.

4. **Not open to learning? Make repeated efforts to learn from others.** Whatever the causes are, people view you as not open to learning. Until you signal repeatedly that you are open to others, interested in what they have to say, share things you don't have to share, invite people to talk with you and then listen, little will come of this effort. You will have to persevere, endure some rejection, and perhaps some angry or dismissive remarks in order to balance the situation. Mentally rehearse so you're not blindsided by this. It would be a rare group of people who would respond to your new overtures without making you squirm a bit because they have seen you as closed up to this point.

5. **Need a new bag of tricks? Experiment with some new techniques with people.** Many excellent personal learners have a bag of engaging techniques they use: They give reasons for everything they say, saving any solution statements or conclusions for last. They ask more questions than make statements, speak briefly, summarize often, and when disagreeing, they put it in conditional terms: "I don't think so, but what do you think?" The point of these is to elicit as much information about the reactions of others as they can. They are loading their files so they can change behavior when needed.

6. **Stuck in a rut? Expand your repertoire.** Stretch yourself. Do things that are not characteristic of you. Go to your limits and beyond. By expanding the number of behaviors you have access to, you can become more effective across a larger number of situations.

7. **Ready to try something new? Be an early adopter of something.** Find some new thing, technique, software, tool, system, process, or skill relevant to your activity. Privately become an expert in it. Read the books. Get certified. Visit a location where it's being done. Then

Factor: N/A
Cluster M: Trouble with people
Career staller and stopper 102: Blocked personal learner

102

surprise everyone and be the first to introduce it into your world. Sell it. Train others. Integrate it into your work.

8. **Don't know where to start? Pick three tasks you've never done before and go do them.** If you don't know much about customers, work in a store or handle customer complaints; if you don't know what engineering does, go find out; task trade with someone. Meet with your colleagues from other areas and tell each other what, and more importantly, how you do what you do.

9. **Need a broader perspective? Volunteer for task forces.** Task forces/ projects are a great opportunity to learn new things in a low-risk environment. Task forces are one of the most common developmental events listed by successful executives. Such projects require learning other functions, businesses, or nationalities well enough that in a tight time frame, you can appreciate how they think and why their area/position is important. In so doing, you get out of your own experience and start to see connections to a broader world—how international trade works or, more at home, how the pieces of your organization fit together.

10. **Need to also stretch in your personal life? Expand your horizons.** Do you eat at the same restaurants? Vacation at the same places? Holidays are always done the same as in the past? Buy the same make or type car over and over again? Have the same insurance agent your father had? Expand yourself. Go on adventures with your family. Travel to places you have not been before. Never vacation at the same place again. Eat at different theme restaurants. Go to events and meetings of groups you have never really met. Go to ethnic festivals and sample the cultures. Go to athletic events you've never attended before. Each week, you and your family should go on a personal learning adventure. See how many different perspectives you can add to your knowledge.

|

102

Factor: N/A
Cluster M: Trouble with people
Career staller and stopper 102: Blocked personal learner

Job assignments

- Attend a self-awareness/assessment course that includes feedback.

- Study some aspect of your job or a new technical area you haven't studied before that you need in order to be more effective.

- Attend a course or event which will push you personally beyond your usual limits or outside your comfort zone (e.g., Outward Bound, language immersion training, sensitivity group, public speaking).

- Volunteer to do a special project for and with a person you admire and who has a skill you need to develop.

- Teach/coach someone how to do something you are not an expert in.

102

"*It is impossible to withhold education from the receptive mind, as it is impossible to force it upon the unreasoning.* **"**

Agnes Repplier – American essayist

Factor: N/A
Cluster M: Trouble with people
Career staller and stopper 102: Blocked personal learner

102

Learning resources

Bennis, W. G., & Thomas, R. J. (2007). *Leading for a lifetime: How defining moments shape leaders of today and tomorrow*. Boston, MA: Harvard Business School Press.

Blakeley, K. (2007). *Leadership blind spots and what to do about them*. Hoboken, NJ: John Wiley & Sons, Inc.

Cashman, K. (2008). *Leadership from the inside out: Becoming a leader for life* (2nd ed.). San Francisco, CA: Berrett-Koehler Publishers.

Eichinger, R. W., & Lombardo, M. M. (2004). Learning agility as a prime indicator of potential. *Human Resource Planning, 27,* 12-15.

Eichinger, R. W., Lombardo, M. M., & Stiber, A. (2005). *Broadband talent management: Paths to improvement*. Minneapolis, MN: Lominger Limited.

Gardner, H. (2006). *Five minds for the future*. Boston, MA: Harvard Business School Press.

Kotter, J., & Rathgeber, H. (2006). *Our iceberg is melting: Changing and succeeding under any conditions*. New York: St. Martin's Press.

Kourdi, J. (2007). *Think on your feet: 10 Steps to better decision making and problem solving at work*. London, England: Cyan Communications.

McCall, M. W., Lombardo, M. M., & Morrison, A. M. (1988). *The lessons of experience*. Lexington, MA: Lexington Books.

Merriam, S. B., Caffarella, R. S., & Baumgartner, L. M. (2006). *Learning in adulthood: A comprehensive guide*. San Francisco, CA: Jossey Bass.

Rimanoczy, I., & Turner, E. (2008). *Action reflection learning: Solving real business problems by connecting learning with earning*. Mountain View, CA: Davies-Black Publishing.

Thomas, R. J. (2008). *Crucibles of leadership: How to learn from experience to become a great leader*. Boston, MA: Harvard Business School Press.

Wick, C., Pollock, R., Jefferson, A., & Flanagan, R. (2006). *The six disciplines of breakthrough learning: How to turn training and development into business results*. San Francisco, CA: Pfeiffer.

Wilkinson, D. (2006). *The ambiguity advantage: What great leaders are great at*. Hampshire, UK: Palgrave Mcmillan.

103. *Lack of* ethics and values

Being seen as having questionable ethics means the values and ethics you are operating under are not in line with those of the people around you. On the more negative side, it could mean you have unacceptable values and ethics in a more absolute sense; that is, most would reject them. You may hedge or operate too close to the edge for people to feel comfortable with you. Most of us haven't thought out our values/ethical stances well; we are on autopilot from childhood and our collective experience. People deduce your values and ethics by listening to what you say and, more importantly, watching what you do.

" Ethics is knowing the difference between what you have the right to do and what is right to do. "

Potter Stewart – Former Supreme Court Justice of the United States

103

Factor: N/A
Cluster M: Trouble with people
Career staller and stopper 103: *Lack of* ethics and values

A problem

- Lacks the necessary sensitivity to the operating ethics and values of the organization.
- Operates too close to the margins.
- Pushes the limits of tolerance.
- Doesn't operate within the norms.

Not a problem

- Values and ethics are generally aligned with the organization's.
- Operates within boundaries most others would agree to.
- Looked to for guidance on standards and norms.
- Stays steady through crises involving close calls on ethics.
- Can articulate own and others' values.
- Helpful to others in making close calls on values/ethical matters.
- Projects a consistent set of values.

Some possible causes

- Operates close to the edge.
- Overly ambitious.
- Overly independent.
- Pragmatic to a fault.
- Sets own rules of conduct.
- Not consistent across situations; situational ethics.

Other causes

Being less skilled at, or overusing, some competencies may also be the cause of an issue with *Lack of* ethics and values.

Being less skilled at:

14. *Values* differences
26. *Being* resilient
29. *Demonstrates* self-awareness
36. *Instills* trust

Factor: N/A
Cluster M: Trouble with people
Career staller and stopper 103: *Lack of* ethics and values

103

Overusing:

19. *Cultivates* innovation

23. Organizational savvy

28. *Drives* results

37. *Drives* vision and purpose

Tips to overcome *Lack of* ethics and values

1. **Unsure of the real issues? Diagnose the problem.** Make sure you know exactly what your problem is. The range of possibilities is great. Get 360 feedback on this specific issue by having a human resource professional or outside consultant poll people to find out what your difficulty is. As a less severe problem, you may be just stubborn and rigid, tied to the values of the past, out of tune with the times, pragmatic to a fault, seen as not helpful enough to others, pushing your own agenda, playing favorites, or being reluctant to speak up. As a more severe problem, you might be cutting corners to look good, setting your own rules, blaming others for things you should take responsibility for, sabotaging your rivals, hedging the truth, or showing little concern for others.

2. **Ready to admit it? Take corrective action.** The worst case—your ethics really are questionable. You hedge, sabotage others, play for advantage, set up others and make others look bad. You may be devious and scheming and overly political. You tell yourself it's OK because you are getting the results out on time. You really believe the end justifies the means. If any of this is true, this criticism should have also happened to you in the past. This is not something that develops overnight. You need to find out if your career with this organization is salvageable. The best way to do this is to admit that you know your ethics and values are not the same as the people you work with and ask a boss or a mentor whether it's fixable. If they say yes, contact everyone you think you've alienated and see how they respond. Tell them the things you're going to do differently. Ask them if the situation can be repaired. Longer-term, you need to seek some professional counsel on your values and ethics.

3. **Unpredictable? Be consistent across situations and groups.** You might just be inconsistent in your value stances and actions. You change your mind based on mood or who you talked with last. That may confuse and bother people. You may express a pro people value in one instance (people you manage) and an anti people value

103

Factor: N/A
Cluster M: Trouble with people
Career staller and stopper 103: *Lack of* ethics and values

in another (people from another unit). You may rigidly adhere to a high moral code in one transaction (with customers) and play it close to the acceptable margin in another (with vendors). You may match your values with your audience when managing up and not when you're managing down. You may play favorites. People are more comfortable with consistency and predictability. Look for the three to five areas where you think these inconsistencies play out. Write down what you did with various people so you can compare. Did you do different things in parallel situations? Do you hold others to a different standard? Do you have so many values positions that they have to clash? Do you state so few that people have to fill in the blanks with guesses? Try to balance your behavior so that you are more consistent across situations.

4. **Sending mixed messages? Avoid "do as I say, not as I do" behavior.** Another possibility is that there is a sizable gap between what you say about your ethics and values and what the ethics and values of others should be and what you actually do in those same situations. Many people get themselves in trouble by giving motivating values and ethics speeches, high-toned, passionate, charismatic, gives you goose bumps—until you watch that person do the opposite or something quite different in practice. Examine all the things you tend to say in speeches or in meetings or casual conversations that are values and ethics based. Write them down the left side of a legal pad. For each one, see if you can write three to five examples of when you acted exactly in line with that value or ethic. Can you write down any that are not exactly like that? If you can, it's the gap that's the problem. Either stop making values and ethics statements you can't model or bring your values into alignment with your own statements.

5. **Muddled values? Get clarity about your values.** You may not think in terms of values much, and your statements may not clearly state your values. To pass the test of a thoughtfully held value, you should be able to state it in a sentence and give five examples of how it plays out—both the situation and consequences. State what is the opposite of the value—what is dishonesty, for example—and demonstrate how you follow the value. Since you are having trouble in this area, it may be a good exercise to try to capture your value system on paper so you can practice delivering a clear statement of it to others. If you ignore obvious values implications, people may assume you don't care.

6. **Time to change? Thoughtfully and intentionally adopt values and ethics.** Remember, behavior is 10 times more important than words.

482 |

Factor: N/A
Cluster M: Trouble with people
Career staller and stopper 103: *Lack of* ethics and values

103

What values do you want? What do you want your ethics to be? Write them down the left-hand side of the page. I want to be known as a fair manager. Then down the right side, what would someone with that value do and not do? Wouldn't play favorites. Would offer everyone opportunities to grow and develop. Would listen to everyone's ideas. Would call for everyone's input in a staff meeting. Would apportion my time so everyone gets a piece of it. Hold everyone to the same standards. Have someone you trust check it over to see if you are on the right track. Then start to consistently do the things you have written on the right-hand side.

7. **Struggling with close calls? Bring focus and clarity to the gray areas.** Sometimes people get in trouble because they don't understand the underlying mismatch between values. Few people have any trouble with clear-cut values clashes; it's the close calls where ill-thought-through positions get us in trouble. You should be able to pro and con various values. You should be able to help people think through when to break a confidence or when loyalty to the organization supersedes loyalty to an individual. What are the common values clashes you deal with? In these situations, you need to be able to argue both sides of the question. Hedging on your tax return and padding of an expense account—is that the same or different? Working with or firing a marginal performer? Cutting quality or raising the price? Firing someone for drug abuse and serving alcohol at company functions?

8. **Too independent? Recognize that you don't operate in a vacuum.** You set your own rules, smash through obstacles, see yourself as tough, action- and results-oriented. You get it done. The problem is, you wreak havoc for others; they don't know which of your actions will create headaches for them in their own unit or with customers. You don't often worry about whether others think like you do. You operate from the inside out. What's important to you is what you think and what you judge to be right and just. In a sense, admirable. In a sense, not smart. You live in an organization that has both formal and informal commonly held standards, beliefs, ethics, and values. You can't survive long without knowing what they are and bending yours to fit. To find out, focus on the impact on others and how they see the issue. This will be hard at first since you spend your energy justifying your own actions.

9. **Constrained by your own point of view? Go beyond the facts to consider the values of others.** You may be a fact-based person. Since to you the facts dictate everything, you may be baffled as to why people would see it any differently than you do. The reason

103

103

Factor: N/A
Cluster M: Trouble with people
Career staller and stopper 103: *Lack of* ethics and values

they see it differently is that there are different values at work. People compare across situations to check for common themes, equity, and parity. They ask questions like who wins and loses here, who is being favored, is this a play for advantage? Since you are a here-and-now person, you will look inconsistent to them across slightly different situations. You need to drop back and ask what will others hear, not what you want to say. Go below the surface. Tell them why you're saying something. Ask them what they think.

10. **Stuck in the past? Adapt when it makes sense.** This is a tough one. Times change. Do values change? Some think not. That may be your stance. What about humor? Could you tell some ribald jokes in the past that would get you in trouble today? Has television and 24-hour news changed our worldview? Is there still lifelong employment? How long does a college education last today versus 20 years ago? Values run pretty deep. They don't change easily. When did you form your current values? Over 20 years ago? Maybe it's time to examine them in light of the new today to see whether you need to make any midcourse corrections.

Job assignments

103

- Manage the assigning/allocating of office space in a contested situation.
- Make peace with an enemy or someone you've disappointed with a product or service or someone you've had some trouble with or don't get along with very well.
- Resolve an issue in conflict between two people, units, geographies, functions, etc.
- Be a member of a union-negotiating or grievance-handling team.
- Work on a team looking at a reorganization plan where there will be more people than positions.

"Our deeds determine us,
as much as we determine our deeds. **"**

George Eliot – English novelist

Factor: N/A
Cluster M: Trouble with people
Career staller and stopper 103: *Lack of* ethics and values
103

Learning resources

Bellingham, R. (2003). *Ethical leadership: Rebuilding trust in corporations*. Amherst, MA: HRD Press.

Bennis, W., Goleman, D., & O'Toole, J. (with Ward Biederman, P.). (2008). *Transparency: How leaders create a culture of candor*. San Francisco, CA: Jossey-Bass.

Boatright, J. R. (2006). *Ethics and the conduct of business* (5th ed.). Upper Saddle River, NJ: Prentice Hall.

Brown, M. T. (2005). *Corporate integrity: Rethinking organizational ethics and leadership*. New York, NY: Cambridge University Press.

Buckner, M. L. (2007). *The ABCs of ethics: A resource for leaders, managers, and professionals*. Lincoln, NE: iUniverse.

Cooper, C. (2008). *Extraordinary circumstances: The journey of a corporate whistleblower*. Hoboken, NJ: John Wiley & Sons, Inc.

Ferrell, O. C., Fraedrich, J., & Ferrell, L. (2006). *Business ethics: Ethical decision making and cases* (7th ed.). Boston, MA: Houghton Mifflin.

Heineman, B. W., Jr. (2008). *High performance with high integrity*. Boston, MA: Harvard Business School Press.

Klann, G. (2007). *Building character: Strengthening the heart of good leadership*. San Francisco, CA: John Wiley & Sons.

Knapp, J. C. (Ed.). (2007). *Leaders on ethics: Real-world perspectives on today's business challenges*. Westport, CT: Praeger.

Lubit, R. H. (2004). *Coping with toxic managers, subordinates, and other difficult people: Using emotional intelligence to survive and prosper*. Upper Saddle River, NJ: Financial Times Prentice Hall.

Porter, M. E., & Kramer, M. R. (2006). Strategy and society: The link between competitive advantage and corporate social responsibility. *Harvard Business Review, 85*, 136-137.

Showkeir, J., & Showkeir, M. (2008). *Authentic conversations: Moving from manipulation to truth and commitment*. San Francisco, CA: Berrett-Koehler.

Spinello, R., & Tavani, H. T. (Eds.). (2004). *Readings in cyberethics* (2nd ed.). Sudbury, MA: Jones & Bartlett.

Terris, D. (2005). *Ethics at work: Creating virtue at an American corporation*. Waltham, MA: Brandeis University Press.

104. Failure to build a team

There is more talk of teams than there are well-functioning teams. Most managers grow up as strong individual contributors. That's why they get promoted. They weren't like the rest of the members of the team. They were not raised in teams. They owe little of their success to teams. As a matter of fact, most of them could tell you stories about how some past team held them back from getting things done. But teams, although strange and uncomfortable to many, are the best way to accomplish some tasks such as creating systems that cross boundaries, producing complex products, or sustained coordinated efforts. It's really rewarding to be a member of a well-functioning, high-performance team. Well-functioning teams can outproduce the collective of what each individual could do on their own. Most individuals would choose to work for a boss who was able to build a well-functioning team.

"A great person attracts great people and knows how to hold them together."

Johann Wolfgang von Goethe – German poet, scientist, and diplomat

104

Factor: N/A
Cluster N: Doesn't inspire or build talent
Career staller and stopper 104: Failure to build a team

A problem

- Doesn't believe much in the value of teams.
- Doesn't pull the group together to accomplish the task.
- Delegates pieces and parts.
- Doesn't resolve problems within the team.
- Doesn't share credit for successes.
- Doesn't celebrate.
- Doesn't build team spirit.
- Treats people more as a collection of individuals than as a team.

Not a problem

- Usually operates in a team format.
- Talks "we," "us," and "the team" versus "I."
- Gets the whole team motivated and enthused.
- Runs participative meetings and processes.
- Shares credit with the team for successes.
- Adds people to strengthen the team.
- Team performance doesn't suffer when a key person moves on.
- Trusts the team to perform.

Some possible causes

- Can't set common cause.
- Can't resolve conflict among direct reports.
- Doesn't believe in teams.
- Doesn't have the time.
- Doesn't want to deal with the conflict.
- More comfortable one-on-one.
- The idea of a team is resisted by people.
- Poor time management; too busy.
- Too serious.

Factor: N/A
Cluster N: Doesn't inspire or build talent
Career staller and stopper 104: Failure to build a team

104

Other causes

Being less skilled at, or overusing, some competencies may also be the cause of an issue with Failure to build a team.

Being less skilled at:

13. Develops talent

15. Directs work

16. *Drives* engagement

34. *Builds effective* teams

Overusing:

2. Action oriented

5. Business insight

8. *Manages* complexity

35. Tech savvy

Tips to overcome Failure to build a team

1. **Prefer an individualistic approach? Find the value in teams.** If you don't believe in teams, you are probably a strong individual achiever who doesn't like the mess and sometimes the slowness of due-process relationships and team processes. You are very results oriented and truly believe the best way to do that is manage one person at a time. To balance this thinking, observe and talk with three excellent team builders and ask them why they manage that way. What do they consider rewarding about building teams? What advantages do they get from using the team format? Read *The Wisdom of Teams* by Katzenbach and Smith. If you can't see the value in teams, none of the following tips will help much.

2. **No time? Make the time and reap the benefits.** Don't have the time, teaming takes longer. That's true and not true. While building a team takes longer than managing one person at a time, having a well-functioning team increases results, builds in a sustaining capability to perform, maximizes collective strengths and covers individual weaknesses, and actually releases more time for the manager because the team members help each other. Many managers get caught in the trap of thinking it takes up too much time to build a team and end up taking more time managing one-on-one.

104

104

Factor: N/A
Cluster N: Doesn't inspire or build talent
Career staller and stopper 104: Failure to build a team

3. **Not a people person? Focus on basic people skills.** Many managers are better with things, ideas, and projects than they are with people. They may be driven and very focused on producing results and have little time left to develop their people skills. It really doesn't take too much. There is communicating. People are more motivated and do better work when they know what's going on. They want to know more than just their little piece. There is listening. Nothing motivates more than a boss who will listen, not interrupt, not finish your sentences, and not complete your thoughts. Increase your listening time 30 seconds in each transaction. There is caring. Caring is questions. Caring is asking about me and what I think and what I feel. Ask one more question per transaction than you do now.

4. **Want to optimize team performance? Study the characteristics of high-performing teams.** High-performance teams have four common characteristics: (1) They have a shared mindset. They have a common vision. Everyone knows the goals and measures. (2) They trust one another. They know others will cover them if they get in trouble. They know other team members will pitch in and help, even though it may be difficult for them. They know others will be honest with them. They know people will bring problems to them directly and won't go behind their backs. (3) They have the talent collectively to do the job. While not any one member may have it all, collectively they have every task covered. (4) They know how to operate efficiently and effectively. They have good team skills. They run effective meetings. They have efficient ways to communicate. They have ways to deal with internal conflict.

5. **Want to raise the odds that the team will excel? Inspire the team.** Follow the basic rules of inspiring others as outlined in classic books like *People Skills* by Robert Bolton or *Thriving on Chaos* by Tom Peters. Communicate to people that what they do is important, say thanks, offer help and ask for it, provide autonomy in how people do their work, provide a variety of tasks, "surprise" people with enriching, challenging assignments, show an interest in their careers, adopt a learning attitude toward mistakes, celebrate successes, have visible accepted measures of achievement, and so on. Try to get everyone to participate in the building of the team so they have a stake in the outcome.

6. **Unsure of how to assign team roles? Allow roles within the team to evolve naturally.** Cement relationships. Even though some—maybe including you—will resist it, parties, games nights, picnics and outings help build group cohesion. Allow roles to evolve naturally rather than being specified by job descriptions. Some research indicates

Factor: N/A
Cluster N: Doesn't inspire or build talent
Career staller and stopper 104: Failure to build a team

104

that people gravitate naturally to eight roles and that successful teams are not those where everyone does the same thing. Successful teams specialize, cover for each other, and only sometimes demand that everyone participate in identical activities.

7. **Want to know the secret to team building? Delegate and empower others.** One true team builder is giving people tough tasks to do, the resources to do them, and the authority to make decisions about it. Delegating increases motivation, releases your time to move on to other things, and gets more work done. Delegating is scary at first. They probably can't do it the first time as well as you can. But with coaching and support, they will learn and eventually either do it as well as you can or, better yet, do it better.

8. **Focused on the individual? Leverage the power of words and rewards.** Use *we* instead of *I*. Use *team, us, together*, more. Say *let us*. Let's get together. We can do it. We're all in this together. Signal that you are thinking team. Do you talk teams and reward individuals? To the extent that you can, reward the team more. Take some incentive money and divide it equally among the team members. Set team goals and line up team rewards.

9. **Team stuck in a rut? Create a climate of innovation and experimentation.** Don't prescribe how to do everything. How things are done should be as open as possible. Studies show that people work harder and are more effective when they have a sense of choice. Encourage quick experiments. Most innovations and experiments will fail, so communicate a learning attitude toward mistakes and failures.

104

10. **Need an outside perspective? Engage a team coach.** Because a team coach is external to the team, they can objectively help you problem solve and provide you with feedback to avoid some of the temptations that can demotivate a team. The team coach could be a human resources partner or an external professional who specializes in coaching.

11. **All work and no play? Build a sense of joy and fun for the team.** Research noted in *The Wisdom of Teams* by Katzenbach and Smith found there were several common threads among high-performing teams, including having fun. Fun is a by-product of the team's sense of commitment to each other and performance. If your team doesn't seem to be having fun, look for likely causes. Are the team members committed to the goals of the team? Are the team members

104

Factor: N/A
Cluster N: Doesn't inspire or build talent
Career staller and stopper 104: Failure to build a team

committed to one another? Fixing one or both of these issues might result in more fun.

12. **Ready to lead? Set the standard by modeling it.** Use your behavior to shape the behavior and performance of others. You have an opportunity to set the standard for the team. Many people resist developing new behaviors if they don't see those behaviors rewarded or demonstrated by more senior people. If behavior changes are required to improve team performance, they must start with you.

13. **Team in a downward spiral? Study the characteristics of low-performing teams.** Much research has been done on why teams fail. Your team is probably not unique. Read *The New Why Teams Don't Work* by Robbins and Finley and determine if your team has fallen into one of the common team traps and work to create a strategy to get the team back on track.

Job assignments

- Manage a group of low-competence or low-performing people through a task they couldn't do by themselves.
- Manage a group of people who are older and/or more experienced to accomplish a task.
- Assemble a team of diverse people to accomplish a difficult task.
- Manage a group of people involved in tackling a fix-it or turnaround project.
- Build a multifunctional project team to tackle a common business issue or problem.

"It's amazing what you can accomplish if you don't care who gets the credit."

Harry S. Truman – 33rd President of the United States

Factor: N/A
Cluster N: Doesn't inspire or build talent
Career staller and stopper 104: Failure to build a team

104

Learning resources

Capretta, C. C., Eichinger, R. W., & Lombardo, M. M. (2009). *FYI® for teams* (2nd ed.) Minneapolis, MN: Lominger International: A Korn Ferry Company.

Duarte, D. L., & Snyder, N. T. (2006). *Mastering virtual teams: Strategies, tools, and techniques that succeed* (3rd ed.). San Francisco, CA: Jossey-Bass.

Dyer, W. G., Dyer, W. G., Jr., & Dyer, J. H. (2007). *Team building: Proven strategies for improving team performance* (4th ed.). San Francisco, CA: Jossey-Bass.

Gibson, C. B., & Cohen, S. G. (Eds.). (2003). *Virtual teams that work: Creating conditions for virtual team effectiveness*. San Francisco, CA: Jossey-Bass.

Guttman, H. M. (2008). *Great business teams: Cracking the code for standout performance*. Hoboken, NJ: John Wiley & Sons.

Hackman, J. R. (2002). *Leading teams: Setting the stage for great performances*. Boston, MA: Harvard Business School Press.

Halverson, C. B., & Tirmizi, S. A. (Eds.). (2008). *Effective multicultural teams: Theory and practice* (Series: Advances in group decision and negotiation, Vol. 3). New York, NY: Springer.

Katzenbach, J. R., & Smith, D. K. (2003). *The wisdom of teams: Creating the high-performance organization*. New York, NY: HarperBusiness.

Klann, G. (2004). *Building your team's morale, pride, and spirit*. Greensboro, NC: Center for Creative Leadership.

Leigh, A., & Maynard, M. (2002). *Leading your team: How to involve and inspire teams*. Yarmouth, ME: Nicholas Brealey.

Lencioni, P. (2005). *Overcoming the five dysfunctions of a team: A field guide for leaders, managers, and facilitators*. San Francisco, CA: Jossey-Bass.

Parker, G. M. (2008). *Team players and teamwork: New strategies for the competitive enterprise* (2nd ed.). San Francisco, CA: Jossey-Bass.

Robbins, H., & Finley, M. (2000). *The new why teams don't work— What goes wrong and how to make it right*. San Francisco, CA: Berrett-Koehler.

Thompson, L. L. (2004). *Making the team: A guide for managers* (2nd ed.). Upper Saddle River, NJ: Pearson.

Van Ness, G., & Van Ness, K. (2003). *Being there without going there: Managing teams across time zones, locations, and corporate boundaries*. Boston, MA: Aspatore Books.

105. Failure to staff effectively

There is no substitute for a talented team all pulling in one direction accomplishing great things. Anything less than that is inefficient and ineffective. Getting there is a combination of hiring people against both a short-term and long-term staffing plan and having people with the necessary variety of skills and talents to do today's job with reserve to tackle tomorrow. You need the variety because no single profile or person is going to have it all.

" If you think it's expensive to hire a professional to do the job, wait until you hire an amateur. "

Red Adair – American oil well firefighting expert

105

Factor: N/A
Cluster N: Doesn't inspire or build talent
Career staller and stopper 105: Failure to staff effectively

A problem

- Does not assemble skilled staff either from inside or outside the organization.
- Uses inappropriate criteria and standards.
- May select people too much like self.
- Is not a good judge of people.
- Is consistently wrong on estimates of what others may do or become.

Not a problem

- Good judge of people.
- Hires for diversity and balance of skills.
- Describes people in a textured manner.
- Uses a broad set of criteria in staffing.
- Objective track record better than most on selections.
- Takes their time to find the right person.

Some possible causes

- Impatient.
- Narrow perspective.
- Non-strategic.
- Poor people-reading skills.
- Unfocused.
- Unwilling to take negative people actions.

105 Other causes

Being less skilled at, or overusing, some competencies may also be the cause of an issue with Failure to staff effectively.

Being less skilled at:

4. Attracts top talent
13. Develops talent
14. *Values* differences
34. *Builds effective* teams

Factor: N/A
Cluster N: Doesn't inspire or build talent
Career staller and stopper 105: Failure to staff effectively

105

Overusing:

2. Action oriented

3. *Manages* ambiguity

5. Business insight

35. Tech savvy

Tips to overcome Failure to staff effectively

1. **Going with your gut? Use proven interview techniques.** You just can't seem to make accurate appraisals based upon interviews and reference checks. Sound interviewing is a known technology. Read a book on interviewing techniques and successful practices and go to a course that teaches interviewing skills, preferably one with videotaped practice and feedback. Also, have others interview the candidates using standard competency rating scales and seek their counsel.

2. **Not sure what you're looking for? Define the skills that are required for success.** You don't have a feel for what skills and talents are required. Ask someone from human resources for help. Ask other bosses of units like yours what they look for. Benchmark with peers in other firms to see what they look for.

3. **Shortsighted? Make sure your success profile takes a long-term view.** Your people choices work out in the short-term but become less effective longer-term. This usually means you are using a success profile that is too narrow over time. It could also be that your organization only pays for current skills and you have trouble hiring the best people. In this case, try to hire people who have the current skills needed and are eager to learn new skills. Add "What did you learn?" and "How have you applied that?" questions to your interviews to try to hire current doers and future learners.

4. **Hesitant to take action? Address people problems promptly.** You inherited the team and some of the people are just not up to standard and you don't want to pull the trigger. If you don't, it just means more work for you and the rest of the team. The sooner you address people problems, the better off everyone will be, even the people involved.

5. **Impatient? Give yourself a choice of candidates.** You are impatient to fill empty spots on your team and tend to take the first acceptable

105

105

Factor: N/A
Cluster N: Doesn't inspire or build talent
Career staller and stopper 105: Failure to staff effectively

or near-acceptable candidate that comes along. That means you will make compromises and probably never meet the best candidate. Always try to wait long enough for multiple candidates and a real choice.

6. **Always scrambling to fill vacancies? Recruit proactively.** Finding someone to fill a gap in the team can be tough. The pressure's on. Results are at risk. Don't wait for someone to leave to look at the talent out there. Find people before you need them. Use your network to identify potential future candidates. Build a pipeline. Keep in touch with people; keep them interested.

7. **Need diversity? Avoid hiring clones.** You tend to hire too much in your own image. You prefer working with people who think and act as you do, so the team ends up skilled in only a few areas. You may load up on friends, people you have worked with in the past, or favorites. If you clone yourself in terms of skills, beliefs, background, or orientation, you and your team will not have the variety and diversity for truly great performance.

8. **Ready to learn best practices? Study high-performing teams.** Look to teams around you that you feel are the best-performing teams. What does the talent look like? What does the hiring model look like? Are the team members more the same or are they different from one another? Do they have the same background or come from a variety of situations? How do those team managers hire? Ask them what they do when filling an opening.

9. **Not challenged? Stretch yourself and your team.** You spend too little time worrying about improving the team. You may as well just do the important things yourself and let the team fend for itself. This is a very short-term strategy—one that will usually get you in more trouble as the situation continues. A good rule of thumb to follow is that your team should spend 20% of its time working outside its (and perhaps your) comfort zone. Stretching assignments are the prime source or reason for improvement.

10. **Trouble saying no? Stick to your criteria for candidates.** You take the easy way out and are hesitant to go against the grain and reject internal candidates. You can't say no to people more senior than you. You will be better able to do this if you have criteria for success for the job—ones that you can discuss easily. It's far easier to take a stand if you can say, "This candidate is strong in these competencies but not in these; we need someone who can do these as well."

Factor: N/A
Cluster N: Doesn't inspire or build talent
Career staller and stopper 105: Failure to staff effectively
105

Discussions of criteria get discussions off individuals and onto what it takes to do the job. Beyond this, you have to take a stand. Prepare a brief list of what you are looking for and stick to it calmly. Invite input on criteria, not people.

Job assignments

- Do a study of successful executives in your organization, and report the findings to top management.
- Do a study of failed executives in your organization, including interviewing people still with the organization who knew or worked with them, and report the findings to top management.
- Train and work as an assessor in an assessment center.
- Work on a team that's deciding whom to keep and whom to let go in a layoff, shutdown, delayering, or merger.
- Build a multi-functional project team to tackle a common business issue or problem.

" If you hire only those people you understand, the company will never get people better than you are. Always remember that you often find outstanding people among those you don't particularly like. "

Soichiro Honda – Japanese engineer and industrialist

105

105

Factor: N/A
Cluster N: Doesn't inspire or build talent
Career staller and stopper 105: Failure to staff effectively

Learning resources

Adler, L. (2007). *Hire with your head: Using performance-based hiring to build great teams.* Hoboken, NJ: John Wiley & Sons.

Charan, R., Lorsch, J. W., Khurana, R., Sorcher, M., Brant, J., Bennis, W., & O'Toole, J. (2005). *Hire the right CEO* (HBR OnPoint Collection). Boston, MA: Harvard Business Review.

Dimitrius, J., & Mazzarella, M. C. (2008). *Reading people: How to understand people and predict their behavior: Anytime, anyplace.* New York, NY: Ballantine Books.

Fields, M. R. A. (2001). *Indispensable employees: How to hire them, how to keep them.* Franklin Lakes, NJ: Career Press.

Guion, R. M., & Highhouse, S. (2006). *Essentials of personnel assessment and selection.* Mahwah, NJ: Lawrence Erlbaum Associates.

Hallenbeck, G. S., Jr., & Eichinger, R. W. (2006). *Interviewing right: How science can sharpen your interviewing accuracy.* Minneapolis, MN: Lominger International: A Korn Ferry Company.

Harvard Business Essentials. (2002). *Hiring and keeping the best people.* Boston, MA: Harvard Business School Press.

Harvey, M., Novicevic, M. M., & Garrison, G. (2004). Challenges to staffing global virtual teams. *Human Resource Management, 14,* 275-294.

Levin, R. A., & Rosse, J. G. (2001). *Talent flow: A strategic approach to keeping good employees, helping them grow, and letting them go.* New York, NY: John Wiley & Sons.

Michaels, E., Handfield-Jones, H., & Axelrod, B. (2001). *The war for talent.* Boston, MA: Harvard Business School Press.

Rosenberger, L. E., & Nash, J., (with Graham, A.). (2009). *The deciding factor: The power of analytics to make every decision a winner.* San Francisco, CA: Jossey-Bass.

Sears, D. (2003). *Successful talent strategies: Achieving superior business results through market-focused staffing.* New York, NY: AMACOM.

Smart, B. D. (2005). *Topgrading: How leading companies win: Hiring, coaching and keeping the best people* (Rev. ed.). New York, NY: Prentice Hall.

Still, D. J. (2001). *High impact hiring: How to interview and select outstanding employees.* Dana Point, CA: Management Development Systems.

105

Factor: N/A
Cluster N: Doesn't inspire or build talent
Career staller and stopper 105: Failure to staff effectively

105

Wylie, K. (2005). *Hiring the right candidate: Forms, FAQs, and resources for every employer*. Port Orchard, WA: Windstorm Creative.

105

106. Key skill deficiencies

New and different jobs, roles, geographies, business units, and organizations require new and different skills and abilities. Many times as we move up, in, out, down, and sideways, we are caught without the requisite skills needed to perform well. Some go about the business of learning the new skills and others wait to see if they can get through without building new skills. Most of the time, you can't wait. Those who wait too long get rated as having Key skill deficiencies.

“Faults are more easily recognized in the works of others than in our own.”

Leonardo da Vinci - Italian Renaissance painter, sculptor, architect, inventor, and writer

A problem

- Lacks one or more key job-required talents or skills needed to perform effectively.

Not a problem

- Skilled in most if not all of the mission-critical areas of the job.
- Scopes out what skills are required to perform.
- Works to improve and expand skill set.
- Open to tutors, courses, any learning mode to improve proficiency.

Some possible causes

- Counting backwards to retirement.
- Inexperienced.
- Lack of technical/functional skills.
- Narrow perspective.
- New to the job or function.
- Not interested in self-development.

Other causes

Being less skilled at, or overusing, some competencies may also be the cause of an issue with Key skill deficiencies.

Being less skilled at:

8. *Manages* complexity
22. Nimble learning
29. *Demonstrates* self-awareness
31. Situational adaptability

Overusing:

N/A

Tips to overcome Key skill deficiencies

1. **Unsure about your needs? Ask for feedback.** You need to find out what it is that people think you are missing. The best way to do that is to volunteer for a 360 feedback process. Find out what skills others think are important to do the job and compare your feedback against that standard. You can also simply ask your boss for that gap information.

2. **Unreceptive? Listen to feedback.** Sometimes you miss essential feedback about what you need to build because you didn't listen. Turn off your evaluator and listen to what you're being told. Don't dismiss a comment just because you don't agree with it. Think about what's behind the comment. What truth could there be in it? Why might the other person perceive you this way?

3. **Need to take action? Act on feedback.** Sometimes you hear the feedback but you choose not to do anything about it. That's your choice, but think carefully about the comments. How could taking action improve your performance? Your interaction with people? What could be the consequences of continuing to do things the way you have been? Think about the benefits of changing—to you and to others around you.

4. **Resisting? Stop being defensive.** Sometimes people try to deliver feedback to help you, and you fight it. Why are you resisting? Is it because you don't like what you hear? The truth can be painful sometimes. But it was probably uncomfortable for the other person to give you that feedback. They did it to help you develop. Don't fight it. Welcome it as an opportunity to grow. Don't make excuses for your behavior or your performance. Hold your hand up. Take responsibility. And, hardest of all, thank them for their feedback.

5. **No time? Prioritize and manage your time.** Sometimes you know what you need to develop or build but you don't have the time. Well, you can't afford to *not* make the time. Build time into your working week for your development. To reflect on your work. To consider the feedback you receive. To think about how you might modify your approach. What are you doing each week that you could spend less time on or eliminate altogether to allow time for your development? How much time do you waste on trivia? Is part of your week spent doing something that should really be delegated to someone else? Scrutinize how you use your time and be ruthless.

106

6. **Don't know how? Work on continuous improvement.** Sometimes you know what you need but don't know how to go about building it. If you come up against something you don't know how to do, don't just work around it or dismiss it. Think about what you need to learn to tackle it. Who can help? Where can you go for input and information? Always be looking to expand your skill toolkit and grow.

7. **Ready to learn from a master performer? Identify and observe experts in your area.** Look to what others in your role or job have that you don't have. What skills do they apply to the job that you don't as yet have? Talk to your mentor and ask them for information about what you are missing. Seek their guidance on how you can fill the skill gap.

8. **Curious? Make a commitment to learning.** Learn how to become a learner. Reflect on how you have learned best in the past. Read up on different learning styles. What methods of learning do you enjoy most? What approaches are most productive for you? What approaches to learning could you build into your regular routine going forward? Search online for information about learning to learn. Become a learning junkie.

9. **Need functional expertise? Identify functional skills required.** Talk to someone more experienced who can advise you on what skills are required for success. How have they developed these? What have they not yet developed that they need in order to do the best job they can? Where can you go to develop these functional skills?

10. **Need new technical skills? Identify technical skills required.** Sometimes the missing skills are technical. What are they? Think ahead, not just about the here and now. What technical skills are likely to become important for success in the future? How can you get ahead of the curve with these? Perhaps you have technical skills already that you can build upon further. Who can help?

Job assignments

- Find and spend time with an expert to learn something in an area new to you.

- Study some aspect of your job or a new technical area you haven't studied before that you need in order to be more effective.

- Work closely with a higher-level manager who is very good at something you need to learn.

- Volunteer to do a special project for and with a person you admire and who has a skill you need to develop.

- Study and summarize a new trend, product, service, technique, or process, and present and sell it to others.

" When you have faults, do not fear to abandon them. "

Confucius – Chinese philosopher

106

| 507

Learning resources

Argyris, C. (2008). *Teaching smart people how to learn*. Boston, MA: Harvard Business School Press.

Bell, A. H., & Smith, D. M. (2002). *Motivating yourself for achievement*. Upper Saddle River, NJ: Prentice Hall.

Bunker, K. A., Kram, K. E., & Ting, S. (2002). The young and the clueless. *Harvard Business Review, 80* (12), 80-88.

Colvin, R. (2008). *Building expertise: Cognitive methods for training and performance improvement*. San Francisco, CA: Pfeiffer.

Finkelstein, S. (2003). *Why smart executives fail: And what you can learn from their mistakes*. New York, NY: Portfolio.

Furnham, A. (2005). *The incompetent manager: The causes, consequences, and cures of management failure*. London, England: John Wiley & Sons.

Goldsmith, M., & Reiter, M. (2007). *What got you here won't get you there: How successful people become even more successful*. New York, NY: Hyperion.

Lizotte, K. (2007). *The expert's edge: Become the go-to authority people turn to every time*. New York, NY: McGraw-Hill.

Lombardo, M. M., & Eichinger, R. W. (2011). *The leadership machine* (10th Anniversary ed.). Minneapolis, MN: Lominger International: A Korn Ferry Company.

Rossiter, A. P. (2008). *Professional excellence: Beyond technical competence*. New York, NY: John Wiley & Sons, Inc.

Swisher, V. V., Hallenbeck, G. S., Jr., Orr, E. O., Eichinger, R. W., Lombardo, M. M., & Capretta, C. C. (2013). *FYI® for learning agility*. Minneapolis, MN: Lominger International: A Korn Ferry Company.

Waitzkin, J. (2008). *The art of learning: An inner journey to optimal performance*. New York, NY: Free Press.

Wick, C., Pollock, R., Jefferson, A., & Flanagan, R. (2006). *The six disciplines of breakthrough learning: How to turn training and development into business results*. San Francisco, CA: Pfeiffer.

Woller, L., & Woller, J. (2008). *The skill: The most critical tool needed to increase your potential, performance, and promotability*. Victoria, Canada: Trafford Publishing.

107. Non-strategic

There are a lot more people who can take a hill than there are people who can accurately predict which hill it would be best to take. There are more people good at producing results in the short-term than there are visionary strategists. Both have value but we don't have enough strategists. It is more likely that your organization will be outmaneuvered strategically than that it will be outproduced tactically. Most organizations do pretty well what they do today. It's what they need to be doing tomorrow that's the missing skill. Part of every manager's job is to be strategic. The higher you go, the more critical the requirement.

" *Strategy without tactics is the slowest road to victory. Tactics without strategy is the noise before defeat.* **"**

Sun Tzu – Chinese military strategist

A problem

- Can't create effective strategies.
- Can't deal effectively with assignments that require strategic thinking.
- Gets mired in tactics and details.
- Prefers the tactical over the strategic, simple versus complex.
- Isn't a visionary.
- Lacks broad perspective.

Not a problem

- Can think and talk strategy with the best.
- Intrigued and challenged by the complexity of the future.
- Likes to run multiple "what if" scenarios.
- Very broad perspective.
- Counsels others on strategic issues.
- Can juggle a lot of mental balls.
- Isn't afraid to engage in wild speculation about the future.
- Can bring several unrelated streams of information together to form a compelling vision.
- Good at meaning making.
- Produces distinctive and winning strategies.

Some possible causes

- Doesn't like complexity.
- Doesn't think the future is knowable.
- Inexperienced.
- Lack of perspective.
- Low-variety background.
- Low risk taker; doesn't like uncertainty.
- New to the area.
- Too busy with today's tasks.
- Too narrow.
- Very tactical.

510 |

Other causes

Being less skilled at, or overusing, some competencies may also be the cause of an issue with Non-strategic.

Being less skilled at:

12. Decision quality

18. Global perspective

33. Strategic mindset

37. *Drives* vision and purpose

Overusing:

2. Action oriented

20. Interpersonal savvy

Tips to overcome being Non-strategic

1. **Problems with presentation? Use strategic language.** In some rare cases, we have found people who could think strategically but were not identified as such because they either didn't know, rejected, or chose not to use what they considered the latest strategic buzzwords. Strategy is an emerging and ever-changing field. At any time, there are gurus (at present probably Michael Porter, Ram Charan, Gary Hamel, Fred Wiersema, and Vijay Govindarajan) in vogue who create new words or concepts (values disciplines, strategic intent or destination, value migration, co-evolution, market oligarchy, core capabilities, strategic horizon) to describe strategic thinking. If you don't use those words, then others won't know you're being strategic. New words can be found in books by these gurus, in the *Harvard Business Review*, and in *Strategy and Leadership*—a publication of the Strategic Leadership Forum. And, yes, most of the words are bigger words for things we used to call something else with smaller words. Nevertheless, if you want to be seen as more strategic, you have to talk more strategically. Every discipline has its lexicon. In order to be a member, you have to speak the code.

2. **Rejecting strategy? Recognize the value of strategic planning.** There are people who reject strategic formulation as so much folly. They have never seen a five-year strategic plan actually happen as projected. They think the time they use to create and present strategic plans is wasted. They think it's where the rubber meets the sky. While it's true that most strategic plans never work out as planned, that doesn't mean that it was a wasted effort. Strategic

plans lead to choices about resources and deployment. They lead to different staffing actions and different financial plans. Without some strategic planning, it would be a total shot in the dark. Most failed companies got buried strategically. They picked the wrong direction or too many directions. Not being able to produce a quality product or service today is generally not the problem.

3. **Don't think about the future? Be curious and imaginative.** Many managers are so wrapped up in today's problems that they aren't curious about tomorrow. They really don't care about the future. They believe there won't be much of a future until we perform today. Being a visionary and a good strategist requires curiosity and imagination. It requires playing "what ifs." What are the implications of the growing gap between rich and poor? The collapse of retail pricing? The increasing influence of brand names? What if it turns out that there is life on other planets and we get the first message? What will that change? Will they need our products? What will happen when a larger percentage of the world's population is over the age of 65? The effects of terrorism? What if cancer is cured? Heart disease? AIDS? Obesity? What if the government outlaws or severely regulates some aspect of your business? True, nobody knows the answers, but good strategists know the questions. Work at developing broader interests outside your business. Subscribe to different magazines, pick new shows to watch, meet different people, join a new organization. Look under some rocks. Think about tomorrow. Talk to others about what they think the future will bring.

4. **Narrow perspective? Broaden your perspective.** Some people are sharply focused on what they do and do it very well. They have prepared themselves for a narrow but satisfying career. Then someone tells them their job has changed and they now have to be strategic. Being strategic requires a broad perspective. In addition to knowing one thing well, it requires that you know about a lot of things somewhat. You need to understand business. You need to understand markets. You need to understand how the world operates. You need to put all that together and figure out what it means to your organization. And then you have to create a strategy.

5. **Too busy? Delegate the tactical and make time for strategy.** Strategy is always last on the list. Solving today's problems, of which there are many, is job one. You have to make time for strategy. A good strategy releases future time because it makes choices clear and leads to less wasted effort, but it takes time. Delegation is usually the key. Give away as much tactical, day-to-day stuff as you can. Ask your people what they think they could do to give you more time for strategic reflection. Another key is better time management. Put an hour a

week on your calendar for strategic reading and reflection throughout the year. Don't wait until one week before the strategic plan is due. Keep a log of ideas you get from others, magazines, etc. Focus on how these impact your organization or function.

6. **Avoiding ambiguity? Embrace the uncertainty.** Strategic planning is the most uncertain thing managers do. It's speculating on the near-unknown. It requires projections into foggy landscapes. It requires assumptions about the unknown. Many conflict avoiders don't like to make statements in public that they cannot back up with facts. Most strategies can be questioned. There are no clean ways to win a debate over strategy. It really comes down to one subjective estimate versus another.

7. **Addicted to the simple? Embrace the complexity.** Strategy ends up sounding simple—five clean, clear statements about where we want to go with a few tactics and decisions attached to each. Getting there is not simple. Good strategists are complexifiers. They extend everything to its extreme before they get down to the essence. Simplifiers close too early. They are impatient to get it done faster. They are very results oriented and want to get to the five simple statements before strategic due process has been followed. Be more tolerant of unlimited exploration and debate before you move to close.

8. **Don't know how to be strategic? Become a student of strategy.** The simplest problem is someone who wants to be strategic and wants to learn. Strategy is a reasonably well-known field. Read the gurus—Michael Porter, Ram Charan, C. K. Prahalad, Gary Hamel, Fred Wiersema, and Vijay Govindarajan. Scan the *Harvard Business Review* regularly. Read the three to five strategic case studies in *Bloomberg Businessweek* every issue. Go to a three-day strategy course taught by one of the gurus. Get someone from the organization's strategic group to tutor you in strategy. Watch CEOs talk about their businesses on cable. Volunteer to serve on a task force on a strategic issue.

9. **Can't think strategically? Practice strategic thinking.** Strategy is linking several variables together to come up with the most likely scenario. It involves making projections of several variables at once to see how they come together. These projections are in the context of shifting markets, international affairs, monetary movements, and government interventions. It involves a lot of uncertainty, making risk assumptions, and understanding how things work together. How many reasons would account for sales going down? Up? How are advertising and sales linked? If the dollar is cheaper in Asia, what

does that mean for our product in Japan? If the world population is aging and they have more money, how will that change buying patterns? Not everyone enjoys this kind of pie-in-the-sky thinking and not everyone is skilled at doing it.

10. **Don't want to be strategic? Get some help.** Some just don't feel they want to ramp up and learn to be strategic. But they like their job and want to be considered strategically responsible. Hire a strategic consultant once a year to sit with you and your team and help you work out your strategic plan. Accenture. The Boston Consulting Group. McKinsey. Booz Allen Hamilton. Strategos. Plus many more. Or delegate strategy to one or more people in your unit who are more strategically capable. Or ask the strategic planning group to help. You don't have to be able to do everything to be a good manager. You like your nest? Some people are content in their narrow niche. They are not interested in being strategic. They just want to do their job and be left alone. They are interested in doing good work in their specialty and want to advance as far as they can. That's OK. Just inform the organization of your wishes and don't take jobs that have a heavy strategic requirement.

Job assignments

- Do a competitive analysis of your organization's products or services or position in the marketplace, and present it to the people involved.

- Do a postmortem on a successful project, and present it to the people involved.

- Do a feasibility study on an important opportunity and make recommendations to those who will decide.

- Monitor and follow a new product or service through the entire idea, design, test market, and launch cycle.

- Study and summarize a new trend, product, service, technique, or process, and present and sell it to others.

" *What's the use of running if you are not on the right road?* **"**

– German proverb

Learning resources

Apgar, D. (2008). *Relevance: Hitting your goals by knowing what matters*. San Francisco, CA: Jossey-Bass.

Barney, J., & Hesterly, W. S. (2007). *Strategic management and competitive advantage: Concepts and cases* (2nd ed.). Upper Saddle River, NJ: Prentice Hall.

Camillus, J. C. (2008). Strategy as a wicked problem. *Harvard Business Review, 86*(5), 98-107.

Charan, R. (2005). *Boards that deliver: Advancing corporate governance from compliance to competitive advantage*. San Francisco, CA: John Wiley & Sons.

Eichinger, R. W., Ruyle, K. E., & Ulrich, D. O. (2007). *FYI® for strategic effectiveness: Aligning people and operational practices to strategy*. Minneapolis, MN: Lominger International: A Korn Ferry Company.

Freedman, M. (with Tregoe, B. B.). (2003). *The art and discipline of strategic leadership*. New York, NY: McGraw-Hill.

Hughes, R. L., & Beatty, K. M. (2005). *Becoming a strategic leader: Your role in your organization's enduring success*. San Francisco, CA: John Wiley & Sons.

Hunger, J. D., & Wheelen, T. (2006). *Essentials of strategic management* (4th ed.). Upper Saddle River, NJ: Prentice Hall.

Krames, J. A. (2003). *What the best CEOs know: 7 Exceptional leaders and their lessons for transforming any business*. New York, NY: McGraw-Hill.

Nolan, T. N., Goodstein, L. D., & Goodstein, J. (2008). *Applied strategic planning: An introduction* (2nd ed.). San Francisco, CA: Pfeiffer.

Pearce, J. A., & Robbins, D. K. (2008). Strategic transformation as the essential last step in the process of business turnaround. *Business Horizons, 51*, 121-130.

Prahalad, C. K., & Ramaswamy, V. (2004). *The future of competition: Co-creating unique value with customers*. Boston, MA: Harvard Business School Press.

Stalk, G. (2008). *Five future strategies you need right now (Memo to the CEO)*. Boston, MA: Harvard Business School Press.

Thompson, A. A., Jr., Strickland, A. J., III., & Gamble, J. E. (2007). *Crafting and executing strategy* (16th ed.). New York, NY: McGraw-Hill.

Welborn, R., & Kasten, V. (2003). *The Jericho principle: How companies use strategic collaboration to find new sources of value.* New York, NY: John Wiley & Sons.

108. Overdependence on an advocate

The most successful men in studies of managerial success usually didn't have a single long-term mentor or advocate. They were more likely to have multiple advocates at various stages of their careers. Women have reported a higher incidence of having single mentors because of being pioneers in a new arena. They needed one to get into the "Club." There's good news and bad news. Having an advocate/mentor is a great way to get into the mainstream of an organization, be privy to fresh information, and get advantages—promotions, choice assignments, invitations to events, etc. Having a strong advocate is also one of the best ways to stall your career long-term. People wonder if you can do it on your own—can you stand alone without the advocate and be successful? How much of your success was windfall? What would happen to you if your advocate/mentor left or fell from grace?

> **"** *All charming people have something to conceal, usually their total dependence on the appreciation of others.* **"**
>
> Cyril Connolly – English intellectual, literary critic, and writer

A problem

- Has been with the same boss, champion, mentor, advocate too long.
- Isn't seen as independent.
- Others question whether he/she could stand up to a tough assignment or situation without help.
- Might not do well in the organization if the advocate lost interest, lost out, or left the organization.

Not a problem

- Has largely done it on his/her own.
- Has multiple advocates and champions.
- No one questions whether he/she could go it alone.
- Independent, resourceful person.
- Doesn't use a champion's influence to get things done.
- Has moved around a lot; has not been with one boss very long.
- Has survived an advocate or two leaving the organization.

Some possible causes

- Dependent.
- Doesn't get results alone.
- Has become lazy.
- Narrow experience base.
- Not tough.
- Overly loyal.

Other causes

Being less skilled at, or overusing, some competencies may also be the cause of an issue with Overdependence on an advocate.

Being less skilled at:

21. *Builds* networks
23. Organizational savvy
27. Resourcefulness
32. *Balances* stakeholders

Overusing:

30. Self-development

35. Tech savvy

Tips to overcome Overdependence on an advocate

1. **In a rut? Determine how long is too long.** Being trapped with an advocate/mentor starts innocently enough. Two people take a liking to each other. They respect each other. A bond is formed. One helps the other break in. The other works hard to reward the advocate/mentor. The advocate/mentor gets promoted. They take you along. You pass up other opportunities to stay with this positive and supportive person. The advocate/mentor doesn't put you up for other jobs because they really appreciate what you can do. And it's so easy working for each other. Each of you is in the groove and in your comfort zone. How long is too long? When others begin to question whether you could perform alone. When your advocate/mentor turns down opportunities for you. When your advocate/mentor keeps you for their own comfort. When you aren't learning anything new. When you don't have to push yourself to please them. Then it's time to break free. Volunteer for a job change. Ask your advocate/mentor for help in getting another assignment. Ask human resources about how you can market yourself for another opportunity.

2. **Can't change jobs? Spread your wings.** Volunteer for task forces or projects your advocate/mentor is not involved in. If the project is important, is multi-functional and has a real outcome which will be taken seriously, it is one of the most common developmental events listed by successful executives. Such projects require learning other functions, businesses, or nationalities. You can get out of your own experience and start to see connections to a broader world—how international trade works or how the pieces of your organization fit together. Your performance will also be seen as yours and part of the project's and not connected with your advocate/mentor.

3. **Ready to explore? Try something new.** Do things in your job that you have not done before. Broaden your experience base. In your unit there are things to start up or fix, problems to confront, etc. Pick three tasks you've never done and volunteer to do them. If you don't know much about customers, work in a store or handle customer complaints; if you don't know what engineering does, go find out; task trade with someone; write a strategic plan for your unit.

4. **Need variety? Locate some additional role models.** You have learned great stuff from your advocate/mentor but it's time to add some new stuff. Pick a person in the organization who is different in some aspects from your advocate/mentor. Observe what they do and how they do it. They are as successful as your advocate/mentor but do it in other ways. If possible, ask for a meeting/lunch to discuss their success and the things they have learned. See if they have any interest in teaching you something and being a temporary coach. Get to know other potential advocates on- and off-work. Go for maximum variety in the towering strengths they possess.

5. **Ready to take on more responsibility? Perform more independently.** What do you take for granted that your advocate/mentor does for you? How are they helpful? Do they help you make final decisions? Start making the decisions yourself. Get you invitations to special events? Get them on your own. Share interesting information? Get it from other sources. Help you prepare important presentations? Do a few by yourself. Cover your mistakes? Fix them yourself. Pass on feedback from others to you? Go talk to the originators on your own. Try to think about all the things you rely on your advocate/mentor for and try to begin to perform more independently.

6. **Seen as a proxy for your manager? Avoid overusing your advocate/mentor.** One common problem of being with a boss or advocate too long is that you might get in the habit of acting in their absence or on their behalf. You may take on their authority. You might even get in the lazy habit of saying "Larry" would like it this way or "Larry" would approve or not approve of this when that isn't literally true. People may get in the habit of passing information to you because they know it will get to Larry. People may pass things by you and ask how you think Larry would react to it. People may ask you what Larry is really like because they are having some difficulty with him. All of these types of things are natural consequences of your special relationship with Larry, but they can just as well backfire longer-term in your career. Don't use Larry's name, use your own.

7. **Need to develop courage? Take more risks.** If you have trouble standing alone because you have been overly dependent upon an advocate/mentor, increase the risks you take on your own. Stake out a position on an issue that will require some courage and where you know there will be some detractors. Prepare by rehearsing for tough questions, attacks, and countering views. Don't use your advocate/mentor. Talk to yourself. Pump yourself up by focusing on your strengths.

8. **Need to break a habit? Try new approaches.** Stuck in the ways the advocate/mentor passed on to you? Do you approach situations much the same every time? Then switch approaches. Do something totally different next time. If you visited the office of someone you have difficulties with, invite them to your office next time. Compare the situations and see which was more valuable. Develop three different ways to get the same outcome. For example, to push a decision through, you could meet with stakeholders first, go to a key stakeholder, study and present the problem to a group, call a problem-solving session, or call in an outside expert. Be prepared to do them all when obstacles arise.

9. **Need an advocate? Engage, but also establish your independence.** A mentor, guide, or advocate can be an invaluable resource to help you thrive in an organization. The advice and feedback they provide can contribute significantly to your career progression. However, the trick is to take advantage of this special relationship long enough to get plugged in and comfortable but not so long that you question whether you could have done it on your own. That usually means unplugging before you want to. Before you become too comfortable. Before the mentor has taught you everything you need to know. Before you get evaluated as being overdependent on an advocate. Start early to find multiple models, multiple advocates. Make sure at least five key figures know who you are and what you can do.

10. **Ready to say good-bye? Know when to move on.** One situation involves what to do when your advocate/mentor stumbles, falls, fails, or leaves. Many times, the person may ask you to join them in the next company. Think very carefully about that. There are many cases of entourages of people following a general manager from company to company. You will be an outsider. Your career will be closely tied to the person you are following. The same thing will happen to you in the next company, only faster. If they fall out of favor but stay, be supportive but keep out of it. It's not your problem. Don't go around defending your advocate/mentor. You will get tainted too. The other situation occurs when you decide to change jobs within your organization. Advocates/mentors may not buy the fact that you have to establish a performance track on your own to be truly successful. They may think or say that they can counsel you to the top. You don't need to take another job. You don't need to work for someone else. Remember that these kinds of wonderful relationships have advantages for both sides. They get things they need from you also. You are in no way rejecting or devaluing your advocate/mentor by breaking free. In a sense, it's a celebration of the success the advocate/mentor has had with you. You are now

fully prepared to go it on your own. Be appreciative. Keep a light in the window. And move on to new vistas.

Job assignments

• Make peace with an enemy or someone you've disappointed with a product or service or someone you've had some trouble with or don't get along with very well.

• Become a referee for an athletic league or program.

• Be a change agent; create a symbol for change; lead the rallying cry; champion a significant change and implementation.

• Run (chair) a task force on a pressing problem.

• Handle a tough negotiation with an internal or external client or customer.

108

"_It is not inequality which is the real misfortune, it is dependence._ **"**

Voltaire – French Enlightenment writer, historian, and philosopher

Learning resources

Badowski, R. (with Gittines, R.). (2003). *Managing up: How to forge an effective relationship with those above you*. New York, NY: Currency.

Baker, W. E. (2000). *Networking smart*. New York, NY: Backinprint.com

Bell, C. R. (2002). *Managers as mentors: Building partnerships for learning*. San Francisco, CA: Berrett-Koehler.

Butler, T. (2007). *Getting unstuck: How dead ends become new paths*. Boston, MA: Harvard Business School Press.

Chaleff, I. (2003). *The courageous follower: Standing up to and for our leaders*. San Francisco, CA: Berrett-Koehler.

Champy, J., & Nohria, N. (2000). *The arc of ambition*. Cambridge, MA: Perseus Publishing.

Darling, D. (2005). *Networking for career success*. New York, NY: McGraw-Hill.

Ensher, E. A., & Murphy, S. E. (2005). *Power mentoring: How successful mentors and protégés get the most out of their relationships*. San Francisco, CA: Jossey-Bass.

Ferrazzi, K., & Raz, T. (2005). *Never eat alone: And other secrets to success, one relationship at a time*. New York, NY: Doubleday

Gardner, H. (2006). *Five minds for the future*. Boston, MA: Harvard Business School Press.

Ibarra, H. (2003). *Working identity: Unconventional strategies for reinventing your career*. Boston, MA: Harvard Business School Press.

Kouzes, J. M., & Posner, B. Z. (2007). *The leadership challenge* (4th ed.). San Francisco, CA: Jossey-Bass.

Warrell, M. (2007). *Find your courage! Unleash your full potential and live the life you really want*. Austin, TX: Synergy Books.

Wendleton, K. (2006). *Navigating your career: Develop your plan, manage your boss, get another job inside*. New York, NY: The Five O'clock Club.

Zigarmi, D., Blanchard, K., O'Connor, M., & Edeburn, C. (2005). *The leader within: Learning enough about yourself to lead others*. Upper Saddle River, NJ: Prentice Hall.

109. Overdependence on a single skill

We are comfort zone creatures. We build nests. We go where it feels safe and good. Most of us don't like taking chances. Most of us don't venture onto alien ground comfortably. For those reasons, many of us take the safe career track, we think, of learning one thing and doing that well. In our early careers, that gets us good pay and promotions up the career ladder. We are promoted over people who are not as deeply skilled as we are. We play the one skill, one technology, one business, one function or one talent (e.g., selling) all the way. Trouble is, it doesn't go all the way. All things change. One of the requirements for higher-level management and career fulfillment is broadness and diversity. If you succeed long enough, you'll manage or work closely with new functions and businesses. A single skill is never enough.

" Jack of all trades, master of none, certainly better than a master of one. "

– English folk couplet

A problem

- Relies too much on a single strength for performance and career progression.
- Uses the same core talent, function, or technology to leverage self.
- Acts as if they can make it all the way on one strength.

Not a problem

- Has a broad and varied background.
- Has moved around a lot.
- Relies on several different skills to get the job done.
- Has multiple functional exposures.
- Has worked in different business units.
- Always looking to learn more.
- Works on adding more skills.

Some possible causes

- Counting backwards to retirement.
- Inexperienced.
- Lazy.
- Lives in the glory of the past.
- Narrow perspective.
- Not interested in broadening or self-development.
- Too comfortable.

Other causes

Being less skilled at, or overusing, some competencies may also be the cause of an issue with Overdependence on a single skill.

Being less skilled at:

6. Collaborates
15. Directs work
29. *Demonstrates* self-awareness
31. Situational adaptability

526 |

Overusing:

2. Action oriented

Tips to overcome Overdependence on a single skill

1. **Need a change? Plan your next assignment.** Think carefully about your next natural point for an assignment change. This time, press your boss, business unit, or organization for something different. Could be different geography, same job but different business unit, same job but different assignments, or a completely different job. Sometimes if you have been in something too long, you may have to take a lateral or even a short-term downgrading to get on a different track.

2. **Want to see alternatives? Broaden your perspective.** Volunteer for task forces and study teams outside your area. Be brave and consider things you've never even thought of being involved in before. Go beyond your comfort zone. Look into joining groups involved in things that don't even relate to what you are used to doing. Investigate those that would require you to stretch and learn skills you never thought you would need.

109

3. **Ready to learn from others? Learn from other functions.** Attend off-sites and meetings of functions and units other than yours. Build relationships with people you don't normally interact with. Be curious about their area of the organization. Ask lots of questions to learn as much as you can. Be prepared to reciprocate so the door is kept wide open. Keep up-to-date with what they're doing. Relate their activities to your own area. What impact do the two areas have on each other?

4. **Reading narrowly? Expand your reading selections.** In addition to the literature you now read in your specialty, expand to a broader selection of journals and magazines. What trade journals are there for your industry? Visit the library and dip into the trade press for other industries. Read journals that will expand your knowledge more broadly, such as *Harvard Business Review*, the *Wall Street Journal*, *Bloomberg Businessweek*, *Forbes*, *Time*, *Fortune*. Read ones with global coverage like *Commentary*, the *Economist*, *Monocle*, or the *International New York Times*. Follow business social media and blogs. Browse through the business section of any good quality newspaper. Read the latest business books. No time to sift through?

Subscribe to Soundview Executive Book Summaries and read summaries of the current best sellers.

5. **Curious? Take a class.** Take a seminar or workshop outside your area just for the fun of it. What do you know nothing about, but would like to learn? Find out what sessions colleagues have found helpful. Go online and see what's available. Watch some TED (Technology, Entertainment, Design) Talks on subjects you know nothing about. Broaden your mind outside of work. Join a martial arts group. Take a painting class. Learn the art of French cuisine.

6. **Need a vacation? Explore new destinations.** Vacation more broadly. Get out of your comfort zone and explore new places. If you can arrange it, vacation outside of your home country. Where have you always been slightly nervous about going? Get the brochure. Where would you feel most culturally out of place? Book a flight. Always gone five star and never "roughed it"? Find a hostel.

7. **Ready to teach in order to learn? Organize a knowledge exchange.** Find someone who is as specialized as you are who is also seeking expansion and teach your specialties to each other. Get together a small group and have each person agree to present a new technology or business topic each month to the group. Teaching something new for you is one of the best ways to learn it yourself.

8. **Got what it takes? Observe higher-level general managers.** Look to some people in your area who are in more senior jobs than you are. Are they as specialized as you are? Are they struggling in their new roles because they are as specialized as you are? Read *Career Mastery* by Harry Levinson.

9. **Want to learn the field? Interview an expert.** Find some experts in what you need to learn. Interview them. Find out how they think about their area. Ask them about the challenges they have faced. How have they figured out what to do? What did they find most difficult when they were first learning in this field? What's most fun about their area? Most frustrating? Where do they go for information? Who are their go-to people? What are the five key things they look for when they're faced with a problem? What do they wish they'd known before they started working in this area? What has been their biggest learning in the last year?

10. **Want to learn about alternatives? Interview a generalist.** Pick three people who are broadly skilled. Ask them how they got to be that

way. What motivated them to become a generalist, rather than specialize? What job experiences have they had? What do they read? Watch on TV? Who do they like to learn from? How do they continue to grow their knowledge and expertise in so many areas? Who do they recommend you contact to learn about an area in more depth?

Job assignments

- Study some aspect of your job or a new technical area you haven't studied before that you need in order to be more effective.

- Work closely with a higher-level manager who is very good at something you need to learn.

- Work short rotations in other units, functions, or geographies you've not been exposed to before.

- Study and summarize a new trend, product, service, technique, or process, and present and sell it to others.

- Benchmark innovative practices, processes, products, or services of competitors, vendors, suppliers, or customers, and present a report making recommendations for change.

109

Specialization is for insects.

Robert Heinlein – American science fiction writer

Learning resources

Cashman, K. (2008). *Leadership from the inside out: Becoming a leader for life* (2nd ed.). San Francisco, CA: Berrett-Koehler Publishers.

Champy, J., & Nohria, N. (2000). *The arc of ambition*. Cambridge, MA: Perseus Publishing.

Charan, R., Drotter, S., & Noel, J. (2000). *The leadership pipeline: How to build the leadership powered company*. San Francisco, CA: Jossey-Bass.

DuFour, R., DuFour, R., Eaker, R., & Many, T. (2006). *Learning by doing: A handbook for professional learning communities at work*. Bloomington, IN: Solution Tree.

Friedman, T. L. (2006). *The world is flat 3.0: A brief history of the twenty-first century* (Updated ed.). New York, NY: Farrar, Straus and Giroux.

Goldsmith, M., & Reiter, M. (2007). *What got you here won't get you there: How successful people become even more successful*. New York, NY: Hyperion.

Kaplan, B., & Kaiser, R. (2006). *The versatile leader: Make the most of your strengths—without overdoing it*. San Francisco, CA: Pfeiffer.

Lombardo, M. M., & Eichinger, R. W. (2011). *The leadership machine* (10th Anniversary ed.). Minneapolis, MN: Lominger International: A Korn Ferry Company.

McCall, M. W., Lombardo, M. M., & Morrison, A. M. (1988). *The lessons of experience*. Lexington, MA: Lexington Books.

Morrison, A. M., White, R. P., Van Velsor, E., & the Center for Creative Leadership. (1992). *Breaking the glass ceiling: Can women reach the top of America's largest corporations?* Reading, MA: Addison-Wesley.

Rothwell, W., Jackson, R. D., Knight, S. C., & Lindholm, J. E. (2005). *Career planning and succession management: Developing your organization's talent – for today and tomorrow*. Westport, CT: Praeger.

Waitzkin, J. (2008). *The art of learning: An inner journey to optimal performance*. New York, NY: Free Press.

110.   Political missteps

Organizations are a complex maze of constituencies, issues, and rivalries peopled by strong egos, sensitive personalities, and empire protectors. People who are politically savvy accept this as the human condition and deal with it by considering the impact of what they say and do on others. Political savvy involves getting things done in the maze with the minimum of noise. Political mistakes come in a variety of shapes and sizes. The most common is saying things that you shouldn't. This comes in two shapes—you knew it was wrong but you couldn't hold it back, or you didn't know it was wrong to say and were surprised at the reaction. Next, are actions that are politically out of line and not right for the context. Worst, are politically unacceptable moves, initiatives, tactics, and strategies. You tried to get something done in the organization and went about it in the wrong way. Last are unnecessary conflicts, tensions, misunderstandings, and rivalries created because you provoked a specific person or group.

" Every political system is an accumulation of habits, customs, prejudices, and principles that have survived a long process of trial and error and of ceaseless response to changing circumstances. "

Edward C. Banfield – American political scientist and author

110

Factor: N/A
Cluster M: Trouble with people
Career staller and stopper 110: Political missteps

A problem

- Can't get things done in complex political settings and environments.
- Lacks sensitivity to people and organizational politics.
- Doesn't recognize political due process requirements.
- Says and does the wrong things.
- Shares sensitive information and opinions with the wrong people.

Not a problem

- Is politically smooth and noiseless.
- Reads individuals and groups well; knows how they are affected.
- Modifies approach when resistance is met.
- Keeps confidences.
- Can maneuver through rough water without getting wet.
- Uses multiple ways to get things done.
- Adjusts to the realities of the political situation.
- Counsels others on political approaches.
- Usually knows the right thing to do and say.

Some possible causes

- Competitive with peers.
- Doesn't read others or their interests well.
- May be too candid to curry favor.
- May share wrong/sensitive information.
- Misunderstands what political savvy is.
- No patience with due process.
- Poor impulse control.
- Poor interpersonal skills.
- Poor negotiator.
- Seen as a strident advocate.

Other causes

Being less skilled at, or overusing, some competencies may also be the cause of an issue with Political missteps.

Factor: N/A
Cluster M: Trouble with people
Career staller and stopper 110: Political missteps

110

Being less skilled at:

6. Collaborates

20. Interpersonal savvy

21. *Builds* networks

36. *Instills* trust

Overusing:

2. Action oriented

19. *Cultivates* innovation

28. *Drives* results

35. Tech savvy

Tips to overcome Political missteps

1. **Can't hold back? Work on impulse control.** Many people get into political trouble because they find it difficult to hold things back. It's not that they didn't know what they were about to say was going to cause noise, they just have weak impulse control. They say almost everything that occurs to them to say. It's even possible that others in the room or in the meeting were thinking the same thing. The difference is that they kept it to themselves. When you dump everything before you put it through a political filter, much of what you say will cause noise and will be seen as poor political judgment by others. One rule is to let others speak first and follow their lead before you dump.

2. **Humor seen as offensive? Keep it in good taste.** Many people get into political trouble with their humor. Times have changed. Workplace demographics have changed. Humor that was once seen as OK is now politically unacceptable and possibly illegal. The guidelines are simple. Refrain from using humor that hurts or demeans others. Don't use any type of humor that involves prejudice, such as racial comments, making fun of someone's disability, physical appearance, or gender-biased humor. No humor that is critical or sarcastic is acceptable. This doesn't mean that people should avoid humor in the workplace. Humor can have a positive impact. It releases stress, spurs creative thinking, increases productivity. Encourage appropriate humor.

110

Factor: N/A
Cluster M: Trouble with people
Career staller and stopper 110: Political missteps

3. **Want to avoid politics? Evaluate your attitude toward politics.** Many people confuse the terms political savvy and being political. When someone criticizes you for not being political, you might interpret it as the bad political. Being bad political means that your motives should not be trusted. Being bad political means saying one thing and meaning another. It means being devious and scheming. Being politically savvy means saying and doing things that fit into the commonly held beliefs people have around you about what's appropriate and wise and what is not. It's about a set of standards that most people around you would agree to. Being politically savvy means you can transact with others and get things done in the maze with minimum noise and without triggering an unnecessary negative reaction from others.

4. **Stuck with a predictable approach? Adjust to the situation and the audience.** In any culture or organization, there are multiple ways you can get things done. You could use a direct attack. You could get an ally first. You could send in a more acceptable substitute for yourself. Some of these tactics are more effective and acceptable than others. Some people get into trouble because they treat all situations the same. They don't do any research about the most effective ways to get things done for each event. People who are politically savvy operate from the outside in—starting with the audience, person, group, organization. They pick their pace, style, tone, and tactics based upon an evaluation of what would work best in each situation. We all have a number of ways in which we can behave if we want to. It's the one-trick ponies that get into political trouble because they don't adjust what they say and do to each audience.

5. **Too honest? Decide whether candor is appropriate.** Candor can be a mission-critical requirement in a 9 a.m. meeting and politically unwise and unacceptable in a 10 a.m. meeting. Many people get themselves into political trouble with either too much candor that ends up hurting others and causing noise, or too little candor seen as holding back something important. Many often say, "I just say what I think. I've always believed in saying exactly what I mean. Consequences be damned. If they don't like it, they shouldn't have asked me about it." While that might get good marks for integrity, it would fail the political savvy test. Each situation must be examined on the candor scale. Are the right people here? Is this the best time for candor? Should I let someone else start before I do? Did the speaker who asked for candor really mean it?

Factor: N/A
Cluster M: Trouble with people
Career staller and stopper 110: Political missteps

110

6. **Don't know the key players? Navigate the politics of the organization.** Who are the movers and shakers in the organization? Who are the major gatekeepers who control the flow of resources, information and decisions? Who are the guides and the helpers? Get to know them better. Do lunch. Who are the major resisters and stoppers? Either avoid them or sidestep them or make peace with them. Every maze has its solution. Being politically savvy means finding that least distant path through the organizational maze.

7. **Sharing too much? Make sure comments are relevant and proper.** Are you sharing things inappropriately to cement a relationship, to get something you need, to feel like an important insider, or because you just don't think it through? Monitor yourself closely and ask these questions: "Why am I sharing this? Does it move a problem along? Do people really need to know this? Will this make someone else look bad or will it be obvious where I got it? Am I name dropping? Have I labeled facts as facts and opinions as opinions? Will this be considered grousing, gossiping, or cutting down another person or group? In the worst case, how could this person use this information in a way that would reflect badly on me?" A general rule of thumb is that you can be as candid as you like as long as comments refer to specific problems/issues and you're not violating confidences and the person you are giving the information to can be trusted.

8. **Talking about people? Refrain from gossiping.** A lot of political noise comes from sharing private views of others in the wrong settings and with the wrong people. All things come around that go around. In closed organizations, people quickly find out what you have said about them. If you are having trouble with this, the simplest rule is never to share any negative information about another person unless it is a formal evaluation process in the organization.

110

9. **Dealing with executives? Approach top management with extra care.** In the special case of dealing with top management, sensitivities are high, egos can be big, and tensions can be severe. There is a lot of room for making statements or acting in ways that would be seen as exhibiting poor political judgment. There usually isn't a second chance to make a good first impression. Plan your approach carefully. Consider what this audience is looking for. Be respectful of their time. Share information clearly and concisely. Express opinions tactfully. Practice your message in advance. It might also be valuable to talk to experienced colleagues about the sensitivities, priorities, and preferences of top management. What are their hot-button issues? What pitfalls do you need to avoid? How can you adjust your style to engage with them as effectively as possible?

110

Factor: N/A
Cluster M: Trouble with people
Career staller and stopper 110: Political missteps

10. **Strong point of view? Temper your advocacy and make the business case.** Strident advocates don't usually fare well in organizations because their perspectives are seen as rigid and narrow. To avoid being seen this way, make the business or organizational case first. Be more tentative than you actually are so others have room to get comfortable and negotiate and bargain. People who have trouble with this tend to state things in such an extreme that others are turned off and can't save face, even if they agree with more than 50% of what you are pushing for.

Job assignments

- Integrate diverse systems, processes, or procedures across decentralized and/or dispersed units.

- Manage the interface between consultants and the organization on a critical assignment.

- Prepare and present a proposal of some consequence to top management.

- Manage the assigning/allocating of office space in a contested situation.

- Work on a team that's deciding whom to keep and whom to let go in a layoff, shutdown, delayering, or merger.

" Politics is the art of looking for trouble,
finding it whether it exists or not,
diagnosing it incorrectly
and applying the wrong remedy. **"**

Sir Ernest Benn – British publisher and writer

Factor: N/A
Cluster M: Trouble with people
Career staller and stopper 110: Political missteps
110

Learning resources

Bradberry, T., & Greaves, J. (2005). *The emotional intelligence quick book*. New York, NY: Fireside.

Brandon, R., & Seldman, M. (2004) *Survival of the savvy: High-integrity political tactics for career and company success*. New York, NY: Free Press.

Buchanan, D. A. (2008). You stab my back, I'll stab yours: Management experience and perceptions of organizational political behavior. *British Journal of Management, 19,* 49-65.

Buchanan, D. A., & Badham, R. (2008). *Power, politics, and organizational change: Winning the turf game*. London, England: Sage.

Cashman, K. (2008). *Leadership from the inside out* (2nd ed.). San Francisco, CA: Berrett-Koehler.

de Janasz, S. C., Dowd, K. O., & Schneider, B. Z. (2008). *Interpersonal skills in organizations* (3rd ed.). New York, NY: McGraw-Hill.

Dimitrius, J., & Mazzarella, M. C. (2008). *Reading people: How to understand people and predict their behavior: Anytime, anyplace*. New York, NY: Ballantine Books.

Douglas, C., & Ammeter, A. P. (2004). An examination of leader political skill and its effect on ratings of leader effectiveness. *Leadership Quarterly, 15,* 537-551.

Fritz, S. M., Lunde, J. P., Brown, W., & Banset, E. A. (2004). *Interpersonal skills for leadership* (2nd ed.). Upper Saddle River, NJ: Prentice Hall.

Harvard Business School Press. (2008). *Managing up*. Boston, MA: Harvard Business School Press.

Hawley, C. F. (2008). *100+ Tactics for office politics* (2nd ed.). New York, NY: Barrons Educational Series.

Kissinger, H. (1994). *Diplomacy*. New York, NY: Simon & Schuster.

Klaus, P. (2007). *The hard truth about soft skills: Workplace lessons smart people wish they'd learned sooner*. New York, NY: HarperCollins.

McIntyre, M. G. (2005). *Secrets to winning at office politics: How to achieve your goals and increase your influence at work*. New York, NY: St. Martin's Press.

Ranker, G., Gautrey, C., & Phipps, M. (2008). *Political dilemmas at work: How to maintain your integrity and further your career*. Hoboken, NJ: John Wiley & Sons.

110

Appendix A

Developmental difficulty matrix

All competencies are not created equal. Some are harder for people to develop than others. The following charts show, on a five-point scale, how difficult it would be for a typical professional person to develop any of the 38 Competencies. The charts also show the average skill rating of the average population for each competency. This information lets you know what you're up against so you can adjust your development plan, remedies, and time line accordingly. As you put your plan together:

- Take into account how difficult it is to develop the competencies you are considering building into your plan. As you prioritize, keep in mind that focusing on several competencies that are harder or hardest to develop could mean you are overloading yourself. Try to strike a balance between difficulty and the importance to your role.

- Also consider the skill rating of the general population. If you focus on developing a competency that, on average, has a low skill rating in the general population, then developing your strength in this area could help to differentiate you.

The data is provided for six levels:

Entry level individual contributor	Individuals who perform predefined responsibilities or deal with technical/functional problems according to established standards and processes with limited discretionary performance or decision-making authority.
Mid-senior level individual contributor	Functional and/or technical experts given the authority to develop tools and processes or provide specialized skills; may often serve as advisors or project leaders, though they have no direct reports to manage.
First level leader or supervisor	Those in first-line management positions who have individual contributors reporting to them.
Mid-level leader	Managers and directors who lead other managers within a business or corporate function, product line, or region.
Business unit leader	Leaders with full responsibility for a P&L unit, a function, or managing multiple functions (e.g., general manager, managing director).
Senior executive	Executives responsible for enterprise-wide leadership of a business group or function (e.g., senior corporate functional executives).

- This shows the average skill level for the general population from low to high.

- Competencies in this cell are hardest to develop and most people are low in these skills.

- This shows how difficult it is to develop a competency from easiest to hardest.

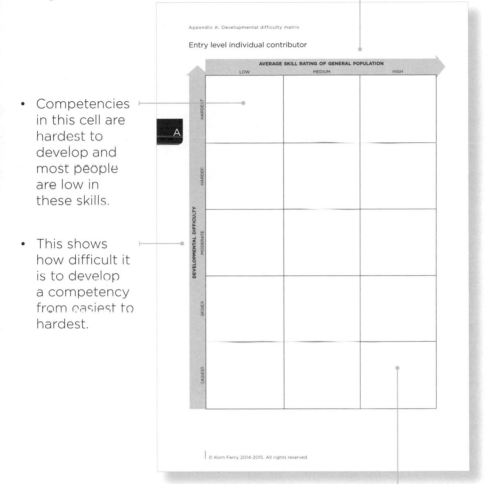

Appendix A: Developmental difficulty matrix

Entry level individual contributor

AVERAGE SKILL RATING OF GENERAL POPULATION

LOW — MEDIUM — HIGH

DEVELOPMENTAL DIFFICULTY

HARDEST
HARDER
MODERATE
EASIER
EASIEST

- Competencies in this cell are easiest to develop and most people are high in these skills.

Entry level individual contributor

	AVERAGE SKILL RATING OF GENERAL POPULATION		
	LOW	MEDIUM	HIGH
HARDEST	8. *Manages* conflict 21. *Builds* networks 31. Situational adaptability 33. Strategic mindset	3. *Manages* ambiguity 19. *Cultivates* innovation 34. *Builds effective* teams	
HARDER	10. Courage 13. Develops talent 37. *Drives* vision and purpose	23. Organizational savvy 24. Persuades	14. *Values* differences 20. Interpersonal savvy
MODERATE	16. *Drives* engagement 18. Global perspective 38. *Optimizes* work processes	4. Attracts top talent 5. Business insight 29. *Demonstrates* self-awareness	8. *Manages* complexity 22. Nimble learning 26. *Being* resilient 30. Self-development
EASIER	15. Directs work	1. *Ensures* accountability 7. Communicates effectively 12. Decision quality 27. Resourcefulness	6. Collaborates
EASIEST		25. Plans and aligns	2. Action oriented 11. Customer focus 28. *Drives* results 35. Tech savvy 36. *Instills* trust

DEVELOPMENTAL DIFFICULTY

Normative data pending
17. Financial acumen – easiest
32. *Balances* stakeholders – easier

Mid-senior level individual contributor

	AVERAGE SKILL RATING OF GENERAL POPULATION		
	LOW	MEDIUM	HIGH
HARDEST	3. *Manages* ambiguity 9. *Manages* conflict 21. *Builds* networks 31. Situational adaptability 33. Strategic mindset 34. *Builds effective* teams	19. *Cultivates* innovation	
HARDER	10. Courage 13. Develops talent 37. *Drives* vision and purpose	20. Interpersonal savvy 23. Organizational savvy 24. Persuades	14. *Values* differences
MODERATE	16. *Drives* engagement	4. Attracts top talent 5. Business insight 18. Global perspective 29. *Demonstrates* self-awareness 30. Self-development 38. *Optimizes* work processes	8. *Manages* complexity 22. Nimble learning 26. *Being* resilient
EASIER	15. Directs work	7. Communicates effectively 12. Decision quality	1. *Ensures* accountability 6. Collaborates 27. Resourcefulness
EASIEST		25. Plans and aligns	2. Action oriented 11. Customer focus 28. *Drives* results 35. Tech savvy 36. *Instills* trust

DEVELOPMENTAL DIFFICULTY

Normative data pending
17. Financial acumen – easiest
32. *Balances* stakeholders – easier

First level leader or supervisor

AVERAGE SKILL RATING OF GENERAL POPULATION →

DEVELOPMENTAL DIFFICULTY ↑

	LOW	MEDIUM	HIGH
HARDEST	9. *Manages* conflict 19. *Cultivates* innovation 21. *Builds* networks 31. Situational adaptability 33. Strategic mindset	3. *Manages* ambiguity 34. *Builds effective* teams	
HARDER	10. Courage 13. Develops talent 37. *Drives* vision and purpose	14. *Values* differences 20. Interpersonal savvy 24. Persuades	23. Organizational savvy
MODERATE	4. Attracts top talent 16. *Drives* engagement 29. *Demonstrates* self-awareness	5. Business insight 18. Global perspective 30. Self-development 38. *Optimizes* work processes	8. *Manages* complexity 22. Nimble learning 26. *Being* resilient
EASIER		1. *Ensures* accountability 7. Communicates effectively 15. Directs work	6. Collaborates 12. Decision quality 27. Resourcefulness
EASIEST		25. Plans and aligns	2. Action oriented 11. Customer focus 28. *Drives* results 35. Tech savvy 36. *Instills* trust

Normative data pending

17. Financial acumen – easiest

32. *Balances* stakeholders – easier

Mid-level leader

	AVERAGE SKILL RATING OF GENERAL POPULATION		
	LOW	MEDIUM	HIGH
HARDEST	9. *Manages* conflict 19. *Cultivates* innovation 31. Situational adaptability 33. Strategic mindset 34. *Builds effective* teams	3. *Manages* ambiguity 21. *Builds* networks	
HARDER	13. Develops talent 37. *Drives* vision and purpose	10. Courage 14. *Values* differences 20. Interpersonal savvy 24. Persuades	23. Organizational savvy
MODERATE	4. Attracts top talent 16. *Drives* engagement 29. *Demonstrates* self-awareness 38. *Optimizes* work processes	18. Global perspective 30. Self-development	5. Business insight 8. *Manages* complexity 22. Nimble learning 26. *Being* resilient
EASIER	15. Directs work	1. *Ensures* accountability 6. Collaborates 7. Communicates effectively 12. Decision quality	27. Resourcefulness
EASIEST		25. Plans and aligns	2. Action oriented 11. Customer focus 17. Financial acumen 28. *Drives* results 35. Tech savvy 36. *Instills* trust

DEVELOPMENTAL DIFFICULTY

A

Normative data pending

32. *Balances* stakeholders – easier

Business unit leader

| | AVERAGE SKILL RATING OF GENERAL POPULATION | | |
	LOW	MEDIUM	HIGH
HARDEST	9. *Manages* conflict 19. *Cultivates* innovation 31. Situational adaptability 34. *Builds effective* teams	3. *Manages* ambiguity 21. *Builds* networks 33. Strategic mindset	
HARDER	10. Courage 13. Develops talent 37. *Drives* vision and purpose	14. *Values* differences 20. Interpersonal savvy 24. Persuades	23. Organizational savvy
MODERATE	4. Attracts top talent 16. *Drives* engagement 29. *Demonstrates* self-awareness 38. *Optimizes* work processes	18. Global perspective 30. Self-development	5. Business insight 8. *Manages* complexity 22. Nimble learning 26. *Being* resilient
EASIER	15. Directs work	6. Collaborates 7. Communicates effectively 12. Decision quality 27. Resourcefulness	1. *Ensures* accountability
EASIEST		25. Plans and aligns	2. Action oriented 11. Customer focus 17. Financial acumen 28. *Drives* results 35. Tech savvy 36. *Instills* trust

*(left axis: **DEVELOPMENTAL DIFFICULTY**)*

Normative data pending
32. *Balances* stakeholders – easier

Senior executive

	AVERAGE SKILL RATING OF GENERAL POPULATION		
	LOW	MEDIUM	HIGH
HARDEST	9. *Manages* conflict 19. *Cultivates* innovation 31. Situational adaptability 34. *Builds effective* teams	3. *Manages* ambiguity 33. Strategic mindset	21. *Builds* networks
HARDER	10. Courage 13. Develops talent	14. *Values* differences 20. Interpersonal savvy 24. Persuades 37. *Drives* vision and purpose	23. Organizational savvy
MODERATE	4. Attracts top talent 16. *Drives* engagement 29. *Demonstrates* self-awareness 38. *Optimizes* work processes	30. Self-development	5. Business insight 8. *Manages* complexity 18. Global perspective 22. Nimble learning 26. *Being* resilient
EASIER	6. Collaborates 15. Directs work	1. *Ensures* accountability 7. Communicates effectively 12. Decision quality 27. Resourcefulness	
EASIEST		25. Plans and aligns 35. Tech savvy	2. Action oriented 11. Customer focus 17. Financial acumen 28. *Drives* results 36. *Instills* trust

DEVELOPMENTAL DIFFICULTY

A

Normative data pending
32. *Balances* stakeholders – easier

Notes

Ensures accountability

1. Tapia, A. T. (2013). *The inclusion paradox* (2nd ed.), pp. 106-108. Publisher: Author.

Action oriented

2. Sullivan, B., & Thompson, H. (2013, May 3). Brain, interrupted. *The New York Times*. Retrieved from http://www.nytimes.com/ 2013/05/05/opinion/sunday/a-focus-on-distraction.html?_r=0

Manages ambiguity

3. Rock, D. (2009). *Your brain at work: Strategies for overcoming distraction, regaining focus, and working smarter all day long*. New York, NY: HarperCollins Publishers.

Attracts top talent

4. Great Rated!™. (2014). *Google, Inc*. Great Rated!™ Reviews. Retrieved from http://us.greatrated.com/google-inc

5. Wikipedia. (n.d.). *Google*. Retrieved from http://en.wikipedia.org/ wiki/Google

Business insight

6. Perth Leadership Institute. (2008). *The role of business acumen in leadership development* [White Paper, p. 8]. Retrieved from http://www.perthleadership.org/documents/Business_Acumen_ WP_Updated.pdf

Collaborates

7. Vivona, J. M. (2009). Leaping from brain to mind: A critique of mirror neuron explanations of countertransference. *Journal of the American Psychoanalytic Association, 57*(3), 525-550.

Communicates effectively

8. Gallo, C. (2013). How Martin Luther King improvised "I have a dream." *Forbes*. Retrieved from http://www.forbes.com/sites/carminegallo/2013/08/27/public-speaking-how-mlk-improvised-second-half-of-dream-speech/

9. Wikipedia. (n.d.). *I have a dream*. Retrieved from http://en.wikipedia.org/wiki/I_Have_a_Dream

Manages complexity

10. Rock, D. (2009). *Your brain at work: Strategies for overcoming distraction, regaining focus, and working smarter all day long*. New York, NY: HarperCollins Publishers.

Courage

11. Sweeney, M. S. (2009). *Brain: The complete mind: How it develops, how it works, and how to keep it sharp*. Washington, DC: National Geographic.

Customer focus

12. Anders, G. (2012). Inside Amazon's idea machine: How Bezos decodes customers. *Forbes*. Retrieved from http://www.forbes.com/sites/georgeanders/2012/04/04/inside-amazon/

13. Wikipedia. (n.d.). *Amazon.com*. Retrieved from http://en.wikipedia.org/wiki/Amazon.com

14. Yahoo Finance. (n.d.). Current and historical Amazon stock price. Retrieved from http://finance.yahoo.com/q/hp?s=AMZN

Decision quality

15. Kahneman, D. (2011). *Thinking, fast and slow*. New York, NY: Farrar, Straus and Giroux.

Develops talent

16. Hamori, M., Cao, J., & Koyuncu, B. (2012). Why top young managers are in a nonstop job hunt. *Harvard Business Review*. Retrieved from http://hbr.org/2012/07/why-top-young-managers-are-in-a-nonstop-job-hunt/ar/1

17. Mourdoukoutas, P. (2012). The career-development gap: Why employers fail to retain top talent. *Forbes*. Retrieved from http://www.forbes.com/sites/panosmourdoukoutas/2012/07/11/1-career-development-gap-why-employers-fail-to-retain-top-talent/

Values differences

18. Derks, B., Scheepers, D., & Ellemers, N. (Eds.). (2013). *Neuroscience of prejudice and intergroup relations*. New York, NY: Psychology Press.

Directs work

19. Khallash, S. (2013, March 18). *How does leadership vary across the world?* Global Talent Strategy. Retrieved from http://globaltalentstrategy.com/en/article/how-does-leadership-vary-across-the-world-360

20. Ladimeji, K. (2013, March 18). *How leadership styles vary around the world* [Study]. thecareercafe.co.uk. Retrieved from http://thecareercafe.co.uk/blog/?p=7522

Drives engagement

21. Best Companies™. (n.d.). *UKRD Group Limited*. Retrieved from http://www.b.co.uk/Company/Profile?Company=305561#.U3usbLROXAU

22. Faragher, J. (2013, May). Employee engagement: The secret of UKRD's success. *Personnel Today*. Retrieved from http://www.personneltoday.com/hr/employee-engagement-the-secret-of-ukrds-success/

23. UKRD Group. (n.d.). *Meet the exec team*. Retrieved from http://www.ukrd.com/ukrdpeople/execteam.php

24. Wikipedia. (n.d.). *UKRD Group*. Retrieved from http://en.wikipedia.org/wiki/UKRD_Group

Financial acumen

25. Keevy, M. (2012). *From CFO to CEO: A pathway to leadership*. The Korn Ferry Institute. Retrieved from http://www.kornferryinstitute.com/sites/all/files//documents/briefings-magazine-download/From%20CFO%20to%20CEO_Korn%20Ferry_12Nov%2012.pdf

26. Saunders, J. S. (2011). The path to becoming a Fortune 500 CEO. *Forbes*. Retrieved from http://www.forbes.com/sites/ciocentral/2011/12/05/the-path-to-becoming-a-fortune-500-ceo/

Global perspective

27. Unruh, G. (2012). Being Global II: Global leaders have a global mind. *Forbes*. Retrieved from http://www.forbes.com/sites/csr/2012/04/19/being-global-ii-global-leaders-have-a-global-mind/

Cultivates innovation

28. ThinkingAllowedTV. (2010, August 10). Mihály Csíkszentmihályi: Flow, creativity & the evolving self. Thinking Allowed DVD w/ Mishlove [YouTube]. Retrieved from https://www.youtube.com/watch?v=7dSzKnf5WWg

29. Wikipedia. (n.d.). *Flow (psychology)*. Wikipedia. Retrieved from http://en.wikipedia.org/wiki/Flow_(psychology)

552 |

Interpersonal savvy

30. Iacoboni, M. (2008). *Mirroring people: The new science of how we connect with others*. New York, NY: Farrar, Straus and Giroux.

Builds networks

31. Lieberman, M. D. (2013). *Social: Why our brains are wired to connect*. New York, NY: Crown Publishers.

Nimble learning

32. Lillard, A., & Erisir, A. (2011). Old dogs learning new tricks: Neuroplasticity beyond the juvenile period. *Developmental Review, 31*(4), 207-239.

Notes

Organizational savvy

33. Adachi, Y. (2010, May 21). Business negotiations between the Americans and the Japanese. *Global Business Languages*: Vol. 2, Article 4. Retrieved from http://docs.lib.purdue.edu/cgi/viewcontent.cgi?article=1018&context=gbl

34. btrax Staff. (2010, December 15). *10 Cultural contrasts between US & Japanese companies*. Freshtrax. Retrieved from http://blog.btrax.com/en/2010/12/15/10-cultural-contrasts-between-us-and-japanese-companies-a-personal-view/

35. Flannery, N. P. (2011, November 2). Japanese business culture and why good governance matters. *Forbes*. Retrieved from http://www.forbes.com/sites/nathanielparishflannery/2011/11/02/japanese-business-culture-and-why-good-governance-matters/

36. Kwintessential. (n.d.). *Doing business in Japan*. Retrieved from http://www.kwintessential.co.uk/etiquette/doing-business-japan.html

37. World Business Culture. (n.d.). *Japanese management style*. Retrieved from http://www.worldbusinessculture.com/Japanese-Management-Style.html

| 553

Persuades

38. Falk, E. B., Morelli, S. A., Welborn, B. L., Dambacher, K., & Lieberman, M. D. (2013). Creating buzz: The neural correlates of effective message propagation. *Psychological Science, 24*(7), 1234-1242.

39. Stephens, G. J., Silbert, L. J., & Hasson, U. (2010). *Speaker-listener neural coupling underlies successful communication.* Proceedings of the National Academy of Sciences, 107, 14425-14430.

Plans and aligns

40. Bivins, F., & De Smet, A. (2013). Making time management the organization's priority. *McKinsey Quarterly*. Retrieved from http://www.mckinsey.com/insights/organization/making_time_management_the_organizations_priority

Resourcefulness

41. Swisher, V. S., Hallenbeck, G. S., Jr., Orr, J. E., Eichinger, R. W., Lombardo, M. M., & Capretta, C. C. (2013). *FYI® for learning agility* (2nd ed.), p. 218. Minneapolis, MN: Lominger International: A Korn Ferry Company.

42. Wikipedia. (n.d.). *Jugaad*. Retrieved from http://en.wikipedia.org/wiki/Jugaad

Drives results

43. Schwartz, T. (2013, February 9). Relax! You'll be more productive. *The New York Times*. Retrieved from http://www.nytimes.com/2013/02/10/opinion/sunday/relax-youll-be-more-productive.html

Demonstrates self-awareness

44. Cashman, K. (2012). *The pause principle: Step back to lead forward*. San Francisco, CA: Berrett-Koehler Publishers, Inc.

45. Rock, D. (2009). *Your brain at work: Strategies for overcoming distraction, regaining focus, and working smarter all day long*. New York, NY: HarperCollins Publishers.

Self-development

46. Kahneman, D. (1973). *Attention and effort*. Upper Saddle River, NJ: Prentice-Hall.

Situational adaptability

47. One. (n.d.). *Bono*. Retrieved from http://www.one.org/us/person/bono/

48. U2, & McCormick, N. (2009). *U2 by U2*. New York, NY: HarperCollins Publishers.

Balances stakeholders

49. Business Case Studies. (n.d.). *Shell. Balancing stakeholder needs*. Retrieved from http://businesscasestudies.co.uk/shell/balancing-stakeholder-needs/introduction.html

50. Huffington Post Business. (2013). Fortune Global 500: Top 10 most profitable companies in the world. *Huffington Post*. Retrieved from http://www.huffingtonpost.com/2013/07/08/fortune-global-500_n_3561233.html

Strategic mindset

51. Kabacoff, R. (2014, February 7). Develop strategic thinkers throughout your organization. *Harvard Business Review Blog Network*. Retrieved from http://blogs.hbr.org/2014/02/develop-strategic-thinkers-throughout-your-organization/

52. Yakowicz, W. (2014, February 10.). How to get your employees to think strategically. *Inc.* Retrieved from http://www.inc.com/will-yakowicz/how-to-foster-strategic-thinking-in-employees.html

Builds effective teams

53. Official Disney Store Blog. (2012, April 6.). *Flashback Friday: Disney's Nine Old Men*. Disney Store's The Buzz. Retrieved from http://blog.disneystore.com/blog/2012/04/flashback-friday-disneys-nine-old-men.html

54. Palfini, J. (2008, June 17). *Walt Disney and his "Nine Old Men."* CBS Money Watch. Retrieved from http://www.cbsnews.com/news/four-great-teams-in-business-history/

Tech savvy

55. Haggerty, N. (2012, July/August). On becoming an IT savvy CEO. *Ivy Business Journal*. Retrieved from http://iveybusinessjournal.com/topics/leadership/on-becoming-an-it-savvy-ceo

Instills trust

56. Boyatzis, R. E., Smith, M., & Blaize, N. (2006). Developing sustainable leaders through coaching and compassion. *Academy of Management Learning & Education, 5*(1), 8-24.

57. Rock, D. (2009). *Your brain at work: Strategies for overcoming distraction, regaining focus, and working smarter all day long*. New York, NY: HarperCollins Publishers.

Drives vision and purpose

58. de Vries Hoogerwerff, M. (2007, November 7). Interview with Lee Kuan Yew [YouTube]. Retrieved from http://www.youtube.com/watch?v=B3YFl-dY9Qg

59. Wikipedia. (n.d.). *Lee Kuan Yew*. Retrieved from http://en.wikipedia.org/wiki/Lee_Kuan_Yew

Optimizes work processes

60. Liker, J. K. (n.d.). *The Toyota Way: 14 Management principles from the world's greatest manufacturer*. ROI Communications. Retrieved from http://www.roibg.com/en/?cat=3&sub=11&id=9

61. Wikipedia. (n.d.). *The Toyota Way*. Retrieved from http://en.wikipedia.org/wiki/The_Toyota_Way

62. Wikipedia. (n.d.). *Toyota*. Retrieved from http://en.wikipedia.org/wiki/Toyota

Index

The Index is designed to include key development themes that a manager or learner might want to explore in greater detail. Each entry directs learners and coaches to a chapter and remedy number that is pertinent to the theme. For example, if a learner looks up "Attracts top talent" they will see entries that pertain to "global talent pools, 4.14; hiring wisely, 4.2; talent pipeline, 4.12". If hiring wisely is the issue at hand, the learner can go to chapter four and read remedy number two. Please note: Index entries in italics are not alphabetized.

Index

Index

Index

Index

|

Index

| 577

Index